DIGITAL TRANSFORMATION, STRATEGIC RESILIENCE, CYBER SECURITY AND RISK MANAGEMENT

CONTEMPORARY STUDIES IN ECONOMIC AND FINANCIAL ANALYSIS

Series Editor: Simon Grima

Volume 98:	Contemporary Issues in Finance: Current Challenges from Across Europe *Edited by Simon Grima, Frank Bezzina, Inna Romānova and Ramona Rupeika-Apoga*
Volume 99:	Governance and Regulations' Contemporary Issues *Edited by Simon Grima and Pierpaolo Marano*
Volume 100:	Contemporary Issues in Business and Financial Management in Eastern Europe *Edited by Simon Grima and Eleftherios Thalassinos*
Volume 101:	Contemporary Issues in Behavioral Finance *Edited by Simon Grima, Ercan Özen, Hakan Boz, Jonathan Spiteri and Eleftherios Thalassinos*
Volume 102:	Contemporary Issues in Audit Management and Forensic Accounting *Edited by Simon Grima, Engin Boztepe and Peter J. Baldacchino*
Volume 103:	Global Street Economy and Micro Entrepreneurship *Edited by Simon Grima, Osman Sirkeci and Kamuran ElbeyoĞlu*
Volume 104:	Contemporary Issues in Business, Economics and Finance *Edited by Simon Grima, Ercan Özen and Hakan Boz*
Volume 105:	Contemporary Issues in Public Sector Accounting and Auditing *Edited by Simon Grima and Engin Boztepe*
Volume 106:	Contemporary Issues in Social Science *Edited by Simon Grima, Ercan Özen and Hakan Boz*
Volume 107:	A New Social Street Economy: An Effect of the COVID-19 Pandemic *Edited by Simon Grima, Osman Sirkeci and Kamuran Elbeyoğlu.*
Volume 108A:	Managing Risk and Decision Making in Times of Economic Distress *Edited by Simon Grima, Ercan Özen and Inna Romānova*
Volume 108B:	Managing Risk and Decision Making in Times of Economic Distress *Edited by Simon Grima, Ercan Özen and Inna Romānova*
Volume 109A:	The New Digital Era: Digitalisation and Emerging Risks and Opportunities *Edited by Simon Grima, Ercan Özen and Hakan Boz*
Volume 109B:	The New Digital Era: Digitalisation and Emerging Risks and Opportunities *Edited by Simon Grima, Ercan Özen and Hakan Boz*
Volume 110A:	Smart Analytics, Artificial Intelligence and Sustainable Performance Management in a Global Digitalised Economy *Edited by Pallavi Tyagi, Simon Grima, Kiran Sood, B. Balamurugan, Ercan Özen and Thalassinos Eleftherios*
Volume 110B:	Smart Analytics, Artificial Intelligence and Sustainable Performance Management in a Global Digitalised Economy *Edited by Pallavi Tyagi, Simon Grima, Kiran Sood, B. Balamurugan, Ercan Özen and Thalassinos Eleftherios*

CONTEMPORARY STUDIES IN ECONOMIC AND FINANCIAL ANALYSIS VOLUME 111A

DIGITAL TRANSFORMATION, STRATEGIC RESILIENCE, CYBER SECURITY AND RISK MANAGEMENT

EDITED BY

SIMON GRIMA
University of Malta, Malta

ELEFTHERIOS THALASSINOS
University of Piraeus, Greece

MIRELA CRISTEA
University of Craiova, Romania

MARTA KADŁUBEK
Czestochowa University of Technology, Poland

DIMITRIOS MADITINOS
International Hellenic University, Greece

and

LĪGA PEISENIECE
BA School of Business and Finance, Latvia

emerald PUBLISHING

United Kingdom – North America – Japan
India – Malaysia – China

Emerald Publishing Limited
Emerald Publishing, Floor 5, Northspring, 21-23 Wellington Street, Leeds LS1 4DL.

First edition 2023

British Library Cataloguing in Publication Data
A catalogue record for this book is available from the British Library

ISBN: 978-1-80455-254-4 (Print)
ISBN: 978-1-80455-253-7 (Online)
ISBN: 978-1-80455-255-1 (Epub)

ISSN: 1569-3759 (Series)

Printed and bound by CPI Group (UK) Ltd, Croydon, CR0 4YY

INVESTOR IN PEOPLE

CONTENTS

ABOUT THE EDITORS

Simon Grima is the Deputy Dean of the Faculty of Economics, Management and Accountancy, Associate Professor and the Head of the Department of Insurance and Risk Management which he set up in 2015 and started and coordinates the MA and MSc Insurance and Risk Management degrees together with the BCom in Insurance at the University of Malta. He is also a Professor at the University of Latvia, Faculty of Business, Management and Economics and a Visiting Professor at UNICATT Milan. He served as the President of the Malta Association of Risk Management and President of the Malta Association of Compliance Officers between 2013 and 2015 and between 2016 and 2018, respectively. Moreover, he is the Chairman of the Scientific Education Committee of the Public Risk Management Organization and the Federation of European Risk Managers. His research focus is on governance, regulations and internal controls and has over 30 years of experience varied between financial services, academia and public entities. He has acted as Co-chair and is a member of the scientific programme committee on some international conferences and is a chief editor, editor and review editor of some journals and book series. He has been awarded outstanding reviewer for *Journal of Financial Regulation and Compliance* in the 2017 and 2022 Emerald Literati Awards. Moreover, he acts as an Independent Director for Financial Services Firms, sits on Risk, Compliance, Procurement, Investment and Audit Committees and carries out duties as a Compliance Officer, Internal Auditor and Risk Manager.

Eleftherios Thalassinos, PhD (UIC, Chicago, USA, 1983), DHC Degrees in Economics (Danubius University of Galati, Romania, 2013; University of Craiova, Romania, 2015; and Rostov State University of Economics, Russia, 2018), MBA (De-Paul U Chicago, USA, 1979) and BA (U of Athens, Greece, 1976), a Jean Monnet Chair Professor experienced in European Economic Integration and International Finance. He is Editor-in-Chief of ERSJ, IJEBA, Editor of IJFIRM and Chair of ICABE. His professional experience includes quantitative analysis, technical and financial analysis, banking, business consulting, project evaluations, international business, international finance and maritime economics. He has a long track of publications in several journals, collective volumes and chapter books. Among them a publication as a chapter book in the *World Scientific Handbook* in *Financial Economics Series*, Vol. 5, is dedicated to the memory of Late Milton Miller, Nobel prize winner in Economics in 1990. Parallel to the academic career, he has performed as Bank Director for 12 years, Ministerial Advisor for 6 years, Public Servant for 4 years and Independent Consultant for a long time.

Mirela Cristea is a Professor at the University of Craiova (Romania), Faculty of Economics and Business Administration, Department of Finance, Banking and Economic Analysis and Center for Economic, Banking and Financial Research (CEBAFI). Her main research directions and teaching activities are insurance and private pension funds, banking administration and interdisciplinary research in economics. She is also a PhD Coordinator within the Doctoral School of Economics at the University of Craiova by obtaining the PhD habil. in Economics. She obtained the scientific title of PhD in Economics at the University of Craiova and graduated the Post-Doctoral School in Economics and Applied Sciences in Economics at the Romanian Academy from Bucharest on the subject of private pension system in Romania. She received two awards from the Faculties on Economics Association from Romania in 2007 and 2013 for two books on life insurance and pension system subjects. In addition, she is a reviewer and member of the scientific and organisational committees for numerous journals and conferences.

Marta Kadłubek is an Assistant Professor at the Department of Logistics at the Faculty of Management, the Częstochowa University of Technology in Poland. She completed her studies with honours at the Czestochowa University of Technology, PhD in Management, Master's in Economics and Enterprise Management (in Polish language), Master's in Management (in English language) and Master's in Enterprise on International Market (in English language), respectively. The scientific fields of her interest are logistics management, supply chain management, transportation enterprises, logistics service providers and logistics customer service. She has 20 years of teaching and research experience in higher education. She is an author of over 200 scientific publications including books, book chapters, journal papers and proceedings presented at international conferences. She is a member of scientific and review boards of several journals and conferences and a member of numerous research and scientific societies.

Dimitrios Maditinos holds a degree with specialisation in Business Administration and Informatics from Lund University, Sweden, and a PhD in Finance and Financial Modelling from Greenwich University, London, UK. Currently, he is a Professor in Business Administration and Informatics at International Hellenic University. His research interests are in financial modelling, performance measurement, investors behaviour, e-business and e-commerce, applications and internet use, digital business, management information systems, SCM and business digitalisation, with three books, more than 60 published papers in international scientific journals and more than 90 papers presented in international conferences. Moreover, he serves as a Scientific board member in many International Scientific Journals. His appears in Scopus with 31 published papers, 839 citations and *h*-index of 13, while in Google Scholar he appears with 3,100 references, *h*-index 23 and i10-index 37 (31 October 2022).

Liga Peiseniece Dr. Sc. Admin. is the Rector at BA School of Business and Finance (BASBF), Latvia. She holds a Master's degrees in Mathematics and Public Management. She has been conferred a Doctoral degree in Business Management at the University of Latvia. She has gained extensive experience in Professional Higher Education Management, as well as expertise in the Human Resources Management. For eight years L. Peiseniece has worked as a HR manager in various organisations which gave her enormous practical experience in the field of management. For 10 years, as a Vice Rector for Academic Affairs at BA School of Business and Finance, L. Peiseniece contributed to the development and modernisation of higher education through her immense motivation and intensive research done. She is program director of the joint doctoral program 'Business Management' run by BA School of Business and Finance and RISEBA (Latvia). Apart from her job in the field of management, L. Peiseniece is one of the leading Associate Professors delivering lectures on HR Management, Leadership, and Innovation Management. As a researcher of CRANET Association, that unites members from more than 50 countries, she focuses on HR Management issues, actively publishing research articles and participating in international conferences. She is the author of 18 publications. L. Peiseniece has represented BA School of Business and Finance and contributed to socially important issues such as financial literacy development in Latvia, as well as participated in 'Junior Achievement Latvia' activities to promote entrepreneurial drive among young generation. Her high-level commitment to business education was also demonstrated through her active participation in special international projects. Being a responsible leader of BASBF for the European international association PRIME Networking gave her the opportunity to support high quality international project developments to enhance European dimension in teaching and learning not only at BASBF but on a wide professional higher education scale. She is also an active Board Member of the Baltic Management Development Association (BMDA).

ABOUT THE CONTRIBUTORS

Gani Asllani holds MA and PhD in Finance from the University of Pristina, Kosovo. He is regular Professor at University 'Haxhi Zeka', Peja within the Law Faculty. He teaches public finance, taxation and competition rights. During his 20 years of experience, he has contributed to the creation of the tax system in Kosovo, making tax analysis and expertise, participating in several working groups at international level (IMF, OECD and Robert Shuman Center for Advance Studies).

Dzintra Atstāja is a Professor at the Department of Management at BA School of Business and Finance (Latvia), a Scientific Expert in Economics and Management Sciences of the Latvian Council of Science. She specialises in economics and design of sustainability; green entrepreneurship, business control systems and management and business sustainability; corporate social responsibility; civil defense and work safety. She has more than 25 years of experience in business consulting.

Ieva Auzina is a Security Management Team Lead at Atea Global Services in Riga, Latvia. She holds a Master's degree in Cybersecurity Management as well as CompTIA security certification. Her work involves leading five highly experienced security professionals whose main goal is to ensure security and compliance services across Nordic countries. She has overall six years of experience in cybersecurity, including various security tools and solution implementation in complex business environments.

Lochan Chavan is currently working as an Assistant Professor at Smt. Kamala Mehta V.W.A. College of Commerce, Versova, Mumbai, India and holds a Master's degree in Commerce and is also a Law Graduate. She is currently pursuing her PhD in Business Management from Chitkara University, Punjab, India. She has contributed four years in teaching.

Shkelqesa Citaku works as a Legal Advisor at EU Institution in Kosovo. In addition, she worked as Lecturer at the University of Prizren. She holds MA and PhD in Financial Law at the University of Pristina, Law Faculty. The expertise and analyses she performed in the field of financial law were a great accomplishment for her academic and professional development.

Mirela Cristea is a Professor at the University of Craiova (Romania), Faculty of Economics and Business Administration, Department of Finance, Banking and Economic Analysis and Center for Economic, Banking and Financial

Research (CEBAFI). Her main research directions and teaching activities are insurance and private pension funds, banking administration and interdisciplinary research in economics. She is also a PhD Coordinator within the Doctoral School of Economics at the University of Craiova by obtaining the PhD habil. in Economics. She obtained the scientific title of PhD in Economics at the University of Craiova and graduated the Post-Doctoral School in Economics and Applied Sciences in Economics at the Romanian Academy from Bucharest on the subject of private pension system in Romania. She received two awards from the Faculties on Economics Association from Romania in 2007 and 2013 for two books on life insurance and pension system subjects. In addition, she is a reviewer and member of the scientific and organisational committees for numerous journals and conferences.

Arnaud Denis is a Consultant in Industrial (ICS/OT) Cybersecurity at Accenture in Riga, Latvia. He holds a Master's degree in Cybersecurity Management. His work involves helping customers identify and deploy security solutions in varied fields like energy, consumable goods and others. He has prior experience in the global marketing of electrical control systems and their associated software and services.

Biruta Dzerve is Assistant Professor of the Economics and Finance Department at BA School of Business and Finance since 2000. Her previous experience includes work in tax administration. In recent years, her scientific studies relate to the impact of the development of information technologies on the process of higher education studies. She is also the author and co-author of a number of scientific publications and a member of international scientific conferences. She has been the director of the finance programmes for many years and has been responsible for the BA study process. For the last few years, she has been performing the duties of Vice-Rector of Studies and researching the positive and negative effects of information technology on the study process.

Simon Grima is the Deputy Dean of the Faculty of Economics, Management and Accountancy, Associate Professor and the Head of the Department of Insurance and Risk Management which he set up in 2015 and started and coordinates the MA and MSc Insurance and Risk Management degrees together with the BCom in Insurance at the University of Malta. He is also a Professor at the University of Latvia, Faculty of Business, Management and Economics and a Visiting Professor at UNICATT Milan. He served as the President of the Malta Association of Risk Management and President of the Malta Association of Compliance Officers between 2013 and 2015 and between 2016 and 2018, respectively. Moreover, he is the Chairman of the Scientific Education Committee of the Public Risk Management Organization and the Federation of European Risk Managers. His research focus is on governance, regulations and internal controls and has over 30 years of experience varied between financial services, academia and public entities. He has acted as Co-chair and is a member of the scientific programme committee on some international conferences and is a chief editor,

editor and review editor of some journals and book series. He has been awarded outstanding reviewer for *Journal of Financial Regulation and Compliance* in the 2017 and 2022 Emerald Literati Awards. Moreover, he acts as an Independent Director for Financial Services Firms, sits on Risk, Compliance, Procurement, Investment and Audit Committees and carries out duties as a Compliance Officer, Internal Auditor and Risk Manager.

Camelia-Daniela Hategan is Professor PhD habil. of Accounting at Faculty of Economics and Business Administration, West University of Timisoara, Accounting and Auditing Department. The author's areas of research interest include financial accounting, international financial reporting standards, financial audit, entrepreneurship in the accounting profession and corporate social responsibility. She is a member of a Professional Accounting Association, the Chamber of Financial Auditors of Romania. She has published and presented numerous papers in this field in scientific journals indexed on Web of Science or other relevant databases and conference proceedings. She has reviewed many articles for relevant journals, for example, *Sage Open*, *Economic Research*, *International Journal of Emerging Markets, Sustainability, Education*, *Journal of Risk and Financial Management*, *International Journal of Financial Studies* and conferences, for example, *International Business Information Management Association*.

Gunta Innuse is Assistant Professor of the Economics and Finance Department at BA School of Business and Finance, Certified accountant and member of the Association of Accountants of the Republic of Latvia. In parallel with academic work in higher education, she provides accountants' professional services to businesses and the public sector. Her recent activities include (1) participation in international activities as the head of development and mobility project department; (2) regular lectures at partner's universities; and (3) inter-university student project management. She is co-authoring a number of scientific publications on accounting and tax issues, and actively presenting the results of their studies at international conferences during last years.

Narayanage Jayantha Dewasiri is a Professor attached to the Department of Accountancy and Finance, Sabaragamuwa University of Sri Lanka. Further, he currently serves as the Brand Ambassador at Emerald Publishing, UK, and the Secretary of the Sri Lanka Institute of Marketing. He is a pioneer in applying triangulation research approaches in the management discipline. He is currently serving as the Co-Editors-in-Chief of the *South Asian Journal of Marketing* published by Emerald Publishing, Managing Editor of the *Asian Journal of Finance* and *South Asian Journal of Tourism and Hospitality* published by the Faculty of Management Studies, Sabaragamuwa University of Sri Lanka.

Priya Jindal is currently working as an Associate Professor at Chitkara Business School, Chitkara University, Punjab, India and holds a Master's degree in commerce and economics. She earned her Doctorate in Management. She has contributed more than 15 years in teaching. She supervised four PhD research scholars and two MPhil candidates. There are numerous research papers to her credit in leading journals; among them seven research papers have been published in *Scopus Indexed Journal*. Her areas of research include banking, finance and insurance. She has filed more than 21 patents and one copyright. She is the Editor of two books under IGI publications and one book indexed in *Scopus*.

Marta Kadłubek is an Assistant Professor at the Department of Logistics at the Faculty of Management, the Częstochowa University of Technology in Poland. She completed her studies with honours at the Czestochowa University of Technology, PhD in Management, Master's in Economics and Enterprise Management (in Polish language), Master's in Management (in English language) and Master's in Enterprise on International Market (in English language), respectively. The scientific fields of her interest are logistics management, supply chain management, transportation enterprises, logistics service providers and logistics customer service. She has 20 years of teaching and research experience in higher education. She is an author of over 200 scientific publications including books, book chapters, journal papers and proceedings presented at international conferences. She is a member of scientific and review boards of several journals and conferences and a member of numerous research and scientific societies.

Arvinder Kaur is working as an Assistant Professor at the University School of Business, Chandigarh University, in the field of Finance since 2016. She has done her Master's in Finance and Control with distinction and graduation in Commerce. She is currently pursuing PhD from Chandigarh University. She has seven years of academic experience and expertise in teaching specialised subjects like taxation, financial accounting, corporate accounting and GST. She has presented (in national and international conferences) nine research papers and published in various renowned journals and also published five book chapters. She attended 16 faculty development programmes and workshops in her tenure. Her area of interest is Fintech.

Pawan Kumar has 16 years of experience in teaching. He obtained his highest degree from Kurukshetra University in India and worked in educational institutions. At present, he is working as an Associate Professor in Finance at the University School of Business Chandigarh University Mohali, India. He has presented more than 30 papers at various national and international conferences and published more than 25 research papers in various reputed journals. He also has two patents in his credit. He has published three books on the Indian financial system, economics and insurance fundamentals and principles. Moreover, he supervises five PhD scholars.

Jekaterina Kuzmina is Dr Sc. Administr. – assisting Professor at BA School of Business and Finance. She holds a PhD in Business Administration. She is a Scientific Expert in Economics and Management Sciences at the Latvian Council of Science and an investment analyst at an asset management company. Her research interests are related to financial management and sustainability concepts' integration into financial decision-making, risk management, asset management and sustainability. She has been involved in several research projects as a project leader or member of project teams. She has been working with qualitative methods such as case studies and document analysis and with various quantitative methods including modelling in Matlab.

Dimitrios Maditinos holds a degree with specialisation in Business Administration and Informatics from Lund University, Sweden, and a PhD in Finance and Financial Modelling from Greenwich University, London, UK. Currently, he is a Professor in Business Administration and Informatics at International Hellenic University. His research interests are in financial modelling, performance measurement, investors behaviour, e-business and e-commerce, applications and internet use, digital business, management information systems, SCM and business digitalisation, with three books, more than 60 published papers in international scientific journals and more than 90 papers presented in international conferences. Moreover, he serves as a Scientific board member in many International Scientific Journals. His appears in Scopus with 31 published papers, 839 citations and *h*-index of 13, while in Google Scholar he appears with 3,100 references, *h*-index 23 and i10-index 37 (31 October 2022).

Maria Moraru is an Associate Professor at the West University of Timisoara, Faculty of Economics and Business Administration, Department of Accounting and Audit. She published her doctoral thesis titled *Accounting Management of Public Treasury* in 2005 and has been teaching and guiding students through their learning curriculum through accounting in public institutions, private companies, financial bank institutions and non-governmental organisations. She is an active scholar who has published several scientific papers in co-authorship with other university department colleagues. In recently published papers, her focus has been on the economic deficiencies in Romania when compared to other European countries and the necessary actions to be taken.

Vithyalani Muthusamy is a Lecturer in Banking and Insurance in the Department of Accountancy and Finance, Faculty of Management Studies, at the Sabaragamuwa University of Sri Lanka, since 2016. She obtained her first degree, BSc, in Banking and Insurance (Special) with First Class Division from the Sabaragamuwa University of Sri Lanka in 2015. She also won the gold medal for the highest final grade point average and the best performance in the Bachelor of Science in Banking and Insurance Special Degree Examination. She holds a Master of Science in Applied Finance from the University of Sri

Jayawardenepura. She completed TKT-CLIL with band III in 2021. Her research interest areas are mainly general insurance and banking. Her major teaching areas are banking and insurance.

Graţiela Georgiana Noja is the Vice-Dean of the Faculty of Economics and Business Administration, West University of Timisoara, Romania, in charge of academic and student affairs, and Full Professor, PhD habil., at the same faculty, Department of Marketing and International Economic Relations. She is also a PhD Coordinator within the Doctoral School of Economics and Business Administration. She completed her studies with the highest honours at the West University of Timisoara, a PhD habil. in Economics, PhD in Economics, a Master's in Management and European integration and BA in International Economic Relations. She was the Manager of the Erasmus+ Project 'Coordinated higher education institutions responses to digitalisation' (2019-1-RO01-KA203-063214) implemented during 2019–2021 and developed several national and international projects throughout the years. She has around 30 publications indexed in the Web of Science Core Collection and a couple dozen of other publications in relevant international journals/books/collective volumes. Also, she is an active member of the International Strategic Management Association and has a wide membership in various educational organisations, research networks, scientific and review committees of top-tier journals, and international conferences. Her main research and teaching activities are developed within the framework of Economics and International Business area, with a keen focus on European economic integration, international migration, digital transformation and sustainable economic development.

Diego Norena-Chavez holds a postdoctoral degree in management from the University of Piraeus, Greece. He earned his Doctorate in Business Administration with honors from the Paris School of Business, France, and a Doctorate in Strategic Business Administration (Magna Cum Laude) from the Pontifical Catholic University of Peru. He also holds a Master of Business Administration from the Ramon Llull University-ESADE Business School, Spain, and another Master's degree from Adolfo Ibáñez University, Chile. Furthermore, Dr. Norena-Chavez has a Master's in Applied Statistics for Data Science with R software from Nebrija University, Spain. He completed his Bachelor's degree in Business Administration with a specialization in human resources at the University of Lima, Peru. Additionally, he has an Executive Certificate in Management and Leadership from the Massachusetts Institute of Technology, United States. He has also graduated from the Senior Management Program at INCAE Business School, Costa Rica, and is a Reserve Officer of the Peruvian Army. Dr. Norena-Chavez has pursued specialized studies at various institutions, including OAS (Organization of American States), China Europe International Business School, University of Seville, MIT, University of Szczecin, National Defense University, U.S. Special Operations Command South. He has also completed the Aerospace and Cyberspace Strategic Management Program at the Peruvian

Air War College and the Strategic Leadership and Crisis Management Course offered by the Peruvian Naval War College and the William J-Perry Center for Hemispheric Defense Studies. Dr. Norena-Chavez has served as a visiting professor at the Universidad San Buena Ventura, Universidad Externado, Peruvian Army War College, Peruvian Air War College. He is currently the CEO of Dinor General Services S.A.C. He is also a member of editorial boards and acts as a referee for several journals. Additionally, he holds the position of Director of the Doctorate in Administration at the University of Lima, Peru. He has previously held teaching positions in doctorate and master's degree programs at CENTRUM PUCP Business School and has been recognized as one of the top part-time professors.

Ercan Özen received his BSc in Public Finance (1994), MSc in Business-Accounting (1997), and PhD in Business Finance (2008) from the University of Afyon Kocatepe. Now he is Associate Professor of Finance in Department of Banking and Finance, School of Applied Sciences, University of Uşak, Turkey. His current research interests include different aspects of finance. He has (co-)authored five book chapters and more than 40 papers. He has participated in more than 30 conferences and is member of International Programme Committee of three conferences and workshops. He is Chair of International Applied Social Sciences Congress. He is also a certificated accountant, member of Aegean Finance Association and member of TEMA (Turkey Combating Soil Erosion, for Reforestation and the Protection of Natural Resources Foundation).

Peterson K. Ozili, PhD, is an Economist in the Economic Policy Office of the Central Bank of Nigeria. He works extensively in policymaking and is actively involved in academic research. He has experience in economic policy, financial inclusion, financial stability, financial innovation, banking regulation and supervision. His areas of specialisation are: financial economics, international development, accounting, development finance, the economics of financial markets, banking and financial reporting. He has published extensively in many accounting and finance journals such as the *British Accounting Review*, *Journal of Applied Accounting Research*, *Journal of Accounting in Emerging Economies*, *International Journal of Managerial Finance* and *European Journal of Finance*.

Sandra Ozolina is Assistant Professor and the Head of Foreign Language Department, teaching German for Specific Purposes and has been working for BA School of Business and Finance since 1993 and also has developed long-term cooperation with Goethe Institute. She is a member of *German Teachers' Association* and member of *Deutsche Auslandsgesellschaft*. She has participated in scientific conferences and is the co-author of the glossary *Banking Operations, Bank Settlements* (in German language). For the last few years, she has been researching the training process of German universities and the impact of IT on the study process, analysing the opinions of students and lecturers as well as conducting surveys of BA students about the role and impact of IT in the training process of foreign languages and other study courses.

K. M. Rajeewa Chanaka Lankanatha is a graduate of the Department of Accountancy and Finance, Faculty of Management Studies, Sabaragamuwa University of Sri Lanka. He got trained for his second-class lower division degree, BSc in Banking and Insurance, from the Sabaragamuwa University of Sri Lanka. He has completed DCM, DABF and DBIRM in the Institute of Bankers of Sri Lanka (IBSL) and he is also an Associate and Fellow member of the IBSL. Currently, he works as an Executive Officer – Enterprise Risk Management under the risk and compliance department in a reputed finance company in Sri Lanka. His research areas of interest are risk management in both the insurance and banking sector.

Kristian Pultz Schlosser is Lean Six Sigma and strategic consultant who has won multiple awards for his work and research. He has practical experience in leadership working in leading global enterprises, such as SEB Group, Genpact and Airbnb, across multiple countries. He is focussing on people-centred and large-scale data-driven transformations, implementation of new technologies and sustainability advocacy. He is currently a portfolio business owner, spanning from executive education, consultancy and investments. He is a student at RISEBA Doctoral Programme. His PhD topic is focussed on strategic leadership and its impact on delivering financial and social value in large and medium-sized enterprises.

Kiran Sood is a Professor at Chitkara Business School, Chitkara University, Punjab, India. She received her undergraduate and postgraduate degrees in Commerce from Panjabi University in 2002 and 2004, respectively. She earned her Master of Philosophy degree in 2008 and Doctor of Philosophy in Commerce with a concentration on Product Portfolio Performance of General Insurance Companies in 2017 from Panjabi University, Patiala, India. Before joining Chitkara University in July 2019, she had served four organisations with a total experience of 18 years. She has published various articles in various journals and presented papers at various international conferences. She serves as an Editor of the refereed journal, particularly the *International Journal of BioSciences and Technology*, *International Journal of Research Culture Society* and *The Journal of Corporate Governance, Insurance, and Risk Management* 2021. Her research mainly focusses on regulations, marketing and finance in insurance, insurance management, economics and management of innovation in insurance. She has edited more than 10 books with various international publishers such as Emerald, CRC, Taylors & Francis, AAP, WILEY Scrivener, IET, Rivers Publishers and IEEE.

Aivars Spilbergs is the Head of the Economics and Finance Department at BA School of Business and Finance. His previous experience includes working in economics and finance research (1976–1995 in the University of Latvia) and professional work in the banking sector (1995–2016 as the Head of Risk Management Department in SEB Bank). His recent activities include (1) Project Manager of a scientific project of BA School of Business and Finance; (2) participation in scientific projects of LSC and others; and (3) Council Member in global lending conference (2015–2018). He is the author of a number of scientific articles and presentations of research results on conferences during last years.

Astride Stonane is Assistant Professor of Foreign Language Department, teaching English for Specific Purposes to the students of Finance department and Business Process management students since 1998. She is responsible for updating study programme materials. She has participated in Erasmus+ mobility projects, and this has provided the opportunity to notice and compare the problems lecturers have in teaching business English abroad, like in Germany, Portugal and Denmark. The acquired knowledge has been compiled and selected in the form of study materials for the students of different language knowledge. At present, she has started researching the ways on how to organise effective work in the conditions of COVID-19 understanding the importance of IT technologies used in the process of teaching business issues to students. In parallel to her work with students, she has participated in scientific conferences organised by BA and is a co-author of several scientific publications. She is the co-author of the glossary *Banking Operations, Bank Settlements.*

Eleftherios Thalassinos, PhD (UIC, Chicago, USA, 1983), DHC Degrees in Economics (Danubius University of Galati, Romania, 2013; University of Craiova, Romania, 2015; and Rostov State University of Economics, Russia, 2018), MBA (De-Paul U Chicago, USA, 1979) and BA (U of Athens, Greece, 1976), a Jean Monnet Chair Professor experienced in European Economic Integration and International Finance. He is Editor-in-Chief of ERSJ, IJEBA, Editor of IJFIRM and Chair of ICABE. His professional experience includes quantitative analysis, technical and financial analysis, banking, business consulting, project evaluations, international business, international finance and maritime economics. He has a long track of publications in several journals, collective volumes and chapter books. Among them a publication as a chapter book in the *World Scientific Handbook* in *Financial Economics Series*, Vol. 5, is dedicated to the memory of Late Milton Miller, Nobel prize winner in Economics in 1990. Parallel to the academic career, he has performed as Bank Director for 12 years, Ministerial Advisor for 6 years, Public Servant for 4 years and Independent Consultant for a long time.

Georgiana Ioana Tircovnicu is a highly motivated and goal-driven financial analyst while being a PhD student at Doctoral School of Economics Sciences and Business Administration, West University of Timisoara, Romania, in the field of Accounting and Auditing Department. Her topic of Doctoral thesis is Enterprise Risk Management Challenges in Assessment and Reporting. Now, she has completed the first year of Doctoral studies, the period in which she taught Ethics and Accounting of credit institutions to students from years 1 and 3 at the faculty. She is a German speaker who just participated in an Erasmus Plus programme in Lithuania this summer.

Nazli Tyfekçi is a Faculty of Philology at the University of Gjakova 'Fehmi Agani', where she has been a faculty member since 2006. She is the Head of the English Language Department in the same faculty. She has obtained her PhD at St. Kiril and Methodius University in Northern Macedonia and her Master's and undergraduate studies at Pristina University in Kosovo. Her research interests lie in the area of language methodology in general and metacognition as a reading methodology in specific as well as bilingualism in multicultural environments ranging from theory to design and implementation. She has collaborated actively with researchers in several other disciplines of social sciences, particularly business administration, where her research interest spam was over English language importance in the business environment. Recently she is researching teaching with documentary movies and has published a guide for university professors on the same topic. She is Co-Editor-in-Chief in International Scientific Journal *Prizren Social Science Journal*, which has been indexed by important research criteria. For more since 2016, she is the Executive Director of NGO 'Association of Scientists and Intellectuals in Kosovo'. She has served on plenty of conference and workshop programme committees. In addition, she was Visiting Lecturer at John Von Neumann University in Hungary and Ondokuz Mayis University in Samsun Turkey. She lives with her husband, and their two children, in Prizren, the cultural capital city of Kosovo.

Emil Velinov is Assistant Professor at SKODA AUTO University, Department of Marketing and Management in Mlada Boleslav, the Czech Republic, adjunct Associate Professor at RISEBA University of Applied Sciences in Riga, Latvia, member of the Academy of International Business community, member of the European Academy of International Business community, an active reviewer in the *Journal for Eastern European Management Studies* and *European Journal of International Management* and Management Consultant hired by SUEZ Belgium. His research topics are international business, top management teams, virtual learning in international business and diversity management.

Tatjana Volkova is a Professor of Strategic Management and Innovation Management and a leading researcher at BA School of Business and Finance in Riga, Latvia. Her research findings have been published in several peer-reviewed books and journals nationally and internationally and presented at numerous international conferences. She is also a member of the Editorial Committee of Scientific Journals (e.g. Editor and Reviewer of *Journal of Business Management*, *SBS Journal of Applied Business Research* and *Banks and Banks System Journal*) and has participated in numerous international research projects.

Serap Vurur has 18 years of experience in teaching. At present, she is working as an Associate Professor in Finance at the Faculty of Bolvadin Applied Sciences, University of Afyon Kocatepe, Turkey. She has presented more than 25 papers at various national and international conferences and published more than 20 research papers in various reputed journals. She has published five books with the titles financial system, economics and cost stickiness.

FOREWORD

The book innovatively enhances several advanced researches performed to provide accurate solutions to the on-going challenges faced worldwide that have brought digital transformation, cyber security and risk management into a fierce debate and at the core of comprehensive resilience strategies.

The current ongoing challenges faced at the global level have brought digital transformation, cyber security and risk management into a fierce debate both scientists and public discourse rendering global the keen need for strategic resilience through new innovative measures and coordinated risk management approaches. The current COVID-19 pandemic has an outburst on the global economy, making digitalisation even more relevant and a key milestone to overcome these challenges and enhance sustainable economic development. Digitalisation notably shapes the world economy, impacting individuals, businesses, industries, labour markets, education systems and governments. On the one hand, digital transformations and technological progress are transforming the skills needed by individuals to actively engage in the world of online work in a modern economy and, especially, post-pandemic crisis. On the other hand, digital technologies have become an important enabler for innovation, thus bringing value added for companies and broad industries, along with numerous opportunities and capabilities for growth and increased performance. However, these are also associated with risks and deterring factors that must be managed wisely to ensure an effective digital environment, strategic resilience and sustainability.

Digitisation of economic and management processes allows for new value delivery and higher efficiency in implementing their strategic goals. However, it involves the need to reconfigure, reconstruct or build new business models. This is due to the inclusion of digital technologies in the existing rules of functioning among partners involved in the flow of resources and their readiness for digital transformation. Maximising the benefits of digitising processes can be achieved when data and information from multiple sources within cyber security are analysed and shared. In this way, it is possible to increase the transparency of flows, reduce costs from a global perspective and reduce uncertainty and risks arising both within the processes and in their environment. Such solutions may also counteract the negative effects of crises caused by unforeseen circumstances like the COVID-19 pandemic.

A significant challenge, in practical, organisational and scientific terms, is to understand the opportunities and threats resulting from digital transformation, to identify optimal strategies for the development of business entities in new economic and management conditions, taking care to adopt collateral and proper management of new risks and to attempt to set further directions of their evolution.

For this reason, it is important to present a book like this, in which very important issues are addressed in this contemporary social and technological context.

Addressing this challenge to the readers – in this book, the authors of the chapters indicate the latest theoretical and practical achievements in the above-mentioned scientific areas. The proposal book is a synthetic look at the complex digital transformation processes of the modern world both in terms of the underlying causes and the vast effects of the transformations and digitisation of social and economic life.

The book covers important topics such as ESG integration as a risk management tool for the financial decision-making process, multimedia sustained benefits for financial services and unveiling the potential of blockchain technology in the domain of research. Education is another important section of this book including the potential of the Romanian market in the adoption of blockchain technology, strategic leadership attributes for adopting digital technology, adapting information security policy, the liquidity position of the banking sector during the COVID-19 pandemic of western Balkan countries, the impact of COVID-19 on the stock market in BRIC countries, fiscal deficit, shift in paradigm and the financial education under the influence of digital transformation.

Moreover, it leaps into technologies including the Internet of Things (IoT), artificial intelligence (AI), Big Data analytics and blockchain, and the book also shows how enterprises can take advantage of them and ultimately beat the competition.

This book is an invaluable resource for postgraduate and undergraduate students of digital business, innovation and transformation. Showing how to initiate digital transformation across an organisation will prepare business owners, directors and management of small- and medium-sized businesses to take strategic advantage of new and emerging technologies to stay ahead of their competition.

Kiran Sood
Chitkara Business School, Chitkara University, Punjab, India

ACKNOWLEDGEMENT

We, the editors of this book, wish to thank Prof. Kiran Sood of Chitkara Business School, Chitkara University for the help in compiling this book.

CHAPTER 1

TRENDS IN ENTERPRISE RISK MANAGEMENT RESEARCH: A BIBLIOMETRIC ANALYSIS

Georgiana Ioana Tircovnicu and
Camelia-Daniela Hategan

West University of Timisoara, Romania

ABSTRACT

The need for an efficient enterprise risk management (ERM) has never been greater than today when organisations face complex and interconnected risks targeting their business models. Macroeconomics and geopolitical uncertainties, digital transformations of industries and sectors, cybersecurity, and climate change, among other trends, present significant uncertainties. This article aims to analyse the scientific papers on research specific to ERM and review the links between the researched area and market or corporate governance topics. Risk management is underdeveloped in many organisations; the current standard for risk management is a reactive approach. It is usually treated in isolation rather than as a core competency and a strategic asset. As a result, risk management processes are ineffective and seen as adding value to decision-making and responding to uncertainties. Based on the literature, the scope is to set up the framework for future research on ERM by building a bibliometric analysis and examining articles collected from the Web of Science Core Collection database. The study identified the essential research on this topic based on the citations of the papers and the author's countries with the highest

Digital Transformation, Strategic Resilience, Cyber Security and Risk Management
Contemporary Studies in Economic and Financial Analysis, Volume 111A, 1–20

Published under exclusive licence by Emerald Publishing Limited
ISSN: 1569-3759/doi:10.1108/S1569-37592023000111A001

number of publications and citations. VOSviewer software analysed the ERM system based on keywords, citations, geographical distribution, and authorships. The research proves a strong connection between the ERM and corporate governance topics considering the stage where most countries are regarding this subject.

Keywords: Enterprise risk management; bibliometric mapping; VOSviewer; corporate governance; market; trends

JEL classifications: M40; D81; G32

1. INTRODUCTION

The continuous development of technology induces the need for companies to control all the risks that could negatively affect a company. From this idea, more and more entities have implemented a risk management system, aiming to maintain a balance against the negative influences that may appear during the life of an enterprise.

The current topic represents an area that has not yet been fully explored, nationally and internationally. The state of the economy today provides us with an unpredictable environment, which is why so many managers focus on implementing an appropriate risk management strategy. In other words, risk management involves using various techniques and methods to reduce possible future risks. A good risk management strategy starts with a good knowledge of the business environment. It is also necessary for those charged with corporate governance to understand the entity's risk management capacity and to identify challenges that may arise at the financial assessment and reporting stage.

Regardless of whether it is a small business or a 'global player', each company can be affected by the occurrence of possible risks if there is a process to manage them. Risks can be very different; therefore, their effects can be more or less damaging to the company. Sometimes the consequences can be, in the worst scenario, existential. It is reasonable for a company to consider which risk is tolerable and which is not systematic. This systematic consideration is called risk management. Risk is frequently defined as a combination of damage capacity and appearance probability. In the process of minimising risks, there are two options:

a) To reduce the extent of the prejudice.
b) To reduce the probability of happening.

The goal is not to eliminate all risks because this is impossible but to achieve an optimal ratio.

The concept of ERM has undergone numerous interpretations and studies, creating the foundations for a process that can significantly influence a company's performance. Although the concept has been highly debated over the years, it is only seen as an asset in organisational management. As we will demonstrate later in this paper, North America and Europe are the pillars on which the foundations of the ERM concept were formed. The ERM idea has always been linked to studies such as sustainability, corporate governance, growth of the MSME sector, etc. Emerging countries have also begun investing time and research in this field. In a highly globalised corporate world, the consequences of various risks keep hampering businesses.

Risk management at the organisational level implies a universal vision of the business environment and the company's capabilities, which aims at strategic research to identify the most promising areas of activity.

Top management and CEOs must pay considerable attention to ERM practices, as this can lead to competitive advantage and, why not, increased company profits.

Undoubtedly, every business organisation is inclined towards making a profit. To this end, every small, large, or medium-sized company strives to gain an advantageous position in the market and, therefore, better performance. To achieve this goal, a firm may need enormous resources that can lead to high risks. The ERM process will never get results until the top management is fully aware of your financial issues and policies (Inder, Sood, & Grima, 2022).

The debate of this paper is done in two stages. In the first part of this article, we describe the concept of risk management and ERM. Based on the literature review, this concept is presented through the lens of its objective. These aspects are approached from several perspectives regarding the purpose of implementing such a process. In the second part of this article, we find a bibliometric analysis regarding the concept of ERM, followed by conclusions and personal opinions.

The objective was to establish the conceptual map for future research on the subject and examine the articles considered in constructing the bibliometric analysis.

The study identified essential research based on the number of citations of the works and the authors who significantly impacted the analysed field. For the case study, we used the VOSviewer software, which analysed the concept of ERM based on the relationship between the keywords used in the literature, citations, geographical distribution, as well as the working connection created by researchers from all over the world.

2. LITERATURE REVIEW

In Bernardi and Pincus's view (1996), every company should start from the premise that risks have a strategic basis for developing a risk management programme. Strategic threats are related to the organisation's future, with specific issues that are not current. It is necessary to distinguish between strategic risks for approximately stable periods of crisis and those that may arise unexpectedly throughout life. Brodeur et al. (2010) suggest that the relationship between the company's growth direction and the risk management system is reflected in the idea that they complement each other. Such a relationship suggests the likelihood of taking risks into account and taking steps to manage them. Second, that risk management is an essential component of overall corporate governance. In the face of uncertainty, risk management decisions must be compatible with decisions about the operation of a company.

Fabbian (2020) believes that when an organisation's financial position is assessed, resources are analysed, thus prioritising various strategies to manage the possible risks. The main task of an entrepreneur in this field is to find an option that offers the optimal combination of risk and income for a particular project. The characteristics of the risk management system are established by the relationship between its growth vision and the market in which the company operates. The company's growth strategy could be establishing a new niche business or maintaining a stable financial position.

Risk management does not refer to risk reduction but its control. Management must decide what risks to take beyond the settled tolerability of the implemented risk strategy. There is a single risk management option for the entire company. This aspect depends very much on the cultural climate of each entity according to studies conducted by Adibah, Mohamat, and Norman (2020).

A growing company approaches the implementation process of a risk management system at all levels of management. Risk management is not annexed to the general management structure of the organisation but is its central feature. Implementing the planning process involves an anti-risk strategy to mitigate the negative phenomena (Schmitz & Wittenberg, 2012). The further the training goes, the more inaccurate the data. Therefore, strategic planning translates into risk planning, considering the impact of risks on achieving the organisation's objective. Also, changes in the external environment, such as political nature or changes in consumer behaviour, can significantly impact a company's risk management strategy. Those who run a company need to know the 'business language' very well, according to a study by Tyagi (2021). As in many other professions, those involved in corporate governance often develop a language to communicate with others. Conversations about likelihood, impact, inherent and residual risk, degree of risk, and risk tolerance have become commonplace among risk management leaders. However, they may not be fully understood by all people and may not be well understood by other staff Sood, Seth, and Grima (2022).

Some risk management leaders forget the importance of using a language with a low level of difficulty so that the communication in the organisation is as good as possible. Some executives rethink their language to ensure business leaders hear and understand them. Learning and then using the business language used in an organisation can contribute to the involvement of business leaders in important risk management tasks.

Holland and Sylvis (2021) studied the complexity of business and concluded that it could exceed a person's ability to assess risk. Geopolitical events, cyber threats, disruptive innovation, and regulatory change are only a few issues that can pose significant risks to an organisation. Any of these risk factors is complex in itself.

Each of the above factors can trigger a chain reaction, causing other risks to arise, which adds to the complexity of the risk management challenge. In many cases, the number of factors that need to be assessed to analyse the likelihood of a risk impact accurately may exceed the ability of any individual.

The relationship between the strategy and the risk monitoring process must be as stable as possible. Unfortunately, Mashael (2020) noted a connection between an organisation's risk management and strategic planning activities in many organisations. In many organisations, risk management is seen as a mandatory regulatory activity that must be done to meet the demand outside the company.

This aspect often means that the risk management process is degraded to a lower, non-strategic position, which addresses critical issues, but does not address issues related to the strategy for addressing possible risks. According to Karnes's (2017) studies, an organisation's efforts in terms of risk management are inadequately correlated with the company's strategic plan. This is partly how risk managers have focused their efforts on identifying and assessing risks.

The perspective on ethical culture can lead to one of the most significant risks for an organisation. The business culture varies from organisation to organisation, and it is essential to understand how it can affect the organisation's risk management efforts. Although most organisations have a set of defined business values, there are situations where management's behaviour and decisions do not reflect those values.

In this case, Seshagiri (2021) concludes that risk management can contribute by recognising situations where ethical values are not respected and implicitly drawing attention to this fact. Of course, this can be a significant risk for risk managers if there is little support from those with crucial governance roles such as the board. As the risk management process is integrated into the organisation, communication between the entity and the board becomes efficient and meaningful. External pressure is causing boards to become increasingly involved in risk oversight activities. The risk management process positively and significantly influences a company's performance. Organisations that integrate ERM into strategic planning benefit from the characteristics of the risk management process in several areas. Some of the advantages of this process are presented in Table 1.

Following the literature review, it can be stated that risk management policy is the art of risk management in an unpredictable economic situation. The approach to risk management in the development policy of organisations should be systematic. Based on progressive changes, the risk management strategy focuses on long-term research to reduce risks. A mixture of values improves the efficiency of decisions in practice (Yerpudee et al., 2022).

Strategic risk preparedness is the management mechanism that creates and manages strategic communication between the organisation's mission, priorities, future opportunities, and threats. Each organisation establishes the risk preparation activities according to the object of activity of the entity. Implementing a company's risk policy consists of two stages (the strategic risk planning and management processes).

Table 1. The Advantages of Implementing a Risk Management Process

Financial benefits	Infrastructure benefits	Market advantages	Reputation benefits
Cost reduction	Reducing operating costs	Maximising business opportunities	Compliance with regulatory requirements
Increasing the company's profitability.	The risk management process helps organisations stay effective and provides a competitive advantage.	Better customer satisfaction.	Advantages of advertising – The public notices effective implementation, which helps to establish public confidence in the company.
Accuracy in the reporting process of the organisation's financial risks.	The risk management process helps organisations stay efficient and provides a competitive advantage.	Adverse effects can be reduced.	Structured risk identification and remediation approach; regular monitoring and communication ensure customer confidence.

Source: Author's creation.

Moldovan and Neamţu (2016) concretise the idea that a well-developed risk management process can increase the level of performance, thus contributing to:

- Creating greater security in the business process
- More efficient provision of products and services
- The efficiency of the management process in terms of the environment
- Decreasing the degree of pollution
- Efficient use of resources in the organisation, including financial ones
- Loss reduction

Halil (2012) mentions that good risk management involves identifying the risks specific to each objective and evaluating and establishing the means of control to mitigate their occurrence.

Lamptey and Singh (2018) considers that the management policy of an organisation should be aimed to adopt the best practices for identifying and assessing the risks associated with specific objectives to reduce them to a level as acceptable as possible that does not affect the quality of products, the quality of services provided, or even the well-being of the entire organisation.

Risks need to be known and managed as efficiently as possible. This phase is the first step in building a risk profile (the direction they are heading). This stage can only occur if we assume that in the previous stage, different objectives related to the environment or the qualitative nature corresponding to the field of the organisation were established. In that case, various activities or actions will be documented to achieve these objectives and the risks during the development.

According to Moshesh, Niemann, and Kotzé (2017), each identified risk can have significance for several objectives. The possibility of this risk being realised differs depending on the importance of each objective. Once the objectives are identified and found in the organisation's strategy, they must be closely correlated with the activities in each department and complemented by the associated risks.

Branson (2015) indicates that risk assessment is done through a thorough analysis. The probability of materialisation of the risks and, at the same time, the influence that they may have on the previously established objectives are evaluated.

The hierarchy of risks is established according to the level of specialised departments and tolerance towards risk. Various ways of dealing with risks and the people responsible for managing them will be implemented.

The review process assures that all aspects of the risk management process are reviewed at least annually. According to the authors of Agrawal and Chadha (2005), the risks must be reviewed with an appropriate frequency; this process must be in accordance with the fluidity of the circumstances and the different procedures to be put into operation.

Nichita and Vulpoi (2016) mention in their studies the existence of two categories of research methods that consider financial reporting, namely:

1. The annual financial statements shall be used as a source of analysis for risk reporting.
2. Analysis of internal reports specific to management.

As mentioned above, the risks are subject to specific objectives. They form a well-defined system, interdependently linked to the overall objectives so that activity levels can support each other. Risk management aims to manage events that could harm the organisation's objectives and implicitly on its resources of any kind.

Therefore, we can say that the implementation of risk management in an organisation comes from the following three scenarios:

A. Uncertainty is a daily reality = the reaction to uncertainty becomes a constant concern of management.
B. The analysis of the consequences does not remedy the causes = the materialised risks will occur in the future more quickly.
C. Regular risk review = the organisation's efforts focus on what is essential, and the resources are not used in areas irrelevant to its purposes.

The uncertainty created by the evolution of the COVID-19 virus has triggered a complex area of risk that affects virtually all aspects of most entities. According to van der Meulen (2020), only now people in charge of organisations have realised the implications of being less prepared to deal with a situation caused by an event as significant as the COVID-19 pandemic.

Pandemic risk has long been recognised as central to risk management in practice. However, the COVID-19 pandemic has shown that generic pandemic risk has been underestimated in terms of its size and potential impact. The role of ERM is to assess and define risks that may affect an organisation's success in achieving its strategic objectives. ERM does this by helping the board and managers understand the organisation's risk appetite, identifying risks, assessing their impact, and developing a risk response. Ultimately, ERM is about helping management and the board create and sustain value.

The COVID-19 pandemic has shown that adverse effects are difficult to estimate reliably. At the same time, it is challenging to analyse such an event's persistence level. In this sense, pandemic risk should be perceived as a severe threat to an entity's strategic objectives. With this phenomenon, many companies have substantially re-examined their risk management approaches. Unsurprisingly, the COVID-19 pandemic has become a focus for risk management professionals and will likely remain a focus for businesses, governments, and universities as it has unleashed challenges across the board.

In response to the pandemic crisis, organisations across the globe have reviewed their risk identification, analysis, and assessment processes to minimise negative impacts on organisational performance. Shareholders communicated with managers and investors to better connect risk management with the company's development strategy. Furthermore, the crisis highlighted the importance of treating the subject of ERM not just as a mandatory regulatory requirement but as an integral part of the strategic process.

The initial response to the pandemic was more of a short-term action to stabilise the organisation through the first wave of the crisis. Also, the initial response to the pandemic required ensuring the safety of employees but also ways to communicate policies and critical information between associates and third parties. In the second phase, the risk assessment was carried out ensuring compliance with emerging legislation and protocols and examining risk recurrence. In the last phase of responding to the unforeseen, organisations should examine and implement changes to ensure the sustainability and continued success of the organisation. An initial response that organisations should consider in the third phase is examining their risk identification process (Sood, Kaur, & Grima, 2022). Risk identification methods are a fundamental part of ERM implementation. Many organisations have been surprised by the depth and severity of the pandemic has had on their organisations.

With this in mind, it is vital for organisations to develop possible scenarios that describe the types of events the world is facing today in terms of pandemic situations as a result of demographic, economic, operational, and strategic risks. It is necessary to examine the risk scenarios, especially how the organisation's most valuable assets are affected to maintain the value factors in future crises to support its viability.

Company management oversees and monitors the corporation's operational viability, legal compliance, and financial performance. They should monitor the impact of COVID-19 regularly and understand how management assesses it, taking into account the acceptability of managers' responses to the pandemic.

In this regard, the ERM process can be strengthened through more effective communication and establishing a risk culture. Due to this, we might say there is significant room for improvement in the risk management process in many organisations. In risk identification and analysis, it is necessary to address the ability to understand such events and, therefore, the development of cloud scenarios responsible for dealing with these types of risk events in the future.

3. RESEARCH METHODOLOGY

The continuous growth of risks that could impact the efficiency of an enterprise determined us to evaluate and review different articles regarding risk management and ERM, using a statistical method such as a bibliometric analysis. We collected the data from the Web of Science (WoS) Core Collection, one of the highest qualitative research information sources. The WoS information network contains some of the most vigorously verified academic papers, so we created our database using this source of information. The outcome of our database was achieved using terms such as 'enterprise risk management', 'ERM', and 'risk management'.

Our findings are based on all articles (from the economy, management, and business finance) published between 2013 and 2022. The sample consists of 34,297 articles. The bibliometric visualisation network was created using the free VOSviewer, establishing a study based on keywords (keywords that arise under the abstract), quotations, geographical representation, and authorship. Through this evaluation, we should be able to identify the nature of the connection between the writers and the research subject by assessing occurrences and co-citations.

While using VOSviewer, it was crucial to understanding the software's terminology. Each constructed map comprises items. For example, items can be identified as researchers or publications representing the object of interest. The connection between items is outlined through different types of links. These links are bibliographic coupling links for published papers, researchers' co-authorship links, and terms' co-occurrence links. When the association is strong, every link is symbolised by its force, defined by a specific mathematical value. With their links, items can be classified into different clusters (groups). It may occur when not all items on the chart are grouped into clusters, which means those elements do not relate to any defined clusters. The clusters are marked with a different colour, while each element has assigned a specific feature. We might notice that the programme uses attributes such as 'score' or 'weight'. The purpose of these attributes is to classify the elements as essential or less significant depending on the attribute received; for example, an increased score stands for more extensive meaning than decreased score.

4. RESULTS

4.1. Keywords Review

The keyword study identifies several keywords based on the selected criteria. The identified keywords illustrate the most used elements in the selected database. In the first stage of the case study, we tried to identify and highlight the most essential and questioned theories associated with the 'ERM' concept. Even though our WoS extracted database consisted of 34,297 articles, the programme we used (VOSviewer) underlined 145 keywords after further analysis. Fig. 1 illustrates these elements through the links between them. The larger dots signify a higher occurrence of the keywords. The lines represent the connection between the keywords, and the thicker a line, the more those keywords were identified together in the same article.

The distance within the dots characterises the strength of the connection. If the difference between the two dots is slight, then the connection within the concepts (keywords) is more substantial. Ultimately, it is vital to observe that each colour marks a different group (cluster) of keywords generated by the software.

The VOSviewer visualisation network has returned four clusters due to using a rate of 50 occurrences of keywords. Table 2 portrays the four clusters; each is represented by the top 10 significant keywords placed in descending order based on their frequency.

Based on the presented information, we notice the four top keywords: 'risk' (with 7815 occurrences), 'model' (with 3735 occurrences), 'competition' (with 780 occurrences), and 'firm' (with 1682 occurrences). The red cluster, governed by the

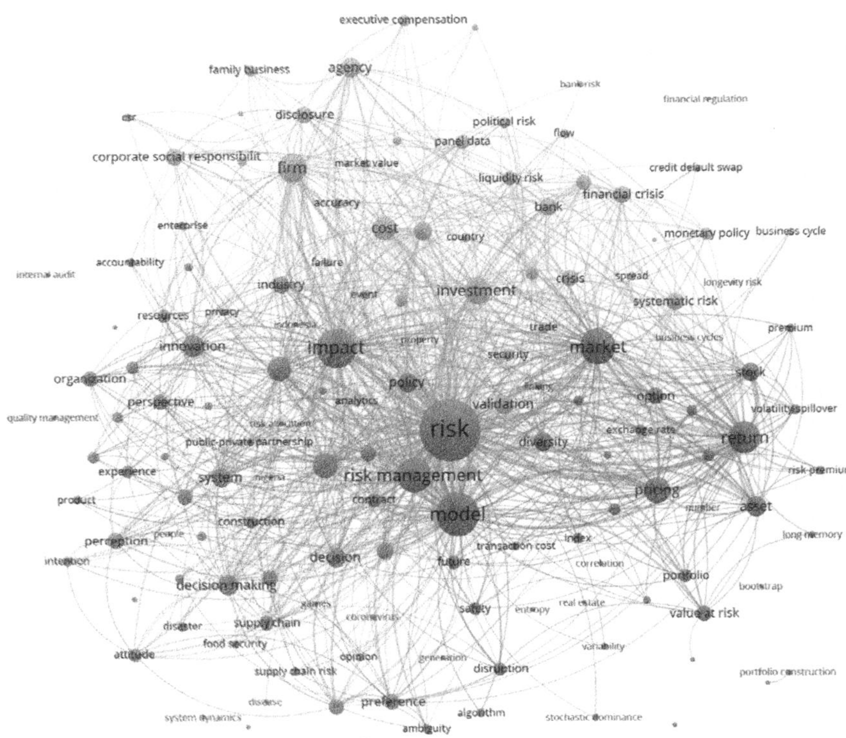

Fig. 1. Co-occurrence Map of Author Keywords Regarding ERM System.
Source: Author's computation in VOSviewer.

Table 2. Clusters of Keywords

Cluster 1 (Red)	Cluster 2 (Green)	Cluster 3 (Blue)	Cluster 4 (Yellow)
Risk	Model	Competition	Firm
Impact	Market	Validation	Investment
Strategy	Risk management	Bank	Cost
Behaviour	Return on investment	Systematic risk	Agency
Innovation	Pricing	Crisis	Corporate social responsibility
Decision-making	Asset	Insurance	Disclosure
System	Stock	liquidity risk	Board
Policy	Diversity	Panel data	Empirical analysis
COVID-19 pandemic	Option	Emerging market	Accuracy
Industry	Value at risk	Monetary policy	Executive compensation

Source: Author's computation.

word 'risk', includes 59 elements. It is essential to mention that the VOSviewer software has integrated several types of risks under the keyword 'risk' such as business risk, crash risk, financial risk, etc. After all, all these subcategories represent threats that companies face and must be eliminated. From our perspective, the first cluster presents the most vital connections between the elements. As the table above shows, each cluster contains items influencing or impacting the research topic (ERM). On an important notice, we managed to observe that the first cluster creates the foundation of a risk management system based on innovation (with 1041 occurrences), ethical behaviour (with 1225 occurrences), good policy (with 740 occurrences), and advanced strategy plan (with 1300 occurrences).

Furthermore, we realise that COVID-19 pandemic had a significant impact on the ERM system since we identified a significant number of 631 occurrences and 1193 total link strength. This can only mean that researchers have noticed considerable influences worth studying. The keyword 'decision-making' has reached 1569 occurrences, which implies that in this process, it is always about making decisions; the important thing is to make decisions in favour of the company. The second cluster (green) refers to a conducive business environment. The keyword 'market' is the second most vital element from the green cluster (with 2538 occurrences), indicating a solid connection with the research topic. The green cluster contains 41 elements including pricing (with 1377 occurrences), stock (with 721 occurrences), and asset (with 809 occurrences). The third category of elements (blue cluster) includes 26 items and represents the existence of a competitive environment (with 780 occurrences), where various types of risks can occur such as systematic risks (with 609 occurrences), liquidity risks (with 455 occurrences) and all other types of crises (with 579 occurrences) that may lead to the need to implement different types of insurance. We also notice the keyword 'bank' (with 725 occurrences) here, which makes sense because many companies take out loans from banks when they become financially unavailable. The fourth group connects the rest of the elements with aspects found in the governing process and contains 19 keywords. Among the keywords used for the governance environment of a company, we find items such as investment (with 1522 occurrences and 4062 total link strength), corporate social responsibility (with 628 occurrences and 1501 total link strength), board (with 473 occurrences and 1127 total link strength) and executive compensation (with 281 occurrences and 590 total link strength). The image in Fig. 1 shows that the red and green clusters are positioned close. The dots are thicker than the other, which means that these two groups of elements have a closer connection. At the same time, their keywords were most often used in the analysed articles.

4.2. Country Co-author Review

During the second part of our study, we imposed a minimum of 20 published documents per country and a minimum of 10 citations as a selection criterion. The programme selected from the database (34,297 articles) 86 countries that met the requirements. We considered the citation per country helped us notice how strong some connections between authors worldwide are. The research teams from different countries have built a stable collaboration network, creating the foundation for future research on the 'ERM' topic. In Fig. 2, we might notice that some dots are more significant than others. This means that some countries have published more papers on this subject, showing a greater interest in it. The density of each line is a sign of qualitative cooperation among researchers.

According to the second bibliometric visualisation network, we identified five clusters. The cluster elements are reflected in Table 3. Each cluster is represented by the top 10 essential countries, placed in descending order according to the strength of the cooperation between writers, the number of published documents per country, and the number of citations.

Following the presented table, we established our top five countries where the subject of ERM has been highly disputed: England (with 56,414 citations and 3988 published documents), Australia (with 25,096 citations and 2261 published documents), Germany (with 30,984 citations and 2428 published documents), Spain (with 12,671 citations and 1050 published documents), and the USA (with 155,879 citations and 10,081 published documents). Even if the highest point found on the bibliometric map is in the last cluster (purple), the first cluster (red) is the most widespread, containing in its network 41 countries. This group of countries is led by England, while cluster two, led by Australia, and cluster three (blue), led by Germany, contain 17 and 12 items. Cluster four, led by Spain, is formed out of 10 elements, while cluster five, led by the United States, has grouped only six countries. Out of the five clusters, the United States (cluster 5) finds itself in the centre of the bibliometric visualisation network with 155,879 references and 10,081 published documents, having the highest link strength (7326) in the citations network. China follows the USA in the same cluster, where 5397 published documents on the ERM system have been analysed. Ecuador, Argentina, Peru, and Mexico (cluster four) represent the countries where the ERM is not yet a topic of interest. The number of WoS-indexed articles in these countries

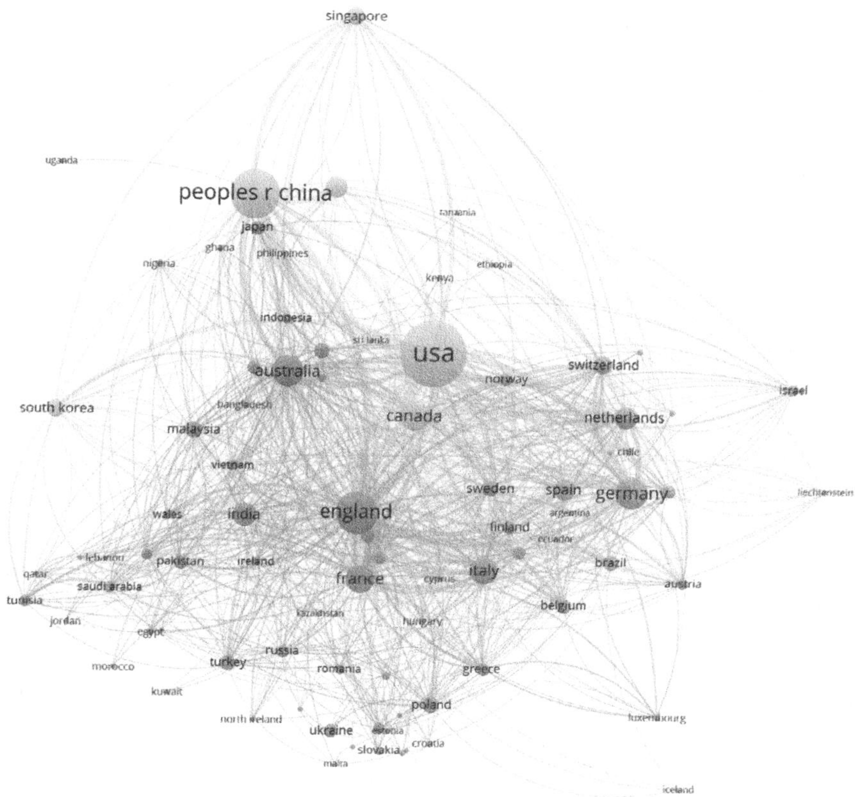

Fig. 2. Countries' Co-authorship Bibliometric Map.
Source: Author's computation in VOSviewer.

is 204 papers. This proves that this field is still developing, and it is still worth researching. Taking a look at cluster three (blue), we notice some of the most developed countries of the world such as Germany (with 30,984 quotations and 2428 published papers), the Netherlands (with 18,588 quotations and 1145 published papers), Switzerland (with 11,695 quotations and 809 published papers), Sweden (with 7599 quotations and 622 published papers), Denmark (with 6671 quotations and 417 published papers), Norway (with 5309 quotations and 431 published papers), and Finland (with 5248 quotations and 380 published papers) showing considerable interest in the subject. Observing the distance between the representative dots and the thickness of the lines between these, we can conclude that there is strong cooperation between researchers from the USA, China, Canada, Germany, England, and France. To outline the results of the second part of the analysis, we conclude that the trends of ERM systems cover a wide geographical area, demonstrating a massive interest in this subject. Accordingly, this result creates the foundation of the ERM trends.

Table 3. Clusters of References Per State.

Cluster 1 (Red)	Cluster 2 (Green)	Cluster 3 (Blue)	Cluster 4 (Yellow)	Cluster 5 (Purple)
England	Australia	Germany	Spain	USA
France	New Zealand	Netherlands	Israel	China
Scotland	Malaysia	Italy	Portugal	Canada
India	Japan	Switzerland	Brazil	Singapore
Turkey	South Africa	Sweden	Argentina	Taiwan
Greece	Vietnam	Denmark	Chile	South Korea
Poland	Thailand	Austria	Mexico	
Pakistan	Indonesia	Belgium	Colombia	
United Arab Emirates	Bangladesh	Norway	Peru	
Saudi Arabia	Nigeria	Finland	Ecuador	

Source: Author's computation.

4.3. Author Co-citation Network Review

The following stage of our bibliometric visualisation network emphasises the leading authors and researchers in risk management. The analysis per author quotations confirms who are the most quoted authors regarding ERM and risk management scientific articles. Considering the extracted database (34,297 articles) and the enforced criteria (min. 15 published articles per author as the first author); (min. 10 citations of an author), the VOSviewer programme has returned 52 researchers. According to Fig. 3, the top five authors with some of the most robust link connections are Mensi, Walid (with 42 total link strength), Olson, David l. (with 41 total link strength), Hammoudeh S. (with 38 total link strength), Ji, Qiang (with 36 total link strength) and Kang Sang Hoon (with 33 total link strength).

According to the third bibliometric visualisation network, we recognised five clusters. The cluster elements are reflected in Table 4, where each cluster is represented by the top 10 most quoted authors of scientific papers placed in descending order.

The first cluster contains 10 researchers and looking at the bibliometric map; we see a solid connection between Mensi W. (with 1192 citations), Hammoudeh S. (with 1069 citations), Kang S.H. (with 646 citations), Shahzad S.J.H (with 537 citations), and Uddin G.S. (with 516 citations). As far as we can see in Fig. 3, the links between these authors, grouped in cluster three (blue), are thicker than any other lines, and according to the citation criteria, cluster four is the most valuable. According to the citation criteria, we identify the first cluster as the most significant due to the most quoted author, Ji Q., with 1815 references. We also find Choi T.M. (with 1100 references) and Fan Y. (with 743 references) in this cluster. Reboredo J. (with 1402 citations) is the second most quoted author regarding ERM topics according to the quotation numbers. In the yellow cluster, we identify Fabozzi F.J., the author with the highest number of published articles (52 released documents) regarding the ERM trends. The last cluster (purple) is formed out of nine authors with a lower number of citations or published documents, indicating

Fig. 3. Author Co-citation Map Regarding ERM.
Source: Author's computation in VOSviewer

Table 4. Clusters of References Per Author

Cluster 1 (Red)	Cluster 2 (Green)	Cluster 3 (Blue)	Cluster 4 (Yellow)	Cluster 5 (Purple)
Ji, Qiang	Bouri, Elie	Reboredo, Juan c.	Fabozzi, Frank J.	Wang, Gang-Jin
Choi, Tsan-Ming	Lee, Chien-Chiang	Mensi, Walid	Wong, Wing-Keung	Wang, Yudong
Fan, Ying	Gupta, Rangan	Hammoudeh, Shawkat	Mcaleer, Michael	Ma, Feng
Wang, Shouyang	Lee, chi-Chuan	Duc Khuong Nguyen	Umar, Zaghum	Li, Jing
Tiwari, Aviral Kumar	Han, Liyan	Kang, sang Hoon	Zaremba, Adam	Wei, Yu
Kumar, Satish	Xiong, Xiong	Shahzad, Syed Jawad Hussain	Caporin, Massimilia	Liu, Li
Olson, David l.	Yang, Jinqiang	Uddin, Gazi Salah	Yousaf, Imran	Chevallier, Julien
Liu, Jia	Liu, yang	Boubaker, Sabri	Ali, Shoaib	Zhang, Yaojie
Chen, Rongda	Wang, Chih-Wei	Yoon, Seong-Min	Gubareva, Mariya	Wu, Chongfeng
Lai, kin Keung	Sornette, Didier	Sensoy, Ahmet		

Source: Author's computation.

their incipient path in the research of this subject. We observe Wang Y. with 408 citations, 26 published documents, and 28 total link strengths.

4.4. University Co-Author Review

The last part of our study is meant to analyse the behaviour of the research team in institutions and evaluate their network connection. For this stage of our bibliometric review, we developed a University Co-Author analysis to underline the collaboration within universities worldwide. Considering our database of 34,297 articles and the required selection (a minimum of 10 papers per University and 50 citations per University), the VOSviewer software has returned to 113 universities. Looking at Fig. 4, we notice that the bibliometric visualisation network does not highlight a particular Institution; the representative dots are similar in size. However, we can identify the top five most-cited universities regarding ERM trends: Erasmus University Rotterdam (with 4175 citations and 297 published papers), Cornell University (with 4536 citations and 265 published papers), the National University of Singapore (with 4742 citations and 253 published papers), National Bureau of Economic Research (with 8280 citations and 249 published papers), and the last classified Institution is Hong Kong Polytech University (with 4413 citations and 253 published papers).

According to the last bibliometric visualization network, we grouped our Institutions into five clusters. The cluster items are reflected in Table 5. Each cluster is represented by the top 10 most quoted universities, where researchers have shown interest in the trends of ERM topics.

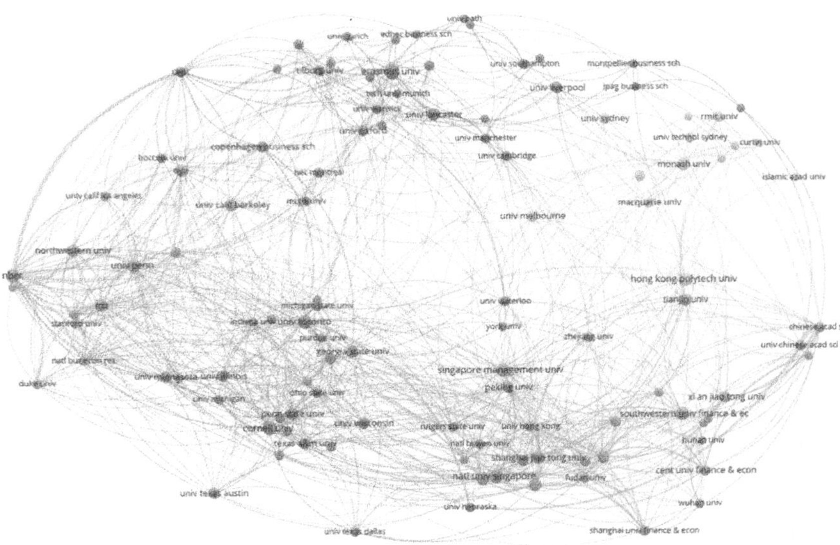

Fig. 4. Universities' Co-authorship Map on ERM.
Source: Author's computation in VOSviewer.

Table 5. Clusters of References Per Institution.

Cluster 1 (Red)	Cluster 2 (Green)	Cluster 3 (Blue)	Cluster 4 (Yellow)	Cluster 5 (Purple)
Erasmus University	Cornell University	National University of Singapore	National Bureau of Economic Research	Hong Kong Polytech University
CEPR	Penn State University	City University Hong Kong	Stanford University	Monash University
Copenhagen Business School	Indiana University	Chinese ACAD Science	National Bureau of Economic Research	University Melbourne
Bocconi University	Ohio State University	Chinese University Hong Kong	NYU	RMIT University
City University London	Georgia State University	Hong Kong University Sci & Technology	MIT	Curtin University
IPAG Business School	Arizona State University	Hunan University	Northwestern University	Macquarie University
Frankfurt School Finance & Management	Michigan State University	Huazhong University Sci & Technology	Harvard University	Deakin University
Katholieke University Leuven	Natl Taiwan University	Fudan University	Duke University	Massey University
HEC Montreal	Natl Chengchi University	Cent University Finance & Economics	Columbia University	Griffith University
EDHEC Business School	Florida State University	Beihang University	Boston University	Islamic Azad University

Source: Author's computation.

According to the network review, the Institution with the highest published and cited articles is the National Bureau of Economic Research Institution, with 249 published papers and 8280 quotations. Also, the National Bureau of Economic Research Institution has the highest total link strength (362) out of the selected sample. Another great university that has put a lot of effort and resources into researching this field is Sandford University (cluster four), with 143 published documents and 5537 references. Looking closer at the bibliometric representation, we find that cluster four is the most valuable group of Institutions, finding universities like Harvard University (with 4290 citations and 122 published papers) and Duke University (with 3117 citations and 119 published documents). The Erasmus University Rotterdam has the highest number of published documents regarding risk management (297 published papers). Our last network visualization analysis results lead us to conclude that the universities that have approached this subject are spreading all over the globe, an aspect also represented by the shape of the map.

5. CONCLUSIONS

This literature review analyses the progress to date regarding the risk management process in an enterprise. This study was carried out through the VOSviewer software, performing a bibliometric analysis to highlight the incipient state of research on the subject. Studying this area could have a significant impact on future companies. Therefore, the present research reveals the following results.

The keyword analysis was performed to find the most used keywords in the published papers. The VOSviewer programme presented many existing keywords connected with our subject of interest. However, following the imposed criteria, the software returned only 145 keywords, depending on how often they were used. Applicable to our study, the most important terms are described by: 'risk', 'impact', 'competition', and 'firm'. Furthermore, there are other keywords strongly connected to 'enterprise risk management' such as 'strategy', 'decision-making', 'policy', and 'cost'. Through our analysis, we managed to see that there is a strong connection between 'enterprise risk management', 'market', and 'banking Institutions'.

Additionally, according to the country's co-authorship review of ERM published papers, we identified five representative countries (led by the USA, England, Australia, Germany, and Spain). Also, we learned who are the primary authors in this field research with the help of the co-citation analysis. On that account, each of the researchers has brought a significant contribution to the discussed topic. Among the Institutions listed in our database are prestigious organisations such as the National Bureau of Economic Research Institution, Massachusetts Institute of Technology, and Frankfurt School of Finance & Management.

Analysing the results of this research, we realise that although this topic has been researched in various financial fields, there are still gaps, given hidden risks. This study proves an interdependent connection between ERM, market, and banking. For successful performance, the company must consider the changes and recommendations brought by the two areas.

ERM topic is only at the beginning of the research. The COVID-19 pandemic has shown us that we will never be 100 per cent prepared in front of the unknown. Since underdeveloped countries have only begun to show interest in the subject, we can say that there are still difficulties implementing an ERM process in different businesses. This situation limits researchers in this area of expertise but is also an advantage since the area is not thoroughly researched.

Therefore, although the database provided by WoS consists of numerous scientific research and scientific papers, there is enough space for future research. The paper aims to highlight the concept of risk management in the specialised literature through existing materials. Although there has been an increased interest in this field in recent years, we have noticed that the studies are still at the beginning, especially if we consider the accounting side of this subject.

By recognising the links between risk management, ethical behaviour, efficient strategy, and a stable implemented policy, companies can face the risks that can affect their performance and success without shaking their foundations.

The purpose of the paper is thus embodied in the identification of the conceptual frameworks offered by the specialised literature, thus laying the foundations for future research.

The contribution of this article can be seen in light of the fact that there is not much research on this topic, which is why the field can be discussed more widely. Since all the information was extracted from only one database (WoS), this paper faced a series of limitations such as the small number of identified articles.

This article can only be the beginning of a series of research in this area, considering the numerous possibilities for future studies. For future research directions, we can consider using a larger sample and, why not, even use a database with more information about companies listed on the European Capital Exchange. At the same time, we can consider developing a bibliometric analysis, creating a qualitative statistical analysis for an econometric model analysing the factors that influence the content of financial documents.

REFERENCES

Adibah, J., Mohamat, S. H., & Norman, M. S. (2020). Non-financial risk disclosure: From narratives to an index based on Delphi technique. *Asian Journal of Accounting and Governance*, *14*, 123–129. Retrieved from https://ejournal.ukm.my/ajac/article/view/43968/11348

Agrawal, A., & Chadha, S. (2005). Corporate governance and accounting scandals. *The Journal of Law and Economics*, *48*(2), 371–406.

Bernardi, R. A., & Pincus, K. V. (1996). The relationship between materiality thresholds and judgments of fraud risk. *Managerial Finance*, *22*(9), 1–15.

Branson, B. (2015). Reporting key risk information to the board of directors, top risk executives share their practices, ERM Initiative North Carolina State University, Poole College of Management, NC State, Enterprise Risk Management Initiative. Retrieved from https://erm.ncsu.edu/library/article/reporting-key-risk-information-to-the-board-of-directors

Brodeur, A., Buehler, K., Patsalos-Fox, M., & Pergler, M. (2010). *A board perspective on enterprise risk management*. McKinsey Working Papers on Risk, 8. Retrieved from https://www.mckinsey.com/business-functions/risk-and-resilience/our-insights/a-board-perspective-on-enterprise-risk-management

Fabbian, V. (2020). *A systematic literature review on risk disclosure process: Insights, gaps, and evidence from Italian listed companies*. Final Thesis, Master's Degree in Economia e Gestione delle Aziende.

Halil, H. P. (2012). Financial reporting risk. *Global Journal of Management and Business Research*, *XII*(15), 9–13.

Holland, T., & Sylvis, K. (2021). Using the COSO ERM framework to move forward from the pandemic crisis. *Risk Management Magazine*. Retrieved from https://www.rmmagazine.com/articles/article/2021/06/09/using-the-coso-erm-framework-to-move-forward-from-the-pandemic-crisis

Inder, S., Sood, K., & Grima, S. (2022). Antecedents of behavioural intention to adopt internet banking using structural equation modelling. *Journal of Risk and Financial Management*, *15*(4), 157.

Karnes, G. (2017). The 3 common challenges of ERM. Retrieved from https://www.corporatecomplianceinsights.com/3-common-challenges-erm/

Lamptey, E., & Singh, R. (2018). Fraud risk management over financial reporting: A contingency theory perspective. *Journal of Leadership, Accountability and Ethics*, *15*(4). https://doi.org/10.33423/jlae.v15i4.171

Mashael, K. (2020). Simplified enterprise risk management (SERM). *International Journal of Multidisciplinary Research and Publications*, *3*(6), 34–38.

Moldovan D. S., & Neamţu C. V. (2016). Abordarea riscului într-un sistem de management integrat calitate – Mediu. *Revista Calitatea: Acces la Success, Bucharest*, *17*(155), 10–13.

Moshesh, R., Niemann, W., & Kotzé, T. (2017). Enterprise risk management implementation challenges: A case study in a petrochemical supply chain. *South African Journal of Industrial Engineering*, *29*(4), 230–244.

Nichita, M. E., & Vulpoi, M. (2016). Relationship between risk and transparency in the financial statements of professional services entities. *Audit Financiar*, *5*(137), 540–550.

Schmitz, J., & Wittenberg, A. (2012). Dynamic financial planning – Making enterprise risk management matter. *Oliver Wyman Risk Journal*, *2*, 20–27.

Seshagiri, R. V. (2021). *GRC, the backbone of enterprise risk management* (1st ed). San Diego, CA: Templar Shield Inc.

Sood, K., Kaur, B., & Grima, S. (2022). Revamping Indian non-life insurance industry with a trusted network: Blockchain technology. In K. Sood, R. K. Dhanaraj, B. Balamurugan, S. Grima, & R. U. Maheshwari (Eds.), *Big data: A game changer for insurance industry* (pp. 213–228). Bingley: Emerald Publishing Limited.

Sood, K., Seth, N., & Grima, S. (2022). Portfolio performance of public sector general insurance companies in India: A comparative analysis. In S. Grima, E. Özen, & I. Romānova (Eds.), *Managing risk and decision making in times of economic distress, Part B* (pp. 215–229). Bingley: Emerald Publishing Limited.

Tyagi, A. (2021). Enterprise risk management: Benefits and challenges. School of Computer and Information Sciences, University of the Cumberlands. Retrieved from https://papers.ssrn.com/sol3/papers.cfm?abstract_id=3748267

van der Meulen, R. (2020). *COVID-19 Makes a Strong Business Case for Enterprise Risk Management*, April 10, 2020. Available at: https://www.gartner.com/smarterwithgartner/covid-19-makes-a-strong-business-case-for-enterprise-risk-management/.

Yerpudee, S., Sood, K., & Grima, S. (2022). Blockchain-augmented digital supply chain management: A way to sustainable business. *Journal of Risk and Financial Management*, *16*(1), 7.

CHAPTER 2

THE ASSESSMENT OF THE ROMANIAN MARKET REGARDING THE POTENTIAL ADOPTION OF BLOCKCHAIN

Maria Moraru

West University of Timisoara, Romania

ABSTRACT

The COVID-19 pandemic has impacted companies both ways, negatively by testing their ability to adapt in uncertain situations and positively by accelerating the adoption of technology systems. One of the new technologies is represented by blockchain which brings decentralised control, transparency between the involved parties, and two-ways security checks on transactions. The Romanian market has been selected to provide an early assessment of the potential the market has on implementing blockchain technology and becoming more transparent within customer and state interactions. As part of the blockchain network, it brings both numerous benefits such as transparency in interactions with other parties and freedom as it is not regulated by any kind of authority yet.

Keywords: Blockchain; technology; accounting; management; transactions; domain; COVID-19; pandemic

JEL Classifications: G32; N7; M41; O14; O32; Q55

Digital Transformation, Strategic Resilience, Cyber Security and Risk Management
Contemporary Studies in Economic and Financial Analysis, Volume 111A, 21–31

Published under exclusive licence by Emerald Publishing Limited
ISSN: 1569-3759/doi:10.1108/S1569-37592023000111A002

INTRODUCTION

Recent technological advancements have proven to be quite challenging regarding sustainability practices as technology could potentially help decouple environmental degradation from economic growth, while in some cases technology can play a part in both situations (Bergendahl, Sarkis, & Timko, 2018). As a by-product of recent technological advancements, Blockchain technology is on arising path of adoption due to its great implementation behind the Bitcoin cryptocurrency (Kouhizadeh & Sarkis, 2018). Launched after the 2008 financial crisis, the main focus of the blockchain concerned financial applications, its unique characteristics have proven to be very versatile for broader use in different markets and other non-financial purposes. Compared to other information technologies that businesses run, blockchain uses a unique structure of data that stores data as a chain of blocks. When a new transaction is recorded on the system, a block is built and linked to the previous blocks, creating a chain. The chain could be perceived as an electronic coin that contains a network of digital signatures. When talking about a block, refers to a group of items that support the work of a server on timestamping, hashing transactions into an ongoing network of hash-based proof-of-work, accepting as proof of previous operations the moment the nodes are gone (Nakamoto, 2008).

In other words, blockchain can be described as a system based on peer-to-peer electronic transfers and mutual influence due to cryptographic proof without needing a third party or a central institution. Technically speaking, the blockchain network is equivalent to a back-end database having the responsibility of maintaining a distributed ledger that can be examined by everyone. In the business context, the blockchain is represented by an exchange network that transfers funds and processes transactions, values, and assets between the participants as peers of the network, without the involvement of the intermediaries. From a legal point of view, blockchain is a mechanism that validates transactions, this way taking over the role trusted entities previously had (Mougayar & Buterin, 2016).

A little over a decade since its creation, the blockchain has managed to entail a wide variety of broad features, based on key principles necessary for multiple implications of technology including key concepts, generic elements, operating mechanisms, and security and privacy (Nguyen & Do, 2018). A transaction has marked the transfer of value between two contracting parties, from one address known as the identifier to another address, the transferred value is not only related to financing but rather any information or data that has been created and owned by users. One block is composed of multiple transactions and several factors such as block hash and timestamp (Bashir, 2017; Sood, Seth, & Grima, 2022). A block hash, which includes the hash pointer and cryptographic hash of the data, is linked together with the previous block hash (Gupta, 2017), being actually a digital fingerprint, also known as a unique identifier, having a fixed-length output. When it comes to timestamps, this proves the existence of the data at a certain time so it could get into the hash by integrating the previous timestamp and emerging a chain with the additional timestamps, strengthening the previous ones (Nakamoto, 2008; Sood, Kaur, & Grima, 2022). Among the various functions that a node can perform, assuming the responsibility for recommending and validating transactions as well as performing the mining so that it facilitates consensus and secures the blockchain. Other roles that might be assigned could also include simple payment verification and validators. A peer-to-peer network is an essential part of a blockchain, the peers on the network can communicate with each other directly and exchange messages (Bashir, 2017), while the peers act as clients who request a server that provides share and access directly to resources of the others (Steinmetz & Wehrle, 2005).

Blockchain features a shared ledger or distributed ledger technology, shortly known as DLT, which is a digital system that aims recording asset transactions and their associated details in multiple locations simultaneously, blockchains resembling blocks of interactions and transfers used in lifting facilities (Vijai & Wisetsri, 2021). As blocks can represent assets of any digital kind from money, securities, and land titles to information on identity, health, and other personal data, DLT would be able to potentially make a fundamental change in the financial sector by making it more efficient, resilient, and reliable (World Bank, 2018). Adopting on a larger scale the distributed ledger accounting would bring a lot of improvements, eliminating, or redefining the role of external entities such as banks, public institutions, insurance companies, and associations of chartered certified public accountants and auditors (Inghirami, 2020). Through the internet of value which is based on the DLT, the strive aims strictly for a decentralised organisation that has interactivities between peers without needing the support of any centralised platform or intermediaries (Lenz, 2019). DLTs have proven to be more accessible, cost-efficient, and reliable as a transaction platform compared to centralised ledger systems by avoiding intermediaries, distributing ledger control, and providing a tamper-apparent network (Hedera, 2018). At the core of DLT is the encoded and distributed database which acts as a serving ledger recording transactions and storing them is an innovative database approach consisting in a data model which uses cryptography in every transaction update, making verification possible across the specific blockchain network, considering its goal and stakeholders requirements (Vijai & Wisetsri, 2021). Aiming the creation of a decentralised environment and removing trust-related problems makes blockchain technology to be part of many domains due to its distributed database nature and the prospect of audit trails (Zheng, Xie, Dai, Chen, & Wang, 2017). Transactions made through the blockchain network have proven to be much cheaper than by any other equivalent means as this technological architecture allows better traceability and resolution of reliability issues among supply chain members (Kshetri, 2018).

Smart contracts offer the distributed ledgers progressive programmability and improve the tasks which the distributed ledgers could perform and increase massively the range of applications of the blockchain such as digital rights management, digital wallet control, health care data management, and supply chain (Saberi, Kouhizadeh, & Sarkis, 2018). The execution of the smart contracts would start automatically as running a fragment of code by the miners as soon as the contract has been deployed on the blockchain (Zheng et al., 2017), ensured by the use of transparent contracts on several blockchain peers, adding to the trustworthiness improvement (Hawlitschek, Notheisen, & Teubner, 2018).

A recent comparative study based on Digital Economy and Social Index (DESI) done on Romania and nearby countries has revealed the fact that Romania occupies the last position within the European Union when it comes to adopting new technologies and knowledge leveraging in providing better quality services to both public and private sectors (Yerpudee, Sood, & Grima, 2022). With connectivity at the same level as the average European Union level and human capital much lower, Romania raises two issues concerning low levels of digital technology integration and digital public services availability. Also adding to human resources, experienced users should leverage knowledge by increasing the number of basic skilled users so that the Romanian market would catch up with the average European Union on digital intensity, e-commerce, and digital business technologies and become more sustainable and competitive altogether (Moraru, 2022).

Regulatory institutions should have developed a legal framework for controlling blockchain technology, but the situation leaves room for IT companies and supply chain decision-makers to put pressure on the regulatory actors. Few attempts have been made by the United Blockchain Association in order to legislate the blockchain domain in Romania, but the results weren't satisfactory to substantiate the basis of a law project, making the technology very risky in terms of adoption (Ceptureanu et al., 2021).

Besides the fact that companies don't want to invest in their employees' training when it comes to blockchain adoption, there are still many challenges when it comes to high implementation costs or required technical skills, even though it could benefit transactions as well as members of the supply chain (Tapscott & Tapscott, 2017).

Most entrepreneurs involved in supply chain networks lack empirical evidence (Saberi et al., 2018) and a poor understanding of the main concepts and practices regarding blockchain (Andoni et al., 2019) makes them unaware of the benefits that come with the adoption of blockchain by providing a competitive advantage for both networks and own companies. Another improvement expected to be bought by blockchain technology considers the enhancement of the velocity and reliability of the business and managerial processes (Khan & Salah, 2018), becoming more useful in providing inventory management, precise forecast demand, backup at demand, reduction of informational distortion, filtering redundancy, and overloading of the channels (Tjahjono, Esplugues, Ares, & Pelaez, 2017).

The main issues remaining to be solved involve both the sharing information and transaction information as knowledge between the supply chain members with reliability, high speed, and accuracy by using advanced cloud technologies (Wang, Tai, & Grover, 2012). Blockchain is so versatile that it can relate to specific IT applications covering the Internet of Things, smart contracts, public services, big data, security services, reputation systems, or artificial intelligence in order to analyse data generated by business operations (Wu, Yeniyurt, Kim, & Cavusgil, 2006).

As blockchain has an impact on all supply chain processes, business transactions, and managerial transactions between different parties of the network, one of the most important advantages coming from its usage is removing the intermediaries, making more efficient the trading processes among partners (Reinartz, Krafft, & Hoyer, 2004). Issues such as low levels of effectiveness and efficiency in the supply chain flows could be improved through the instruments and techniques available in the supply chain (Grover & Kohli, 2012) saving networks worth millions of EUR (Hofmann, Strewe, & Bosia, 2018).

METHODOLOGY

Our analysis sample contains data extracted from a local database containing randomly selected 60 different entities from almost every county of Romania covering the years 2020 and 2021. As part of assessing the Romanian market situation due to COVID-19 regulations and establishing the level of development, making the potential adoption of blockchain technology implementation either sooner or later. As part of our analysed economic indicator, the selection includes net profit, turnover, liabilities, fixed assets, current assets, equity, and the number of employees to be part of the undergoing analysis. After the determination of the increasing or decreasing percentage among the 60 companies, the data from the Excel file will be further analysed using pivot tables and graphical representations. The results will be presented with graphic figures and relevant observations.

FINDINGS

As part of the analysis, the sample shows an increasing percentage regarding the average values of selected indicators as seen in Fig. 1. The lowest percentage increase has been recorded on the average number of employees, which means that in our sample we have included companies where the number of workers has been kept constant, considering the COVID-19 regulations. On the other hand, as seen in Fig. 1 the biggest increase in percentage has been recorded on the average value of liabilities at 61%, which means companies took a big risk and borrowed money in order to keep the current situation under control rather than expanding the business portfolio. In connection with the level of liabilities, there is an increase of percentage in the average value of fixed assets by 46%, which reveals the fact that despite other companies narrowed their activities, the ones included in our sample have chosen the other way in substantiating their presence on the market and supporting their employees. In other words, the average increased level of indebtedness of 61% within our analysed sample has been successfully capitalised in an average increasing level of fixed assets up to 46% and an average of 27% on the level of current assets.

When looking at the overall average performance registered at the region level, we observe in Fig. 2 that the north-west side has recorded an increase up to an average of 48%, followed closely by the south side with 44%, meaning that these regions were more productive and avoided successfully the issues associated with COVID-19 restrictions. The lowest overall average performance that has been recorded, according to the studied sample, is in the western region which only

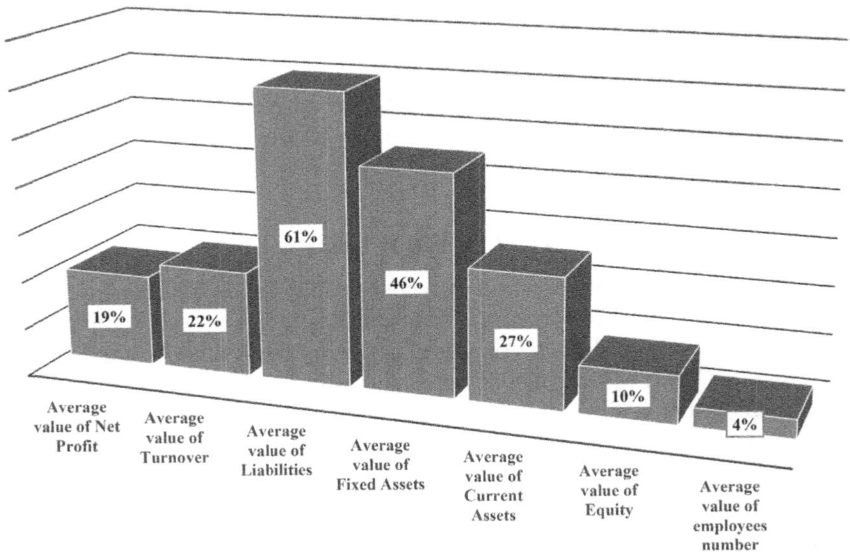

Fig. 1. Average Values on the Selected Sample.
Source: Author research, resulting from the analysis using Microsoft Excel.

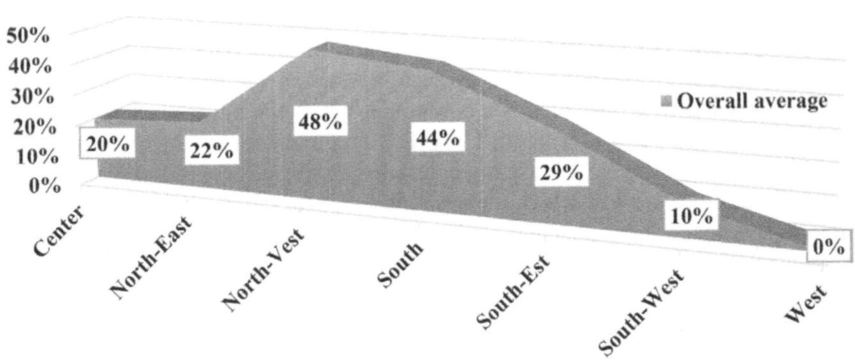

Fig. 2. Regional Performance in Romania Based on the Analysed Sample.
Source: Author research, resulting from the analysis using Microsoft Excel.

managed to stay constant, which could be an interesting subject in continuing this research. The overall average performance represents the average of all analysed indicators of each company that has activity in one of the seven regions of Romania. Considering the levels of overall average performance, we have three scenarios in which each of the seven regions fit, making deeper the gap in overall average performance between the regions.

Connecting the fact that the average overall performance increase has been recorded in the north-west and south regions, according to Fig. 3, on the county level, we reveal another sight of the big picture by having both the highest and lowest overall average performance level in the north-west region due to the selection of random companies from different domains. In this case, even if companies are from different domains with various financial backgrounds, they still compete with each other, but on different markets, services, and even clients. The random selection and uneven distribution of the overall average performance are showing us which regions suffered the most due to COVID-19 pandemic, making it more difficult in understanding if the sample included more companies from different industries and various financial histories.

In the final step of connecting the results, based on the results from Fig. 3, we present in a more detailed manner the contrast image previously revealed on the north-west region and referencing Table 1, in both cases, the highest and lowest overall average performance reveals the fact that there is a shadowed company. The results concerning the shadowed companies were either better or worse, but too small compared to the performance of the other company from the same county. On the county level, according to Table 1, we can see that the company that operates in the domain 'IT services activities' has an outstanding overall average performance, while the company in the 'electric equipment manufacturing' domain has an overall average decrease, affecting very little the overall average results presented. In the same scenario falls the next situation involving

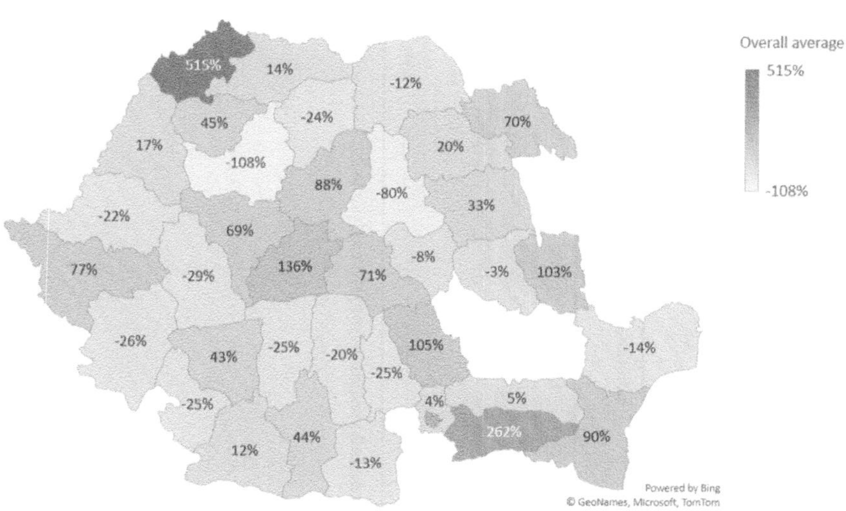

Fig. 3. Overall Average Values on Counties from the Analysed Sample.
Source: Author research, resulting from the analysis using Microsoft Excel.

Table 1. Table of Contrast in North-West Region.

Turnover	Profit Net	Liabilities	Fixed Assets	Current Assets	Equity	Average Number of Employees	CAEN Domain	County	Overall Average	Region
44%	1990%	1247%	108%	183%	80%	0	J 63 IT services activities	Satu Mare	522%	North-West
27%	−116%	22%	−13%	32%	−2%	0	C 27 Electric equipment manufacturing	Satu Mare	−7%	North-West
−23%	−812%	−55%	85%	−44%	−5%	−40%	J 60 Broadcasting activities and programs transmission	Cluj	−128%	North-West
8%	−12%	5%	12%	44%	80%	4%	B 08 Other mining activities	Cluj	20%	North-West

Source: Author research, resulting from the analysis using Microsoft Excel.

the overall average decrease in the company operating on 'broadcasting activities and programmes transmission', while the overall average increase of the company operating in 'other mining activities' is little compared to the overall average decrease of the other company.

CONCLUSIONS

Considering the fact that recent technological advancements have proven to be both disruptive to the way processes usually work within the economy and challenging, seen first more like a potential threat, when it comes to improving activities that already work as intended. First seen in the form of cryptocurrencies, launched right after the 2008 crisis as a solution to the traditional banking system, the technology behind blockchain has become more valuable and versatile as it can optimise both processes and activities in a wide range of services within companies, business relations, and the general public. By featuring a distributed ledger, blockchain facilitates communication and easy transfer of any kind of assets between the users on the same network, making the transfers directly without needing a third-party institution to approve them which enlists the DLT as an important key in the fourth industrial revolution.

Through our analysed sample data containing accounting indicators, we have found that on overall average most of the companies included have not only recorded an increase from 2020 to 2021 on their liabilities but also managed pretty well to capitalise on increasing their assets, resulting in an increase on overall average turnover and net profit levels, qualifying them as potential candidates in blockchain adoption. At the regional level, with randomly selected companies and different industries, we obtained mixed average overall results with some regions like the north-west, south, and south-east having increases up to 48%, while others had slight overall average increases like the centre, north-east, and south-west or even stagnation like in the west. On the county level, we have noticed that the various activities domain had a mixed impact, putting more profitable companies from the same areas like technology, taking as an example the 'IT services activities' domain on the direct competition with its hardware provider from 'electric equipment manufacturing' domain, which in our case has proven to be less profitable on the financial level, putting it in the shadow of a better-developed domain, revealing an uneven distribution where companies with overall average increase take the spotlight and mask the ones with overall average decrease. Based on these results, when it comes to adopting blockchain technology for many companies will prove to be difficult to get done as it will impact all analysed indicators, but mostly starting with the increasing number of IT professionals required to implement the blockchain technology, as well as training required in learning new technologies, increasing expenses and certainly decreasing net profit, even if it will affect budgets on short term until its implementation.

Knowing that the potential benefits of adopting blockchain include increased velocity in transactions, direct communication with other members of the network, and no control of the state or other third parties as part of the usual procedure makes it very risky, taking into consideration the many missed attempts of the regulated institutions to draw a legal framework and support users on their needs. Another aspect worth mentioning when using blockchain involves its potential to decrease the black economy and the direct sharing of benefits between the users as part of an increasing network.

A recommendation in further approaching blockchain adoption will be developing close cooperation between software-producing companies, supply chain members, and researchers in order to develop specific IT solutions that would prove blockchain to be future-proof and sustainable (Ceptureanu et al., 2021).

REFERENCES

Andoni, M., Robu, V., Flynn, D., Abram, S., Geach, D., Jenkins, D., … Peacock, A. (2019). Blockchain technology in the energy sector: A systematic review of challenges and opportunities. *Renewable & Sustainable Energy Reviews*, *100*, 143–174.

Bashir, I. (2017). *Mastering blockchain*. Birmingham: Packt Publishing. ISBN 978-1-78712-544-5.

Bergendahl, J. A., Sarkis, J., & Timko, M. T. (2018). Transdisciplinarity and the food energy and water nexus: Ecological modernization and supply chain sustainability perspectives. *Resources, Conservation and Recycling*, *133*(June), 309–319. https://doi.org/10.1016/j.resconrec.2018.01.001

Ceptureanu, S.-I., Cerqueti, R., Alexandru, A., Popescu, D. I., Dhesi, G., & Ceptureanu, E.-G. (2021). Influence of blockchain adoption on technology transfer, performance and supply chain integration, flexibility and responsiveness. A case study from IT&C medium-sized enterprises. *Studies in Informatics and Control*, *30*, 61–74. doi:10.24846/v30i3y202106

Grover, V., & Kohli, R. (2012). Cocreating IT value: New capabilities and metrics for multiform environments. *MIS Quarterly*, *36*(1), 225–232.

Gupta, M. (2017). *Blockchain for dummies*. Hoboken, NJ: IBM Limited Edition.

Hawlitschek, F., Notheisen, B., & Teubner, T. (2018). The limits of trust-free systems: A literature review on blockchain technology and trust in the sharing economy. *Electronic Commerce. Research Applications*, *29*, 50–63.

Hedera. (2018). What are distributed ledger technologies (DLTs)? Retrieved from https://hedera.com/learning/what-are-distributed-ledger-technologies-dlts

Hofmann, E., Strewe, U. M., & Bosia, N. (2018). *Supply chain finance and blockchain technology*. Heidelberg: Springer International.

Inghirami, I. E. (2020). Accounting information systems: The scope of blockchain accounting. In R. Agrifoglio, R. Lamboglia, D. Mancini, & F. Ricciardi (Eds.), *Digital business transformation organizing, managing and controlling in the information age* (Vol. 38, pp. 107–120). Cham: Springer. https://doi.org/10.1007/978-3-030-47355-6_8

Khan, M. A., & Salah, K. (2018). IoT security: Review, blockchain solutions, and open challenges. *Future Generation Computer Systems*, *82*, 395–411.

Kouhizadeh, M., & Sarkis, J. (2018). Blockchain practices, potentials, and perspectives in greening supply chains. *Sustainability*, *10*, 3652. http://doi.org/10.3390/su10103652.

Kshetri, N. (2018). Blockchain's role in meeting key supply chain management objectives, *International Journal of Information Management*, *39*, 80–89.

Lenz, R. (2019). Managing distributed ledgers: Blockchain and beyond. Retrieved from https://papers.ssrn.com/sol3/papers.cfm?abstract_id=3360655

Moraru, M. (2022). Digitalization: A step closer to sustainability. The case of Romania and neighbor countries from the perspective of DESI components. In *39th IBIMA business conference*, Granada, Spain, 30–31 May.

Mougayar, W., & Buterin, V. (2016). *The business blockchain: Promise, practice, and application of the next internet technology*. Hoboken, NJ: Wiley.

Nakamoto, S. (2008). Bitcoin: A peer-to-peer electronic cash system. Electronic article. Bitcoin. Retrieved from https://bitcoin.org/bitcoin.pdf.

Nguyen, H. H., & Do, L. P. (2018). *The adoption of blockchain in food retail supply chain: Case: IBM food trust blockchain and the food retail supply chain in Malta*. Lahti: Lahti University of Applied Sciences.

Reinartz, W., Krafft, M., & Hoyer, W. D. (2004). The customer relationship management process: Its measurement and impact on performance. *Journal of Marketing Research*, *41*(3), 293–305.

Saberi, S., Kouhizadeh, M., & Sarkis, J. (2018). Blockchain technology and its relationships to sustainable supply chain management. *International Journal of Production Research*, *57*(7), 2117–2135.

Sood, K., Kaur, B., & Grima, S. (2022). Revamping Indian non-life insurance industry with a trusted network: Blockchain technology. In K. Sood, R. K. Dhanaraj, B. Balamurugan, S. Grima, & R. U. Maheshwari (Eds.), *Big data: A game changer for insurance industry* (pp. 213–228). Bingley: Emerald Publishing Limited.

Sood, K., Seth, N., & Grima, S. (2022). Portfolio performance of public sector general insurance companies in India: A comparative analysis. In S. Grima, E. Özen, & I. Romānova (Eds.), *Managing risk and decision making in times of economic distress, part B* (pp. 215–229). Bingley: Emerald Publishing Limited.

Steinmetz, R., & Wehrle, K. (2005). Peer-to-peer systems and applications – Introduction. *Lecture Notes in Computer Science*, *3485*, 1–36.

Tapscott, D., & Tapscott, A. (2017). How blockchain will change organizations. *MIT Sloan Management Review*, *58*(2), 10–13.

Tjahjono, B., Esplugues, C., Ares, E., & Pelaez, G. (2017). What does Industry 4.0 mean to supply chain? *Procedia Manufacturing*, *13*, 1175–1182.

Vijai, C., & Wisetsri, W. (2021). URR blockchain and distributed ledger technology (DLT): The future of accounting. *Journal of Human Kinetics*, *58*, 320–323.

Wang, E., Tai, J., & Grover, V. (2012). Examining the relational benefits of improved inter firm information processing capability in buyer supplier dyads. *MIS Quarterly*, *37*(1), 149–173.

World Bank. (2018). Retrieved from https://www.worldbank.org/en/topic/financialsector/brief/blockchain-dlt

Wu, F., Yeniyurt, S., Kim, D., & Cavusgil, S. T. (2006). The impact of information technology on supply chain capabilities and firm performance: A resource based view. *Industrial Marketing Management*, *35*(4), 493–504.

Yerpudee, S., Sood, K., & Grima, S. (2022). Blockchain-augmented digital supply chain management: A way to sustainable business. *Journal of Risk and Financial Management*, *16*(1), 7.

Zheng, Z., Xie, S., Dai, H., Chen, X., & Wang, H. (2017). An overview of blockchain technology: Architecture, consensus, and future trends. In *Proceedings of the 2017 IEEE international congress on big data (BigData congress)* (pp. 557–564), Honolulu, HI, USA, 25–30 June.

CHAPTER 3

UNVEILING THE BLOCKCHAIN TECHNOLOGY: AN ANALYSIS OF ADOPTION AND INVENTIONS

Arvinder Kaur[a], Pawan Kumar[a], Ercan Özen[b] and Serap Vurur[c]

[a]University School of Business, Chandigarh University, Punjab, India
[b]Dr. University of Usak, Faculty of Applied Sciences, Turkiye (Turkey)
[c]Dr. University of Afyon Kocatepe, Faculty of Bolvadin Applied Sciences, Turkiye (Turkey)

ABSTRACT

The chapter explains the Blockchain and its application in cryptocurrency and in various sectors. It gives an insight into the level of adoption of Blockchain technology globally based upon industry, country, and component. China is leading all nations worldwide, followed by the United States. The study will help to understand future research regarding its applications in different sectors of the economy. The study will also help to understand the significance and complications regarding risk and regulation. Its adoption in the logistics and supply chain is meant to achieve error-free communication and efficient tracking management.

Keywords: Blockchain; cryptocurrency; industry-based adoption; country-level adoption; market capitalisation; Blockchain patent

JEL classification: E00; E42; E52; E58; F10; G00

Digital Transformation, Strategic Resilience, Cyber Security and Risk Management
Contemporary Studies in Economic and Financial Analysis, Volume 111A, 33–48

Published under exclusive licence by Emerald Publishing Limited
ISSN: 1569-3759/doi:10.1108/S1569-37592023000111A003

1. INTRODUCTION

In 2020, the Blockchain market was valued at USD 3.06 billion. COVID-19's global consequence has been unprecedented and catastrophic due to which industry experiencing a drop in demand throughout all areas impacted by the epidemic. However, compared to the average year-on-year growth, the worldwide market grew by 52.4% in 2020. From 2022 to 2030, it is predicted to grow at a compound annual growth rate (CAGR) of 85.9% (Grandview Research, 2021). Financing in Blockchain technology, widespread applications in financial institutions and data security, great acceptance of Blockchain solutions for payout, digital contracts, verifying the identity, and growing public programmes are the foremost motivating aspects paying to the exponential progress rate of this technology (Morkunas et al., 2019). New industrial and business models emerged with the inception of Blockchain technology which was earlier a nightmare. Blockchain is the technology having an advanced feature, which facilitates decentralised and shared ledger enabling a community of users (business enterprises, individuals, and government) to record transactions and information with digital signature into the blocks, which is unalterable and tamper-resistant once it has been published, as long as the Blockchain network is operating normally (Hughes et al., 2019). It ensures secure registration and execution of business contracts among various parties to contract through the smart contract (Pilkington, 2016). Two types of Blockchain technology networks, that is, permissioned and permissionless, put restrictions on the usage of distributed ledger for entering transactions into it (Androulaki et al., 2018). Many industries have started growing interest in Blockchain technology like healthcare, logistics, entertainment media, cyber security, gaming, trading, global transaction, intellectual property, real estate, insurance, stock market, and government services (Casino et al., 2019). Fig. 1 shows the Blockchain technology elements.

The background of Blockchain technology consists of a series of steps. Since its inception began by Stuart Haber and Stornettqo, Bitcoin was the first digital coin/currency introduced in 2008 which works on Blockchain technology (Nakamoto, 2020). Then from 2009 to 2010, the online trade of Bitcoin happened, and it has crossed the trade of USD 1 billion during 2012. It allows permissionless (censor-proof) transactions. It was earlier only used for trading by a few countries, but now its new version, that is, Bitcoin Cash (BTC), has been accepted as a lender tender of exchange in America since September 2019. The second-largest cryptocurrency emerged in 2012, known as Ripple (XRP). As per Geng, Cao, Li, & Han (2022), Ripple facilitates the real-time cryptocurrency trade platform leading to the emergence by Ripple Labs Inc. US-based technology corporation. The third-largest is Ethereum, which was launched in 2015 by Buterin (Somin et al., 2018), who was earlier the programmer of Bitcoin. It provides various ways of exchanging cryptocurrency (i.e. ether), enables smart contracts, and facilitates Ethereum Virtual Machine (Ciampi et al., 2021). During 2015–2017 Linux foundation launched HyperLedger, and JP Morgan introduced Quoram Blockchain technology to provide innovative business solutions. Blockchain as a service industry starts to bloom. From 2008 to 2022, a long list of cryptocurrencies was

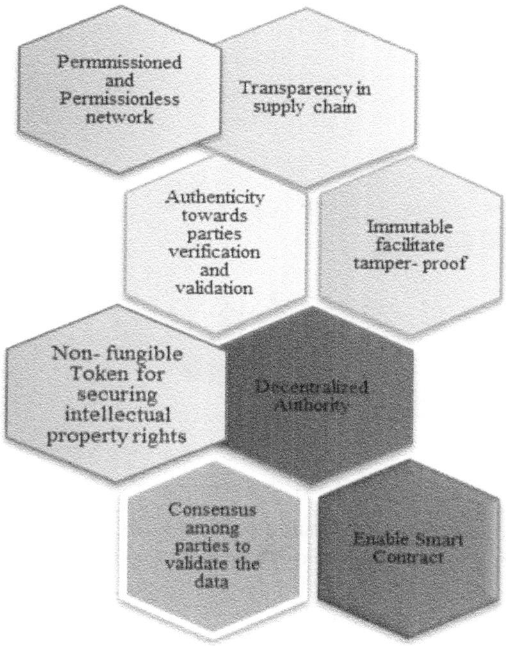

Fig. 1. Blockchain Technology Elements. *Source*: Authors' compilation.

released and traded. The data shown in Figure 2 is about the top 6 crypto currencies and their proportionate market share according to market capitalization. It depicts that Bitcoin serves the largest market share of USD 14,643,548,443.91 billion followed by Ethereum USD 9,501,221,176.92 billion, at third position captured by Bitcoin Cash USD 4,393,440,669.5 billion, BNB having a market cap of USD 1,289,330,237.97 billion, and the remaining share of other cryptocurrencies. Fig. 2 shows the market capitalisation of top six cryptocurrencies.

Fig. 3 shows the size of Bitcoin Blockchain from June 2009 to September 2021. It shows that the size of Bitcoin currency transactions is skyrocketed. During December 2009, the size of Bitcoin transactions was 0.01 GB; it jumped to 4.52 GB in December 2012 within three years of span, and within the next three years in December 2015, it reached 53.16 GB. Now, as of September 2021, it reached 374.23 GB.

Blockchain technology presents the following attributes: (a) Blockchain network; (b) Blockchain category; (c) updating and modification; (d) consensus; (e) hastag; and (f) miners. Blockchain network contains information in two forms; one set is the header used to have metadata containing keys and links to earlier except for the first block, and the second set comprises other information. Transactions can be entered by the users connected through Blockchain networks; it happens through computers executing Blockchain technology. Blockchain category deals with two types of Blockchain categories, that is, permissioned and

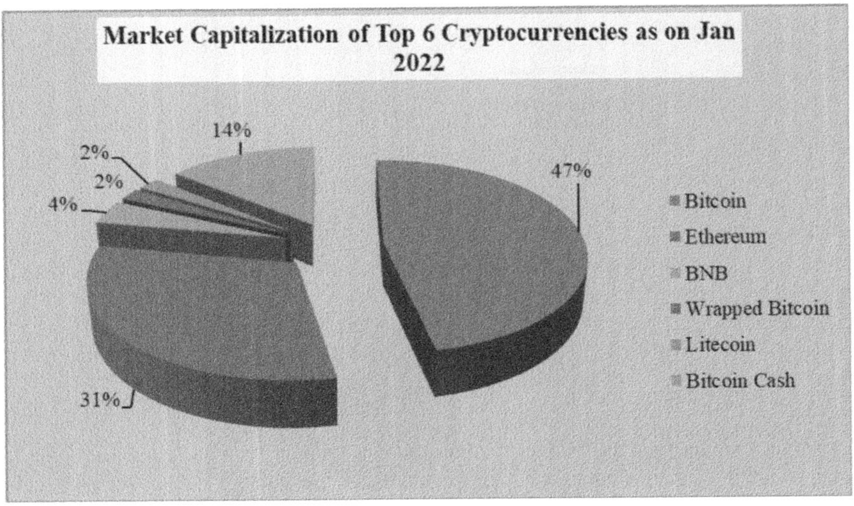

Fig. 2. Market Capitalisation of Leading Cryptocurrencies.
Source: Authors' adaptation from https://coinmarketcap.com.

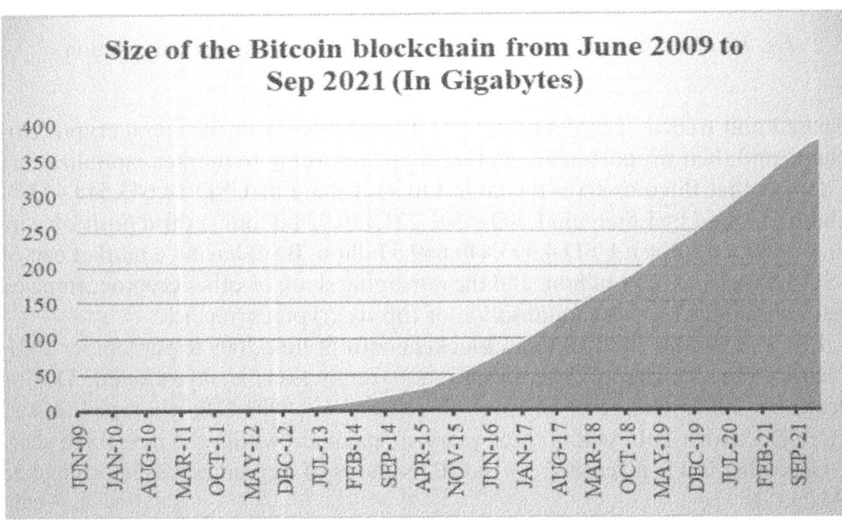

Fig. 3. Size of Bitcoin Blockchain.
Source: Authors' adaptation from Harrity Analytics Report.

permissionless. Permissioned Blockchain access is limited to a specific network of users with checks (Kumar, Reshma, Sharma, & Gandhar, 2022). However, anyone can access permissionless technology for reading and writing transactions. It depends upon the organisation's requirement, which is approachable and valuable to them. Updating and modification, the database query and update function are used to modify or update data. In this, one would get the record of all changes inserted. Implementing Blockchain technology requires a high level of understanding for converting existing data into actual Blockchain data. Consensus refers to the phenomenon when all parties approve the transactions as valid, showing the same information to all users recorded in the previous block and organising them in order. Then the ledger is considered validated. Hashtag is an encryption function that generates codes to secure data. When interacting with massive quantities of data and processes, it is essential. In the case of cryptocurrencies like Bitcoin, hashing means accepting any size intake and producing a set size response. Trades are fed through a hashing algorithm that generates an output with a constant size of 256 bits, regardless of how large or tiny the intake is. Miners are processors or pcs that run the network and authenticate the trades (known as miners) are rewarded. Instead of offering block incentives, Ethereum permits miners to charge the processing commission. The first computer to crack each new node is rewarded with Bitcoins (or a fraction of one).

Blockchain presents the following risks: (a) transparency (information can be exchanged and stored in real-time by all parties within one network); (b) cost-effective (no physical record is required to maintain, so having fewer chances of data manipulation and loss); (c) convenient (all parties in a permissioned peer-to-peer network can work together simultaneously online); (d) secure: transactions are primarily unalterable and verifiable, which reduce the risk of fraud, especially in the case of financial transactions (van Wassenaer, Verdouw, & Wolfert, 2021).

However, Blockchain technology can somehow disrupt and revolutionise transactions, but businesses must overcome critical security, privacy, and control problems. Sharma and Kumar (2022) present that Blockchain transactions are recorded in a distributed public ledger, where attackers can profit from more enormous security vulnerabilities to access crucial and highly confidential information. If a Blockchain solution is used to hold sensitive agreements or financial transactions, copying the file might provide hackers quick and easy access. A hub-and-spoke and a distributed database are used to access the database if a key is compromised. People do not use cryptographic mechanisms. They do not trust Blockchain applications because they do not want to be seen. It has been read in many articles that Blockchain is immutable, but in reality, under some circumstances, it can be altered, and the chains of block cannot be taken as fully immutable. Limited node size: Blockchain consists of a series of blocks/nodes. Information is recorded and stored in each node up to maximise space. Bitcoin was the first Blockchain technology solution, which was having size issues. This issue results in low scalability (expansion of peer network) and low transaction speed. Since its inception, Bitcoin has witnessed tremendous growth in its size. However, each node can hold information electronically with a maximum size of 250 GB.

Nevertheless, it is projected that by 2023 it will cross the 6.5 TB size. Currently, Bitcoin has a 1 MB size limit. Some of the Blockchain users have raised the alarm that Ethereum (another generation solution) required 3× space compared to Bitcoin. Each new block is added to the series every 10 minutes, which means 2.4 TB of data is stored in each Blockchain. The everyday count comes to 350 GB and per year comes to 127 TB. However, pruning is the solution provided to tackle the issue of size, which facilitates the working without even downloading nodes.

Blockchain technology and cryptocurrency is now a popular topic of study and a choice for many industries and businesses. Blockchain can give businesses new advantages and opportunities by making them more efficient, cutting costs, improving integrity and transparency, making security better, and making it easier to track things. Even though the most prominent uses of Blockchain have been in finance and banking, it is now being tried out and used in different ways in other fields (Sood, Kaur, & Grima, 2022; Sood, Seth, & Grima, 2022).

Bitcoin and the Blockchain do not mean the same thing. Blockchain is the system that makes it possible to record and store Bitcoin transactions. Blockchain has many applications other than Bitcoin. Blockchain has been used for the first time with Bitcoin. In Blockchain technology for Dummies (Marzo, Pandolfelli, & Servedio, 2022) it is explained that Bitcoin is built on Blockchain, which is used as the shared ledger for Bitcoin. Think of Blockchain as an operating system, like Macos or Microsoft Windows, and Bitcoin as one of the many programmes that can run on that operating system.

Cryptocurrency is a technology that was made eight years ago. It is a peer-to-peer network that lets people securely trade digital goods (Prakash, Anoop, & Asharaf, 2022). The first and most prominent cryptocurrency, Bitcoin, is paving the path as a disruptive technology to long-standing and unchanged accounting payment solutions that have been in place for decades. Even though traditional fiat currency is not likely to be replaced by cryptocurrencies, it could change how Internet-connected world markets interact by removing barriers around exchange rates and national currencies. Technology changes quickly, and the success of a particular technology depends almost entirely on the market it is trying to improve. Cryptocurrencies could change the way digital markets work by making it possible to trade without fees. Bitcoin, a revolutionary technology that was first shown in late 2008 and began to be used on 3 January 2009, has gotten much attention. Bitcoin was the initial cryptocurrency that a single group did not control. Since then, other cryptocurrencies like Litecoin, altcoins, and many more have emerged. The Blockchain is a list of records that is always getting more prominent and is protected by cryptography. The Blockchain is a public log that keeps track of all the transactions made with Bitcoin.

Hence cryptocurrency is a digital asset meant to be used as a means of exchange and for trading purposes. By investing and trading into cryptocurrency market one can earn high return as compared to others investment avenues but at high risk (Antoniou & Tringides, 2022). It uses cryptography to secure its transactions, control the creation of new units, and verify the transfer of assets. Virtual currencies are a type of cryptocurrency. In place of centralised money and a central banking system, cryptocurrencies use a decentralised control system. Each cryptocurrency's decentralised control works through a Blockchain, which is a database of public transactions that acts as a distributed ledger. At the beginning of 2009, a digital currency called 'Bitcoin' was created. It was the first decentralised cryptocurrency. Jan Lansky says a cryptocurrency is a system that meets all six requirements:

- This system says whether or not new units of cryptocurrency can be made. If a new cryptocurrency unit is made, the system says how it came to be and who owns it. This system says whether or not new units of cryptocurrency can be made. If a new cryptocurrency unit is made, the system says how it came to be and who owns it.
- There is no need for a central authority in the system.
- The system keeps track of the units of cryptocurrency and who owns them.
- Cryptographic method can prove who owns a cryptocurrency unit. In March 2008, the word 'cryptocurrency' was added to the Merriam-Webster Dictionary. Merriam-Webster definition arrived in the 1800s.

Block chain works in cryptocurrencies: (a) to send or get Bitcoin, a user must do a transfer of funds and broadcast it to each portion of the Bitcoin Blockchain; (b) in order for a transaction to go through, the user must always be added to the public digital ledger, also known as Blockchain. The transaction is checked by the network of nodes. (c) Miners collect transaction data and check it against the emerging Blockchain ledger. When they solve a cryptographic puzzle, they can add a new block of transactions to the Blockchain; (d) because so many clients have the same records and can confirm the same transactions, it helps make sure that each block in the public ledger is correct; (e) as was already said, when a new block is made, it is added to the existing chain. When a block is placed on the Blockchain, it stays there forever and is available to everyone.

2. REVIEW LITERATURE

Schuetz and Venkatesh (2020) examined financial inclusion, adoption, and Blockchain research in India. They say four problems need to be solved to end financial exclusion: lack of access to banking services, high costs, inappropriate banking products, and lack of knowledge about money. They say that Blockchain technologies might be able to solve most of these problems. Also, researchers have made a plan for studying what causes adoption, how it happens, and what happens after adoption. Their research's main contribution is a discussion of how Blockchain can help solve the rural India's problem of financial exclusion. This could lead to a way for rural Indians to connect to global supply chain networks.

Hassani et al. (2018) introduced and summarised how three essential ideas in the digital world, Blockchain, cryptocurrency, and Big Data interact with each other. They indicated the outcome of combining Big Data, Blockchain, and cryptocurrency in technological advances, broader uses, and challenges. The article unrevealed the development of applications since 2016 and the chemistry of these technologies. So, we want to assess how cryptocurrency, Blockchain, and

Big Data work together and affect banking data analytics in the future. They also show how signal extraction and filtering are increasingly essential in detecting fraud from the large volume of banking transactions. Blockchain is a distributed ledger to record tamper-proof transactions and is used swiftly and securely in the international fund transfer swiftly and securely.

Lee (2019) demonstrated how the Blockchain technology and cryptocurrencies are changing and how they are linked and collaborating various industry's model and paving the way for emerging a token economy.

Khalil et al. (2021) looked into the adoption of Blockchain and examined concerning a company's digital strategy, innovativeness, profitability, and the moderating effect of IT alignment. The data were analysed statistically using confirmatory factor analysis, the Hayes methodology, and Pearson's correlation analysis. According to the findings of 300 samples, a business's economic performance and innovative business processes are positively correlated with digital company strategy. Blockchain mediates the interaction between digital company strategy, innovative business processes and financial performance (Grima et al., 2021; Yerpudee, Sood, & Grima, 2022). Effective IT alignment moderates the relationship between process innovation and Blockchain adoption.

Saheb and Mamaghani (2021) analysed the organisational advantages and issues of employing Blockchain in financial institutions; the study intends to advance the body of knowledge on the business value of IT. Barriers are identified in three ways: technological, environmental, and organisational. The values generated are knowledge management, business, strategy, and operations. The finding suggests that business operations are the most critical organisational value for Blockchain in the banking sector. According to research, the significant obstacles to the industry's adoption of Blockchain include organisational and marketing noise from the business environment, senior managers' ignorance of the technology, regulatory constraints, and compliances.

Mishra and Kaushik (2021) looked into the ways that Blockchain technology can assist in resolving issues in the banking industry. In order to address these issues, the report provides an overview of Blockchain technology and examines the most prominent problem and issues brought on by Blockchain technology in the financial sector. Traditional systems are considered hazardous, slow, difficult to operate, and mistake-prone. However, people consider the Blockchain more accessible, affordable and efficient. It benefitted the banking sector by cost efficiency, faster speed, security, and clients' incredible services across various activities. Chang et al. (2020) showed how FinTech and Blockchain are causing a revolution in the banking as well as in non-banking sector. The study discussed three important and ethical problems using Blockchain technology. It describes the real reasons why banks are interested in Blockchain and the problems they face. A qualitative method was used in which 16 experts of industry were interviewed. The theory of planned behaviour method was used to figure out why it was common for people to hide information on Blockchain. The analysis showed that people hide information because of how they feel, what they do, and what they think. Albayati et al. (2020) determined how helpful Blockchain technology is by examining how customers' behaviour affects their plans for Blockchain-based cryptocurrency transactions. They suggested the collaboration of some external variables regarding adoption of Blockchain technology with TAM model, that is, Technology Acceptance Model considering the complexity of the technology for its fuller penetration. Their results show that two strong ideas make customers more likely to trust Blockchain-based apps.

Bhimani et al. (2022) looked at the relationship between specific measures of macro-national development and the use of cryptocurrencies in 137 countries. Linear regressions find specific links between the use of cryptocurrencies and other things. It has positive effect Human Development Index, GDP, Network Readiness Index, and education level. Negative effect posed on Economic Freedom Index and Corruption Perception Index. Ante (2020) provided an insight on network building in terms of research conducted on Blockchain technology. From the WOS Core Collection, 467 cryptocurrency and Blockchain research studies collected from the economics and business fields, then analysed to learn more about the theoretical basis, prevalent applications, and future research directions of the discussion. Using factor analysis and social network analysis, it garnered the research field with animportant aspect of market efficiency, valuation pricing of cryptocurrency.

Yadav et al. (2020) depicted that large multinationals were officially told how they could use Blockchain technology in their daily work. Of the three squares, the money part moved fastest, followed by the promotion and market parts. When Blockchain technologies are used, digital copies can be made available to all parties in a transaction that are safe and easy to access. Smart contracts can manage the approval process and automatically transfer payment when all signatures are collected. This shows that Blockchain technology is accurate.

Fratric, Sileno, Klous, and van Engers (2022) demonstrated the workings of several trading strategies adopted by trade agents based on historical price data and manipulating the market and the limit order book market. The model check against the Bitcoin price, the number of Bitcoins the fraudster got, and the amount of Bitcoins that were traded. The results of the simulation fit historical data well. The actions of the dishonest trader can explain several drops in price and strange changes in volume. In order to make Bitcoin prices shoot up, as happened in late 2017, the role of fraudulent traders is inevitable. The model's insights, especially the link between liquidity and the effectiveness of manipulation, led to a discussion about how to stop the illegal behaviour.

3. OBJECTIVES OF THE STUDY AND RESEARCH METHODOLOGY

This research presents the next objectives: (a) to investigate the adoption level of Blockchain technology based on industry, country, and component; (b) to assess the level of invention for Blockchain technology worldwide with leading countries and companies; and (c) to examine the market capitalisation of various cryptocurrencies.

We utilised secondary research to assess and forecast the Blockchain technology industry. Throughout this step, we gathered and examined large amounts of data from reliable, reputable articles and journals, additional studies, institutions and government reports, industry publications, and commercial sources of information. The following are some of the secondary data sources we used for our research: (a) white paper on Bitcoin; (b) frontier business insight; (c) deloitte survey report on Blockchain; and (d) Harrity Analytics Report.

4. RESULTS

BFSI, administration, electricity and telecommunications, production, medical and biosciences, aviation and transportation, telecom, warehousing and distribution goods, film and music, and media industries make up the market. With banks and other financial institutions adopting distributed ledger solutions and services to improve efficiency, the firm will likely have a significant market share (Campbell-Verduyn & Hütten, 2021; Wamba, Queiroz, & Trinchera, 2020). The consumer and business products business are expected to grow fastest throughout the estimated period. Medical and Lifesciences, power and resources, administration, manufacturing, travel, and transportation are other multiple industries expected to increase. Fig. 4 depicts the highest share of 60% of Blockchain utilisation in the Banking and Financial service sector (BFSI), followed by the public sector at 15%; healthcare is at third position with 12% stake and logistics having a stake of 8% for the adoption of Blockchain. Some leading logistics and supply chain companies are SyncFab, RoadLauch, CargoCoin, EverLedger, and Skuchain. They are estimated to grow with a compounded annual growth return of 63.9% and forecasted to reach 14,180 million USD by 2028. Table 1 shows the Blockchain utilisation in various sectors.

Fig. 4 shows the industry-based adoption of Blockchain.

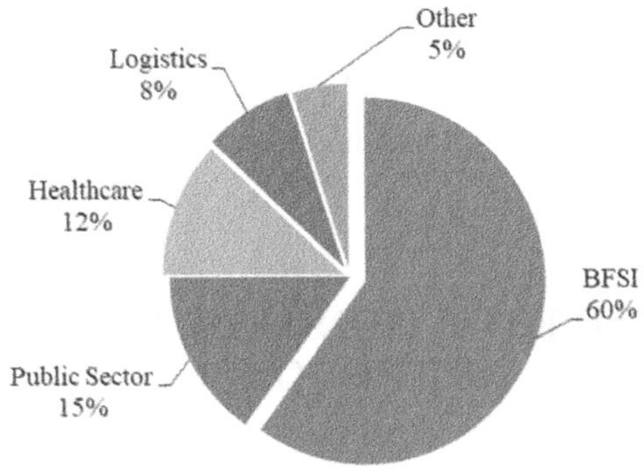

Fig. 4. Industry-based Adoption of Blockchain in India.
Source: Authors compilation adapted from NASSCOM report.

Table 1. Blockchain Utilisation in Various Sectors.

Field	Description
Payment and transaction system	Utilisation of Blockchain in fund transfer Fraud detection out of large data
Financial services	Include Blockchain utilisation in stock trading and banking services
Business administration	Application towards making contract and other related transactions
Shopping and E-commerce	Usage in online gaming and purchase and sale online
Encryption and security	Used in data protection and integrity
Networking and data transmission	Technology used in dissemination of information between Blockchain network
Health sector	Storing patient's electronic medical record Tracing diseases and medicines Genomics management
Logistic and supply chain sector	Reducing communication errors Supplementing the tracking management of location, price, quality, date, and other related information Invoice raising, financing, and accuracy judgement based on effective tracking

Source: Authors compilation.

North America, Europe, Asia Pacific, the Middle East and Africa, and Latin America are the five critical areas the global Blockchain market is segmented (Wang, Li, & Zhan, 2021). They are broken down even further into countries. According to market data, North America led the global Blockchain technology industry during 2021. Large firms in the United States such as IBM Corporation, Microsoft Corporation, Oracle Corporation, AWS, Digital Asset Management, and others may be described to the considerable share. Europe is now in the second position on the market and predicted to rise gradually throughout the forecasted period. Digital currencies are being significantly invested in by governments and private firms in France, Germany, Italy, Spain, Luxembourg, the Netherlands, and other countries. The Asia Pacific is expected to increase fastest during the anticipated period. Manufacturing firms in China, Japan, Oceania, South Korea, and Southeast Asia boosted their technological expenditures and involved themselves in inventing products and services supporting Blockchain technology. In addition, many nations get a considerable amount and variety of digital ledger technology. Fig. 5 depicts the top 10 countries in the Blockchain patent landscape, and China has the highest total number of patents of 34,562, out of which 6,086 patents are granted, and 28,476 is pending for application for inventing services that support Blockchain technology. Whereas the United States bagged the second position with 8,759 patents filled, of which 3,218 patents are granted; however, 5,541 patents are pending to be granted so far. At third position bagged by Korea with a total of 4,035 patents filled of which 1,911 patents are granted with 2,124 as pending. Europe follows this number with total patents 2,288, WIPO has 2,018 patents, Japan has filled 1,649 patents, Taiwan with 1,244 patents, Singapore has a total of 789 patents, Canada with a total of 725 patents, and Australia with 685 patents.

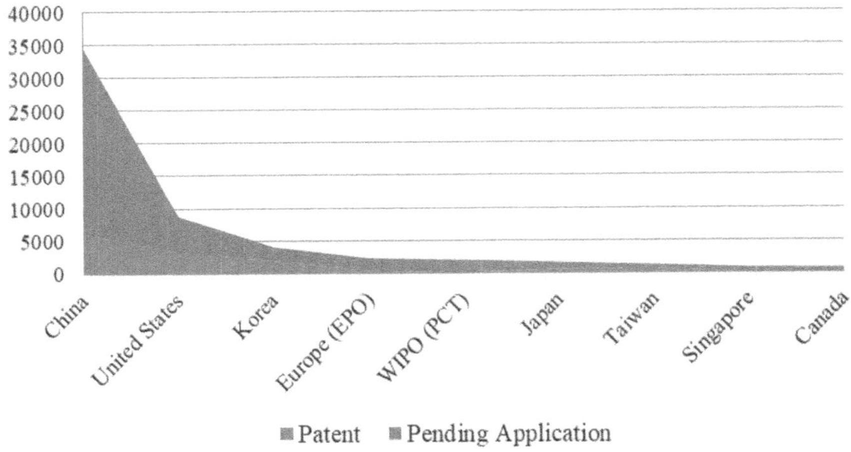

Fig. 5. Top Countries in Blockchain Patents 2021. *Source*: Authors' compilation adapted from Deloitte survey Report 2020.

Fig. 6 depicts that Blockchain technology started to bloom in 2018, and the size of Blockchain transactions shows a growing trend and is predicted to be raised exponentially. During 2018, the market size of Blockchain transactions

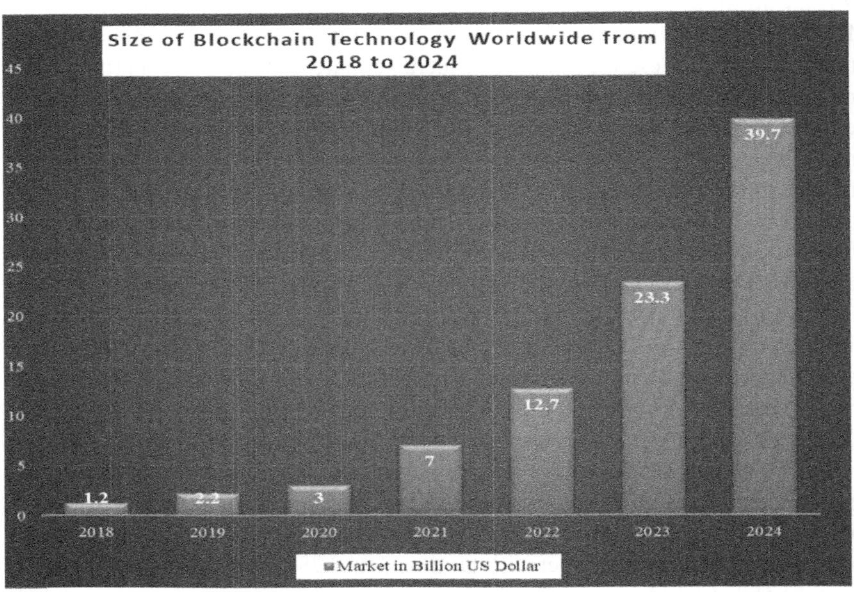

Fig. 6. Size of Blockchain Worldwide from 2018 in USD Billion. *Source*: Authors' compilation adapted from Harrity Analytics Report 2021.

Table 2. Leading Companies with Highest Patents in Blockchain.

Rank	Company	Active Worldwide Patents and Pending Application
1	Alibaba Group Holding Ltd.	2,588
2	Ping An Insurance (Group); Company of China, Ltd.	2,075
3	Advanced New Technologies Co., Ltd.	1,914
4	Tencent Holdings Ltd.	1,703
5	Nchain Holdings Ltd.	1,196
6	Alipay.com Co., Ltd.	1,094
7	International Business Machines Corp.	962
8	Shenzhen Oneconnect Technology Co., Ltd.	587
9	China United Network Communications Group Company Ltd.	516
10	Baidu, Inc.	429

Source: Authors' compilation.

was just USD 1.2 billion, whereas it reached USD 2.2 billion during 2019, which further increased to USD 7 billion during 2021 and is predicted by researchers to be reached at USD 39.7 billion by 2024.

Table 2 shows the leading companies with highest patents in Blockchain.

5. DISCUSSION AND CONCLUSION

Producers of digital ledger infrastructure and systems can utilise the technology to make specialised distributed ledger networks for end-users due to the growing market in many fields for platforms like HyperLedger Fabrics, Ethereum, R3 Cords, Ripple, and others. According to the component, the market is segmented into two divisions: Blockchain as a service and platform/solution.

Whereas, due to increased business use of cloud-based applications like smart contracts, crowdfunding, crypto e-wallet development and others, blockchain as a service is expected to grow at the quickest level (Olleros & Zhegu, 2016; Vadgama & Tasca, 2021).

Various researches have shown that the topmost barrier in adoption is replacing the legacy system, regulatory issues, potential security threat, lack of skilled workforce, deficiency of captivating solicitation of the technology, unproven technology and many enterprises it is not considered as a business priority so far (Wamba et al., 2020). Often, organisational level and country-level restrictions could become the reasons for lower adoption. How a nation's government supports it and what type of tax benefits and duties are imposed on the trade of cryptocurrency gives directions towards its adoption level.

Blockchain adoption level can be assessed by the data representing the level of growth. Nowadays, almost every industry uses Blockchain technology to facilitate easy trade on securable terms due to its advanced features like decentralised, immutability and transparency. The following parts indicate the level of adoption of Blockchain technology in various sectors worldwide through large-scale inventions to support the goal of this technology. From 2022 to 2030, the worldwide Blockchain market is estimated to reach USD 1,431.54 billion, increasing at a CAGR of 85.9%. The rising digitisation of the BFSI industry is responsible for the market's rise. Additionally, the market is likely to be driven by the increasing adoption of contactless Blockchain digital ticketing at various events. The expanding usage of cryptocurrencies throughout the globe is expected to fuel industry expansion. It is since Blockchain technology supports cryptocurrencies like Ethereum and Bitcoin. The popularity of Blockchain is growing due to its many advantages including ease of trade, inflationary protection, and better data security, high acceptance of Blockchain solutions for payout, smart contracts, and verifying the identity, and growing public programmes are the critical aspects responsible for the high growth rate of the Blockchain market. It is indeed worth noting that the increasing prevalence of cryptocurrencies, particularly Bitcoin, has a favourable impact on the adoption of Blockchain technology, resulting in increased funding by significant banking and no-banking financial intermediaries in the expansion of distributed ledger initiatives. However, while considering the benefits of Blockchain technology, the key restrictions and hazards must be considered. A lack of technological understanding, particularly beyond the banking world, may hinder investment in technology development, high initial expenditures and safety privacy. The adoption of this innovation in trade execution requires stringent cryptography and safety protocols. To provide secrecy, every information collected in a decentralised system must be linked to unique identifiers. A legislative structure controls the usage of the technology among diversified areas of the world industry. An institutional barrier where several organisations are already creating their Blockchain-based initiatives, which have so far greatly reduced the possibilities of exploiting the network effect, as when the success of platform-mediated networks and services is strong relative to the amount of the party's framework.

REFERENCES

Albayati, H., Kim, S. K., & Rho, J. J. (2020). Accepting financial transactions using blockchain technology and cryptocurrency: A customer perspective approach. *Technology in Society*, *62*, 101320. https://doi.org/10.1016/J.TECHSOC.2020.101320

Androulaki, E., Barger, A., Bortnikov, V., Muralidharan, S., Cachin, C., Christidis, K., & Yellick, J. (2018). Hyperledger fabric: A distributed operating system for permissioned blockchains. In *Proceedings of the 13th EuroSys conference, EuroSys 2018, April 23–26, 2018, Porto, Portugal*, January. https://doi.org/10.1145/3190508.3190538

Ante, L. (2020). A place next to Satoshi: Foundations of blockchain and cryptocurrency research in business and economics. *Scientometrics*, *124*(2), 1305–1333. https://doi.org/10.1007/S11192-020-03492-8

Antoniou, J., & Tringides, O. (2022). Financial data, blockchain, decision-making and quality of experience. In *EAI/Springer innovations in communication and computing* (pp. 19–35). Cham: Springer International Publishing. https://doi.org/10.1007/978-3-031-06870-6_2

Bhimani, A., Hausken, K., & Arif, S. (2022). Do national development factors affect cryptocurrency adoption? *Technological Forecasting and Social Change*, *181*, 121739. https://doi.org/10.1016/J.TECHFORE.2022.121739

Campbell-Verduyn, M., & Hütten, M. (2021). The formal, financial and fraught route to global digital identity governance. *Frontiers in Blockchain*, *4*, 627641. https://doi.org/10.3389/FBLOC.2021.627641/FULL

Casino, F., Dasaklis, T. K., & Patsakis, C. (2019). A systematic literature review of blockchain-based applications: Current status, classification and open issues. *Telematics and Informatics*, *36*, 55–81. https://doi.org/10.1016/J.TELE.2018.11.006

Chang, V., Baudier, P., Zhang, H., Xu, Q., Zhang, J., & Arami, M. (2020). How blockchain can impact financial services – The overview, challenges and recommendations from expert interviewees. *Technological Forecasting and Social Change*, *158*, 120166. https://doi.org/10.1016/J.TECHFORE.2020.120166

Ciampi, M., Esposito, A., Marangio, F., Sicuranza, M., & Schmid, G. (2021). Modernizing healthcare by using blockchain. *Applications of Blockchain in Healthcare*, *83*(1), 29–67. https://doi.org/10.1007/978-981-15-9547-9_2

Fratric, P., Sileno, G., Klous, S., & van Engers, T. (2022). Manipulation of the bitcoin market: An agent-based study. *Financial Innovation*, *8*(1), 1–29. https://doi.org/10.1186/S40854-022-00364-3

Geng, Z., Cao, Y., Li, J., & Han, Y. (2022). Novel blockchain transaction provenance model with graph attention mechanism. *Expert Systems with Applications*, *209*, 118411. https://doi.org/10.1016/J.ESWA.2022.118411

Grandview Research. (2021). Blockchain technology market size report, 2022–2030. Retrieved from https://www.grandviewresearch.com/industry-analysis/blockchain-technology-market

Grima, S., Kizilkaya, M., Sood, K., & ErdemDelice, M. (2021). The perceived effectiveness of blockchain for digital operational risk resilience in the European Union insurance market sector. *Journal of Risk and Financial Management*, *14*(8), 363.

Hassani, H., Huang, X., & Silva, E. (2018). Big-crypto: Big data, blockchain and cryptocurrency. *Big Data and Cognitive Computing*, *2*(4), 34. https://doi.org/10.3390/BDCC2040034

Hughes, A., Park, A., Kietzmann, J., & Archer-Brown, C. (2019). Beyond bitcoin: What blockchain and distributed ledger technologies mean for firms. *Business Horizons*, *62*(3), 273–281. https://doi.org/10.1016/J.BUSHOR.2019.01.002

Khalil, M., Khawaja, K. F., & Sarfraz, M. (2021). The adoption of blockchain technology in the financial sector during the era of fourth industrial revolution: A moderated mediated model. *Quality & Quantity*, *56*(4), 2435–2452. https://doi.org/10.1007/S11135-021-01229-0

Kumar, P., Reshma, Sharma, K. K., & Gandhar, A. (2022). A block-chain excellency in the mining of crypto currency. *Journal of Information and Optimization Sciences*, *43*(1), 123–130. https://doi.org/10.1080/02522667.2022.2037281

Lee, J. Y. (2019). A decentralized token economy: How blockchain and cryptocurrency can revolutionize business. *Business Horizons*, *62*(6), 773–784. https://doi.org/10.1016/J.BUSHOR.2019.08.003

Marzo, G. D., Pandolfelli, F., & Servedio, V. D. P. (2022). Modeling innovation in the cryptocurrency ecosystem. *Scientific Reports*, *12*(1), 12942. https://doi.org/10.1038/s41598-022-16924-7

Mishra, L., & Kaushik, V. (2021). Application of blockchain in dealing with sustainability issues and challenges of financial sector. *Journal of Sustainable Finance & Investment*, 1–16. https://doi.org/10.1080/20430795.2021.1940805.

Morkunas, V. J., Paschen, J., & Boon, E. (2019). How blockchain technologies impact your business model. *Business Horizons*, *62*(3), 295–306. https://doi.org/10.1016/J.BUSHOR.2019.01.009

Nakamoto, S. (2020). *Bitcoin. A peer-to-peer electronic cash system*. Hovedstaden: Klaus Norbdy.

Olleros, F. X., & Zhegu, M. (2016). *Research handbooks on digital transformations* (pp. 1–462). Cheltenham: Edward Elgar. https://doi.org/10.4337/9781784717766

Pilkington, M. (2016). Blockchain technology: Principles and applications. In F. X. Olleros & M. Zhegu (Eds.), *Research handbooks on digital transformations* (pp. 225–253). Cheltenham: Edward Elgar. https://doi.org/10.4337/9781784717766.00019

Prakash, R., Anoop, V. S., & Asharaf, S. (2022). Blockchain technology for cybersecurity: A text mining literature analysis. *International Journal of Information Management Data Insights*, *2*(2), 100112. https://doi.org/10.1016/j.jjimei.2022.100112

Saheb, T., & Mamaghani, F. H. (2021). Exploring the barriers and organizational values of blockchain adoption in the banking industry. *Journal of High Technology Management Research*, *32*(2), 100417. https://doi.org/10.1016/J.HITECH.2021.100417

Schuetz, S., & Venkatesh, V. (2020). Blockchain, adoption, and financial inclusion in India: Research opportunities. *International Journal of Information Management*, *52*, 101936. https://doi.org/10.1016/J.IJINFOMGT.2019.04.009

Sharma, M., & Kumar, P. (2022). Adoption of blockchain technology: A case study of Walmart. In R. Bansal, P. Malyadri, A. Singh, A. Pervez (Eds.), *Blockchain technology and applications for digital marketing* (pp. 210–225). IGI Global. https://doi.org/10.4018/978-1-7998-8081-3.CH013

Somin, S., Gordon, G., & Altshuler, Y. (2018). Social signals in the Ethereum trading network. Retrieved from https://arxiv.org/abs/1805.12097v1

Sood, K., Kaur, B., & Grima, S. (2022). Revamping Indian non-life insurance industry with a trusted network: Blockchain technology. In K. Sood, R. K. Dhanaraj, B. Balamurugan, S. Grima, & R. U. Maheshwari (Eds.), *Big data: A game changer for insurance industry* (pp. 213–228). West Yorkshire: Emerald Publishing Limited.

Sood, K., Seth, N., & Grima, S. (2022). Portfolio performance of public sector general insurance companies in India: A comparative analysis. In S. Grima, E. Özen, & I. Romānova (Eds.), *Managing risk and decision making in times of economic distress, Part B*. (pp. 215–229). West Yorkshire: Emerald Publishing Limited.

Vadgama, N., & Tasca, P. (2021). An analysis of blockchain adoption in supply chains between 2010 and 2020. *Frontiers in Blockchain*, *4*, 8. https://doi.org/10.3389/FBLOC.2021.610476/BIBTEX

van Wassenaer, L., Verdouw, C., & Wolfert, S. (2021). What blockchain are we talking about? An analytical framework for understanding blockchain applications in agriculture and food. *Frontiers in Blockchain*, *4*, 653128. https://doi.org/10.3389/FBLOC.2021.653128/FULL

Wamba, S. F., Queiroz, M. M., & Trinchera, L. (2020). Dynamics between blockchain adoption determinants and supply chain performance: An empirical investigation. *International Journal of Production Economics*, *229*, 107791. https://doi.org/10.1016/J.IJPE.2020.107791

Wang, Q., Li, R., & Zhan, L. (2021). Blockchain technology in the energy sector: From basic research to real world applications. *Computer Science Review*, *39*, 100362. https://doi.org/10.1016/J.COSREV.2021.100362

Yadav, S. P., Agrawal, K. K., Bhati, B. S., Al-Turjman, F., & Mostarda, L. (2020). Blockchain-based cryptocurrency regulation: An overview. *Computational Economics*, *59*(4), 1659–1675. https://doi.org/10.1007/S10614-020-10050-0

Yerpudee, S., Sood, K., & Grima, S. (2022). Blockchain-augmented digital supply chain management: A way to sustainable business. *Journal of Risk and Financial Management*, *16*(1), 7.

CHAPTER 4

CALCULATING FINANCIAL WELL-BEING: THE CASE OF YOUNG ADULTS IN LATVIA

Jekaterina Kuzmina[a], Dzintra Atstāja[b], Simon Grima[c], Graţiela Georgiana Noja[d], Mirela Cristea[e] and Eleftherios Thalassinos[f]

[a]*Department of Economics and Finance, BA School of Business and Finance, Riga, Latvia*
[b]*Department of Management, BA School of Business and Finance, Riga, Latvia*
[c]*Department of Insurance and Risk Management, Faculty of Economics, Management and Accountancy, University of Malta, Malta*
[d]*Department of Marketing and International Economic Relations, Faculty of Economics and Business Administration, West University of Timisoara, Timisoara, Romania*
[e]*Department of Finance, Banking and Economic Analysis, Faculty of Economics and Business Administration, University of Craiova, Craiova, Romania*
[f]*University of Piraeus, Faculty of Maritime and Industrial Studies, Piraeus, Greece and University of Malta, Faculty of Economics Management and Accountancy, Msida, Malta*

ABSTRACT

To achieve success and results satisfying a wide range of stakeholders, the management and other decision-makers must consider that one of the central elements in the process mentioned above is the employee. Therefore, the employee's well-being should play a crucial role in the management process (be a core stone in the decision-making process), and consequently, it should be considered an appropriate instrument to keep existing talents within the company and attract new ones. The main objectives of this chapter are to discover

Digital Transformation, Strategic Resilience, Cyber Security and Risk Management
Contemporary Studies in Economic and Financial Analysis, Volume 111A, 49–59

Published under exclusive licence by Emerald Publishing Limited
ISSN: 1569-3759/doi:10.1108/S1569-37592023000111A004

the level of the financial well-being of young adults in Latvia (the group of people responsible for the future sustainable development of the country) and to determine the factors influencing the level of financial well-being to create a prototype of financial well-being index. Based on an online questionnaire, the process first involves applying different statistical tests and regression analysis built-in MatLab programming. Second, we intend to create a prototype of the financial well-being index based on a three-step optimisation approach that allows determining the weightings for the factors selected as most important to influence the state of financial well-being and the scoring scale for each of the factors.

Keywords: Financial well-being; young adults; Latvia; financial well-being index; Matlab; the hierarchy of needs

INTRODUCTION

The concept of well-being is extensively debated in the scientific literature. The best-known approach to determining well-being is Maslow's hierarchy of needs. The concept developed in the previous century by American scientists is grounded in the needs of individuals. These needs are grouped and presented as a hierarchy. Each step of the hierarchy can be achieved successively, as described by Maslow (1948), starting with physiological needs, followed by security, social needs, and social recognition, while the final step is self-implementation.

The above-mentioned hierarchy of needs is one of the most cited concepts; many researchers are contributing to the topic of well-being and discussing and developing the concept mentioned above further. Some of the works should be mentioned here as the authors discussed the concept of well-being and proposed ways to measure the degree of well-being (Abeltina, Rascevska, & Stokenberga, 2021; Adler & Seligman, 2016; Stockenberg & Sultán, 2018; Tay & Diener, 2011). Analysing the research mentioned above, one can conclude the importance of the theory developed for the current research even though it does not allow for solving all the issues. On the one hand, the concept of well-being is well-settled and widely elaborated; on the other hand, the concept of financial well-being, in particular, is less advanced. It is worth considering that the definitions of financial well-being are not unified; therefore, many authors have proposed their own. Furthermore, it is necessary to underline that the concept of well-being is only recently introduced in the Latvian academic research environment. The introduction of the concept was facilitated by its frequent usage in foreign literature, and currently, it is in the development stage.

An important aspect is that even with no homogeneous definition, there are significant parallels between the ideas of each author of the definition. After reading works by Brüggen, Hogreve, Holmlund, Kabadayi, and Löfgren (2017), Tenney and Kalenkoski (2019), and Barrafrem, Västfjäll, and Tinghög (2020), among others, the authors of the current chapter would like to offer their definition of financial well-being that will be applied in the following research steps: the capacity to avoid and manage financial and economic risks as well as one's comfort level with their financial condition are indicators of one's financial well-being.

This definition includes a person's current financial situation (expressed as the ability to avoid and overcome economic and financial risks) and comfort (considered comfort about their current and future financial situation), which covers the most important aspects of financial well-being as concluded from the analysed literature.

Last but not the least, based on the literature analysis, the authors of this chapter determined the number of factors to evaluate the level of financial well-being including well-being at the workplace; level of overall optimism; social-anthropology factors; financial behaviour; level of self-control and level of financial literacy. All the mentioned factors will be studied to determine the level of financial well-being. It is worth considering that the study is limited to the young adults in Latvia, as this group of people is responsible for the country's further sustainable economic development and society's development. Seeing the importance of the group and being aware that the group's behaviour pattern has not been studied, the authors are willing to contribute to the research and close the existing gap.

The purpose of the current research chapter is to determine the level of the financial well-being of young adults in Latvia and to find the factors influencing the level of financial well-being (as it is going to increase the chances of finding tools and methods to make improvements in the future) as well as to create a prototype of financial well-being index.

METHODOLOGY OF RESEARCH

Factors Influencing Financial Well-being

The research methodology is developed as empirical research conducted by questionnaires to acquire the respondents' answers to specific statements by completing an online questionnaire. The data were analysed by applying several statistical tests and regression analysis. The online questionnaire of 326 young adults was conducted (the period of the survey includes Spring-Summer 2021).

The development of the questionnaires was based on the results of the literature analysis, discussing the factors influencing financial well-being. It should be noted that there is a wide range of research discussing these factors, while the authors propose several interpretations and application possibilities. The paper by Vlaev and Elliott (2014) and other scientists suggests that financial security and financial anxiety should be used to determine financial well-being. Both these factors hold the power to measure a person's financial situation and provide more insight into how a person feels about his current financial situation. Further discussion about financial anxiety could be found by Shapiro and Burchell (2012) and Strömbäck, Lind, Skagerlund, Västfjäll, and Tinghög (2017) while financial security is discussed by Mcknight (2019). These two main factors, financial anxiety and security, are influenced by other factors. A general understanding of the concept is synthesised in Fig. 1, which describes financial well-being as a composite of two issues issued by several variables factors (six factors are selected for further study).

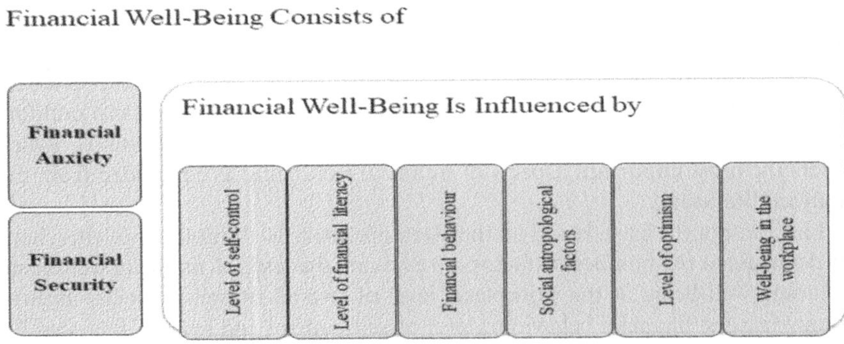

Fig. 1. General Description of the Concept. *Source*: Created by authors.

The summary of factors determining the level of financial well-being is provided in Table 1. One should consider that the authors created the list of factors based on the literature available for analysis at the time of research and represent

Table 1. Factors Influencing Financial Well-being Based on the Literature Analysis. An Overview.

The Factor Determining the Financial Well-being	Definition and/or Explanation of the Factor
Level of self-control	Self-control depends on three things: (1) standards (goals, intentions, norms, etc.); (2) monitoring process (keeping track of behaviour); and (3) the operational capacity to alter one's behaviour. Self-control is a factor that would tie in with financial well-being, and it could strongly impact individuals' financial well-being as it affects all areas of life (spending, working, saving money, investing, etc.)
Level of financial literacy	Financial literacy is described in the literature by dividing it into five components, namely (1) financial knowledge; (2) financial communication ability; (3) ability to use financial knowledge for decision making; (4) usage of financial instruments (financial behaviour); and (5) financial confidence
Financial behaviour	Each individual may have different financial behaviour, depending on character qualities and understanding of what is happening in the past and present. Financial behaviour plays an important role in well-being because understanding the goals allows one to plan the coming steps easily
Social anthropological factors	These factors show how personal and family experience, academic ability, and childhood experience affect financial literacy. These factors are related to the early phase of a person's life when the first knowledge of finances is acquired
Level of optimism	Optimism affects many aspects of life from a positive perspective including a positive effect on financial well-being since it influences personal approaches including dealing with finances or rating satisfaction
Well-being in the workplace	Well-being in the workplace has an important role in a person's life and affects financial situations

Source: Created by authors.

the authors' opinion regarding the relevance for further analysis. The list could be used as a starting point for future analysis.

Prototype of Financial Well-being Index

In the second part of the research, the authors intend to create a prototype of the financial well-being index, and the first results will be shared below. The prototype of the financial well-being index is built based on a three-step optimisation approach proposed by Becker, Saisana, Paruolo, and Vandecasteele (2017). The approach allows determining the weightings of the selected factors to influence the state of financial well-being (Sood, Seth, & Grima, 2022).

Moreover, the authors propose to introduce weighting and scoring scale for each factor similar to the approach described by Kuzmina, Natrins, Ziemele, and Kivrina (2021). The scoring process requires the determination of the threshold levels that, on the one hand, allow better understanding and broader usage of the index in the coming periods but, on the other hand, allow making some estimations and adjustments. The scoring scale runs from 1 (standing for a minimum level) up to 10 (indicating the maximum level).

RESEARCH RESULTS

Level of Financial Well-being by Young Adults in Latvia

In the first stage of the research, the authors determined the level of the financial well-being of the young adults (based on the self-evaluation applying the scale from 1 – poor to 5 – excellent). The results are presented in Fig. 2, where the lowest level of financial well-being equals 1.1, and the highest level equals 4.9.

Assuming that the situation could be different due to the COVID-19 pandemic, the same question was asked to determine the current level of financial well-being while society struggles to diminish the pandemic's negative effects. The results are displayed in Fig. 3.

One can note that there is no significant change in the level of financial well-being experienced by young adults; while the distribution of answers between categories has changed, the overall level is still the same (between 2.7 and 3.3), showing the average level as experienced by young adults in Latvia.

Moreover, the authors have tested if the COVID-19 pandemic seriously impacted financial well-being in the short run, and no significant impact was determined based on the Student's t-test: t equal to -1.252; df equal to 99 and p equal to 0.213. One can conclude that the level of financial well-being is stable, which is a positive sign.

Evaluation of Factors Influencing the Level of Financial Well-being as Experienced by Young Adults in Latvia

In the second stage, the authors verified the factors prompting the level of the financial well-being of Latvian young adults (the factors are chosen based on the

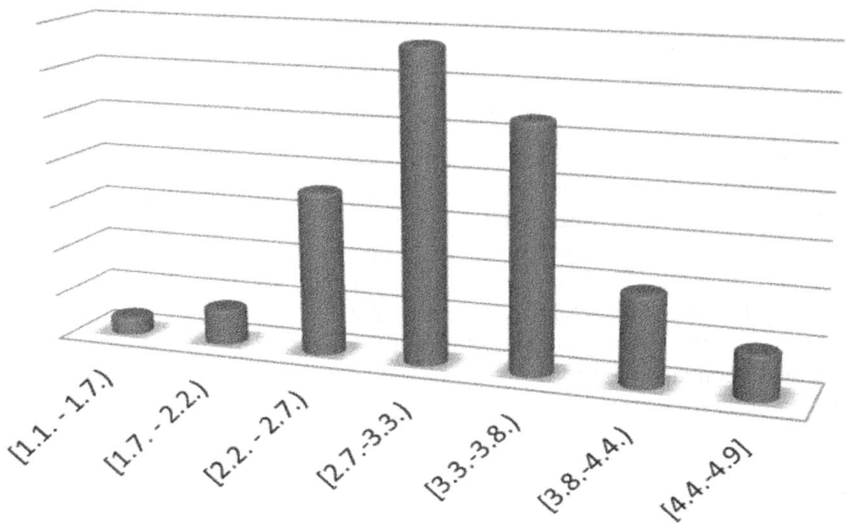

Fig. 2. State of Financial Well-being as Experienced by Young Adults Before COVID-19. *Source*: Created by authors.

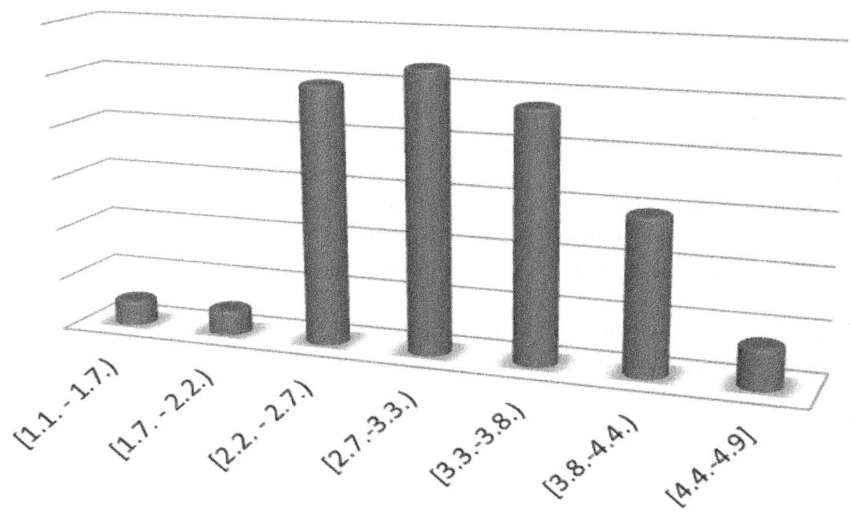

Fig. 3. Current State of Financial Well-being as Experienced by Young Adults. *Source*: Created by authors.

literature analysis). The most important factors are presented in Table 2, and one can notice that only three out of six are significant in comprehending and controlling the level of financial well-being among young adults (Grima, Kizilkaya, Sood, & ErdemDelice, 2021).

Table 2. Determining the Significance of Factors.

Relative Factors	Partial Regression Coefficient	Standard Error	Standardised Partial Regression Coefficient	*t*	*p*
Monthly income in EUR	0.1894	0.0892	0.2020	2.1161	0.0370
Level of self-control as determined by individuals (by answering three questions)	0.342	0.0961	0.3551	3.5740	0.0010
Level of overall optimism as determined by individuals (by answering five questions)	0.163	0.0743	0.2053	2.2130	0.0300
Level of financial literacy as determined by individuals (by answering five questions)	0.125	0.0511	0.2200	2.4331	0.0170

Source: Created by authors.
Note: R^2 =0.706 (F = 6.275; $p < 0.001$). The questions for the study were selected based on the Cronbach α equal or above 0.6.

The significant factors are shown in the table as they will play a crucial role in the coming step. Furthermore, the authors could define that the level of monthly net income plays a rather important role and should be measured while calculating the overall level of financial well-being.

The authors tested the factors selected for further analysis, and the following conclusions are gained. By creating the box-whisker plots, further tests were performed where the level of self-control is divided into two groups: 0 – the group, where the respondents' level of self-control is below the median and 1 – the group, where the respondents' level of self-control is above the median to determine the difference and the impact on the financial well-being.

From the obtained results, one can conclude that the level of well-being of young adults with self-control below the median is lower than those above the median (Fig. 4).

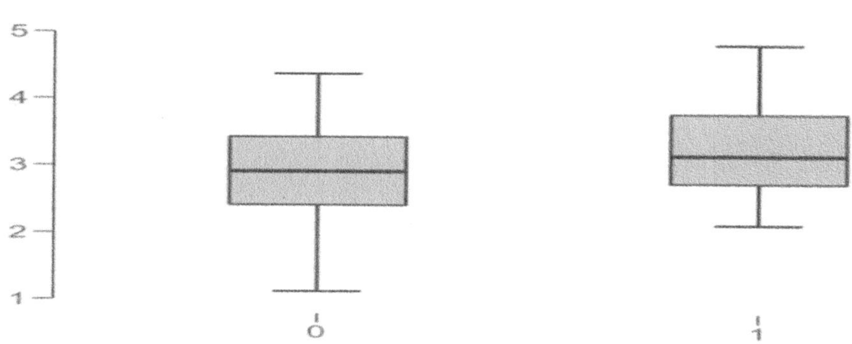

Fig. 4. Level of Self-control. *Source*: Created by authors.

By creating the box-whisker plots, further tests were performed where the level of overall optimism is divided into two groups: 0 – the group where the respondents' optimism is below the median, and group 1 – where the respondents' optimism is above the median to determine the difference and the impact on the financial well-being. From the obtained results, one can conclude that the level of well-being of young adults whose optimism is below the median is lower than those whose optimism is above the median (Fig. 5).

By creating the box-whisker plots, further tests were performed where the level of financial literacy is divided into two groups: 0 – the group, where the respondents' level of financial literacy is below the median, and the group 1 – where the respondents' level of financial literacy is above the median to determine the difference and the impact on the financial well-being.

From the obtained results, one can conclude that the level of well-being of young adults whose financial literacy is below the median is lower than those whose financial literacy is above the median. It is important to mention that this factor shows a much smaller range for financial well-being. As a result, the level of financial well-being fluctuates less (Fig. 6).

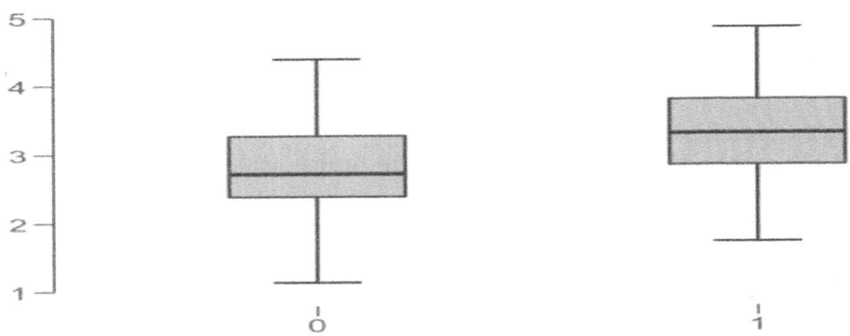

Fig. 5. Level of Overall Optimism. *Source*: Created by authors.

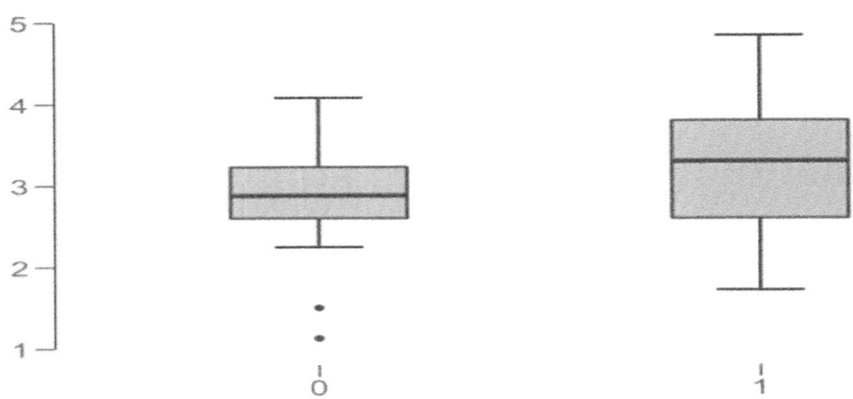

Fig. 6. Level of Financial Literacy. *Source*: Created by authors.

Creating Prototype of Financial Well-being Index

In the third stage, it was necessary to generate the so-called financial well-being index (a prototype for further research) that could support observing the level of financial well-being. The factors influencing the financial well-being of young adults should be considered in the index resulting from the above-mentioned research.

To resolve the weight determination problem, the authors applied methods described by Becker et al. (2017), who studied indexes and settled approaches allowing the expansion of factors to differentiate the influence of weights.

By applying the methods above, the following weights were determined based on the optimisation algorithm within Matlab programming space [eqs. (1)–(4)]:

$$X1 = 26\% \text{ (where X1 is the net monthly income)} \quad (1)$$

$$X2 = 41\% \text{ (where X2 is the level of self-control)} \quad (2)$$

$$X3 = 20\% \text{ (where X3 is the level of overall optimism)} \quad (3)$$

$$X4 = 13\% \text{ (where X4 is the level of financial literacy)} \quad (4)$$

All the composite well-being index weights are rounded up to the full number. It is worth mentioning that index weights are skewed towards the level of self-control that could be improved via self-studying and personal development and therefore is valued as being positive.

To create the composite well-being index in the fourth step, the following procedure is required: every factor's median observation determined previously should be divided by the strength of the factor and multiplied by the weight of the factor determined based on the model mentioned above. The scoring scale determines the weights of the factors and strength factors. The scoring scale runs from 1 (minimum level) up to 5 (indicating the maximum level). The results are demonstrated in Table 3.

The financial well-being index is determined as 3.48, showing the above-average level of the financial well-being of Latvian young adults, which should be considered a positive sign, while there is still a place for improvement. The improvements

Table 3. Scoring and Weighting Parameters for the Financial Well-being Index.

Factor/Scoring Scale	1	3	5	Weight of Each Factor (%)
Net monthly income	<500 EUR	<1,000 EUR	Starting from 1,000 EUR	26
Level of self-control	1.7100	3.0900	4.5500	41
Level of overall optimism	1.8100	3.5800	4.9000	20
Level of financial literacy	Below 60%	Between 60% and 80%	Above 80%	13

Source: Created by authors.

could be initiated by politicians, non-profit organisations, and companies, and individuals could contribute to achieving higher goals and standards.

Moreover, the authors would like to propose that similar measures should be performed on an annual basis which would contribute to a better understanding of the issue and allow taking necessary steps to achieve higher results in a timely manner.

It is worth considering that the result gained is preliminary as the scoring parameters are proposed by authors based on overall knowledge and previous experience in the research field. Further justifications or proofs would be necessary to claim the usability of the proposed tool for further research and implementation in practice (Sood, Kaur, & Grima, 2022).

CONCLUSIONS

The authors claim that financial well-being is not just about the level of financial security but also about the level of financial comfort experienced by individuals. Therefore, it is necessary to re-determine the approach (and the tools) to how the phenomena – financial well-being of young adults in Latvia and factors influencing it – are analysed. The proposed solution in the current chapter should contribute to a better understanding of the issue, increase the interest in the topic and make the task of different interesting parts of studying the issue easier to accomplish.

The influencing factors found in this study that affect the financial well-being of young adults in Latvia are self-control, optimism, and financial literacy. Based on the research, the authors can determine that the level of self-control has a positive effect on financial well-being, the level of financial knowledge has a positive effect on financial well-being, and the level of overall optimism has a positive effect on financial well-being of young adults in Latvia. All the factors are statistically significant and important for current and future research. The research findings could be interesting for business representatives willing to attract new talented employees and politicians and decision-makers understanding the necessity to diminish the emigration of young adults from Latvia.

Moreover, the authors presented a prototype of the financial well-being index. Even though it is still a work in progress (being a preliminary theoretical concept tested on the previously gained data set), it will contribute to further understanding of the issue and propose a tool to be used in measurement and management processes.

ACKNOWLEDGEMENTS

The authors would like to express their gratitude to Lāsma Zaikovska – BA School of Business and Finance (Class 2022) – for her assistance in preparing the questionnaire and acquiring the data for further analysis in the current research chapter.

REFERENCES

Abeltina, M., Rascevska, M., & Stokenberga, I. (2021). Mental health and work engagement as predictors of different burnout conceptualizations in a multi-occupational sample from Latvia. *International Journal of Psychology and Psychological Therapy*, *21*(3), 323–345.

Adler, A., & Seligman, M. E. (2016). Using well-being for public policy: Theory, measurement, and recommendations. *International Journal of Wellbeing*, *6*(1), 1–35. https://doi.org/10.5502/ijw.v6i1.429

Barrafrem, K., Västfjäll, D., & Tinghög, G. (2020). Financial well-being, COVID-19, and the financial better-than-average-effect. *Journal of Behavioral and Experimental Finance*, *28*, 100410–100410. https://doi.org/10.1016/j.jbef.2020.100410

Becker, W., Saisana, M., Paruolo, P., & Vandecasteele, I. (2017). Weights and importance in composite indicators: Closing the gap. *Ecological Indicators*, *80*, 12–22. https://doi.org/10.1016/j.ecolind.2017.03.056

Brüggen, E. C., Hogreve, J., Holmlund, M., Kabadayi, S., & Löfgren, M. (2017). Financial well-being: A conceptualization and research agenda. *Journal of Business Research*, *79*, 228–237. https://doi.org/10.1016/j.jbusres.2017.03.013

Grima, S., Kizilkaya, M., Sood, K., & ErdemDelice, M. (2021). The perceived effectiveness of blockchain for digital operational risk resilience in the European Union insurance market sector. *Journal of Risk and Financial Management*, *14*(8), 363.

Kuzmina, J., Natrins, A., Ziemele, A., & Kivrina, E. (2021). Developing financial efficiency index for higher education institutions. In M. H. Bilgin, H. Danis, E. Demir, & C. D. García-Gómez (Eds.), *Eurasian business and economics perspectives* (Eurasian Studies in Business and Economics, Vol. 19). Cham: Springer. https://doi.org/10.1007/978-3-030-77438-7_2

Maslow, A. H. (1948). "Higher" and "lower" needs. *The Journal of Psychology*, *25*(2), 433–436. https://doi.org/10.1080/00223980.1948.9917386

Mcknight, A. (2019). *Financial resilience among EU households*. Belgium: European Commission, Brussels, Directorate-General for Employment, Social Affairs and Inclusion Social Situation Monitor.

Shapiro, G. K., & Burchell, B. J. (2012). Measuring financial anxiety. *Journal of Neuroscience, Psychology, and Economics*, *5*(2), 92–103. https://doi.org/10.1037/a0027647

Sood, K., Kaur, B., & Grima, S. (2022). Revamping Indian non-life insurance industry with a trusted network: Blockchain technology. In K. Sood, R. K. Dhanaraj, B. Balamurugan, S. Grima, & R. U. Maheshwari (Eds.), *Big data: A game changer for insurance industry* (pp. 213–228). Bingley: Emerald Publishing Limited.

Sood, K., Seth, N., & Grima, S. (2022). Portfolio performance of public sector general insurance companies in India: A comparative analysis. In S. Grima, E. Özen, & I. Romānova (Eds.), *Managing risk and decision making in times of economic distress, part B* (pp. 215–229). Bingley: Emerald Publishing Limited.

Stockenberg, F., & Sultán, A. (2018). Key performance indicators in construction projects identification. Retrieved from https://hdl.handle.net/20.500.12380/256614

Strömbäck, C., Lind, T., Skagerlund, K., Västfjäll, D., & Tinghög, G. (2017). Does self-control predict financial behavior and financial well-being? *Journal of Behavioral and Experimental Finance*, *14*, 30–38. https://doi.org/10.1016/j.jbef.2017.04.002

Tay, L., & Diener, E. (2011). Needs and subjective well-being around the world. *Journal of Personality and Social Psychology*, *101*(2), 354–354.

Tenney, J. A., & Kalenkoski, C. M. (2019). Financial ratios and financial satisfaction: Exploring associations between objective and subjective measures of financial well-being among older Americans. *Journal of Financial Counseling and Planning*, *30*(2), 231–243. https://doi.org/10.1891/1052-3073.30.2.231

Vlaev, I., & Elliott, A. (2014). Financial well-being components. *Social Indicators Research*, *118*(3), 1103–1123. https://doi.org/10.1007/s11205-013-0462-0

CHAPTER 5

A SHIFT IN PARADIGM: THE FINANCIAL EDUCATION UNDER THE INFLUENCE OF DIGITAL TRANSFORMATION

Biruta Dzerve[a], Aivars Spilbergs[a], Gunta Innuse[a], Sandra Ozolina[a], Astride Stonane[a] and Dimitrios Maditinos[b]

[a]*BA School of Business and Finance, Latvia*
[b]*International Hellenic University, Greece*

ABSTRACT

The chapter explores the challenges in the financial education of the new generation under the influence of digital transformation, building awareness, and compliance with the new model of society. The rapid development of technology significantly influences our daily lives, thus making us look at the progress of various processes differently, thus facilitating the social and professional performance of subjects. The need for a comprehensive, fast, and logical personality is growing in a society that can analyse a set of different interconnections, draw logical conclusions, and assess risks. The impact of technology is particularly felt in educating future financiers, as accounting, financial analysis, and financial management decision-making have long been unthinkable without the skills to use various computer programmes, big data processing, and visualisation of financial information using the latest information technology

Digital Transformation, Strategic Resilience, Cyber Security and Risk Management
Contemporary Studies in Economic and Financial Analysis, Volume 111A, 61–82

Published under exclusive licence by Emerald Publishing Limited
ISSN: 1569-3759/doi:10.1108/S1569-37592023000111A005

tools. The survey was organised to collect data from student questionnaires. The questionnaire analysis allows for assessing students' digital competences, advantages and drawbacks of the digitalisation process, and university challenges in the digital transformation process as well as detecting the areas that require additional attention to make digital transformation effective. Digital transformation significantly changes the ecosystem, and the level of students' abilities and skills is also a variable. Therefore, it is important to identify the readiness of the participants in the higher education system for new challenges and to use the limited resources as efficiently as possible to prepare the financial specialists necessary for the development of society.

Keywords: Financial education; digital transformation; digital competences; information perception habits; application of technologies in the study process; student

INTRODUCTION

Previous generations of students went into the information in detail, analysed it, and only then came to conclusions and decisions. The twenty-first century generation superficially combines vast amounts of information and perceives only the main idea, often without delving into details. However, this does not prevent them from drawing conclusions and making decisions, which could often be flawed. Is it bad? Yes and no. These risks are likely to increase in the social environment, where you must consider a massive amount of information while having limited time resources. However, assessing the potential loss versus the benefits received is necessary. The task of the higher education system in the next few years will be to prepare financial professionals with sufficient professional knowledge while developing their logical thinking as much as possible, minimising the risks of a mismatch between the vast amount of information and the subject's ability to process it. After graduation, a financially qualified graduate should become a 'universal soldier' who can solve specific professional problems and look at the situation as a whole. Quite often, academics have to 'step out of their comfort zone' to adapt to today's rhythm of modern life and the information perception of young people.

There are no essential differences in the structure of study programmes in the higher educational systems of different countries, though every society has its own specific view on the best model of higher education. International regulations determine the implementation guidelines for higher education in the European Union (EU), while national legislation governing education sets standards to defend the interests of their countries and increase the competitiveness of higher education. Since joining the EU, small countries have learned much from the experience of large countries about how to evolve the level of higher education. They have gained the most experience using various EU-funded instruments. Every six years, when accrediting study programmes, the work done in the previous period as well as the opinions of foreign and local experts are reviewed. The recommendations of experts and professionals as regards the contents of the study programmes have been integrated. Year by year, the cooperation between employers and implementers of higher education programmes becomes closer. It enables the security and creation of study programmes corresponding to the labour market. This cooperation helps foresee whether the educational system can first predict what skills and competencies might be demanded in the labour market. The educational system should outperform the thinking of the labour market. Relevant competences should be predicted first, before changes have happened in the labour market, but this is not the case. According to the latest observations, the opposite trend has been noticed (Sood, Seth, & Grima, 2022). First, new information technology systems and data analysis tools are accepted in the working environment, and only afterwards have learning and teaching been introduced in programmes of higher education. In reality, learning new skills is only possible through practice.

LITERATURE REVIEW

The rapid development of information and communication technologies (ICTs) in recent decades has provided a theoretical framework for the integration and deployment of information systems in diverse business and social ecosystems from simple computer systems to advanced digital technologies such as social, mobile, analytical, cloud, and IoT (Sebastian et al., 2017).

Spante, Hashemi, Lundin, and Algers (2018) present a systematic review of research on digital competence and digital literacy concepts used in higher education research. Review demonstrates that there is a range of definitions used in higher education research and they vary depending on if the concepts are defined by policy, research or both and whether they focus on technical skills or social practices.

Abad-Segura, González-Zamar, Infante-Moro, and García (2020) analyse the trends of the last 30 years in research on digital transformation (DT) in higher education (Grima, Kizilkaya, Sood, and ErdemDelice, 2021). The authors point to an exponential trend in recent years.

Higher education institutions have long been developing digital solutions by introducing information systems such as registers of students, study courses, and results such as BigBlueButton, Moodle, Blackboard, GoToMeeting, etc., and academic staff have digitised their study courses (Crawford et al., 2020). DT in the study process means the evolution of the type of learning and adaptation to the new needs of the student (Du Toit & Verhoef, 2018).

Kim, Hong, and Song (2019) examine university students' perceptions of e-learning, based on their experiences, and the mediating roles of academic engagement and digital readiness within the university context of an e-learning environment for academic achievement. Research shows that although students positively perceived e-learning experiences on campus, they must have strong digital skills to perform academic work and commit to effortful involvement in the context of academic learning (Inder, Sood, & Grima, 2022).

Santos, Batista, and Marques (2019) analyse the students' perspective on using digital technologies to communicate with their teachers. Research results show that solutions that allow interpersonal communication as well as publishing and sharing are preferred by students.

Sjöberg and Lilja (2019) investigate how theoretical assumptions about technology integration in education relate to Swedish universities' teaching practice. Research results indicate that the teachers are hesitant yet positive towards using digital technology in their pedagogical practice and that ambivalence surrounds the issue at hand.

Aristovnik, Keržic, Ravšelj, Tomaževic, and Umek's (2020) study of the impact of the first wave of COVID-19 on the learning process across 62 countries reveals that students were most satisfied with the public relations provided by teachers and universities when switching to online learning support. At the same time, the lack of computer skills and the perception of heavier workloads prevented them from achieving the best performance. The students were worried about their future professional careers, experiencing boredom, anxiety, and frustration.

Another study (Crawford et al., 2020), which analysed higher education's response to COVID-19 in 20 countries, concludes that responses from higher education providers have ranged from non-response to social isolation strategies on campus and the rapid transformation of curricula to fully deliver online offerings. The results of the study suggest that there are significant opportunities to learn from the pedagogical achievements of other universities to strengthen the collective response to COVID-19 now and in the future.

Gonzalez-Zamar and Abad-Segura (2020) analyse the research from 2000 to 2019 on implementing information technologies for sustainable education in the context of higher education. Authors apply bibliometric techniques to a sample of 1,814 articles selected from the Scopus database and show an exponential trend, mainly in the last five years.

Papouli, Chatzifotiou, and Tsairidis (2020) explore Greek social work students' views on using digital technology during their stay at home due to the coronavirus lockdown. The results describe aspects of using digital technology and its connections to learning interactions, communication with others, self-fulfilment, and well-being. Researchers highlight the critical role digital technology played in numerous aspects of students' daily lives, helping them discover new ways to navigate the unprecedented new reality formed due to the COVID-19 pandemic.

Goulart, Liboni, and Cezarino (2021) evaluate the relationship between the professional profile required by companies and what students are taught on IT-related programmes in higher education institutions. The analysis reveals that universities must go beyond the transfer of knowledge and technical qualification in IT, promoting a comprehensive education that incorporates personal development goals, focussing on developing social and emotional skills.

Monteiro and Leite (2021) identify university students' digital competences and the uses and effects of digital literacy in developing personal and social skills.

The research results show good information search and data editing skills and less developed abilities to create and develop new digital solutions. The low involvement of teachers in the available pedagogical support is reported as an obstacle to an adequate DT in higher education.

In contrast, the study on the impact of COVID-19 on education (Kumar, Alshazly, Idris, & Bourouis, 2021) examines both the positive and negative consequences of combining the opportunities offered by digital technologies with traditional teaching to improve communication between teachers and students.

Bygstad, Øvrelid, Ludvigsen, and Dæhlen's (2022) study by the University of Oslo focusses on identifying digital learning space, distinguishing two main aspects: digitalisation of education and digitalisation of subjects. The study allows us to conclude that the alignment of digital education and digital subjects provided a technical foundation for DT, the digital learning space allows to clarify the roles between students and teachers, allowing for new and deeper forms of learning.

Rodríguez-Abitia, Martínez-Pérez, Ramírez-Montoya, and López-Caudana (2020) analyse how higher education institutions in Spain and Mexico have taken on the challenge of introducing and using technology in education. The study's results suggest that contextual factors play a key role in an institution's ability to benefit from DT and help ensure the quality of the educational process.

Rof, Bikfalvi, and Marques (2020) explore the impact of DT on the universities' business model. Researchers address a research gap at the intersection of DT and the business model in higher education institutions.

Agasisti, Frattini, and Soncin (2021), based on a study of the experience of the Northern Italian School of Management, propose a process model for promoting digital innovation in an emergency. Digital readiness, cultural openness, and a defined strategic orientation are key preconditions for a successful DT.

Alenezi (2021) studies the aspects of DT in higher education institutions and analyses technology integration models in the study process.

Anastasakis, Triantafyllou, and Petridis (2021) explore the difficulties undergraduates faced during the transition to online education in Greek Higher Educational Institutions. Based on online survey data analysis authors conclude that most reported barriers are caused by their lecturers, weak internet connections, and limited social interactions.

García-Morales, Garrido-Moreno, and Martín-Rojas (2021) focus on transformation in higher education institution driven by the need to digitalise education in record time with academics who lack innate technological capabilities for online teaching. Researchers conclude that universities should develop a sophisticated combination of face-to-face and online learning to harness the potential of the technological tools available to meet students' expectations and enhance their learning experience in the current digital environment.

Laufer et al. (2021) investigated how higher education leaders in 24 countries experienced rapid DT. Research identifies the multiple and overlapping factors that contribute to an institution's ability to realise the potential of digital education, in terms of access, learning, and collaboration.

Saikkonen and Kaarakainen (2021) examined the extent to which sociodemographic factors and available resources predict digital information skills and which subgroups emerge as potential targets for interventions. Utilising the multiple regression analysis, the study found that digital activity and age explain most of the variation in teachers' digital information skills.

Sánchez-Caballé, Gisbert-Cervera, and Esteve-Mon (2021) analysed the digital competence content in the curricula of 40 bachelor's degrees. Researchers found that the more technical degrees have the most integrated indicators of technological literacy while the other knowledge areas have a higher level of information literacy.

Silvola, Naykki, Kaveri, and Muukkonen (2021) analysed teachers' needs and expectations for learning analytics to support student engagement on the academic path level. The study results demonstrate how student needs are sometimes contradictory, for example, when students suggest more possibilities for agentic choices in their studies, but similarly more institutional monitoring or their study progression.

Tang et al. (2021) investigate factors related to learning motivation, readiness to learn, and students' self-efficacy in online learning during a coronavirus outbreak. Gender and study level differences are analysed – the results of the study did not reveal statistically significant differences between the sexes, but the study level has an impact on the readiness for online learning.

Toader, Safta, Titirişcă, and Firtescu (2021) study effects of digitalisation on higher education in Romania. The analysis results show the positive effect of digitalisation on tertiary education and the latter's positive impact on sustainable development. Researchers conclude that most of the participants in the university educational process have adapted the online activity.

Ben Youssef et al. (2022) examine the impact of ICT use and digital skills on students' academic performance and explore the digital divide in France. Research shows that poor investment in ICT affects students' results, the ICT training offered by universities has little impact on students' results, and the acquisition of digital skills increases students' academic performance.

Berei and Pusztai (2022) examine the risks of learning using digital technologies. Analysis of survey results from five European countries indicates that more than half of the students never learned by watching tutorials or listening to audio recordings and have significant concentration risks.

Fűzi, Géring, and Szendrei-Pál (2022) investigate the impacts of the COVID-19 pandemic on digitalisation and socialisation in higher education. Research results show the dynamic interconnection between digitalisation and socialisation.

Kedraka, Kaltsidis, Raikou, and Karalis (2022) examine the effects of e-learning and the consequent disruption of the traditional educational function in higher education in Greece with special reference to undergraduates' views. The research results show that students prefer face-to-face courses and provide ideas for developing didactic e-teaching approaches to motivate students on their academic pathways.

Pilotti, El-Moussa, and Abdelsalam (2022) investigate the switch from face-to-face to online study and found differences between female and male students in adopting a changed instruction environment.

Pohlenz, Felix, Berndt, and Seyfried (2022) examine student subgroups' responses to the coercive digitalisation of teaching and learning processes during the pandemic. Researchers identified that student subgroups are proponents, pragmatics, and sceptics of digitalised teaching and learning processes. These subgroups have different preferences concerning teaching and learning modes of delivery, which implies the relevance of individualised educational services and respective quality assurance practices.

Rosak-Szyrocka, Żywiołek, Zaborski, Chowdhury, and Hu (2022) study the worldwide trend of how employees utilise e-learning resources to determine instructors' interest in and attitudes about using them. The researchers provided a detailed overview of e-learning practices during the pandemic and its future prospects from the teacher's point of view. The research results show that the digitalisation of education is no longer a future trend, but today's trend or even a university standard in the education improvement direction.

Stecuła and Wolniak (2022) analysed the influence of the COVID-19 pandemic on the change in the use of innovative e-learning tools in university education in Poland. The authors conclude that the percentage of students familiar with the analysed e-learning tools has increased significantly during the pandemic. The most frequently used e-learning tools during the COVID-19 pandemic have been mainly videoconferencing tools such as MS Teams and Zoom. The author's research identified three hidden factors of the used e-learning tools: popular services and applications adapted to e-learning, popular applications for synchronous meetings adapted to e-learning, and other synchronous and asynchronous e-learning methods. Based on the research results a model of relations between students' interest in innovative e-learning technology and the resources they possess to participate in e-learning classes was developed (Yerpudee, Sood, & Grima, 2022).

Respective variance is discussed in terms of digital inequality and is interpreted as a need to individualise teaching, learning, and quality assurance practices.

Teker, Teker, and Tavman (2022) examine how digitalisation has affected and changed higher education. The authors conclude that a university should support those academics who lead the improvement of digital skills and innovative teaching methods, promote digital literacy in the academia, and encourage the use of learning platforms.

Zagkos et al. (2022) study attitudes of students of five Greek universities towards the distance learning process. Research results show that from students view face-to-face teaching cannot be replaced by distance learning. The findings indicate that students come to a meeting of minds about the educational inequalities worsened by the lack of digital equipment and undeveloped technological infrastructure.

Based on the results of research and analysis of publications obtained in recent years, the following research questions were formulated:

1. Which digital competences are best developed in student's self-assessment and can therefore be used intensively to improve their qualifications without additional investment?
2. Which areas need increased attention in the study process to reduce their negative impact on the development of financial skills?
3. Which digital solutions are not fully used and require adequate solutions in the study process?
4. What are the advantages and disadvantages of DT in studying finance at university?
5. From the student's point of view, what are the most important challenges for the university in implementing the DT?
6. Is there progress in the course of studies in the field of digital competences?
7. Are there observable differences in the assessment of DT in the education process?

DATA AND METHODS

In order to find answers to the research questions, a questionnaire was created, which consists of six parts: (a) study programme and year of the respondent; (b) student's digital competences; (c) usage of digital solutions by students; (d) advantages of DT in studying finance at university; (e) disadvantages of DT in studying finance at university; and (f) challenges in implementing the DT. Digital competences' part of the questionnaire was developed based on adaption of Digital Competence Framework for Citizen (Vuorikari, Kluzer, & Punie, 2022) and (c)–(f) parts, based on the literature review (Levano-Francia et al., 2019; Sillat, Tammets, & Laanpere, 2021; Zhao, Llorente, & Gómez, 2021).

Students were asked to evaluate their digital competences on a 5-point Likert scale (1 – 'None'; 2 – 'Basic'; 3 – 'Medium'; 4 – 'Good'; and 5 – 'High level'), while sections (c)–(f) on a 4-point Likert scale 1 – 'None'; 2 – 'Insignificant'; 3 – 'Important'; and 4 – 'Very important'). The survey was conducted among BA School of Business and Finance students in the spring of 2022.

The distribution of respondents by study programmes is as follows (Fig. 1):

- 20 bachelor study programme 'Finance',
- 14 bachelor study programme 'Business Process Management',
- 14 students of master study programme 'Finance',
- 9 bachelor study programme 'International Finance,
- 8 master study programme 'Entrepreneurship',
- 6 bachelor study programme 'Accounting and Finance',
- 3 bachelor study programme 'Risk Management and Insurance', and
- 3 bachelor study programme 'Financial Management Information Systems'.

The most represented are: 1st year bachelor (25%), 2nd year bachelor (25%), and 1st year magister (22%) study programmes, which largely correspond to the structure of students in BA. Therefore, the survey can be considered as sufficiently representative.

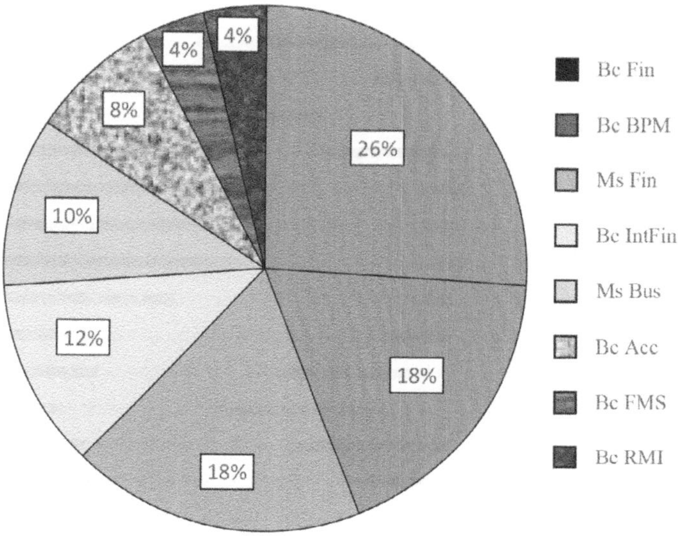

Fig. 1. Distribution of Survey Respondents by Study Programme.
Source: Authors' calculations based on survey results.

In order to assess the progress of students in the field of digital competences and the differences in the assessment of DT in education process, the respondents were divided into two subgroups: first two-year undergraduate students – 'junior' and the rest – 'senior'.

A chi-square test was used to assess differences in response distributions between 'junior' and 'senior' students and test statistic is calculated as follows:

$$\chi^2 = \sum_{i=1}^{k} \frac{(O_i - E_i)^2}{E_i}, \quad (1)$$

where O_i is the observed frequency of respondents answer on *i*th question and E_i the expected frequency of respondents answer on *i*th question.

RESEARCH RESULTS

Fig. 2 shows the distribution of students' self-assessments of digital abilities.

Students value most of their digital competences in the following areas:

- the ability to read digital text,
- the ability to find the digital information needed for work, and
- the ability to communicate and interact with others using technology.

Among the less developed are:

- the ability to detect, avoid, and manage cyber threats,
- the ability to synthesise digital information,

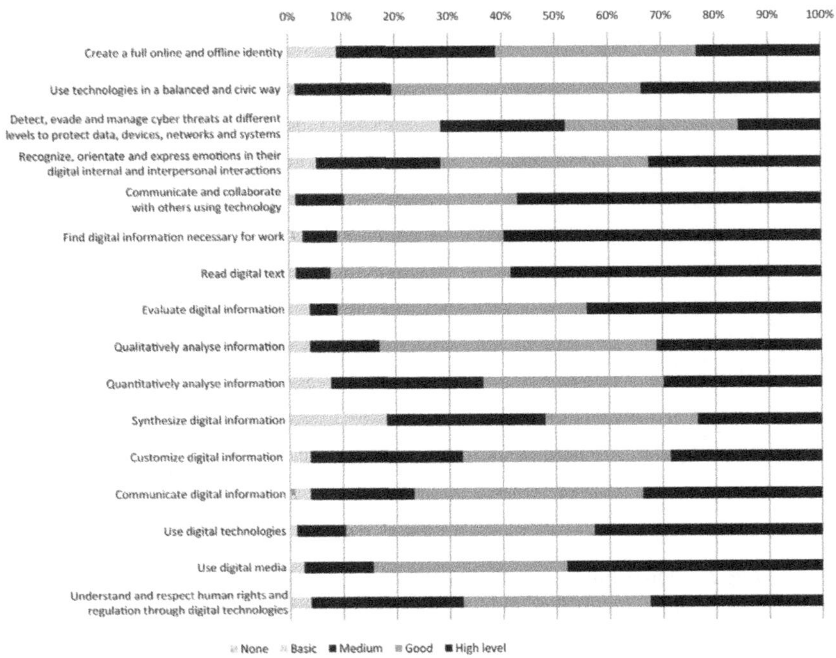

Fig. 2. Distribution of Students' Self-assessments of Digital Abilities.
Source: Authors' calculations based on survey results.

- the ability to customise digital information, and
- the ability to understand and respect human rights and regulation through digital technologies.

Fig. 3 shows the distribution of answers regarding the usage of digital solutions by students.

The results of the survey indicate certain challenges – less than half of students regularly or frequently use digital databases, such as Eurostat, the ECB, the OECD, the IMF, the CSB, the Bank of Latvia, and the FCMC, 18% and 23%, respectively. The situation is similar to the use of databases of scientific publications available on the Internet – 13% and 34%, respectively, and the use of financial portals – 12% and 22%, respectively.

Fig. 4 shows the distribution of answers regarding advantages of DT in studying finance at university.

Respondents note the main advantages of DT in studying finance at university:

- flexibility of the study place,
- study time savings, and
- opportunities for the use of different sources of information.

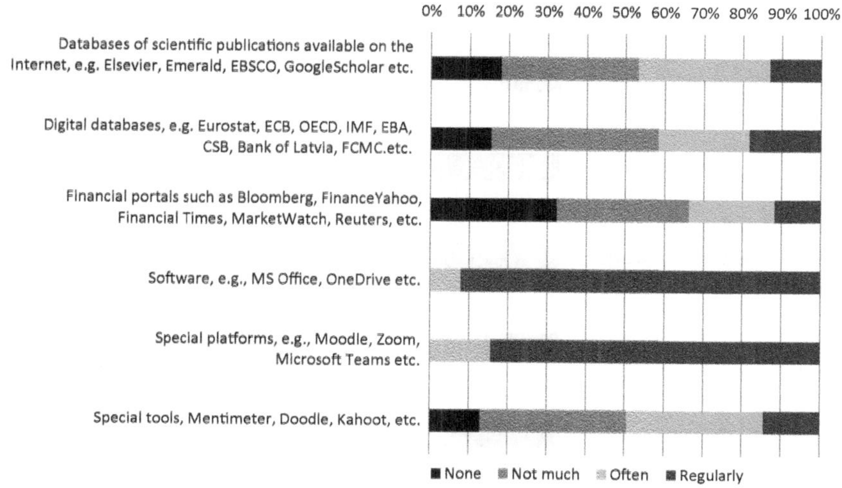

Fig. 3. Distribution of Answers Regarding the Usage of Digital Solutions by Students. *Source*: Authors' calculations based on survey results.

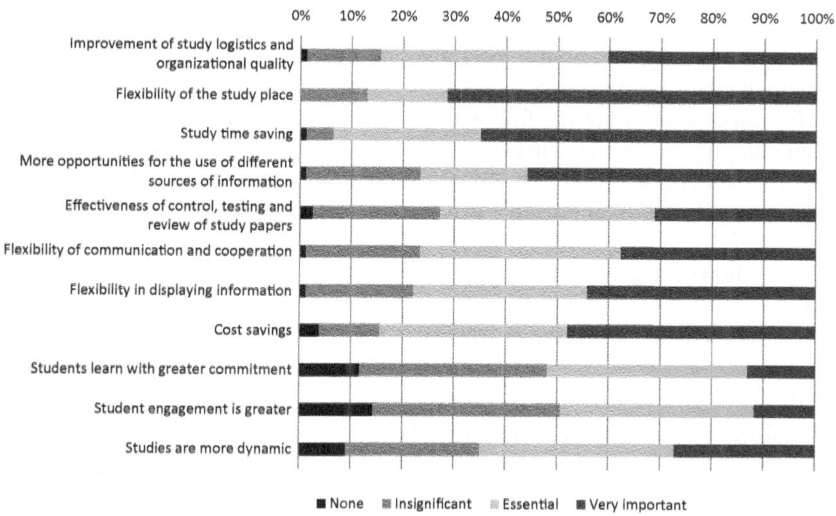

Fig. 4. Distribution of Students' Answers Regarding Advantages of DT in Studying Finance at University. *Source*: Authors' calculations based on survey results.

The following are considered to be less significant:

- student engagement is greater,
- students learn with greater commitment, and
- studies are more dynamic.

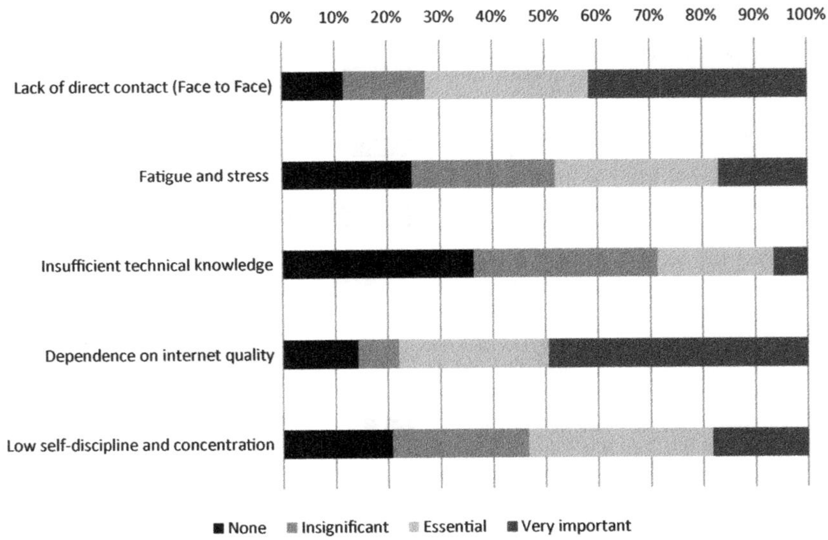

Fig. 5. Distribution of Students' Answers Regarding Disadvantages of DT in Studying Finance at University. *Source*: Authors' calculations based on survey results.

Fig. 5 shows the distribution of answers regarding disadvantages of DT in studying finance at university.

The respondents note the following as the most significant shortcomings of DT in studying finance at university: dependence on the quality of the Internet, lack of direct contact, and low self-discipline and concentration. The following are recognised as less important: insufficient technical knowledge, fatigue, and stress.

Fig. 6 shows the distribution of answers regarding challenges in implementing the DT.

The main challenges of the university in implementing the DT are as follows:

- data security and privacy,
- insufficient funding for the purchase of modern technologies, and
- regulatory requirements and compliance.

Less significant challenges for the university are: students' insufficient digital skills and lack of talent.

Table 1 summarises descriptive statistics of students' self-assessments of digital abilities.

As can be seen from Table 1, on some questions, for example, abilities to create a full online and offline identity, abilities to read digital text, abilities to communicate digital information, and abilities to use media, senior self-assessment is slightly higher, but for the rest – lower. Are these differences statistically

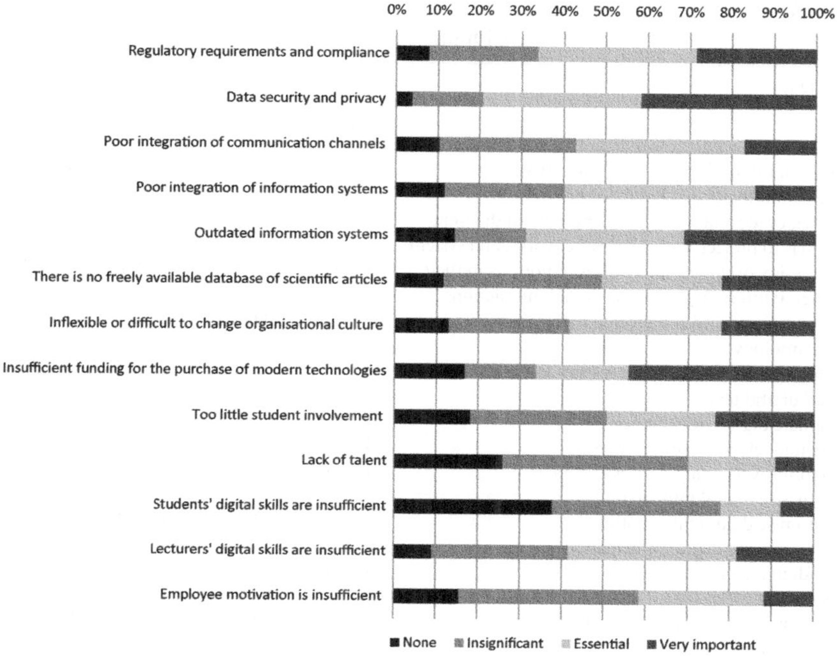

Fig. 6. Distribution of Answers Regarding Challenges in Implementing the DT. *Source*: Authors' calculations based on survey results.

significant? To answer this question, a chi-square test was performed and the results of which are summarised in Table 2.

As can be seen from Table 2, on questions: abilities to create a full online and offline identity; abilities to detect, evade, and manage cyber threats at different levels to protect data, devices, networks, and systems; abilities to recognise, orientate, and express emotions in their digital internal and interpersonal interactions; abilities to find digital information necessary for work; abilities to evaluate digital information; abilities to qualitatively analyse information; abilities to quantitatively analyse information; abilities to communicate digital information; abilities to use digital technologies; and abilities to understand and respect human rights and regulation through digital technologies differences are statistically significant at confidence level of 95%. For the rest of the questions, differences are statistically insignificant.

Table 3 summarises descriptive statistics of students' assessments of usage of digital technologies in financial education.

As can be seen from Table 3, only on question 'Use of special platforms, e.g., Moodle, Zoom, Microsoft Teams, etc.', junior's assessment is slightly higher, but for the rest – lower. Are these differences statistically significant? To answer this question, a chi-square test was performed and the results of which are summarised in Table 4.

Table 1. Mean Values and Standard Deviations of Students' Self-assessments of Digital Abilities.

Variable	Junior		Senior	
	Mean	Stdev	Mean	Stdev
Create a full online and offline identity	3.5385	1.0475	3.9737	0.7161
Use technologies in a balanced and civic way	4.2051	0.7671	4.0526	0.7333
Detect, evade and manage cyber threats at different levels to protect data, devices, networks, and systems	3.4872	1.0729	3.2105	1.0438
Recognise, orientate, and express emotions in their digital internal and interpersonal interactions	4.0513	0.9719	3.9211	0.7844
Communicate and collaborate with others using technology	4.5385	0.6426	4.3421	0.8785
Find digital information necessary for work	4.5641	0.6804	4.3684	0.8829
Read digital text	4.4615	0.6823	4.5263	0.6872
Evaluate digital information	4.3590	0.8425	4.2632	0.6445
Qualitatively analyse information	4.1795	0.8545	4.0263	0.6773
Quantitatively analyse information	4.0256	0.8732	3.6842	0.9893
Synthesise digital information	3.7436	1.0442	3.3947	1.0277
Customise digital information	3.9744	0.8732	3.8684	0.8438
Communicate digital information	4.0000	1.0000	4.1053	0.7274
Use digital technologies	4.3846	0.7114	4.2368	0.6752
Use media	4.1795	0.8231	4.4211	0.7581
Understand and respect human rights and regulation through digital technologies	4.1026	0.9118	3.8158	0.8336

Source: Authors' calculations based on survey results.

Table 2. Chi-squared Statistics of Students' Self-assessments of Digital Abilities

Variable	χ^2-Stat	*p*-Value
Create a full online and offline identity	16.182	0.0010
Use technologies in a balanced and civic way	5.380	0.1461
Detect, evade, and manage cyber threats at different levels to protect data, devices, networks and systems	5.027	0.0106
Recognise, orientate, and express emotions in their digital internal and interpersonal interactions	8.077	0.0444
Communicate and collaborate with others using technology	1.033	05966
Find digital information necessary for work	7.704	0.0212
Read digital text	2.277	0.3203
Evaluate digital information	12.878	0.0049
Qualitatively analyse information	8.697	0.0336
Quantitatively analyse information	9.665	0.0216
Synthesise digital information	6.265	0.0994
Customise digital information	2.910	0.4057
Communicate digital information	11.588	0.0207
Use digital technologies	8.975	0.0113
Use media	4.197	0.2410
Understand and respect human rights and regulation through digital technologies	8.327	0.0397

Source: Authors' calculations based on survey results.

Table 3. Mean Values and Standard Deviations of Students' Assessments of Usage of Digital Technologies in Financial Education

Variable	Junior		Senior	
	Mean	Stdev	Mean	Stdev
Databases of scientific publications available on the Internet, for example, Elsevier, Emerald, EBSCO, GoogleScholar, etc.	2.3077	1.0552	2.5263	0.7965
Digital databases, for example, Eurostat, ECB, OECD, IMF, EBA, CSB, Bank of Latvia, FCMC, etc.	2.3333	1.0596	2.5526	0.8605
Financial portals such as Bloomberg, FinanceYahoo, Financial Times, MarketWatch, Reuters, etc.	2.1282	0.9782	2.3316	1.0442
Software, for example, MS Office, OneDrive, etc.	3.8974	0.3074	3.9474	0.2263
Special platforms, for example, Moodle, Zoom, Microsoft Teams, etc.	3.9487	0.2235	3.7368	0.4463
Special tools, Mentimeter, Doodle, Kahoot, etc.	2.3590	0.9594	2.6579	0.8146

Source: Authors calculations based on survey results.

Table 4. Chi-squared Statistics for Students' Assessments of Usage of Digital Technologies in Financial Education

Variable	χ^2-Stat	*p*-Value
Databases of scientific publications available on the Internet, for example, Elsevier, Emerald, EBSCO, GoogleScholar, etc.	10.455	0.0151
Digital databases, for example, Eurostat, ECB, OECD, IMF, EBA, CSB, Bank of Latvia, FCMC, etc.	10.411	0.0154
Financial portals such as Bloomberg, FinanceYahoo, Financial Times, MarketWatch, Reuters, etc.	8.815	0.0319
Software, for example, MS Office, OneDrive, etc.	1.527	0.6760
Special platforms, for example, Moodle, Zoom, Microsoft Teams, etc.	2.312	0.4218
Special tools, Mentimeter, Doodle, Kahoot, etc.	8.622	0.0348

Source: Authors' calculations based on survey results.

As can be seen in Table 4, on questions: use of databases of scientific publications available on the Internet, for example, Elsevier, Emerald, EBSCO, GoogleScholar, etc.; use of digital databases, for example, Eurostat, ECB, OECD, IMF, EBA, CSB, Bank of Latvia, FCMC, etc.; use of financial portals such as Bloomberg, FinanceYahoo, Financial Times, MarketWatch, Reuters, etc.; and use of special tools, Mentimeter, Doodle, Kahoot, etc. differences are statistically significant at confidence level 95%. For the rest of the questions, differences are statistically insignificant.

Table 5 summarises descriptive statistics of students' assessments of advantages of DT in financial education.

As can be seen from Table 5, only on question regarding advantages of DT in financial education – 'Student engagement is greater', senior's assessment is slightly higher, but for the rest – lower. Are these differences statistically significant? To answer this question, a chi-square test was performed and the results of which are summarised in Table 6.

Table 5. Mean Values and Standard Deviations of Students' Assessments of Advantages of Digital Transformation in Financial Education

Variable	Junior		Senior	
	Mean	Stdev	Mean	Stdev
Improvement of study logistics and organisational quality	3.4359	0.6405	3.3263	0.7880
Flexibility of the study place	3.7949	0.4690	3.5684	0.8517
Study time saving	3.6667	0.6623	3.4737	0.6467
More opportunities for the use of different sources of information	3.5641	0.7180	3.3526	0.9285
Effectiveness of control, testing, and review of study papers	3.2564	0.7853	2.9632	0.7862
Flexibility of communication and cooperation	3.2572	0.8497	3.0126	0.7352
Flexibility in displaying information	3.4103	0.7511	3.1437	0.8383
Cost savings	3.4103	0.8801	3.2579	0.7543
Students learn with greater commitment	2.5385	0.9692	2.5263	0.7618
Student engagement is greater	2.3846	0.9629	2.5526	0.7952
Studies are more dynamic	2.9744	0.9315	2.6842	0.9330

Source: Authors' calculations based on survey results.

As can be seen from Table 6, on questions regarding advantages of DT in financial education: 'Effectiveness of control, testing, and review of study papers'; 'Flexibility of communication and cooperation'; and 'Cost savings' differences are statistically significant at confidence level 95%. For the rest of the questions, differences are statistically insignificant.

Table 7 summarises the descriptive statistics of students' assessments of disadvantages of DT in financial education.

As can be seen in Table 7, on all questions regarding disadvantages of DT in financial education, 'seniors' assessment is more conservative. Are these differences statistically significant? To answer this question, a chi-square test was performed and the results of which are summarised in Table 8.

Table 6. Chi-squared Statistics of Students' Assessments of Advantages of Digital Transformation in Financial Education.

Variable	χ^2-Stat	*p*-Value
Improvement of study logistics and organisational quality	6.507	0.0894
Flexibility of the study place	5.999	0.1116
Study time saving	3.044	0.3850
More opportunities for the use of different sources of information	5.651	0.1299
Effectiveness of control, testing, and review of study papers	13.805	0.0032
Flexibility of communication and cooperation	11.377	0.0099
Flexibility in displaying information	5.135	0.1622
Cost savings	10.239	0.0166
Students learn with greater commitment	2.734	0.4344
Student engagement is greater	4.413	0.2202
Studies are more dynamic	4.411	0.2004

Source: Authors' calculations based on survey results.

Table 7. Mean Values and Standard Deviations of Students' Assessments of Disadvantages of Digital Transformation in Financial Education

Variable	Junior		Senior	
	Mean	Stdev	Mean	Stdev
Lack of direct contact (face-to-face)	2.9231	1.2223	3.1316	0.7771
Fatigue and stress	2.3590	1.1807	2.4474	0.8913
Insufficient technical knowledge	1.8974	1.0710	2.0789	0.7491
Dependence on internet quality	2.8462	1.1594	3.4211	0.8893
Low self-discipline and concentration	2.4359	1.2095	2.5789	0.7929

Source: Authors' calculations based on survey results.

Table 8. Chi-squared Statistics of Students' Assessments of Disadvantages of Digital Transformation in Financial Education.

Variable	χ^2-Stat	*p*-Value
Lack of direct contact (face-to-face)	8.670	0.0340
Fatigue and stress	4.741	0.1918
Insufficient technical knowledge	8.151	0.0430
Dependence on internet quality	10.844	0.0126
Low self-discipline and concentration	6.957	0.0733

Source: Authors' calculations based on survey results.

As can be seen from Table 8, on questions regarding disadvantages of DT in financial education: 'Lack of direct contact (face-to-face)'; 'Insufficient technical knowledge'; and 'Dependence on internet quality' differences are statistically significant at confidence level 95%. For the rest of the questions, differences are statistically insignificant.

Table 9 summarises the descriptive statistics of students' assessments of challenges of DT in financial education.

As can be seen from Table 9, on questions regarding challenges of DT in financial education – 'Outdated information systems'; 'Inflexible or difficult to change organisational culture'; 'Insufficient funding for the purchase of modern technologies'; 'Too little student involvement'; 'Lack of talent'; and 'Lecturers' digital skills are insufficient', 'seniors' assessment is slightly higher, but for the rest – lower. Are these differences statistically significant? To answer this question, a chi-square test was performed and the results of which are summarised in Table 10.

As can be seen from Table 10, on questions regarding challenges of DT in financial education: 'There is no freely available database of scientific articles'; 'Inflexible or difficult to change organisational culture'; 'Too little student involvement'; and 'Employee motivation is insufficient' differences are statistically significant at confidence level 95%. For the rest of the questions, differences are statistically insignificant.

Table 9. Mean Values and Standard Deviations of Students' Assessments of Challenges of Digital Transformation in Financial Education

Variable	Junior		Senior	
	Mean	Stdev	Mean	Stdev
Regulatory requirements and compliance	3.0256	0.9028	2.7105	0.9273
Data security and privacy	3.2051	0.9228	3.1316	0.7771
Poor integration of communication channels	2.7949	0.9509	2.4737	0.7965
Poor integration of information systems	2.6923	0.9502	2.5526	0.7952
Outdated information systems	2.7949	1.0306	2.9211	1.0235
There is no freely available database of scientific articles	2.8462	1.0397	2.3684	0.8194
Inflexible or difficult to change organisational culture	2.5641	1.0953	2.7895	0.8107
Insufficient funding for the purchase of modern technologies	2.6923	1.1955	2.7895	0.8107
Too little student involvement	2.4359	1.1424	2.6579	0.9380
Lack of talent	2.0513	1.0247	2.2105	0.7766
Students' digital skills are insufficient	1.9744	1.0634	1.8684	0.7415
Lecturers' digital skills are insufficient	2.6667	0.9551	2.6842	0.8089
Employee motivation is insufficient	2.4103	1.0187	2.3421	0.7453

Source: Authors' calculations based on survey results.

Table 10. Chi-squared Statistics of Students' Assessments of Challenges of Digital Transformation in Financial Education.

Variable	χ^2-Stat	*p*-Value
Regulatory requirements and compliance	5.195	0.1581
Data security and privacy	5.343	0.1484
Poor integration of communication channels	7.637	0.0541
Poor integration of information systems	4.374	0.2238
Outdated information systems	0.733	0.8654
There is no freely available database of scientific articles	20.714	0.0001
Inflexible or difficult to change organisational culture	9.610	0.0222
Insufficient funding for the purchase of modern technologies	6.020	0.1107
Too little student involvement	9.443	0.0239
Lack of talent	7.379	0.0607
Students' digital skills are insufficient	5.894	0.1169
Lecturers' digital skills are insufficient	3.240	0.3561
Employee motivation is insufficient	9.164	0.0272

Source: Authors' calculations based on survey results.

DISCUSSION AND CONCLUSIONS

1. According to research, technological developments create opportunities to significantly improve financial management processes while reducing costs, but DT is unthinkable without adequate competences.
2. The results of the study show that students' digital competences in some areas, for example, abilities to read digital text, to find the digital information

needed for work, and to communicate and interact with others using technologies are well developed and provide opportunities to use digital solutions more intensively in the study process and to increase the quality of study results.

3. One of the benefits of the COVID-19 pandemic is the increased motivation of students to develop their digital skills. As Fig. 7 shows, seniors' motivation is slightly higher, which can be explained by being in online studies for a longer period during the pandemic.
4. The results of the survey also point to areas where students' digital competences are less developed and require additional attention both in IT-related study courses such as abilities to synthesise and to customise digital information, and in specialised ones such as cybersecurity (ability to detect, avoid' and manage cyber threats) and civil rights (the ability to understand and respect human rights and regulation through digital technologies).
5. The availability of databases has developed rapidly in recent decades, and they have become an integral source of data for supporting financial decisions. However, as the results of the survey show, more progress is possible in this area so that students' abilities are developed according to industry requirements.
6. There are inevitable challenges in the process of DT, and in the students' assessment, the following are mentioned among the most important ones: data security and privacy, insufficient funding for the purchase of modern technologies, and regulatory requirements and compliance.
7. The results of the survey also indicate certain trends that should be taken into account in the organisation of the study process, for example, 'juniors' enter university with better developed abilities, on their self-assessment: (a) to detect, evade, and manage cyber threats at different levels to protect data, devices, networks, and systems; (b) to find digital information necessary for work; (c) to evaluate and communicate digital information; (d) to qualitatively and quantitatively analyse information; and (e) to use digital

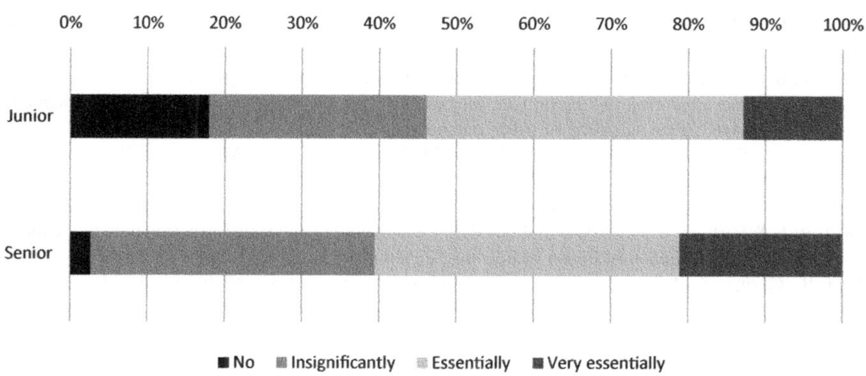

Fig. 7. Distribution of Answers Regarding Motivation to Develop Digital Skills During the Pandemic. *Source*: Authors' calculations based on survey results.

technologies. When analysing the results of the survey, of course, self-assessment bias should also be taken into account.

8. Although the skills of using digital databases improve during the study process, as the results of the study show, progress in this area should be faster to improve the quality of final theses and for graduates to be better prepared for challenges after completing their studies.
9. One of the slightly unexpected results is the higher rating of the 'seniors' for the factor 'Lack of direct contact (face-to-face)', which could have an objective reason – more time was spent in online and/or in hybrid learnings during the pandemic. In any case, this assessment of students indicates the need to organise a significant part of the study process in person. Seniors also evaluate the dependence on the quality of the Internet more critically, which could also have a similar explanation.
10. When evaluating the challenges, a similar relationship appears in the answers to the questions: 'Too little student involvement' and 'Inflexible or difficult to change organisational culture' – 'seniors' assessment is more critical.

REFERENCES

Abad-Segura, E., González-Zamar, M. D., Infante-Moro, J. C., & García, G. R. (2020). Sustainable management of digital transformation in higher education: Global research trends. *Sustainability*, *12*(5), 2107. https://doi.org/10.3390/su12052107

Agasisti, T., Frattini, F., & Soncin, M. (2020). Digital innovation in times of emergency: Reactions from a school of management in Italy. *Sustainability*, *12*, 10312. https://doi.10.3390/su122410312

Alenezi, M. (2021). Deep dive into digital transformation in higher education institutions. *Education Sciences*, *11*, 770. https://doi.org/10.3390/educsci11120770

Anastasakis, M., Triantafyllou, G., & Petridis, K. (2021). Undergraduates' barriers to online learning during the pandemic in Greece. *Technology, Knowledge and Learning*, 1–18. https://doi.org/10.1007/s10758-021-09584-5

Aristovnik, A., Keržic, D., Ravšelj, D., Tomaževic, N., & Umek, L. (2020). Impacts of the COVID-19 pandemic on life of higher education students: A global perspective. *Sustainability*, *12*, 8438. https://doi.10.3390/su12208438

Ben Youssef, A., Dahmani, M., & Ragni, L. (2022). ICT use, digital skills and students' academic performance: Exploring the digital divide. *Information*, *13*, 129. https://doi.org/10.3390/info13030129

Berei, E. B., & Pusztai, G. (2022). Learning through digital devices – Academic risks and responsibilities. *Education Sciences*, *12*(7), 480. https://doi.org/10.3390/educsci12070480

Bygstad, B., Øvrelid, E., Ludvigsen, S., & Dæhlen, M. (2022). From dual digitalization to digital learning space: Exploring the digital transformation of higher education. *Computers & Education*, *182*, 104463. https://doi.org/10.1016/j.compedu.2022.104463

Crawford, J., Butler-Henderson, K., Rudolph, J., Malkawi, B., Glowatz, M., Burton, R., … Lam, S. (2020). COVID-19: 20 countries' higher education intra-period digital pedagogy responses. *Journal of Applied Learning & Teaching*, *3*(1), 1–20. https://doi.org/10.37074/jalt.2020.3.1.7

Du Toit, J., & Verhoef, A. H. (2018). Embodied digital technology and transformation in higher education. *Transformation in Higher Education*, *3*, a52. https://doi.org/10.4102/thev3i0.52

Fűzi, B., Géring, Z., & Szendrei-Pál, E. (2022). Changing expectations related to digitalisation and socialisation in higher education. Horizon scanning of pre-and post-COVID-19 discourses. *Educational Review*, *74*(3), 484–516. https://doi.org/10.1080/00131911.2021.2023101

García-Morales, V. J., Garrido-Moreno, A., & Martín-Rojas, R. (2021). The transformation of higher education after the COVID disruption: Emerging challenges in an online learning scenario. *Frontiers in Psychology*, *12*, 616059. https://doi.10.3389/fpsyg.2021.616059

Gonzalez-Zamar, M. D., & Abad-Segura, E. (2020). Managing ICT for sustainable education: Research analysis in the context of higher education. *Sustainability*, *12*, 8254. https://doi.10.3390/su12198254

Goulart, V. G., Liboni, L. B., & Cezarino, L. O. (2021). Balancing skills in the digital transformation era: The future of jobs and the role of higher education. *Industry and Higher Education*, *36*(2), 1–10. https://doi.10.1177/09504222211029796

Grima, S., Kizilkaya, M., Sood, K., & ErdemDelice, M. (2021). The perceived effectiveness of blockchain for digital operational risk resilience in the European Union insurance market sector. *Journal of Risk and Financial Management*, *14*(8), 363.

Inder, S., Sood, K., & Grima, S. (2022). Antecedents of behavioural intention to adopt internet banking using structural equation modelling. *Journal of Risk and Financial Management*, *15*(4), 157.

Kedraka, K., Kaltsidis, C., Raikou, N., & Karalis, T. (2022). Considerations for university pedagogy: Distance learning one year after the Covid-19 pandemic outbreak. *Journal of Education and Training Studies*, *10*(3), 1–13. https://doi.org/10.11114/jets.v10i3.5445

Kim, H. J., Hong, A. J., & Song, H. (2019). The roles of academic engagement and digital readiness in students' achievements in university e-learning environments. *International Journal of Education Technology in Higher Education*, *16*(21). https://doi.org/10.1186/s41239-019-0152-3

Kumar, V., Alshazly, H., Idris, S. A., & Bourouis, S. (2021). Evaluating the impact of COVID-19 on society, environment, economy, and education. *Sustainability*, *13*, 13642. https://doi.org/10.3390/su132413642

Laufer, M., Leiser, A., Deacon, B., de Brichambaut, P. P., Fecher, B., Kobsda, C., & Hesse, F. (2021). Digital higher education: A divider or bridge builder? Leadership perspectives on Edtech in a COVID-19 reality. *International Journal of Educational Technology in Higher Education*, *18*, 51. https://doi.org/10.1186/s41239-021-00287-6

Levano-Francia, L., Sanchez, S., Guillén-Aparicio, P., Tello-Cabello, S., Herrera-Paico, N., & Collantes-Inga, Z. (2019). Digital competences and education. *Propósitos y Representaciones*, *7*(2), 569-588. http://dx.doi.org/10.20511/pyr2019.v7n2.329

Monteiro, A., & Leite, C. (2021). Digital literacies in higher education: Skills, uses, opportunities and obstacles to digital transformation. *Revista de Educación a Distancia*, *21*(65), 6. https://doi.org/10.6018/red.438721

Papouli, E., Chatzifotiou, S., & Tsairidis, C. (2020). The use of digital technology at home during the COVID-19 outbreak: Views of social work students in Greece. *Social Work Education*, *39*(8), 1107–1115. https://doi.org/10.1080/02615479.2020.1807496

Pilotti, M. A., El-Moussa, O. J., & Abdelsalam, H. M. (2022). Measuring the impact of the pandemic on female and male students' learning in a society in transition: A must for sustainable education. *Sustainability*, *14*(6), 3148. https://doi.org/10.3390/su14063148

Pohlenz, P., Felix, A., Berndt, S., & Seyfried, M. (2022). How do students deal with forced digitalisation in teaching and learning? Implications for quality assurance. *Quality Assurance in Education*, *33*(1), 1108. https://doi.org/10.1108/QAE-02-2022-0041

Rodríguez-Abitia, G., Martínez-Pérez, S., Ramírez-Montoya, M. S., & López-Caudana, E. (2020). Digital gap in universities and challenges for quality education: A diagnostic study in Mexico and Spain. *Sustainability*, *12*, 9069. https://doi.10.3390/su12219069

Rof, A., Bikfalvi, A., & Marques, P. (2020). Digital transformation for business model innovation in higher education – Overcoming the tensions. *Sustainability*, *12*, 4980. https://doi.10.3390/su12124980

Rosak-Szyrocka, J., Żywiołek, J., Zaborski, A., Chowdhury, S., & Hu, Y. C. (2022). Digitalization of higher education around the globe during Covid-19. *IEEE Access*, 10. doi:10.1109/access.2022.3178711

Saikkonen, L., & Kaarakainen, M. T. (2021). Multivariate analysis of teachers' digital information skills – The importance of available resources. *Computers & Education*, *168*, 104206. https://doi.org/10.1016/j.compedu.2021.104206

Sánchez-Caballé, A., Gisbert-Cervera, M., & Esteve-Mon, F. (2021). Integrating digital competence in higher education curricula: An institutional analysis. *Educar*, *57*(1), 241–257. https://doi.org/10.5565/rev/educar.1174

Santos, H., Batista, J., & Marques, R. P. (2019). Digital transformation in higher education: The use of communication technologies by students. *Procedia Computer Science*, *164*, 123–130. https://doi.10.1016/j.procs.2019.12.163

Sebastian, I. M., Mocker, M., Ross, J. W., Moloney, K. G., Beath, C., & Fonstad, N. O. (2017). How big old companies navigate digital transformation. *MIS Quarterly Executive*, *16*(3), 197–213. https://aisel.aisnet.org/misqe/vol16/iss3/6

Sillat, L. H., Tammets, K., & Laanpere, M. (2021). Digital competence assessment methods in higher education – A systematic literature review. *Education Sciences*, *11*(8), 402. https://doi.org/10.3390/educsci11080402

Silvola, A., Naykki, P., Kaveri, A., & Muukkonen, H. (2021). Expectations for supporting student engagement with learning analytics: An academic path perspective. *Computers & Education*, *168*, 104192. https://doi.org/10.1016/j.compedu.2021.104192

Sjöberg, J., & Lilja, P. (2019). University teachers' ambivalence about the digital transformation of higher education. *International Journal of Learning, Teaching and Educational Research*, *18*(13), 133–149. https://doi.org/10.26803/ijlter.18.13.7

Sood, K., Seth, N., & Grima, S. (2022). Portfolio performance of public sector general insurance companies in India: A comparative analysis. In S. Grima, E. Özen, & I. Romānova (Eds.), *Managing risk and decision making in times of economic distress, Part B* (pp. 215–229). Bingley: Emerald Publishing Limited.

Spante, M., Hashemi, S. S., Lundin, M., & Algers, A. (2018). Digital competence and digital literacy in higher education research: Systematic review of concept use. *Cogent Education*, *5*(1), 1519143. https://doi.org/10.1080/2331186X.2018.1519143

Stecuła, K., & Wolniak, R. (2022). Influence of COVID-19 pandemic on dissemination of innovative e-learning tools in higher education in Poland. *Journal of Open Innovation: Technology, Market, and Complexity*, *8*, 89. https://doi.org/10.3390/joitmc8020089

Tang, Y. M., Chen, P. C., Law, K. M., Wu, C. H., Lau, Y., Guan, J., … Ho, G. T. (2021). Comparative analysis of student's live online learning readiness during the coronavirus (COVID-19) pandemic in the higher education sector. *Computers & Education*, *168*, 104211. https://doi.org/10.1016/j.compedu.2021.104211

Teker, S., Teker, D., & Tavman, E. B. (2022). Digital transformation and universities. *Press Academia Procedia*, *15*, 136–137. http://doi.org/10.17261/Pressacademia.2022.1596

Toader, T., Safta, M., Titirişcă, C., & Firtescu, B. (2021). Effects of digitalisation on higher education in a sustainable development framework – Online learning challenges during the COVID-19 pandemic. *Sustainability*, *13*(11), 6444. https://doi.org/10.3390/su13116444

Vuorikari, R., Kluzer, S., & Punie, Y. (2022). *DigComp 2.2: The digital competence framework for citizens – With new examples of knowledge, skills and attitudes*. Luxembourg: Publications Office of the European Union. doi:10.2760/490274

Yerpudee, S., Sood, K., & Grima, S. (2022). Blockchain-augmented digital supply chain management: A way to sustainable business. *Journal of Risk and Financial Management*, *16*(1), 7.

Zagkos, C., Kyridis, A., Kamarianos, I., Dragouni, K. E., Katsanou, A., Kouroumichaki, E., … Stergianopoulos, E. (2022). Emergency remote teaching and learning in Greek Universities during the COVID-19 pandemic: The attitudes of university students. *European Journal of Interactive Multimedia and Education*, *3*(1), e02207. https://doi.org/10.30935/ejimed/11494

Zhao, Y., Llorente, A. M. P., & Gómez, M. C. S. (2021). Digital competence in higher education research: A systematic literature review. *Computers & Education*, *168*, 104212. https://doi.org/10.1016/j.compedu.2021.104212

CHAPTER 6

CHALLENGES TO CREDIT RISK MANAGEMENT IN THE CONTEXT OF GROWING MACROECONOMIC INSTABILITY IN THE BALTIC STATES CAUSED BY COVID-19

Aivars Spilbergs[a], Diego Norena-Chavez[b], Eleftherios Thalassinos[c], Graţiela Georgiana Noja[d] and Mirela Cristea[e]

[a]*Economics and Finance Department, BA School of Business and Finance, Latvia*
[b]*Escuela de Posgrado, Universidad de Lima, Peru*
[c]*University of Piraeus, Faculty of Maritime and Industrial Studies, Piraeus, Greece and University of Malta, Faculty of Economics Management and Accountancy, Msida, Malta*
[d]*The West University of Timisoara, Faculty of Economics and Business Administration, Timisoara, Romania*
[e]*University of Craiova, Faculty of Economics and Business Administration, Craiova, Romania*

ABSTRACT

The COVID-19 pandemic deteriorated the economic situation and raised the issue of the quality of banks' assets and, in particular, the growth of non-performing loans (NPLs). The study approaches a topical subject that is of interest to banks and society at large, as credit availability is likely to be reduced. Over the last 10 years, the Baltic countries' banking sector has significantly improved its risk management policies and practices,

Digital Transformation, Strategic Resilience, Cyber Security and Risk Management
Contemporary Studies in Economic and Financial Analysis, Volume 111A, 83–104

ISSN: 1569-3759/doi:10.1108/S1569-37592023000111A006

increased capital ratios on its balance sheets, and created risk reserves. The current chapter examines the factors affecting NPLs in the Baltic States based on advanced econometric modelling applied to data extracted from the International Monetary Fund (IMF) and Eurostat. The study results show that credit risk management in the Baltic States has significantly improved compared to the period before the global financial crisis (GFC), the capitalisation of credit institutions is one of the highest in the European Union (EU), and banks are liquid and profitable. Lending recovered from the downturn in the first phase of the pandemic, and credit institutions have taken advantage of the European Central Bank's (ECB) long-term funding programme ITRMO III to improve the liquidity outlook. Although the credit quality of commercial banks has not deteriorated, as the exposures of credit institutions in the most affected sectors are insignificant and governments have provided fiscal support to businesses and households, some challenges remain. The increase in credit risk is expected due to rising production prices as well as the rebuilding of disrupted supply chains. The findings allow conclusions to be drawn on the necessary actions to mitigate the credit risk of the banking sector.

Keywords: Credit risk management; macroeconomic instability; econometric modelling; scenario analysis; COVID-19; Baltic states

JEL classifications: G21; O16; C53

1. INTRODUCTION

The COVID-19 pandemic brought significant challenges to economies and financial markets worldwide, and the Baltic States are no exception. It is worth remembering that 'during the global financial crisis (GFC), the Baltic States were among those that received one of the worst shocks in 2008–2010, cumulative GDP decline in Estonia was −17.3%, Latvia −21.9% and Lithuania −10.5%' (IMF, 2022). Although the impact of the pandemic on the macroeconomic situation was significantly milder, all three Baltic countries experienced declining gross domestic product (GDP) in 2020 and a deterioration in banks' asset quality.

On the other hand, the deterioration in asset quality and its consequences, lower profitability, may limit the ability to absorb higher credit losses in the future and reduce the capacity to provide the necessary financing for economic development (Byrne & Kelly, 2019; Çolak & Öztekin, 2021; Czech & Puszer, 2021; Dao & Kang, 2022; Dursun-de Neef & Schandlbauer, 2022; Huljak, Martin, Moccero, & Pancaro, 2022; Miklaszewska, Kil, & Idzik, 2021; Phung, Vu, & Tran, 2022; Teresiene, Keliuotyte-Staniuleniene, & Kanapickiene, 2021; Thornton & Di Tommaso, 2021). In addition, the pandemic has created new challenges, especially in the context of rising inflation starting in the second half of 2021, which will impact customers' ability to repay their loans (Sood, Kaur, & Grima, 2022;

Sood, Seth, & Grima, 2022). Therefore, the bank's managers, supervisors, and monetary and fiscal authorities need to clearly understand the size and quality of banks' assets in different development scenarios when planning the necessary response and possible support measures. In this chapter, these considerations are supported by a simulation analysis that estimates the potential growth of banks' NPLs using a variety of assumptions.

The chapter also examines the future impact on banks' capital adequacy and discusses whether policy responses may be needed to address declining asset quality and capital buffers.

Over the last 10 years, the Baltic countries' banking sector has significantly improved its risk management policies and practices, increased capital ratios on its balance sheets, and created risk reserves (Anginer, Bertay, Cull, Demirgüç-Kuntc, & Mare, 2021; Berger & Demirgüç-Kunt, 2021; Bitar & Tarazi, 2022; Borio, 2020; Borri & Di Giorgio, 2022; Clichici, 2021; Giese & Haldane, 2020; Igan, Mirzaei, & Moore, 2022). IMF data confirm that by the end of 2019, the quality of banking sector assets, capital adequacy, and liquidity had improved significantly (IMF, 2022). However, during this period, the economic environment did not pose significant challenges, and it was only with the onset of the pandemic in 2020 that the issue of the sector's risk resilience came to the fore again. Therefore, it is important to understand whether the significant changes introduced in the regulation of the financial sector and the reforms carried out have significantly improved resilience and contributed to the sustainability of society and the financial sector (Grima, Kizilkaya, Sood, & ErdemDelice, 2021).

Taking into account the specifics of the activity, the Baltic commercial banks' risk structure is strongly dominated by credit risk, which accounts for more than 88% of total risk-weighted assets (ECB, 2022), the main focus of this chapter is on credit risk management challenges.

Fig. 1. The dynamic of GDP in Baltic Countries. *Source*: IMF data.

2. THEORETICAL BACKGROUND

2.1. Economic Cyclicality and COVID-19 Impact on Credit Risk Management

The pandemic crisis and subsequent events create challenges for the banking system both already known and as yet unknown (Beck & Keil, 2022; Goldstein, Koijen, & Mueller, 2021). Although a deterioration in the quality of bank assets is typical of macroeconomic crises, the pandemic revealed several distinctive features: first, it hit industries with close contact in a limited space hard (Demmou, Franco, Calligaris, & Dlugosch, 2022; Kozak, 2021; Laborda & Olmo, 2021); second, significant fiscal support for businesses and households to stabilise their financial situation in 2020 and 2021 (Demirgüç-Kunt, Pedraza, & Ruiz-Ortega, 2021; EC, 2020; Elnahass, Trinh, & Li, 2021), and third, great uncertainty about the future behaviour of the virus and its impact on the economy.

Both direct support from governments for companies affected by restrictions, loan guarantees, a moratorium on loan repayments, and other fiscal support instruments played an important role (Beck & Keil, 2022; Demmou et al., 2022; Didier, Huneeus, Larrain, & Schmukler, 2021; Giese & Haldane, 2020; Kahn & Wagner, 2021; Korzeb & Niedziółka, 2021; Tan, Igan, Peria, Pierri, & Presbitero, 2021). Consequently, the liquidity support and assistance programme for borrowers mitigated the pandemic's negative effects including reduced credit risk growth cost for commercial banks (Inder, Sood, & Grima, 2022). On the other hand, the above solutions had an impact on banks' interest income and thus on profitability. In the long run, extending the credit repayment moratorium may accumulate credit risk and increase write-offs for credit risk according to IFRS 9 (Neisen & Schulte-Mattler, 2021).

Cucinelli, Di Battista, Marchese, and Nieri (2018) researched credit risk management strategies and found that European banks using internal rating-based models could mitigate credit risk better than banks using standardised approach for capital adequacy assessment.

Becker, Bos, and Roszbach (2020) analysed the ability to evaluate borrower's creditworthiness during economic cycle and conclude that corporate defaults are more predictable during the downturn than during the upswing of the economic cycle.

Bischof, Rudolf, and Schmundt (2022) evaluated the development of NPLs in European banks along the economic cycle and indicated substantial differences across countries in the duration and efficiency of the NPLs resolution after the crisis.

High uncertainty in macroeconomic development is an important reason why a scenario analysis approach should be used in credit risk management strategies development and implementation (Apergis, 2022; Baltazar, Reis, & Amorim, 2020; Kostis, 2020; Łasak, 2021).

2.2. Bank Assets Quality Impact on Credit Availability, Bank Stability, and Economic Development

Deterioration in the quality of bank assets reduces profitability and the resource base for new businesses, as they must be reserved to cover expected and unexpected losses. Chiesa and Mansilla-Fernández (2021) analysed effects of NPLs on banks' cost of capital and credit supply and showed that NPLs have consequences on cost of capital both in the short term and long term and thus reduce lending capacity.

De Vincentiis (2021) studied the use of forbearance measures and loan loss provisioning based on the EU-wide Transparency Exercise dataset and found that forbearance measures are frequently used to manage the NPLs portfolio.

Elnahass et al. (2021) examined the pandemic influence on banks' stability and showed that COVID-19 has essentially impacted financial performance and stability. Research provides evidence 'that the implications of COVID-19 for banking stability are mediated by institutional factors and the type of banking business model employed'.

Horobet, Radulescu, Belascu, and Dita (2021) investigated the determinants of banking profitability in Central and Eastern Europe and their findings demonstrate that NPLs rate, concentration rate, and capitalisation rate negatively impact banking profitability.

Miklaszewska et al. (2021) analysed banking sectors of Central, Eastern, and Northern European countries to identify sources of profits and risks and discovered that the initial impact of the COVID-19 pandemic on banks in the analysed region was heterogeneous.

Serrano (2021) studied the stock and flow of NPLs on the lending activities in European banks' and concluded that higher rates of NPLs are associated with lower growth rates of banks performing loans and vice versa.

Tölö and Virén (2021) researched NPLs impact on bank lending in Europe and found that credit supply depends on the level of NPLs. The authors showed that increased NPLs, followed by weak lending decrease bank profits, increase funding costs, and reduce bank capital.

Velliscig, Floreani, and Polato (2022) investigated the relationship of capital and asset quality in terms of provisioning and coverage policies. Researchers point out the crucial role of capital for the overall bank resilience.

Phung et al. (2022) examined the impact of NPLs on bank efficiency and discovered that stronger capital position could mitigate the negative effect on NPLs.

2.3. Determinants of NPLs

NPLs have traditionally been used to assess credit risk and macroeconomic indicators such as GDP growth (Alessi, Bruno, Carletti, Neugebauer, & Wolfskeil, 2021; Apergis, 2022; Ari, Chena, & Ratnovski, 2021; Park & Shin, 2021; Spilbergs, 2022), unemployment (Alessi et al., 2021; Ari et al., 2021; Spilbergs, 2022), inflation rate (Ari et al., 2021; Park & Shin, 2021; Spilbergs, 2022), etc. are most often used as factors influencing NPLs.

Kjosevski and Petkovski (2017) investigated macroeconomic and bank-specific factors of NPLs using data from Baltic banks and concluded that GDP growth, inflation, and credit to the private sector have the most significant impact on NPLs.

Gerlach-Kristen and Lyons (2018) researched the drivers of mortgage loans risk in European countries and concluded that mortgage arrears reduce household's wellbeing and raise social issues.

Szarowska (2018) analysed the impact of macroeconomic determinants of NPLs in Central and Eastern European countries and identified unemployment as the most important determinant for NPLs. Research results confirm a positive effect from unemployment and interest rate, while economic growth, inflation, and exchange rate negatively influence NPLs.

Anastasiou, Louri, and Tsionas (2019) examined the reasons for NPLs and regional differences in vulnerabilities. Researchers found that the increase in NPLs is related to the increase in unemployment and interest rate.

Staehr and Uusküla (2020) studied macroeconomic and macrofinancial factors affecting NPLs in EU countries and showed that leading indicators of NPLs are GDP growth, inflation, and debt.

Ciukaj and Kil (2020) evaluated determinants of the quality of credit exposures in EU countries with a high level of impaired loans using static panel data. The research results show that the NPLs level is statistically significant and affected by macroeconomic factors, for example, GDP, unemployment rate, and bank-specific factors such as the size of the bank or the dynamics of lending. Researchers conclude that, despite differences in banks business models and regulations, the determinants of the NPLs are similar.

Hada, Bărbuţă-Mişu, Iuga, and Wainberg (2020) investigated macroeconomic factors affecting the NPLs in Romania based on data for the period 2009–2019. The regression analysis shows that unemployment rate, inflation rate, and exchange rate have a significant impact on NPLs.

Tatarici, Kubinschi, and Barnea (2020) examined the determinants of NPLs based on panel data of European countries covering the period 2005–2017. Researchers conclude that adverse macroeconomic developments are associated with higher NPLs and countries with higher past loan growth rates experienced higher NPLs in the following periods.

Ari et al. (2021) analysed a large dataset on the dynamics of NPLs since 1990 and used machine learning approach to determine predictors of assets quality deterioration. The authors showed that sound *ex ante* macroeconomic and financial sector policies can significantly reduce NPLs problems.

Karadima and Louri (2021) researched the relationship between economic policy uncertainty and NPLs. Based on major euro area countries banks dataset analysis, researchers concluded that economic policy uncertainty index shows positive correlations, whereas GDP and inflation show negative correlations with NPLs.

Khairi, Bahri, and Artha (2021) presented a literature study of relevant publications and identified several variables that affect NPLs, for example, real GDP growth, inflation, unemployment, etc.

Bischof et al. (2022) studied the development of NPLs in European banks along the economic cycle. Research results prove that NPLs increases are associated with macroeconomic determinants and specifics of banks' business models.

Foglia (2022) investigated the influence of macroeconomics determinants on NPLs in the Italian banking system over the period 2008 Q3–2020 Q4. The research results show that GDP and public debt negatively impact NPLs, and that the unemployment rate and domestic credit positively influence the quality deterioration of loans.

Naili and Lahrichi (2022) provided a structured review of the literature on the determinants of NPLs (Table 1). They argued that

> despite the extensive empirical and theoretical work accomplished over the last decades, the issue of credit risk management remains an unsolved line of inquiry, which leaves ample room for future research.

Based on the literature review, the following hypotheses were formulated:

H1. There is a negative association between NPLs level and GDP growth.
H2. There is a positive association between NPLs and unemployment level.
H3. There is a positive association between NPLs and inflation.
H4. There is a positive association between forborne loans and macroeconomic indicators.
H5. The Baltic banking sector is ready to absorb a significant increase in NPLs during post-COVID-19.

Table 1. NPL Determinants.

Indicator	Source
Interest rates	Alessi et al. (2021), Climent-Serrano (2019), Ciukaj and Kil (2020), Cucinelli et al. (2018), Huljak et al. (2022), Macháček, Melecký, and Šulganová (2018), and Serrano (2021)
Inflation	Alessi et al. (2021), Anastasiou et al. (2019), Ciukaj and Kil (2020), Climent-Serrano (2019), Fallanca, Forgione, and Otranto (2021), Hada et al. (2020), Huljak et al. (2022), Karadima and Louri (2021), Kjosevski and Petkovski (2017), Koju, Koju, and Wang (2020), Macháček et al. (2018), Park and Shin (2021), Salvi, Bussoli, Conca, and Gigante (2018), Staehr and Uusküla (2020), and Szarowska (2018)
GDP growth	Alessi et al. (2021), Anastasiou et al. (2019), Apergis (2022), Bischof et al. (2022), Cerulli, D'Apice, Fiordelisi, and Masala (2020), Chiesa and Mansilla-Fernández (2021), Ciukaj and Kil (2020), Cucinelli et al. (2018), Foglia (2022), Huljak et al. (2022), Karadima and Louri (2021), Kjosevski and Petkovski (2017), Koju et al. (2020), Lee, Chen, Chang, and Chen (2022), Macháček et al. (2018), Park and Shin (2021), Salvi et al. (2018), Serrano (2021), Staehr and Uusküla (2020); Szarowska (2018), and Tatarici et al. (2020)
Unemployment	Alessi et al. (2021), Anastasiou et al. (2019), Ari et al. (2021); Chiesa and Mansilla-Fernández (2021), Ciukaj and Kil (2020), Climent-Serrano (2019), Cucinelli et al. (2018), Foglia (2022), Gerlach-Kristen and Lyons (2018), Hada et al. (2020), Koju et al. (2020), Macháček et al. (2018), Salvi et al. (2018), Staehr and Uusküla (2020); Stanga, Vlahua, and de Haan (2020), Szarowska (2018), and Tatarici et al. (2020)
Government debt	Ari et al. (2021), Bayar (2019), and Foglia (2022)

Source: Authors developed based on literature review.

3. DATA AND METHODS

3.1. Associations Between the NPLs and Macroeconomic Factors

IMF Financial Soundness Indicators (IMF, 2022) data for Baltic States from 2001 to 2021 were used to test research hypotheses. Regression analysis was used to investigate the effect of macroeconomic factors on the NPLs of the Baltic countries. The associations between the NPLs and macroeconomic factors we are analysing are based on the following equation:

$$\mathrm{NPL} = \beta_{0,1} + \beta_{1,1}\mathrm{GDP} + \beta_{2,1}\mathrm{UPL} + \beta_{3,1}\mathrm{CPI} + \ldots + \varepsilon_1, \tag{1}$$

where NPLis the NPLs ratio of all loans; $\beta_{0,1}$, the intercept for first model; $\beta_{1,1}$, $\beta_{2,1}$, $\beta_{3,1}$, the regression coefficients for first model; GDP, the GDP growth; UPL, the unemployment level; CPI, the consumer price inflation; and ε_1, the sampling error for first model.

R package was used to assess the impact of macroeconomic factors on loans quality and to test regression models and parameters (R Core Team, 2022). The stability of the calibrated regression models was evaluated by applying *F*-test and the regression coefficients were assessed using a *t*-test at a confidence level of $\alpha = 0.05$. The Breusch–Pagan test and the Shapiro–Wilk test were used to test the assumptions of the regression models and the variance inflation factor (*vif*) was applied to quantify the effect of collinearity on the variance of regression estimates.

3.2. Associations Between Non-financial Corporate (NFC) and Household (HH) NPLs, and Macroeconomic Factors

The credit portfolios of the Baltic banks are not homogeneous, as can be seen in Fig. 2.

In order to get a more accurate picture of the factors affecting the NPLs and their possible impact on the quality of loans in the future, the two most important sub-portfolios of total loan portfolios will be analysed separately: NFC and HH loans.

ECB consolidated banking data (ECB, 2022) for Baltic States from 2014 to 2021 were used to analyse associations. Regression analysis was used to investigate the effect of macroeconomic factors on the NFC NPLs and HH NPLs of the Baltic countries. The associations between the NFC NPLs and the macroeconomic factors we are analysing are based on the following equation:

$$\mathrm{NFCNPL} = \beta_{0,2} + \beta_{1,2}\mathrm{GDP} + \beta_{2,2}\mathrm{UPL} + \beta_{3,2}\mathrm{CPI} + \ldots + \varepsilon_2, \tag{2}$$

where NFCNPL is NPLs for NFC portfolio; $\beta_{0,2}$, the intercept for second model; $\beta_{1,2}$, $\beta_{2,2}$, $\beta_{3,2}$, the regression coefficients for second model; and ε_2, the sampling error for second model.

The associations between the HH NPLs and the macroeconomic factors we are analysing are based on the following equation:

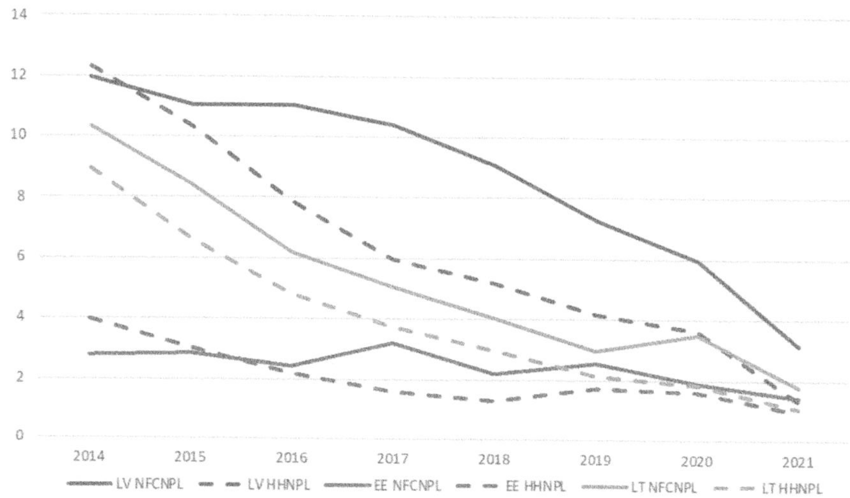

Fig. 2. The dynamic of NFC and HH NPLs in Baltic Countries.
Source: Authors calculations based on ECB data.

$$\text{HHNPL} = \beta_{0,3} + \beta_{1,3}\text{GDP} + \beta_{2,3}\text{UPL} + \beta_{3,3}\text{CPI} + \ldots + \varepsilon_3, \tag{3}$$

where HHNPL is NPLs for HH portfolio; $\beta_{0,3}$, the intercept for third model; $\beta_{1,3}$, $\beta_{2,3}$, $\beta_{3,3}$, the regression coefficients for third model; and ε_3, the sampling error for third model.

3.3. Associations Between Forborne Loans and Macroeconomic Factors

From the point of view of asset quality, it is important to analyse separately also a specific part of credit portfolio namely: forborne loans, especially in the context of their rapid growth during the COVID-19 pandemic period, see Fig. 3.

ECB consolidated banking data (ECB, 2022) for Baltic States from 2014 to 2021 and regression analysis were used to investigate macroeconomic factors' effect on the Baltic countries' forborne loans. The associations between the GFP loans and macroeconomic factors we are analysing are based on the following equation:

$$\text{GFP} = \beta_{0,4} + \beta_{1,4}\text{GDP} + \beta_{2,4}\text{UPL} + \beta_{3,4}\text{CPI} + \ldots + \varepsilon_4, \tag{4}$$

where GFP is the GFP loans ratio; $\beta_{0,4}$, the intercept for fourth model; $\beta_{1,4}$, $\beta_{2,4}$, $\beta_{3,4}$, the regression coefficients for the fourth model; and ε_4, the sampling error for fourth model.

The associations between the gross forborne NPLs (GFN) and macroeconomic factors we are analysing are based on the following equation:

$$\text{GFN} = \beta_{0,5} + \beta_{1,5}\text{GDP} + \beta_{2,5}\text{UPL} + \beta_{3,5}\text{CPI} + \ldots + \varepsilon_5, \tag{5}$$

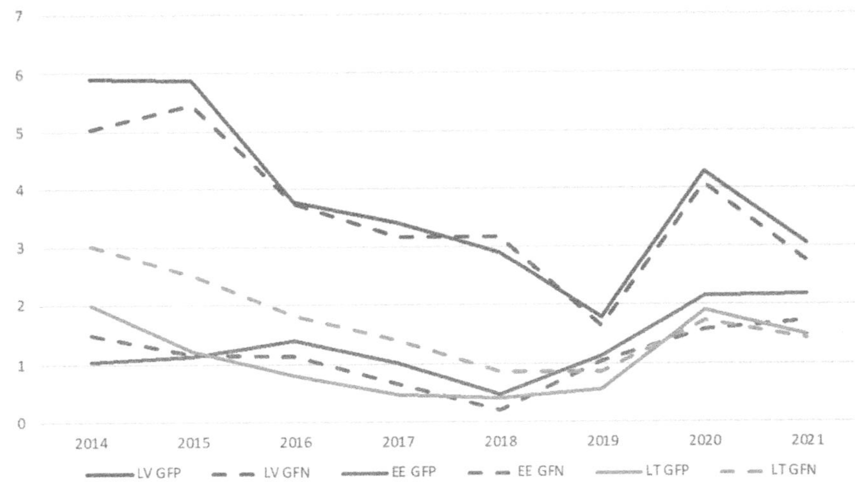

Fig. 3. The dynamic of Gross Forborne Performing (GFP) and NPLs in Baltic Countries. *Source*: Authors calculations based on ECB data.

where GFN is the GFN ratio; $\beta_{0,5}$, the intercept for fifth model; $\beta_{1,5}$, $\beta_{2,5}$, $\beta_{3,5}$, the regression coefficients for fifth model; and ε_5, the sampling error for fifth model.

3.4. Associations of the NPLs and Capital Adequacy of Commercial Banks

ECB consolidated banking data (ECB, 2022) for Baltic States from 2014 to 2021 were used to test research hypotheses. Regression analysis was used to investigate the effect of NPLs on the capital adequacy of the Baltic countries. We use the following regression model to examine the impact of NPLs changes on the capital adequacy of commercial banks in the Baltic States:

$$\mathrm{T1C} = \beta_{0,6} + \beta_{1,6}\mathrm{NPL} + \varepsilon_6, \tag{6}$$

where T1C is the Tier1 capital ratio; $\beta_{0,6}$, the intercept for sixth model; $\beta_{1,6}$, the regression coefficients for sixth model; and ε_6, the sampling error for sixth model.

As economic development is characterised by high uncertainty, two possible development scenarios for the next three years have been developed to estimate possible outcomes:

(1) baseline scenarios based on the IMF financial soundness indicators forecast (IMF, 2022) and
(2) worst case scenarios (one in 20 years) based on macroeconomic indicators volatilities 2001–2021 in Baltic States.

4. RESULTS

4.1. Associations Between the NPLs and Macroeconomic Factors

R package was used to assess the impact of macroeconomic factors on loans quality and to test regression models and parameters (R Core Team, 2022).

F-test results summarised in Table 2 indicate high statistical stability of the calibrated model (1).

Adjusted *R*-squared suggests that 81.9% of the variation in NPL can be explained by the factors included in the model – therefore, it can be concluded that the model fits well and has pretty high predictive power.

Homoscedasticity test results with Breusch–Pagan (BP) give evidence to not reject the null of homoscedasticity and Shapiro–Wilk (W) test gives evidence to not reject the null of residuals normality, see Table 3.

As the *vif* estimates for all three factors are less than 5, see Table 4, it can be concluded that we do not have significant issues with multicollinearity.

Table 5 summarises the results of the regression coefficient tests.

Table 2. Regression Model (1) Estimates.

Res.SE	R^2	Adj.R^2	*F*-stat	*p*-Value
2.4120	0.8423	0.8190	36.06	$<2.2e-16$

Source: Authors' calculations.

Table 3. Homoscedasticity and Residuals Normality Test Results.

BP	*p*-Value	W	*p*-Value
12.3040	0.1381	0.9783	0.3279

Source: Authors' calculations.

Table 4. Regression Coefficients Collinearity Test Results.

GDP	UPL	CPI
1.9780	2.8500	4.8272

Source: Authors' calculations.

Table 5. Regression Model (1) Coefficient Estimates.

Factor	Estimate	St.Error	*t*-Stat	*p*-Value
GDP	−0.3034	0.0778	−3.901	0.0003
UPL	1.3568	0.1365	9.944	8.37e−14
CPI	0.3108	0.0436	7.131	2.52e−09

Source: Authors' calculations.

As can be seen, for all regression coefficients signs are as expected and statistically significant at the confidence level <0.001 and thereof can be safely interpreted and applied.

The result of the regression analysis shows that the unemployment rate has the most significant effect on NPLs growth – if the unemployment rate increases by 1% and the values of other factors remain unchanged, the NPLs ratio will increase by 1.357% on average, and the 95% confidence interval of the effect is from 1.083% to 1.631%. Regarding the CPI, it can be concluded that if the CPI increases by one point and the values of the other factors remain unchanged, the NPLs ratio will increase by 0.311% on average, and the 95% confidence interval of the effect is from 0.223% to 0.398%. On the other hand, if GDP increases by 1% and the values of other factors remain unchanged, the NPLs ratio will decrease by 0.303% on average, and the 95% confidence interval of the effect is from −0.459% to −0.147%.

4.2. Associations Between NFC, HH NPLs, and Macroeconomic Factors

Calibrated model (2) *F*-test results summarised in Table 6 indicate high statistical stability.

Adjusted *R*-squared suggests that 92.5% of the variation in NFC NPLs can be explained by the factors included in the model – therefore, it can be concluded that the model fits well and has high predictive power.

Homoscedasticity test results with Breusch–Pagan (BP) give evidence to not reject the null of homoscedasticity and Shapiro–Wilk (W) test gives evidence to not reject the null of residuals normality, see Table 7.

As the *vif* estimates for all three factors are less than 5, see Table 8, it can be concluded that we do not have significant issues with multicollinearity.

Table 9 summarises the results of the regression coefficient tests.

As can be seen, for all regression coefficients signs are as expected and statistically significant at the confidence level <0.01 and thereof can be safely interpreted and applied.

The result of the regression analysis shows that the unemployment rate has the most significant effect on NFC NPLs growth – if the unemployment rate

Table 6. Regression Model (2) Estimates.

Res.SE	R^2	Adj. R^2	*F*-stat	*p*-Value
0.9699	0.9508	0.9246	36.24	1.913e−08

Source: Authors' calculations.

Table 7. Homoscedasticity and Residuals Normality Test Results.

BP	*p*-Value	W	*p*-Value
6.4387	0.5982	0.9664	0.5792

Source: Authors' calculations.

Table 8. Regression Coefficients Collinearity Test Results.

GDP	UPL	CPI
3.7410	4.1439	4.2498

Source: Authors' calculations.

Table 9. Regression Model (2) Coefficient Estimates.

Factor	Estimate	St.Error	t-Stat	p-Value
GDP	−0.5083	0.1541	−3.298	0.0049
UPL	1.5073	0.3245	4.644	0.0003
CPI	0.9956	0.2819	3.531	0.0030

Source: Authors' calculations.

increases by 1% and the values of other factors remain unchanged, the NPLs ratio will increase by 1.507% on average, and the 95% confidence interval of the effect is from 0.816% to 2.199%. Regarding the CPI, it can be concluded that if the CPI increases by one point and the values of the other factors remain unchanged, the NPLs ratio will increase by 0.996% on average, and the 95% confidence interval of the effect is from 0.395% to 1.596%. On the other hand, if GDP increases by 1% and the values of other factors remain unchanged, the NPLs ratio will decrease by 0.508% on average, and the 95% confidence interval of the effect is from −0.837% to −0.180%.

Calibrated model (3) F-test results summarised in Table 10 indicate high statistical stability.

Adjusted R-squared suggests that 91.2% of the variation in HH NPLs can be explained by the factors included in the model – therefore, it can be concluded that the model fits well and has a high predictive power. Homoscedasticity test results with Breusch–Pagan (BP) give evidence to not reject the null of homoscedasticity and Shapiro–Wilk (W) test gives evidence to not reject the null of residuals normality, see Table 11.

Table 10. Regression Model (3) Estimates.

Res.SE	R^2	Adj.R^2	F-stat	p-Value
0.9289	0.9425	0.9118	30.72	6.045e−08

Source: Authors' calculations.

Table 11. Homoscedasticity and Residuals Normality Test Results.

BP	p-Value	W	p-Value
9.3285	0.3153	0.9613	0.4656

Source: Authors' calculations.

As the *vif* estimates for two factors are less than five and for CPI somewhat above, see Table 12, it can be concluded that we have some issues with multicollinearity.

Table 13 summarises the results of the regression coefficient tests.

As can be seen, for all regression coefficients signs are as expected, but the estimate is statistically significant at the confidence level <0.01 only for unemployment and thereof can be safely interpreted and applied only for this variable.

The result of the regression analysis shows that the unemployment rate has the most significant effect on HH NPLs growth – if the unemployment rate increases by 1% and the values of other factors remain unchanged, the NPLs ratio will increase by 1.47% on average, and the 95% confidence interval of the effect is from 0.944% to 1.996%.

4.3. Associations Between Forborne Loans Ratio and Macroeconomic Factors

Calibrated model (4) *F*-test results summarised in Table 14 indicate high statistical stability.

Adjusted *R*-squared suggests that 73.8% of the variation in performing forborne loans can be explained by the factors included in the model; therefore, it can be concluded that the model fits well and has pretty high predictive power.

Homoscedasticity test results with Breusch–Pagan (BP) give evidence to not reject the null of homoscedasticity and Shapiro–Wilk (W) test gives evidence to not reject the null of residuals normality, see Table 15.

As the *vif* estimates for all three factors are less than 5, see Table 16, it can be concluded that we do not have significant issues with multicollinearity.

Table 12. Regression Coefficients Collinearity Test Results.

GDP	UPL	CPI
4.0748	4.5044	5.2824

Source: Authors' calculations.

Table 13. Regression Model (3) Coefficient Estimates.

Factor	Estimate	St.Error	*t*-Stat	*p*-Value
GDP	−0.1438	0.1541	−0.933	0.3655
UPL	1.4702	0.2468	5.957	2.63e-05
CPI	0.3108	0.2709	1.148	0.2691

Source: Authors' calculations.

Table 14. Regression Model (4) Estimates.

Res.SE	R^2	Adj.R^2	*F*-stat	*p*-Value
0.8267	0.7893	0.7308	13.49	1.473e-05

Source: Authors' calculations.

Table 15. Homoscedasticity and Residuals Normality Test Results.

BP	*p*-Value	W	*p*-Value
8.0500	0.1535	0.9559	0.3611

Source: Authors' calculations.

Table 16. Regression Coefficients Collinearity Test Results.

GDP	UPL	CPI
3.0973	1.7907	3.5433

Source: Authors' calculations.

Table 17 summarises the results of the regression coefficient tests.

As can be seen, for all regression coefficients signs are as expected and estimates of UPL and CPI statistically significant at the confidence level <0.04 and thereof can be safely interpreted and applied.

The result of the regression analysis shows that the unemployment rate has the most significant effect on forborne performing loans growth – if the unemployment rate increases by 1% and the values of other factors remain unchanged, the forborne performing loans ratio will increase by 1.018% on average, and the 95% confidence interval of the effect is from 0.728% to 1.309%. Regarding the CPI, it can be concluded that if the CPI increases by one point and the values of the other factors remain unchanged, the forborne performing loans ratio will increase by 0.447% on average, and the 95% confidence interval of the effect is from 0.032% to 0.861%.

Calibrated model (5) *F*-test results summarised in Table 18 indicate high statistical stability.

Adjusted *R*-squared suggests that 78.1% of the variation in forborne NPLs can be explained by the factors included in the model; therefore, it can be concluded that the model fits well and has a pretty high predictive power.

Table 17. Regression Model (4) Coefficient Estimates.

Factor	Estimate	St.Error	*t*-Stat	*p*-Value
GDP	−0.1787	0.1194	−1.497	0.1517
UPL	1.0182	0.1383	7.361	7.85e−07
CPI	0.4466	0.1972	2.265	0.0361

Source: Authors' calculations.

Table 18. Regression Model (5) Estimates.

Res.SE	R^2	Adj.R^2	*F*-stat	*p*-Value
0.6478	0.8285	0.7808	17.39	2.468e-06

Source: Authors' calculations.

Homoscedasticity test results with Breusch–Pagan (BP) give evidence to not reject the null of homoscedasticity and Shapiro–Wilk (W) test gives evidence to not reject the null of residuals normality, see Table 19.

As the *vif* estimates for all three factors are less than 5, see Table 20, it can be concluded that we do not have significant issues with multicollinearity.

Table 21 summarises the results of the regression coefficient tests.

As can be seen, for all regression coefficients signs are as expected and statistically significant at the confidence level <0.01 only for UPL and thereof can be safely interpreted and applied. CPI estimate statistical significance is at level 7.75% and for GDP at level 14.84%, which is related to pretty high variation for both estimates.

The result of the regression analysis shows that the unemployment rate has the most significant effect on forborne non-performing growth – if the unemployment rate increases by 1% and the values of other factors remain unchanged, the forborne NPLs ratio will increase by 0.902% on average, and the 95% confidence interval of the effect is from 0.674% to 1.130%.

4.4. Associations Between the NPLs and Capital Adequacy of Baltic Banks

The results of the simulation analysis according to the prepared scenarios regarding the expected dynamics of NPLs are as follows: in the baseline scenario the largest relative increase in NPLs is expected in Lithuania 2.5–3.0 times, in Estonia 1.9–2.3 times, and in Latvia 1.7–2.1 times compared to the end of 2021 result. In the coming years, the NPLs in the baseline scenario should gradually decline

Table 19. Homoscedasticity and Residuals Normality Test Results.

BP	*p*-Value	W	*p*-Value
4.3506	0.5001	0.9572	0.3840

Source: Authors' calculations.

Table 20. Regression Coefficients Collinearity Test Results.

GDP	UPL	CPI
3.0973	1.7907	3.5433

Source: Authors' calculations.

Table 21. Regression Model (5) Coefficient Estimates.

Factor	Estimate	St.Error	*t*-Stat	*p*-Value
GDP	−0.1415	0.0937	−1.510	0.1484
UPL	0.9022	0.1085	8.312	1.41e−07
CPI	0.2897	0.1547	1.872	0.0775

Source: Authors' calculations,

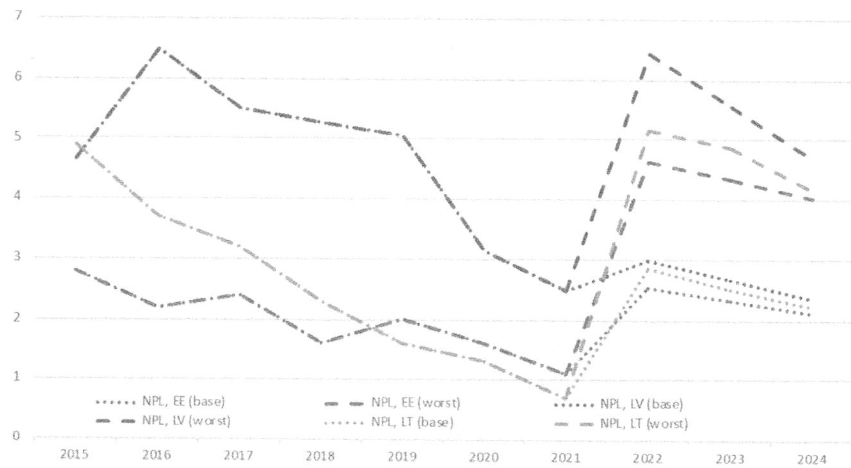

Fig. 4. The dynamic of NPLs and Forecast by Scenarios in Baltic Countries. *Source*: Authors' calculations based on model (6) and IMF data.

in all three Baltic States. In the worst case scenario NPLs are also expected to increase the most 6–7 times in Lithuania, 4–5 times in Estonia, and 3.5–4.5 times in Latvia. The relatively higher growth of NPLs in Lithuania and partly also in Estonia can be explained by a relatively lower level at the end of 2021.

The results of the simulation analysis according to the prepared scenarios regarding the expected dynamics of Tier 1 capital to RWA (T1C) are as follows: in the baseline scenario a larger decrease in T1C is expected in Estonia 15–20%, Lithuania 10–15%, and Latvia 8–12% compared to 2021 year-end results. In the

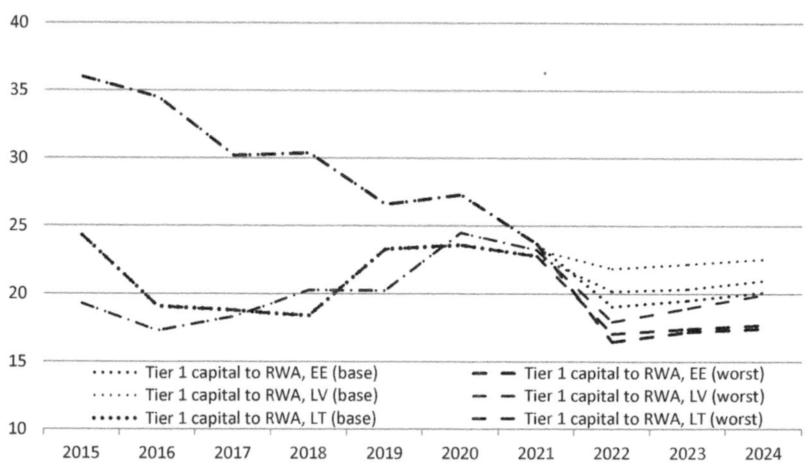

Fig. 5. The dynamic of Tier 1 Capital to RWA and Forecast by Scenarios in Baltic Countries. *Source*: Authors' calculations based on model (6) and IMF data.

coming years, the T1C in baseline scenario is expected to increase gradually in all three Baltic States. Also in the worst case scenario, the largest decrease in T1C is expected in Estonia by 25–30%, in Lithuania by 20–25%, but in Latvia by 18–23%.

The higher level of T1C can explain the larger decrease in T1C in Estonia at the end of 2021.

5. CONCLUSIONS

The effects of COVID-19 on the macroeconomic situation differed significantly from those observed during the GFC. The restrictions caused by the pandemic necessitated liquidity support in sectors directly related to customer service, disrupted supply chains, and consequently, increased credit risk in banks' loan portfolios in related segments.

Governments' fiscal support significantly reduced the pandemic's negative impact on both corporate solvency and unemployment. In turn, the liquidity support provided by central banks enabled commercial banks not to reduce the supply of credit in the financial market.

Calibrated regression models and tests show that rising unemployment and inflation lead to increased NPLs, while GDP growth contributes to declining NPLs. The study results show that the macroeconomic environment's impact on credit quality is not homogeneous. In the conditions of economic recession, the ability of non-financial companies to fulfil credit obligations deteriorates more significantly than that of HHs, and this difference is a significant one.

Taking into account the current macroeconomic trends, especially the rapid increase in inflation, the managers of the Baltic commercial banks need to be aware that an increase in the inflation index by one point causes an increase in the NPLs by 0.31 basis points for total portfolio and 0.996 for NFCs. GDP decline by 1% causes an increase in the NPLs by 0.30 basis points for the total portfolio and 0.51 for NFCs. The difference due to the increase in unemployment is slightly smaller – increase of unemployment level by 1% causes an increase of NPL by 1.51% for NFCs and 1.47% for HHs.

One of the major challenges for Baltic bank managers in the next couple of years will be the adequate application of the forbearance measure. As the study shows, on the one hand, it can be an effective solution to ease the cash flow of borrowers in temporary difficulties and to retain prospective business clients for the bank, but on the other hand, to accumulate future losses and slow down the way out of the crisis by underestimating the business capabilities of partners and continuing to finance 'zombie' firms.

The simulation modelling results confirm that the Baltic States' commercial banks have significantly improved their credit risk management after the GFC and strengthened their capital positions, which allows absorbing even 5–6 times the increase in NPLs and related credit losses. However, this conclusion applies only to the Baltic commercial banking system as a whole in each country, but not to each individual bank, as the study used aggregated data available from the IMF and ECB (ECB, 2022; IMF, 2022).

REFERENCES

Alessi, L., Bruno, B., Carletti, E., Neugebauer, K., & Wolfskeil, I. (2021). Cover your assets: Non-performing loans and coverage ratios in Europe. *Economic Policy*, *36*(108), 685–733. https://doi.org/10.1093/epolic/eiab018

Anastasiou, D., Louri, H., & Tsionas, M. (2019). Nonperforming loans in the euro area: Are core-periphery banking markets fragmented? *International Journal of Finance and Economics*, *24*(1), 97–112. https://doi.org/10.1002/ijfe.1651. Retrieved from https://www.sciencedirect.com/science/article/abs/pii/S1572308921000516?via%3Dihub

Anginer, D., Bertay, A. C., Cull, R., Demirgüç-Kuntc, A., & Mare, D. S. (2021). Bank capital regulation and risk after the global financial crisis. *Journal of Financial Stability*, 100891. https://doi.org/10.1016/j.jfs.2021.100891i

Apergis, N. (2022). Convergence in non-performing loans across EU banks: The role of COVID-19. *Cogent Economics & Finance*, *10*(1), 2024952. https://doi.org/10.1080/23322039.2021.2024952

Ari, A., Chena, S., & Ratnovski, L. (2021). The dynamics of non-performing loans during banking crises: A new database with post-COVID-19 implications. *Journal of Banking & Finance*, *133*, 106140. https://doi.org/10.1016/j.jbankfin.2021.106140

Baltazar, J., Reis, J., & Amorim, M. (2020). Sustainable economies: Using a macro-economic model to predict how the default rate is affected under economic stress scenarios. *Sustainable Futures*, *2*, 1000011. https://doi.org/10.1016/j.sftr.2020.100011

Bayar, Y. (2019). Macroeconomic, institutional and bank-specific determinants of non-performing loans in emerging market economies- A dynamic panel regression analysis. *Journal of Central Banking Theory and Practice*, *8*(3), 95–110. doi: 10.2478/jcbtp-2019-0026

Beck, T., & Keil, J. (2022). Have banks caught corona? Effects of COVID on lending in the US. *Journal of Corporate Finance*, *72*, 102160. https://doi.org/10.1016/j.jcorpfin.2022.102160

Becker, B., Bos, M., & Roszbach, K. (2020). Bad times, good credit. *Journal of Money, Credit and Banking*, *52*(S1), 107–142.

Berger, A. N., & Demirgüç-Kunt, A. (2021). Banking research in the time of COVID-19. *Journal of Financial Stability*, *57*, 100939. https://doi.org/10.1016/j.jfs.2021.100939

Bischof, J., Rudolf, N., & Schmundt, W. (2022). How do nonperforming loans evolve along the economic cycle? The role of macroeconomic conditions and legal efficiency. *European Accounting Review*, *31*(5), 1149–1174. https://doi.org/10.1080/09638180.2022.2071960

Bitar, M., & Tarazi, A. (2022). A note on regulatory responses to COVID-19 pandemic: Balancing banks' solvency and contribution to recovery. *Journal of Financial Stability*, *60*, 101009. https://doi.org/10.1016/j.jfs.2022.101009

Borio, C. (2020). The Covid-19 economic crisis: Dangerously unique. *Business Economics*, *55*, 181–190. https://doi.org/10.1057/s11369-020-00184-2

Borri, N., & Di Giorgio, G. (2022). Systemic risk and the COVID challenge in the European banking sector. *Journal of Banking & Finance*, *140*, 106073. https://doi.org/10.1016/j.jbankfin.2021

Byrne, D., & Kelly, R. (2019) Bank asset quality & monetary policy pass-through. *Applied Economics*, *51*(23), 2501–2521. https://doi.org/10.1080/00036846.2018.1546953

Cerulli, G., D'Apice, V., Fiordelisi, F., & Masala, F. (2020). Benchmarking non-performing loans. *The European Journal of Finance*, *26*(16), 1591–1605. https://doi.org/10.1080/1351847X.2020.1794923

Chiesa, G., & Mansilla-Fernández, J. M. (2021). The dynamic effects of non-performing loans on banks' cost of capital and lending supply in the Eurozone. *Empirica*, *48*, 397–427. https://doi.org/10.1007/s10663-020-09475-5

Ciukaj, R., & Kil, K. (2020). Determinants of the non-performing loan ratio in the European Union banking sectors with a high level of impaired loans. *Economics and Business Review*, *6*(20), 22–45. https://doi.org/10.18559/ebr.2020.1.2

Clichici, D. (2021). The resilience of Central and Eastern European banking systems during the COVID-19 crisis. *Economy and Sociology*, 2, 20–29. https://doi.org/10.36004/nier.es.2021.2-02

Climent-Serrano, S. (2019). Effects of economic variables on NPLs depending on the economic cycle. *Empirical Economics*, *56*, 325–340. https://doi.org/10.1007/s00181-017-1362-y

Çolak, G., & Öztekin, O. (2021). The impact of COVID-19 pandemic on bank lending around the world. *Journal of Banking & Finance*, *133*, 106207. https://doi.org/10.1016/j.jbankfin.2021.106207

Cucinelli, D., Di Battista, M. L., Marchese, M., & Nieri, L. (2018). Credit risk in European banks: The bright side of the internal ratings based approach. *Journal of Banking & Finance*, *93*, 213–229. https://doi.org/10.1016/j.jbankfin.2018.06.014

Czech, M., & Puszer, B. (2021). Impact of the COVID-19 pandemic on the consumer credit market in V4 countries. *Risks*, *9*, 229. https://doi.org/10.3390/risks9120229

Dao, H. T., & Kang, T. (2022). Non-performing loans and the lending channel of shock transmission across countries. *Cogent Business & Management*, *9*(1), 2046239. https://doi.org/10.1080/23311975.2022.2046239

Demirgüç-Kunt, A., Pedraza, A., & Ruiz-Ortega, C. (2021). Banking sector performance during the COVID-19 crisis. *Journal of Banking and Finance*, *133*, 106305. https://doi.org/10.1016/j.jbankfin.2021.106305

Demmou, L., Franco, G., Calligaris, S., & Dlugosch, D. (2022). Liquidity shortfalls during the COVID-19 outbreak: Assessment and policy responses. *Economie et Statistique/Economics and Statistics, 532–33*, 47–61. https://www.insee.fr/en/statistiques/6210400

De Vincentiis, P. (2021). What drives the greater or lesser usage of forbearance measures by banks? *Journal of Banking Regulation*, *22*, 181–190. https://doi.org/10.1057/s41261-020-00136-y

Didier, T., Huneeus, F., Larrain, M., & Schmukler, S. L. (2021). Financing firms in hibernation during the COVID-19 pandemic. *Journal of Financial Stability*, *53*, 100837. https://doi.org/10.1016/j.jfs.2020.100837

Dursun-de Neef, H. O., & Schandlbauer, A. (2022). COVID-19, bank deposits, and lending. *Journal of Empirical Finance*, *68*, 20–33. https://doi.org/10.1016/j.jempfin.2022.05.003

Elnahass, M., Trinh, V. Q., & Li, T. (2021). Global banking stability in the shadow of Covid-19 outbreak. *Journal of International Financial Markets Institutions & Money*, *72*, 101322. https://doi.org/10.1016/j.intfin.2021.101322

European Central Bank. (2022). Consolidated banking data. Retrieved from https://sdw.ecb.europa.eu/browse.do?node=9691533

European Commission. (2020). Commission interpretative communication on the application of the accounting and prudential frameworks to facilitate EU bank lending supporting businesses and households amid COVID-19. COM/2020/169 final. Retrieved from https://eur-lex.europa.eu/legal-content/EN/TXT/?uri=CELEX:52020DC0169

Fallanca, M., Forgione, A. F., & Otranto, E. (2021). Do the determinants of non-performing loans have a different effect over time? A conditional correlation approach. *Journal of Risk and Financial Management*, *14*(1), 21. https://doi.org/10.3390/jrfm14010021

Foglia, M. (2022). Non-performing loans and macroeconomics factors: The Italian case. *Risks*, *10*, 21. https://doi.org/10.3390/risks10010021

Gerlach-Kristen, P., & Lyons, S. (2018). Determinants of mortgage arrears in Europe: Evidence from household microdata. *International Journal of Housing Policy*, *18*(4), 1–23. https://doi.org/10.1080/19491247.2017.1357398

Giese, J., & Haldane, A. (2020). COVID-19 and the financial system: A tale of two crises. *Oxford Review of Economic Policy*, *36*(Suppl 1), S200–S214. https://doi.org/10.1093/oxrep/graa035

Goldstein, I., Koijen, R. S. J., & Mueller, H. M. (2021). COVID-19 and its impact on financial markets and the real economy. *The Review of Financial Studies*, *34*(11), 5135–5148. https://doi.org/10.1093/rfs/hhab085

Grima, S., Kizilkaya, M., Sood, K., & ErdemDelice, M. (2021). The perceived effectiveness of blockchain for digital operational risk resilience in the European Union insurance market sector. *Journal of Risk and Financial Management*, *14*(8), 363.

Hada, T., Bărbuţă-Mişu, N., Iuga, I. C., & Wainberg, D. (2020). Macroeconomic determinants of nonperforming loans of Romanian banks. *Sustainability*, *12*, 7533. https://doi.org/10.3390/su12187533

Horobet, A., Radulescu, M., Belascu, L., & Dita, S. M. (2021). Determinants of bank profitability in CEE countries: Evidence from GMM panel data estimates. *Journal of Risk and Financial Management*, *14*, 307. https://doi.org/10.3390/jrfm14070307

Huljak, I., Martin, R., Moccero, D., & Pancaro, C. (2022). Do non-performing loans matter for bank lending and the business cycle in euro area countries? *Journal of Applied Economics*, *25*(1), 1050–1080. https://doi.10.1080/15140326.2022.2094668

Igan, D., Mirzaei, A., & Moore, T. (2022). Does macroprudential policy alleviate the adverse impact of COVID-19 on the resilience of banks? *Journal of Banking & Finance*, *147*, 106419. https://doi.org/10.1016/j.jbankfin.2022.106419

IMF. (2022). Financial soundness indicators. Retrieved from https://data.imf.org/?sk=388DFA60-1D26-4ADE-B505-A05A558D9A42&sId=1479329132316

Inder, S., Sood, K., & Grima, S. (2022). Antecedents of behavioural intention to adopt internet banking using structural equation modelling. *Journal of Risk and Financial Management*, *15*(4), 157.

Kahn, C. M., & Wagner, W. (2021). Liquidity provision during a pandemic. *Journal of Banking and Finance*, *133*, 106152. https://doi.org/10.1016/j.jbankfin.2021.106152

Karadima, M., & Louri, H. (2021). Economic policy uncertainty and non-performing loans: The moderating role of bank concentration. *Finance Research Letters*, *38*, 101458. https://doi.org/10.1016/j.frl.2020.101458

Kjosevski, J., & Petkovski, M. (2017). Non-performing loans in Baltic States: Determinants and macroeconomic effects. *Baltic Journal of Economics*, *17*(1), 25–44. https://doi.org/10.1080/1406099X.2016.1246234

Khairi, A., Bahri, B., & Artha, B. (2021). A literature review of non-performing loan. *Journal of Business and Management Review*, *2*(5), 366–373. https://doi.10.47153/jbmr25.1402021

Koju, L., Koju, R., & Wang, S. (2020). Macroeconomic determinants of credit risks: Evidence from high-income countries. *European Journal of Management and Business Economics*, *29*(1), 41–53. https://doi.org/10.1108/EJMBE-02-2018-0032

Korzeb, Z., & Niedziółka, P. (2021). Determinants of Differentiation of Cost of Risk (CoR) among Polish Banks during COVID-19 Pandemic. *Journal of Risk and Financial Management*, *14*(3), 110. https://doi.org/10.3390/jrfm14030110

Kostis, P. C. (2020). Increased uncertainty, credit supply, and non-performing loans in the Eurozone. *Journal of Business Accounting and Finance Perspectives*, *2*(1), 7. https://doi:10.35995/jbafp2010007

Kozak, S. (2021). The impact of COVID-19 on bank equity and performance: The case of Central Eastern South European Countries. *Sustainability*, *13*, 11036. https://doi.org/10.3390/su131911036

Laborda, R., & Olmo, J. (2021). Volatility spillover between economic sectors in financial crisis prediction: Evidence spanning the great financial crisis and Covid-19 pandemic. *Research in International Business and Finance*, *57*, 101402. https://doi.org/10.1016/j.ribaf.2021.101402

Łasak, P. (2021). The commercial banking sector in Eurozone after the pandemic: The paths to recovery. *European Research Studies*, *24*(1), 1233–1246. https://doi.org/10.35808/ersj/2101

Lee, J. M., Chen, K. H., Chang, I. C., & Chen, C. C. (2022). Determinants of non-performing loans, firm's corporate governance and macroeconomic factors. *International Journal of Finance & Economics*, *27*(1), 88–98. https://doi.org/10.1002/ijfe.2139

Macháček, M., Melecký, A., & Šulganová, M. (2018). Macroeconomic drivers of non-performing loans: A meta-regression analysis. *Prague Economic Papers*, *27*(3), 351–374. https://doi.org/10.18267/j.pep.656

Miklaszewska, E., Kil, K., & Idzik, M. (2021). How the COVID-19 pandemic affects bank risks and returns: Evidence from EU members in Central, Eastern, and Northern Europe. *Risks*, *9*, 180. https://doi.org/10.3390/risks9100180

Naili, M., & Lahrichi, Y. (2022). The determinants of banks' credit risk: Review of the literature and future research agenda. *International Journal of Finance & Economics*, *27*(1), 334–360. https://doi.org/10.1002/ijfe.2156

Neisen, M., & Schulte-Mattler, H. (2021). The effectiveness of IFRS 9 transitional provisions in limiting the potential impact of COVID-19 on banks. *Journal of Banking Regulation*, *22*, 342–351. https://doi.org/10.1057/s41261-021-00151-7

Park, C. Y., & Shin, K. (2021). COVID-19, nonperforming loans, and cross border bank lending. *Journal of Banking and Finance*, *133*, 106233. https://doi.org/10.1016/j.jbankfin.2021.106233

Phung, Q. T., Vu, H. V., & Tran, H. P. (2022). Do non-performing loans impact bank efficiency? *Finance Research Letters*, *46*, 102393. https://doi.org/10.1016/j.frl.2021.102393

R Core Team. (2022). *R: A language and environment for statistical computing*. Foundation for Statistical Computing. Retrieved from https://www.R-project.org/

Salvi, A., Bussoli, C., Conca, L., & Gigante, M. (2018). Determinants of non-performing loans: Evidence from Europe. *International Journal of Business and Management*, *13*(10), 230–239. https://doi.org/10.5539/ijbm.v13n10p230

Serrano, A. S. (2021). The impact of non-performing loans on bank lending in Europe: An empirical analysis. *The North American Journal of Economics and Finance*, *55*, 101312. https://doi.org/10.1016/j.najef.2020.101312

Spilbergs, A. (2022). Comparative analysis of non-performing loans affecting factors in the Baltic States. *Journal of Economic and Social Development*, *9*(1), 10–17. https://doi.org/10.55539/jesd.9.1.2

Staehr, K., & Uusküla, L. (2020). Macroeconomic and macro-financial factors as leading indicators of non-performing loans: Evidence from the EU countries. *Journal of Economic Studies*, *48*(3), 720–740. https://doi.org/10.1108/JES-03-2019-0107

Sood, K., Kaur, B., & Grima, S. (2022). Revamping Indian non-life insurance industry with a trusted network: Blockchain technology. In K. Sood, R. K. Dhanaraj, B. Balamurugan, S. Grima, & R. U. Maheshwari (Eds.), *Big data: A game changer for insurance industry* (pp. 213–228). Bingley: Emerald Publishing Limited.

Sood, K., Seth, N., & Grima, S. (2022). Portfolio performance of public sector general insurance companies in India: A comparative analysis. In S. Grima, E. Özen, & I. Romānova (Eds.), *Managing risk and decision making in times of economic distress, Part B* (pp. 215–229). Bingley: Emerald Publishing Limited.

Stanga, I., Vlahua, R., & de Haan, J. (2020). Mortgage arrears, regulation and institutions: Cross-country evidence. *Journal of Banking & Finance*, *118*, 105889. https://doi.org/10.1016/j.jbankfin.2020.105889

Szarowska, I. (2018). Effect of macroeconomic determinants on non-performing loans in Central and Eastern European countries. *International Journal of Monetary Economics and Finance*, *11*(1), 20–35. https://doi.org/10.1504/IJMEF.2018.090564

Tan, B., Igan, D., Peria, M. S. M., Pierri, N., & Presbitero, A. F. (2021). Government intervention and bank markups: Lessons from the global financial crisis for the COVID-19 crisis. *Journal of Banking & Finance*, *133*, 106320. https://doi.org/10.1016/j.jbankfin.2021.106320

Tatarici, L., Kubinschi, M., & Barnea, D. (2020). Determinants of non-performing loans for the EEC region. A financial stability perspective. *Management & Marketing. Challenges for the Knowledge Society*, *15*(4), 621–642. https://doi.org/10.2478/mmcks-2020-0036

Teresiene, D., Keliuotyte-Staniuleniene, G., & Kanapickiene, R. (2021). Sustainable economic growth support through credit transmission channel and financial stability: In the context of the COVID-19 pandemic. *Sustainability*, *13*, 2692. https://doi.org/10.3390/su13052692

Thornton, J., & Di Tommaso, C. (2021). The effect of non-performing loans on credit expansion: Do capital and profitability matter? Evidence from European banks. *International Journal of Finance and Economics*, *26*(3), 4822–4839. https://doi.org/10.1002/ijfe.2042

Tölö, E., & Virén, M. (2021). How much do non-performing loans hinder loan growth in Europe? *European Economic Review*, *136*, 103773. https://doi.org/10.1016/j.euroecorev.2021.103773

Velliscig, G., Floreani, J., & Polato, M. (2022). Capital and asset quality implications for bank resilience and performance in the light of NPLs' regulation: A focus on the Texas ratio. *Journal of Banking Regulation*, *24*, 66–88. https://doi.org/10.1057/s41261-021-00184-y

CHAPTER 7

ESG INTEGRATION AS A RISK MANAGEMENT TOOL WITHIN THE FINANCIAL DECISION-MAKING PROCESS

Jekaterina Kuzmina[a], Dimitrios Maditinos[b], Diego Norena-Chavez[c], Simon Grima[d] and Marta Kadłubek[e]

[a]*BA School of Business and Finance, Latvia*
[b]*International Hellenic University, Greece*
[c]*Escuela de Posgrado, Universidad de Lima, Peru*
[d]*University of Malta, Malta*
[e]*Czestochowa University of Technology, Poland*

ABSTRACT

The current chapter deals with the environmental, social, and governance (ESG) integration issue that should contribute to the higher expected investment returns as different kinds of risk are managed in a better and more sufficient way. The goal is to study the ESG risks integration into the decision-making process and test the results. The research chapter intends to contribute to the existing discussion by evaluating some integration techniques. Following the development of the European Taxonomy, one can expect increased interest in integrating ESG risks into the financial forecast and asset valuation. The current chapter deals with Berger and UniCredit Bank's (2010) proposal to include the ESG data as factors influencing the foretasted financial data

Digital Transformation, Strategic Resilience, Cyber Security and Risk Management
Contemporary Studies in Economic and Financial Analysis, Volume 111A, 105–113

Published under exclusive licence by Emerald Publishing Limited
ISSN: 1569-3759/doi:10.1108/S1569-37592023000111A007

in terms of direct costs (like energy, waste, water, and paper expenses; payments for sick leaves and employees' turnover costs); externality costs (like CO_2 *compliance costs) and opportunity costs (ESG provisions; expenses for board compensations). The chapter provides an overview of some integration approaches and discusses the idea of incorporating the ESG criteria into the stock valuation and portfolio management process. It is evident that the classical value investing approach is no more suitable. Nevertheless, the tested sample does not show significantly different results based on the backtesting. The research results could be interesting for authors preparing research on the field of sustainability and risk management as well as for portfolio managers considering the ESG integration to achieve the positive alpha.*

Keywords: Stock valuation; ESG integration; value investing; sustainability; risks; decision-making

INTRODUCTION

According to the significant number of published research papers, there is an increasing number of institutional and private investors willing to include or currently include the ESG factors into the investment decision-making process, asset allocation and portfolio management; in contrast, different kinds of investors are led by various motivations like the trend, requirements, interest, etc. Figs. 1 and 2 illustrate that the impact of sustainability has increased over the past decade within the global growth of sustainable investment strategies and tremendous growth of sustainable assets' volume.

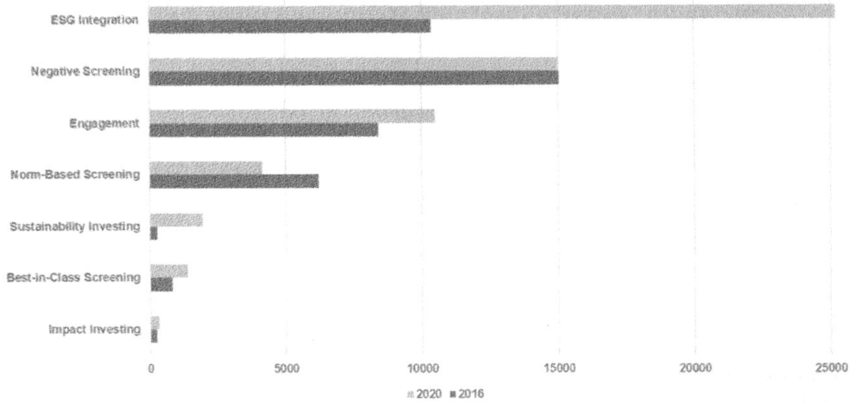

Fig. 1. Global Growth of Sustainable Investing Strategies 2016 Versus 2020. Asset Values Are Expressed in Billions of US Dollars. *Source*: Adapted from Alliance (2021).

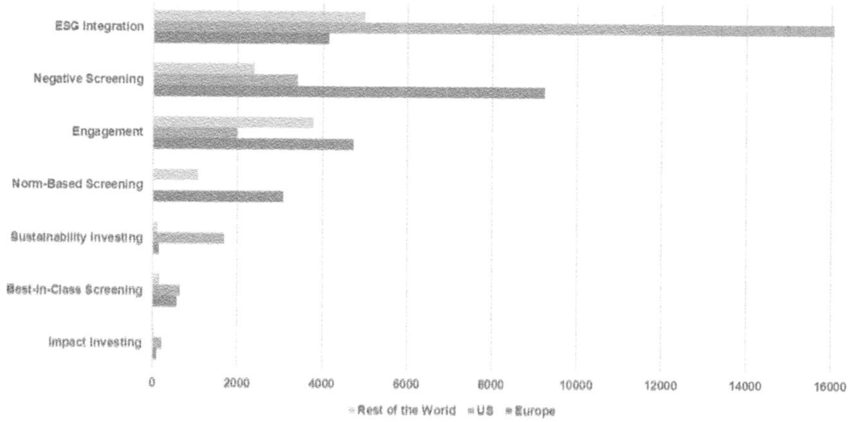

Fig. 2. Sustainable Investing Assets by Strategy and Region as for 2020. Asset Values Are Expressed in Billions of US Dollars. *Source*: Adapted from Alliance (2021).

On the other hand, some investors also believe that the ESG integration will lead to higher returns, even though the last statement is still questionable. In scientific research [e.g. Hastalona and Sadalia (2021); Simone, Petracci, & Piva (2022)] and among practitioners, ESG is used as a synonym for sustainability. Nevertheless, sustainability can be defined broadly by Hallin, Karrbom-Gustavsson, and Dobers (2021) and Ruggerio (2021). It is worth considering that an important question at this point is if the ESG-sensible behaviour of the companies pays off to the different kinds of stockholders. In the case of the positive answer [and the author would like to believe in it, claiming that the findings by several scientists are true, for example, Ahmad, Mobarek, & Roni (2021); Kim and Li (2021); Simone et al. (2022)], various kinds of investors should recognise the added value while putting their money into sustainability and sustainable projects and behaviour.

The current chapter deals with the ESG integration issue that should bring the investor towards higher expected investment returns as different kinds of risk are managed in a better and more sufficient way.

ESG INTEGRATION IN FINANCIAL DECISION-MAKING: OVERVIEW

Considering the potential positive impact of ESG sensibility on the investee company investors, the main concern is about the ESG integration opportunities in the decision-making process even though the ESG strategies could differ significantly as they are based on different viewpoints and values several rather well-defined investment strategies are based on ESG integration.

In the framework of the current paper, it is necessary to provide an overview of these strategies that would allow further understanding of the issue [based on the research conducted by Hebb (2011), Duuren, Plantinga, & Scholtens (2016); Gasperini (2020); Folqué, Escrig-Olmedo, & Santamaría (2021)]. The strategies include the following variants:

1. Exclusion (in some sources also negative screening): exclusion from potential investment universe due to some specific ESG criteria levels.
2. Best-in-class screening (in some sources also positive screening): inclusion into potential investment universe due to some specific ESG criteria's levels compared to industry or sector peer-group.
3. ESG integration: inclusion of the ESG criteria in the investee company valuation and financial analysis (this strategy is going to be considered in the further part of the research).
4. ESG thematic investing: investment strategy includes one or several sustainability issues or goals to be achieved thanks to the investment.
5. Impact ESG investing strategy includes one or several sustainability issues or goals to be achieved thanks to the investment (KPI or measurement parameters are determined and evaluated).
6. Engagement strategy: the investor acts actively to influence/change the company's behaviour considering the ESG factors and sustainability issues.

The strategies are defined; nevertheless, the literature analysis shows that investors do not have clear guidelines about the strategies' usage (and even more integration and engagement) from the practical point of view. The research chapter intends to contribute to the existing discussion by evaluating some of the integration techniques and examining how the ESG factors, among others, are influencing the company's foretasted returns.

Moreover, the chapter addresses the issue of value investing – the skill of purchasing stocks which trade at a significant discount to their intrinsic value – and how the conclusions regarding potential buying targets could be influenced through the ESG integration process. The following methods are used to achieve the objective: a literature analysis to discuss and evaluate ESG factors' integration techniques; Berger and UniCredit Bank's (2010) proposal of ESG incorporation in stock evaluation is used to determine the sustainability impact on the company's value.

RESULTS OF RESEARCH

Introductory Remarks to the Approach

Based on the literature analysis, one can conclude that concerning the ESG integration possibilities, there are some proposals regarding investment strategies in corporate bonds and sovereign asset classes. The main conclusion that could be drawn from the analysis: ESG is complementary to credit ratings in assessing the credit quality of the investment objective so that adjustment to the credit quality and rating is based on the stand of ESG criteria. Further details can be found in Jang, Kang, Lee, and Bae (2020); Gratcheva, Emery, and Wang (2020); Mccarthy

(2021); Morgenstern, Coqueret, and Kelly (2022). In the equity asset class, the integration proposal is constructing smart beta by integrating ESG factors and evaluating their performance. Further, details can be found in Yasmine and Kooli (2022), Kaiser (2020), and Austmo and Eikeland (2021).

Moreover, it is worth considering that in both cases, the investor makes use of so-called traditional accounting while using the fundamental data from the profit and loss statement, the balance sheet and the cash flow statement, while the sustainable approach requires going one step further and analysing the ESG impact (both positive and negative) on the financial statement related positions. Such an approach is less discussed in the scientific literature, but following the development of the European Taxonomy (and increasing the amount of Taxonomy-related data), one can expect increased interest in such an approach. As it was mentioned previously, the current chapter deals with Berger and UniCredit Bank's (2010) proposal to include the ESG data as factors influencing the foretasted financial data in terms of direct costs (like energy, waste, water, and paper expenses; payments for sick leaves and employees' turnover costs); externality costs [like CO_2 compliance costs) and opportunity costs (ESG provisions; expenses for board compensations)]. Fig. 3 demonstrates the approach to be tested and discussed in the coming parts of the current chapter.

	Data (reported by the company &/or researched	MICRO INDICATOR	PRICING FACTOR
Total revenue and other income			
Costs of goods sold			
Gross Profit			
Selling, general and administrative expenses			
Energy expense	*direct costs*	Energy intensity (MWh/sales)	× Electricity price (EUR/MWh)
Waste expense	*direct costs*	Waste intensity (t/sales)	× Waste price (EUR/t)
Rehiring costs	*direct costs*	Workforce replacement rate (%)	× Rehiring cost (EUR/employee)
Water expense	*direct costs*	Water intensity (m³/sales)	× Water price (EUR/m³)
Paper expense	*direct costs*	Paper intensity (t/sales)	× Paper price (EUR/t)
Sick pay	*direct costs*	Accident severity rate (hours/employee)	× Employee salary (EUR/hour)
Employee turnover costs	*direct costs*	Employee turnover (%)	× Employee turnover cost (EUR/employee)
Unusual income item			×
ESG provisions costs	*opportunity costs*	ESG provisions rate (% shareholders' equity)	× ROE (%)
Non-independent board comp. expense	*opportunity costs*	Independent directors (%)	× Exec. board memb comp. (EUR mn/year)
CO_2 compliance costs	*opportunity costs*	GHG intensity (t/sales)	× Electricity price (EUR/MWh)
		Travel CO_2 intensity (t/sales)	× CO_2 price (EUR/t)
EBITDA			

Fig. 3. ESG Incorporation in the Financial Analysis (EBITDA Forecast). *Source*: Created by authors based on Berger and UniCredit Bank (2010).

Selection and Testing of Value Portfolio

To study the potential influence of such an approach, the author decided to use the value investing approach and select an investment portfolio consisting of 15 top-value stocks. The selection criteria can be found in Table 1.

Table 2 represents the results of such an investment portfolio. After selecting the stock portfolio consisting of 15 best-rated stocks (applying criteria for value stocks), it was backtested on the historical data (time period from May 2020 to May 2022). The results show that the portfolio would provide a positive return, but not sufficient if considering the level of risk taken (as Sharp ratio is below one); nevertheless, the investor would benefit from positive alpha and beta below one.

Moreover, it is worth considering that the selected portfolio could be considered only by investors believing in value investing as other criteria were not applied.

ESG Integration

The results presented above show just the classical approach of portfolio selection; as soon as the investor incorporates the ESG criteria and their impact on potential financial positions, the portfolio does not look potentially attractive, as the majority of the positions cannot be included due to ESG incorporation negative impact on foretasted EBITDA for the financial year 2022 and stock price.

The results are presented in Table 3. The evaluation of ESG criteria impact is performed with + standing for positive impact, n – neutral impact and – standing for negative impact.

Table 1. Investment Portfolio Selection Criteria Within the Bloomberg Data Universe.

Selected Screening Criteria	Matches (Number of Stocks)
Security Universe	1,603,260
Trading status: active	548,092
Security attributes: show the primary security of the company only	98,145
Country/territory of domicile: eastern Europe; western Europe	26,963
Top 15 sequential rank – Higher is better (Current market cap [US Dollars])	15
Additional factors to consider for value stocks selection	
Current price-to-book ratio	15
Current price to free cash flow	15
Current price earnings ratio (*P*/*E*)	15
Current periodic EV to trailing 12M EBITDA	15
Current periodic EV to trailing 12M sales	15
BF12M best *P*/*E* ratio	15

Source: Authors creation.

Table 2. Testing on Historical Data Applying Bloomberg Model.

	Statistical Description of Value Stock Portfolio (Top 15)
Total return (%)	28.06
Mean return (%)	13.36
Standard deviation (%)	19.46
Sharp ratio	0.76
Jensen Alpha	4.1
Beta	0.8

Source: Authors creation.

Table 3. ESG Integration and Impact Valuation on Estimated EBITDA and Share Price.

Name of the Company	Impact on Estimated EBITDA for the Year 2022	Impact on the Current Share Price	Environmental Risks (E-Criteria)	Social Risks (S-Criteria)	Governance Risk (G-Criteria)
Shell	−135.02%	192.43%	n	–	n
Astrazeneca	30.93%	40.70%	+	+	n
Total energies	−0.33%	−0.47%	n	n	n
Safoni	−0.66%	−2.18%	+	n	n
HSBC Holdings	Less than 0%	−2.18%	n	n	n
Novartis	0.39%	0.45%	+	n	n
Novo Nordisk	−1.50%	−2.54%	+	–	n
Medtronic	−8.06%	−9.60%	+	–	n
Nestle	−−32.46%	−38.12%	+	–	n
Linde	−1.62%	−2.12%	n	–	n
Roche Holding	−10.05%	−14.78%	+	–	n
LVMH Moet Hennessy Louis Vui	−1.68%	−2.44%	N	–	n
L'Oreal	−0.67%	−0.85	+	–	n
ASML Holding	−1.14%	−1.29%	n	–	n
Accenture	−34.71%	−45.35%	n	–	n

Source: Authors creation.

One can notice that the integration of ESG factors into the evaluation process leads to the following results:

- Due to the potential negative impact, five companies out of 15 do not comply with the value strategy anymore due to the highly negative impact on foretasted EBITDA and stock valuation. Based on this evidence, the investor must exclude Shell; Medtronic; Nestle; Roche Holding, and Accenture. Even though the major parts of other companies show similar negative impact based on ESG integration, it should be seen as less crucial.
- By reducing the portfolio to 10 stocks (assuming that the previous strategy – investing in top-value stocks in Europe – is still reasonable), its performance

Table 4. Testing on Historical Data Applying Bloomberg Model.

Statistical Description of Value Stock Portfolio (Top 10)	
Total return (%)	24.52
Mean return (%)	11.68
Standard deviation (%)	17.01
Sharp ratio	0.79
Jensen Alpha	3.9
Beta	0.8

Source: Authors creation.

should be backtested for comparison reasons. The results show that the portfolio would provide a positive return, but not sufficient if considering the level of risk taken (as Sharp ratio is below one); nevertheless, the investor would benefit from positive alpha and beta below one. No considerable differences from the previous results are present. Follow Table 4 for further details.

- Analysing the results of the ESG integration, one can note that the positive impact mainly comes from environmental factors; while social factors contribute to a major negative impact and neutral governance factors. The environmental issues are probably mainly discussed, and companies are forced to take measures to reduce visible negative footprint; the social factors are less visible and less enforced by regulators (that could change with an introduction of European social taxonomy).

CONCLUSIONS AND DISCUSSIONS

Sustainability is not just a niche or an innovative product; it is a stable part of our everyday life, and also investors have to care about the potential impact of their investment decision on sustainability. On the one hand, there is a growing interest in the topic, and it is widely discussed. On the other hand, the lack of general standards, best practices, and developed methodologies do not allow ESG integration to be used in the financial decision-making process to the full extent.

The chapter contributes to the topic by providing an overview of some integration approaches and discussing the idea of incorporating the ESG criteria into the stock valuation and portfolio management process. It is evident that the classical value investing approach is no longer suitable as soon as an investor integrates the ESG criteria into the decision-making process. Nevertheless, the tested sample does not show any significantly different results based on the backtesting. Excluding the 'high ESG risk', companies from the portfolio do not lead to better financial performance (as measured by risk return) but provide evidence that the created portfolio is more sustainable. Whether this emotional evidence should be considered sufficient to base on other decision-making is still a question.

In the coming papers, it is necessary to test the influence of ESG integration into financial data analysis for the broader investment universe and to evaluate portfolio performance within different market scenarios.

REFERENCES

Ahmad, N., Mobarek, A., & Roni, N. N. (2021). Revisiting the impact of ESG on the financial performance of FTSE350 UK firms: Static and dynamic panel data analysis. *Cogent Business & Management*, *8*(1), 1–18.

Alliance, G. S. I. (2021). Global sustainable investment review 2020. Retrieved from http://www.gsi-alliance.org/wp-content/uploads/2021/08/GSIR-20201.pdf. Accessed on July 15, 2022.

Austmo, J. H., & Eikeland, H. M. (2021). Exploiting ESG information by extending conventional smart beta strategies: An empirical analysis of portfolio performances through the booms and busts in the European equity market. Retrieved from http://research.cbs.dk/en/studentProjects/exploiting-esg-information-by-extending-conventional-smart-beta-s. Accessed on June 25, 2022.

Berger & UniCredit Bank. (2010, November 1). *The Halo's creed.*

Duuren, E. V., Plantinga, A., & Scholtens, B. (2016). ESG integration and the investment management process: Fundamental investing reinvented. *Journal of Business Ethics*, *138*(3), 525–533.

Folqué, M., Escrig-Olmedo, E., & Santamaría, T. (2021). Sustainable development and financial system: Integrating ESG risks through sustainable investment strategies in a climate change context. *Sustainable Development*, *29*(5), 876–890.

Gasperini, A. (2020). Principles for responsible investment (PRI) and ESG factors. In F. W. Leal, A. M. Azul, L. Brandli, P. G. Özuyar, & T. Wall (Eds.), *Climate action. Encyclopedia of the UN sustainable development goals* (pp. 737–749). Cham: Springer.

Gratcheva, E., Emery, T., & Wang, D. (2020). *Demystifying sovereign ESG*. Washington, DC: The World Bank.

Hallin, A., Karrbom-Gustavsson, T., & Dobers, P. (2021). The transition towards and of sustainability – Understanding sustainability as performative. *Business Strategy and the Environment*, *30*(4), 1948–1957.

Hastalona, D., & Sadalia, I. (2021). Literature review ESG and sustainability finance. *Budapest International Research and Critics Institute (BIRCI-Journal): Humanities and Social Sciences*, *4*(3), 3548–3557.

Hebb, T. (2011). The next generation of responsible investing. In T. Hebb (Ed.), *The next generation of responsible investing*. (pp. 1–8) Dordrecht: Springer.

Jang, G. Y., Kang, H. G., Lee, J. Y., & Bae, K. (2020). ESG scores and the credit market. *Sustainability*, *12*(8), 3456–3456.

Kaiser, L. (2020). ESG integration: Value, growth and momentum. *Journal of Asset Management*, *21*(1), 32–51.

Kim, S., & Li, Z. (2021). Understanding the impact of ESG practices in corporate finance. *Sustainability*, *13*(7), 3746–3746.

Mccarthy, T. (2021). ESG and alternative factors in corporate bond returns. Retrieved from http://www.csp.uzh.ch/dam/jcr:c8de28f7-a2a2-41b1-99b2-6f432b910c0e/MA_McCarthy%20-%20CCSF%20Series%20no.%2025.pdf. Accessed on July 29, 2022.

Morgenstern, C., Coqueret, G., & Kelly, J. (2022). Estimating the demand in sovereign sustainability. Retrieved from https://ssrn.com/abstract=4138136. Accessed on May 19, 2022.

Ruggerio, C. A. (2021). Sustainability and sustainable development: A review of principles and definitions. *Science of the Total Environment*, *786*, 147481–147481.

Simone, L., Petracci, B., & Piva, M. (2022). Economic sustainability, innovation, and the ESG factors: An empirical investigation. *Sustainability*, *14*(4), 2270–2270.

Yasmine, B., & Kooli, M. (2022). Smart beta ESG disclosure. *Journal of Asset Management*, *23*(7), 1–14.

CHAPTER 8

ADAPTING INFORMATION SECURITY POLICY MESSAGING STYLES TO THE TARGETED AUDIENCE

Arnaud Denis[a], Tatjana Volkova[b], Simon Grima[c], Graţiela Georgiana Noja[d] and Mirela Cristea[e]

[a]*ICS/OT Consultant, Latvia*
[b]*BA School of Business and Finance, Latvia*
[c]*University of Malta, Malta*
[d]*West University of Timisoara, Romania*
[e]*University of Craiova, Romania*

ABSTRACT

Current research aims to investigate whether it would be possible to identify all information security policy (ISP) writing styles and how these would influence ISP compliance. Almost all businesses use ISPs to establish boundaries and require secure behaviour from their employees. Unfortunately, professional surveys and academic research demonstrate a high level of non-compliance with the ISP. While the justification for the employee's behaviour has been discussed, very few research papers have investigated whether the ISP writing style impacted the intent to comply with ISP. The research methodology incorporates content analysis and a quantitative descriptive review of published papers on ISP and non-IS policy compliance. The theoretical research allowed the identification of five major ISP writing styles: belonging, deterrence, goal, motivation, and specialist, as well as writing style influencers such as timeliness

Digital Transformation, Strategic Resilience, Cyber Security and Risk Management
Contemporary Studies in Economic and Financial Analysis, Volume 111A, 115–131

ISSN: 1569-3759/doi:10.1108/S1569-37592023000111A008

and readability. To achieve a higher level of compliance with the ISP, it was suggested that the writing styles of belonging, goal, and motivation be used primarily. Deterrence is generally discouraged. The study enabled us to determine when ISP writing styles were mentioned and the type of influence on the intent to comply with ISP. It also allowed for comparison and possible differences in ISPs versus standard workplace policies. There are proposals on which writing styles to put forward, along with recommendations on creating an ISP.

Keywords: Information security; information security policies; compliance; ISP writing style; employer's behaviour; ICT governance

INTRODUCTION

ISP informs users of the required behaviour and approaches to safeguard computer systems by keeping information confidential and available and assuring its integrity. Not unlike any other policies, compliance may vary due to many reasons. Unfortunately, as society and businesses become increasingly digitised, this lack of compliance often results in ever-growing negative impacts.

A body of studies often focusses on one reason and does not have an agnostic approach to ensure higher ISP compliance. This chapter will address the issue from a different angle. Daily messages tailored by marketing influence everyone's buying patterns or behaviour. Could a similar approach offer a path to higher ISP compliance?

Since the content must vary from one business to another, the focus shall be on the manner of writing the ISP message. The authors will call it the ISP writing style. The research will seek to identify relevant ISP writing styles. A second step will be to propose a method to use the compliance-friendly writing styles to write an ISP.

DEFINING ISP POLICIES WRITING STYLES

Total ISP policy compliance has eluded many sectors of life. Researching ISP compliance required expanding the research to compare and leverage knowledge created in older fields than ICT. Compliance relies on human nature, and it is a much older field of study. Using existing research on non-compliance provides insights into justifications.

Research such as Bauer, Bernroider, and Chudzikowski (2017) has demonstrated many reasons employees may ignore ISP requirements. Sykes and Matza (1957), in a study related to juvenile delinquency, identified five reasons for non-adherence to regulations or morals:

- denial of responsibility is when someone blames an external influence;
- denial of injury weighs the arm they perceived to be done by not complying;
- denial of the victim accepts harm was done but justifies that it may be a rightful punishment or retaliation where the perpetrator is therefore righteous;

- condemnation of the condemner rejects and judges those declaring an act unacceptable; and
- appeal to higher loyalties puts forward the sense of belonging to a group.

Belonging to a Writing Style

The latter of these neutralisation approaches refers to belonging to a group. According to Aristotle (Jowett, 1885), 'Humans are social animals'. People attach or remove themselves from groups because of culture. A simple example is the need for any business to push diversity and inclusion efforts. These often rely on policies and entail an inherent culture change within the workplace. Da Veiga and Martins (2017) raised the need to address culture and even sub-cultures when writing an ISP. Gaucher, Friesen, and Kay (2011) identified words gender or specific words as having an alienating effect on women. Hence, belonging is the first writing style to be identified.

Deterrence as a Writing Style

The second writing style, deterrence, focusses on preventing non-compliance. This highlighting consequences to individuals, known as deterrence, may appear as a simple solution. Research by Iglesias, Semeshenko, Schneider, and Gordon (2012) seems to support the value of deterrence by demonstrating how the average honesty of the population changes proportionally to crime prevention actions. However, opposing research mitigates the value of deterrence. Park, Ruighaver, Maynard, and Ahmad (2012) demonstrated that employees unaware of actual policy enforcement would, over time, dismiss the risks of non-compliance. Alsaif, Aljaafari, and Khan (2015) found that the lack of violation detection would also neutralise intent to follow the policy requirements.

Goal Writing Style

Alternatively, companies may embed goal-supporting messaging in their ISP. Unlike deterrence, this writing style promotes a communal benefit to the employees, colleagues, and the company. Businesses have largely embraced the idea of corporate social responsibility (CSR). The societal impacts of climate change, the corporate world's response to Russia's unprovoked attack on Ukraine, or the adaptation to a post-pandemic world have further cemented this need. Not only can it drive good behaviour or alienate employees with all the risks of non-compliance.

Motivation as a Writing Style

Motivation as a writing style will emphasise the business goals from an employee and community aspect. However, the greater good is not the driving force for each personal action. Rusu and Avasilcai (2014) defined work motivation as a set of internal and external factors which initiate work behaviour and determine its direction, intensity, and duration. One must consider what may influence an employee with their compliance intent. This writing style will be called motivation.

Specialist Writing Style

Since policies set workplace boundaries, references to regulations and norms are often required. Subject matter experts are usually called upon to write or validate the required information. Human resources, legal, or IT may often use domain-specific language or mentions guiding laws and norms. The typical wording and references lead to naming the specialist writing style.

Writing Styles Influencers: Readability and Timely

While the above definition covers the use of references, another approach centres on the readability of a document. The European Union (EU) and United States of America (USA) laws promote Plain Language and Easy-to-read writing (European Commission, 2011, 2021; US Congress, 2010). The goal is to ensure that the targeted audience understands the policy. The capacity of an employee to understand and thus comply with a policy will not be a writing style. It is an influencer called readability.

The next writing style influencer is timely. Earlier, the goal writing style used the company's targets to address employee compliance with the policies. Doherty and Fulford (2006), along with Box and Pottas (2014), concluded that goal misalignment was responsible for reduced ISP compliance. Similarly, 'specialist' refers to norms and regulations. Timely will refer to content adequacy when an employee reads the policy. For example, whether a stated law is no longer applicable.

Table 1 summarises the writing styles and influencers.

Table 1. Definition of Writing Styles and Influencers

Writing Style	Explanation
Belonging	The message includes employee and company culture(s) and language, for example, details on how the policy aligns with an individual's culture and personal situation. Use of inclusive language
Deterrence	The goal is to explain the issues and consequences and the ISP is meant to define the limits and barriers to an employee's behaviour, for example, constant details on punishment and other consequences to the individual employee
Goal	The message focusses on the company goals and how information security supports this, for example, an explanation of how policies align with and support company goals
Motivation	The message is positive, and the ISP is an enabler for the employee, for example, explanations of individual advantages in policy compliance
Specialist	Where an ISP is written with a language and concepts specialised for the writers or department domain, for example, use of jargon and emphasis on specific regulations
Influencer	**Explanation**
Timely	It will measure how employees may justify non-compliance to an ISP that does not refer to current goals or regulations and standards
Readability	It will measure the ease of reading for any speaker of the language

Source: Created by authors.

THE IMPACT OF WRITING STYLES ON COMPLIANCE INTENT

Research Methodology

Over the last few decades, many researchers studied the reasons for low ISP compliance. There is a much larger body of research addressing all types of policies. This study reviewed research articles that addressed compliance and intent to comply with ISPs and more policies applied to other domains.

The approach was to identify the writing styles and influencers exposed in the research articles. The research consisted of reviewing research articles on Science Direct from 2019 to 2021. Eighty articles were deemed relevant from more than 600 pre-selected. According to the authors, the second step was to record if these had a positive, negative, or mitigating influence.

Overall Results

When looking at overall mentions of the writing styles, the goal was to identify the most studied aspects and compare them between ISPs and regular policies (Figs. 1 and 2).

None of the articles reviewed referred to the seven ISP writing styles aspects studied. The average mentioned two with a median of one. The publication with the highest mention (five) was one of the few to investigate writing approaches (Rostami, Karlsson, & Gao, 2020).

There were some changes in the order they were mentioned. The non-IS research focusses more on belonging, motivational, and goal. On the other hand, IS-related studies keep belonging first. But deterrence, goals, and motivation

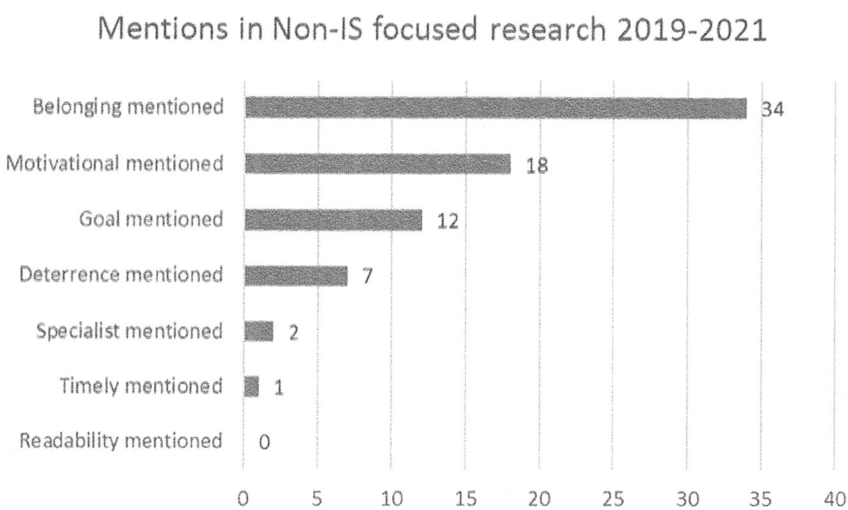

Fig. 1. Mentions of Writing Styles and Influencers in Non-IS-focussed Research. *Source*: Authors' research.

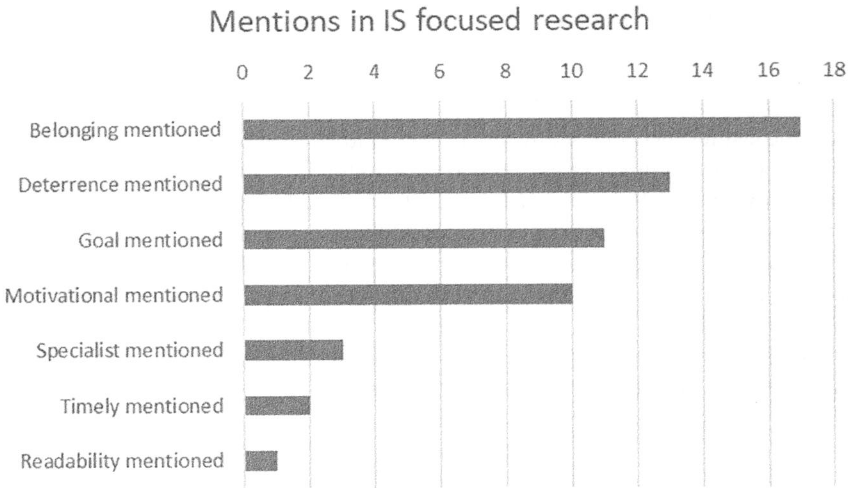

Fig. 2. Mentions of Writing Styles and Influencers in IS-focussed Research. *Source*: Authors' research.

follow. Further research could confirm the reason. It could be due ISPs being a less mature type of policies than generic ones. Or societal pressure to embrace CSR and employee satisfaction is higher with generic policies. ISPs may be looking to be more about consequences to an individual or a business due to their impact. The increase in cybercrime monetisation and regulation adds to the need to protect businesses.

Research lack of mention of readability in non-IS-focussed articles. In IS-focussed investigations, there was only one. Considering new regulatory environments are calling for the use of 'Plain Language', such as Article 12 of the General Data Protection Regulation, with three mentions in Articles 7, 12, and 34 (European Union, 2016).

Perception of Belonging

Being part of an entity causing more relevancy and leading to higher compliance seems simple enough. The study confirmed this writing style to be the most mentioned.

In practice, non-IS-focussed research identifies it as a positive element. IS-focussed articles were slightly less supportive but well within a change due to the low numbers considered (Figs. 3 and 4).

Reasons that support this vary from the importance of CSR (Wang, Hu, & Zhang, 2020) to the benefits of diversity agents (De Silva, Gokhberg, Meissner, & Russo, 2021). Xu and Warkentin (2020) go as far as naming a herd effect.

Another influence of this writing style lies in its capacity to enhance the sense of Belonging. For example, Brink, Eller, and Gao (2021) showed a gender-inclusive

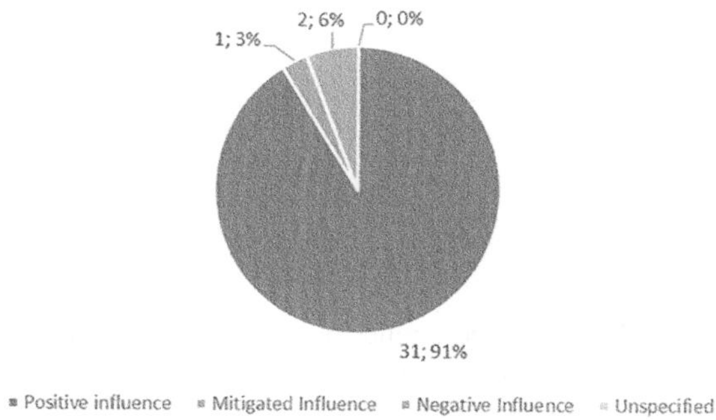

Fig. 3. Influence of Belonging in Non-IS-focussed Research.
Source: Authors' research.

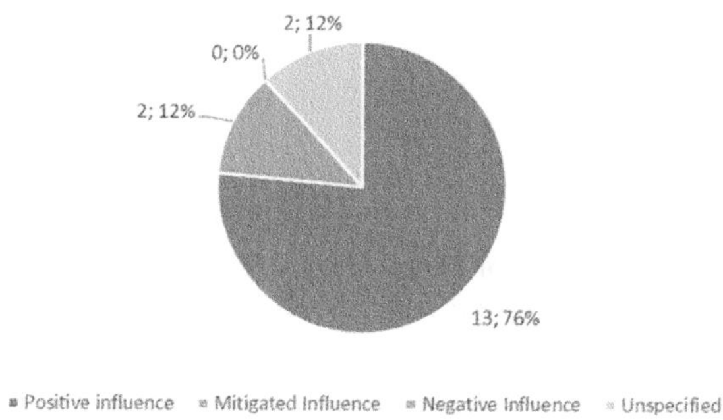

Fig. 4. Influence of Belonging in IS-focussed Research.
Source: Authors' research.

increase in compliance intent. De Silva et al. (2021) also stated the value of co-creation when an employee is involved in the policy design.

Fochmann, Fochmann, Kocher, and Müller (2021) have pointed to the risk of an individual wrongly influencing another individual who would usually comply with tax policies. Karjalainen, Siponen, and Sarker (2020) highlighted the dynamics of individual and cultural characteristics. Changes over time may change and possibly mitigate the intent to comply.

Perception of Deterrence

A clear difference appeared between IS and non-IS articles' use of deterrence. Publications have a more mitigated view of deterrence, but those about non-IS research mention it less (Figs. 5 and 6).

Data are lacking, but the increased incident rate may have pushed forward the need for deterrence in the ISP.

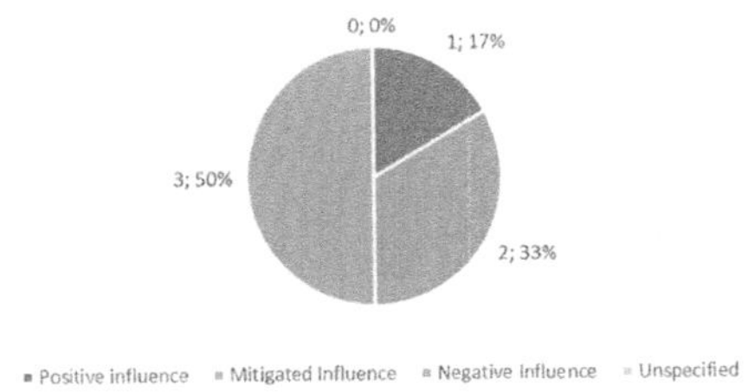

Fig. 5. Influence of Deterrence in Non-IS-focussed Research.
Source: Authors' research.

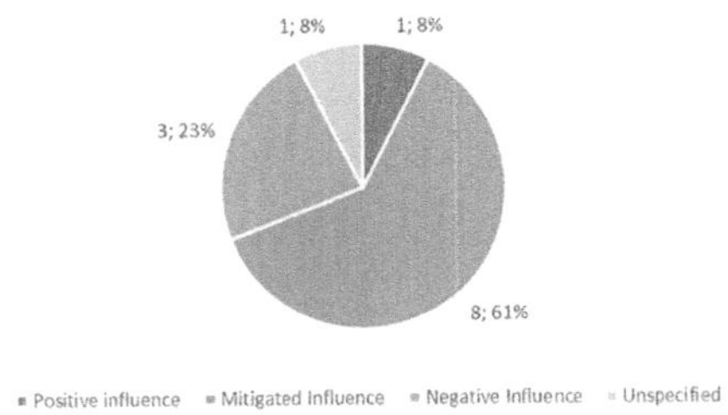

Fig. 6. Influence of Deterrence in IS-focussed Research.
Source: Authors' research.

Regardless of the above, the finding is that Deterrence has a mitigated impact on compliance. Rajab and Eydaghi (2019) wrote:

> Consistent with the prior research, severe sanctions, close management supervision, peer pressure, and attitudes towards information security do not matter as much as perceived vulnerability and response efficacy in ensuring higher levels of intentions to comply with ISPs in organizations.

Nowadays, companies have several justifications for not publicising a failure to comply. Vault (2015) published a survey named: 'Ethics, Security and getting the job done'. Employees revealed that 20 per cent had worked at a place that had hidden a data breach.

At this point, anecdotal information seemed to indicate cultural differences. Some studies promoted a clearer tendency to support punishment and deterrence. The legal possibility of naming incident culprits, or lack thereof, changes the impact and use of deterrence.

Perception of Goal

Workplace policies aim to support the business. Hence, the Goal writing style is always expected. The chapter reviews did not show regular use of this approach.

Over the past three years, non-IS-focussed research referring to company goals in policies has increased. However, the IS-focussed studies remained steady (Figs. 7 and 8).

Guo, Yuan, Archer, and Connelly (2011) came to support a goal approach through their research on non-malicious security violations stated: This study makes several significant contributions to research on security-related behaviour by (first) highlighting the importance of job performance goals and security risk perceptions on shaping user attitudes. Results from this study confirmed the prediction. Each article in both focus groups concluded the goal writing style's positive influence.

Current events highlight the importance of CSR when employee compliance is in play.

Perception of Motivation

Historically management approaches have evolved from a position of strength relationship towards a motivational one.

Research on policies had more non-IS-focussed ones referring to this writing style. In the former case, the interest increased (Figs. 9 and 10).

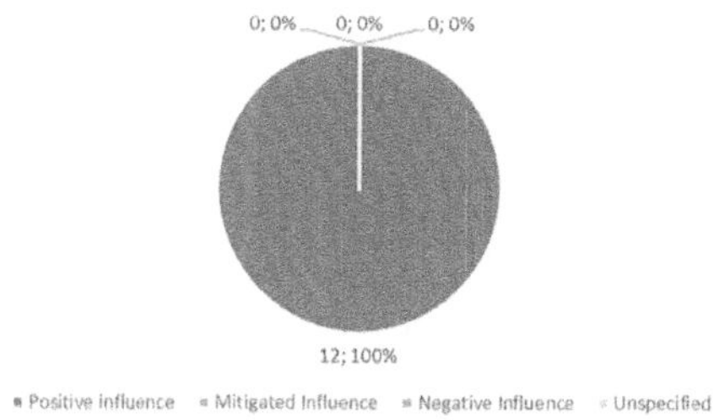

Fig. 7. Influence of Goal in Non-IS-focussed research.
Source: Authors' research.

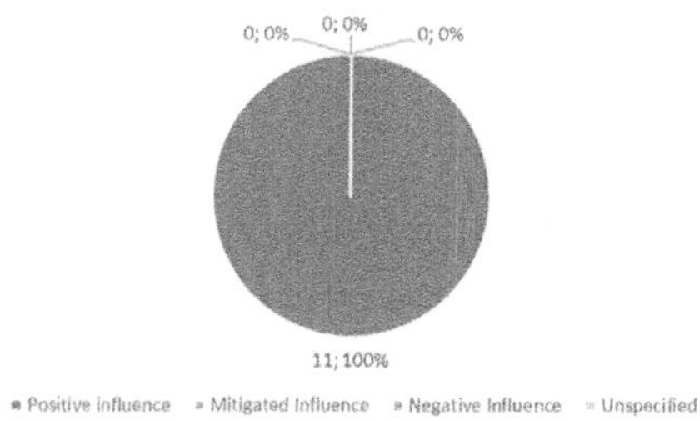

Fig. 8. Influence of Goal in IS-focussed Research.
Source: Authors' research.

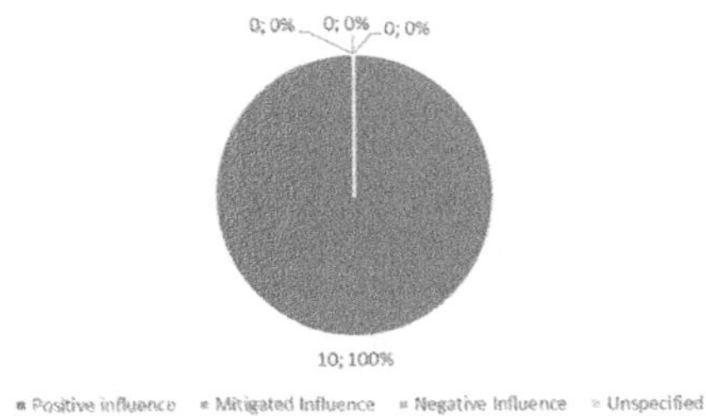

Fig. 9. Influence of Motivation in Non-IS-focussed Research.
Source: Authors' research.

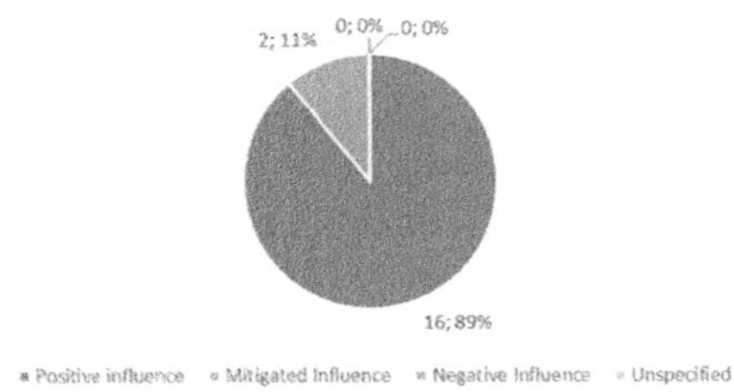

Fig. 10. Influence of Motivation in IS-focussed Research.
Source: Authors' research.

In both focus areas, using the motivation style resulted in a positive impact. Adiguel, Özçınar, and Karadal (2020) studied 'Servant managers' and found that Management with a human side that supports the employees' motivation will eliminate employees' rule-breaking behaviour and positively affect their job satisfaction.

However, some articles pointed to a possible level of neutralisation when the motivation conflicts with business goals. In the case of Health Management Systems in India, Meghani et al. (2021) identified that high-performance pressure coupled with a rigid organisational structure reduced or even negated the local manager's intent to comply. Punitive actions (deterrence) on low-performing managers worsened the situation. There is, therefore, a need to address the motivation and deterrence styles jointly.

Perception of Specialist

A negative impact was expected based on personal and anecdotal data reported by professional contacts. Examples ranged from employees not knowledgeable about regulations mentioned to authors having to rewrite a complete ISP because no one could understand it.

Specialist writing was less mentioned than expected in both the IS and non-IS-focussed research (Figs. 11 and 12).

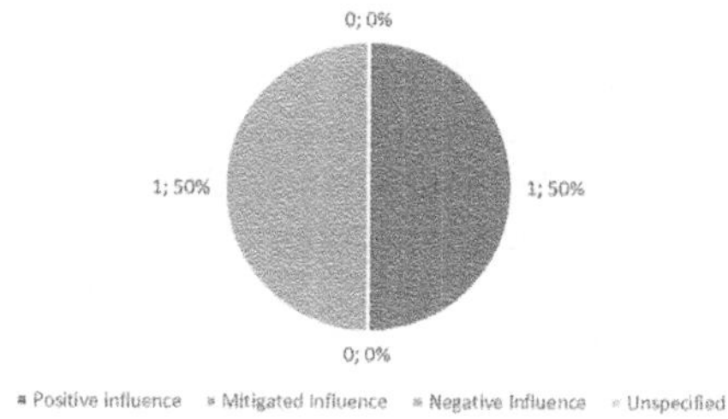

Fig. 11. Influence of Specialists in Non-IS-focussed Research.

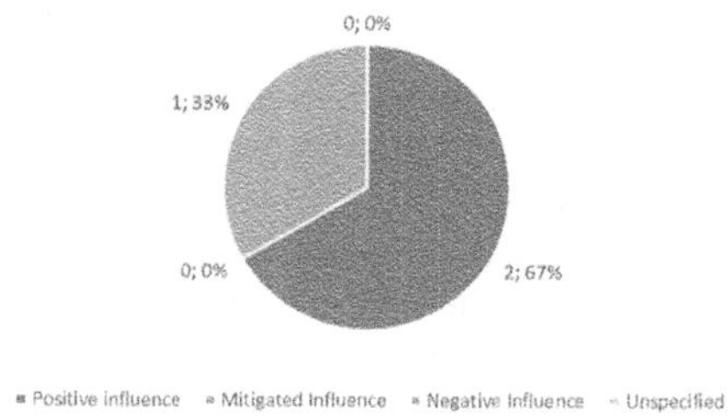

Fig. 12. Influence of Specialist in IS-focussed Research.
Source: Authors' research.

The low number of mentions makes any conclusion on the influence less reliable. Nonetheless, the impact appears mitigated.

The article related to non-IS policies proposed a negative impact. Information security-focussed research identified two documents with a positive view of the Specialist approach. The other document offered an opposite vision of it. Meghani et al. (2021) reported that employees with inadequate computer literacy had difficulties understanding and applying ISPs.

Materials supporting the specialist's writing style rely on the benefit of explaining to employees the regulatory or normative framework limiting the workplace.

Perception of Writing Style Influencer Timely

Many workplace policies worldwide were suddenly obsolete as the COVID-19 pandemic forced employees to work from home. Businesses often had policies that prevented this form of labour. It is an example of the importance of policies to remain relevant in time.

Mentions of timely were so few that it is not easy to conclude their impact. The three references to this *writing style influencer Timely* pointed to a positive effect.

In their research on computerised tools to design ISPs, Rostami et al. (2020) concluded the need to keep the ISP up-to-date. Their findings mentioned the need to keep up-to-date and have ISP reviews with specified updated procedures and mechanisms. The report named: State of Cybersecurity: 2021 by Accenture (2021) identified that top cyber-resilient business had a strong alignment between IS and Business. Tang, Yang, Ye, and Khan (2021) go further in their research. They identified how time references in a policy could lead to better adaptation to innovation.

ISPs must be timely for the business environment. Between the evolving business goals and the risks faced, the ISP content must be kept relevant to limit neutralisation.

Perception of Writing Style Influencer Readability

Countries worldwide are promoting the use of simplified Language in official documents. The EU published a guideline for its documentation and websites (European Commission, 2011). The US government made plain Language a requirement for public-facing documents – Public Law 111-274 – Plain Writing Act of 2010 (US Congress, 2010). The Irish government issued a Plain Language Bill in 2019 (Oireachtas, 2019).

Despite all this public focus on documents and policies having a language comprehension level adapted to the intended audience, the research did not match expectations. The only article found was focussed on ISPs. Rostami et al. (2020) evaluated the requirements to automate ISP creation in this study. In their analysis, the language and writing style is mentioned multiple times as the need for:

- clear communicative objectives;
- clear structure and navigation;
- clearly defined concepts;
- visual appearance; and
- easy to read.

The question is whether the lack of research in the domain is a general oversight or whether the subject is deemed irrelevant. The opinion expressed here is that Readability is critical to policy comprehension and, thus, adoption.

SUGGESTED APPROACHES TO INCREASE COMPLIANCE

Based on the above information, the key will be to leverage employee motivation over any repressive approach. It is also clear that there is no one-size-fits-all solution. Co-creation is crucial to the approach, but smaller entities may not have the overhead capacity to implement it.

Small businesses may be able to reuse some templates that would need to be created. For other companies with restricted resources updating ISPs may be too much to expect. But an up-to-date ISP can help reinforce positive internal messaging. Inclusive Language in policies communicates a more pervasive culture of equality.

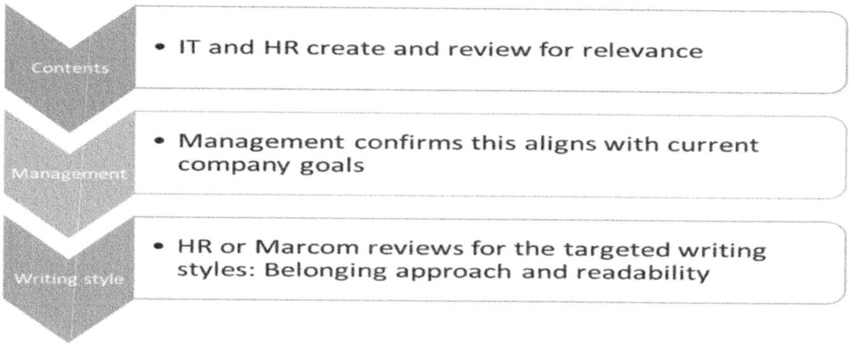

Fig. 13. Minimal Recommended Approach to Creating an ISP.
Source: Authors' research.

Minimal Approach

The research identified belonging, deterrence, and goals as the low-hanging fruits.

The recommendation is to create a small group involving IT, Security, and HR to create a draft ISP. The Management should review the ISP. HR and someone in charge of the company brand or culture will validate and tune the final version. Fig. 13 displays the intended process.

Belonging will be the most relevant writing style in this scenario. Smaller entities are more likely to rely on a family-like culture. An example would be: 'By locking unused workstations, we can protect our company from data theft and the impact on all of us'.

The second aspect is deterrence. Research showed its impact to be mitigated mainly because of the lack of visible implementation. The tonality of deterrence and the chances for miscommunications surrounding its implementation could lead to resentment and neutralisation.

A goal-based ISP writing style will further help justify the security requirements by aligning them with business-supporting aims.

Although not supported by the research, readability remains critical to help the audience understand the ISP. For example, in the case of an educational entity, this would include the workforce, third parties, and students.

Median Approach

This method will apply to larger entities from around one hundred to a few hundred employees. These entities typically have a more defined organisation that can allot more resources to ISP. They are more likely to fall under a higher expectation for proper policy documentation through compliance requirements like ISO 27001 (ISO, 2013).

Here, the focus will remain on using the belonging, goals, and deterrence writing styles. It is also required to consider the timely and readability influencers. Fig. 14 shows the suggested process.

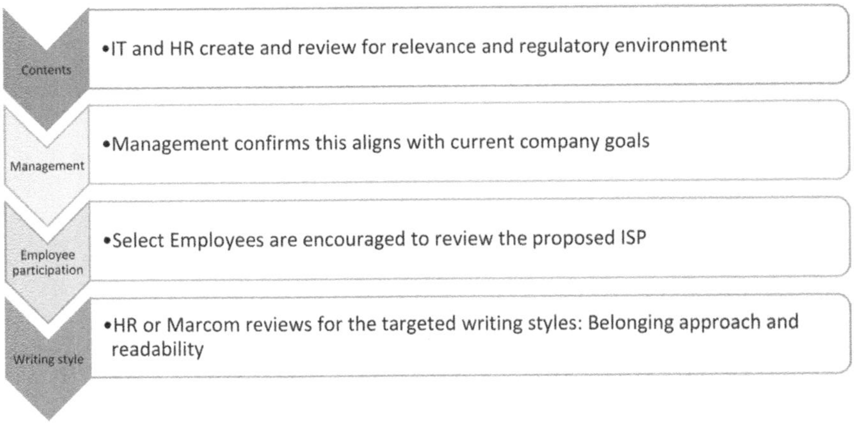

Fig. 14. Median Recommended Approach to Creating an ISP.
Source: Authors' research.

The aim will be to use a positive approach. This approach will leverage further the co-creation method.

In this scenario, an ISP review process will be created and tracked. The Security and HR groups will initiate the document while consulting the IT group. Management will review the document before submitting it to a sample of non-IT employees for review.

Mature Approach

In most maturity models, the key element to reaching the highest levels is the capacity of a business to have all processes documented, repeatable, and applied at all levels of the business. This capacity to be consistent can be borne by documentation but also by automation. Rostami et al. (2020) created a recommendation for the automation of ISP design. While this is tempting, the value of co-creation and adaptation to current times cannot be ignored or replaced by some form of BOT process.

A mature approach would be to have a definition of words and wording a company wants to use to support its view of required writing styles. For example, some companies will refer to: 'employees' as 'associates' both in titles and across the internal documentation. The consistent use of specific language elements and their repetition helps reinforce the message's intent.

The partial automation of the messaging combined with the approved language element will also benefit any business employing multiple languages.

Co-creation will then be vital to validate the language elements. It will also confirm the writing styles. Surveying a few employees on influential writing styles is recommended. Ideally, regular employees participating in the effort shall be diverse and include people identified as having been non-compliant.

The later focus on a writing style is assumed to make it more influential to the outcome. However, readability will remain the last step to consider.

As stated earlier, this method applies to large and more mature companies with adequate resources.

CONCLUSIONS

The research confirmed a possible writing style influence on ISP compliance. The aim is to help define a new ISP writing process that should lead to higher compliance intent. The study identified the following writing styles: belonging, deterrence, goal-setting, motivation, and specialty. Another two influences are timing and readability. This literature review concluded that ISPs must use a multidimensional approach to increase compliance. It means using a 'shared creation' approach where no single group within a business can oversee the ISP's writing. In lieu of this, an article review studied the focus on these writing styles and the expected impact of this approach. As a result, certain writing styles are regarded as influential in policy compliance and for ISPs.

Company dynamics are critical to writing an ISP, but the key to a higher intent to comply will depend on using the gelonging and goal writing styles. Timeliness and readability showed poorly in the research, yet, according to the experts, both are critical to the ISP's usability, even if their definitions may depend on the usage. In conclusion, the authors think the research pointed to the aspects of ISP creation. Ahlan, Lubis, and Lubis (2015) validate the main idea when they state: 'The intention of having security policy was not to persuade users but to convince them, by letting the users reflect on their terms, on why information security is important'.

However, there is a need to validate the research through a study of ISPs and a survey of the employees' intent to comply and perception of the ISP. Then expanding the research by working alongside companies to create new ISPs and measuring their impact on employees. Finally, an expert's suggestion to reduce the size of the ISP by using controls without explaining them in the ISP could be beneficial. It would not only make an ISP shorter, but it would also make its contents easier to understand. If needed, the control can display an explanation.

FUTURE RESEARCH

Future research can include an element of experimentation, which is missing in this chapter. Second, the nature of compliance will vary over time. There seems to be little to no research tracking how compliance evolves through a career as people get exposed to multiple exposures to different ISPs (job change, participation in another activity with its ISP, others). One study by McLeod and Dolezel (2020) studied the capitulation theory and demonstrated that a portion of employees would give up on following an ISP because nothing could change the outcome. They measured how employees who suffered a privacy breach were likely to lose faith in their impact and thus lose their intent to comply. When it comes to future opportunities, the proposal of an automated framework pushed by Rostami et al. (2020) seems very useful. Yet, this may need to combine with the elements of this research. Finally, as demonstrated by Ki-Aries and Faily (2017), the implementation of persona-centric security awareness was positive but could be time-consuming, at least at first. The bigger question is how to scale up or down this research recommendation for the entities considered.

REFERENCES

Accenture. (2021). *State of cybersecurity resilience 2021*. Accenture. Retrieved from https://www.accenture.com/_acnmedia/PDF-165/Accenture-State-Of-Cybersecurity-2021.pdf

Adiguel, Z., Özçınar, M. F., & Karadal, H. (2020). Does servant leadership moderate the link between strategic human resource management on rule breaking and job satisfaction? *European Research on Management and Business Economics*, *26*(2), 103–110. https://doi.org/10.1016/j.iedeen.2020.04.002

Ahlan, A. R., Lubis. M., & Lubis. A. R. (2015). Information security awareness at the knowledge-based institution: Its antecedents and measures. *Procedia Computer Science*, *72*, 361–373. http://dx.doi.org/10.1016/j.procs.2015.12.151

Alsaif, M., Aljaafari, N., & Khan, A. (2015). Information security management in Saudi Arabian organizations. *Procedia Computer Science*, *56*, 213–216. http://dx.doi.org/10.1016/j.procs.2015.07.201

Bauer, S., Bernroider, E. W. N., & Chudzikowski, K. (2017). Prevention is better than cure! Designing information security awareness programs to overcome users' non-compliance with information security policies in banks. *Computers and Security*, *68*, 145–159. http://dx.doi.org/10.1016/j.cose.2017.04.009

Box, D., & Pottas, D. (2014). A model for information security compliant behaviour in the healthcare context. *Procedia Technology*, *16*, 1462–1470. http://dx.doi.org/10.1016/j.protcy.2014.10.166

Brink, A.G., Eller, C. K., & Gao, L. (2021). He wouldn't, but I would: The effects of pronoun-induced language vividness in whistleblowing policies. *Advances in Accounting*, *54*, 100545. https://doi.org/10.1016/j.adiac.2021.100545

Da Veiga, A., & Martins, N. (2017). Defining and identifying dominant information security cultures and subcultures. *Computers and Security*, *70*, 72–94. http://dx.doi.org/10.1016/j.cose.2017.05.002

De Silva, M., Gokhberg, L., Meissner, D., & Russo, M. (2021). Addressing societal challenges through the simultaneous generation of social and business values: A conceptual framework for science-based co-creation. *Technovation*, *104*, 102268. https://doi.org/10.1016/j.technovation.2021.102268

Doherty, N. F., & Fulford, H. (2006). Aligning the information security policy with the strategic information systems plan. *Computers and Security*, *25*(1), 55–63. https://doi.org/10.1016/j.cose.2005.09.009

European Commission. (2011). *Directorate-General for Translation, How to write clearly*. Publications Office. https://data.europa.eu/doi/10.2782/29211

European Commission. (2021). Easy to read summaries of scientific opinions. Retrieved from https://ec.europa.eu/health/scientific_committees/policy/opinions_plain_language_en

European Union. (2016). General data protection regulation. Retrieved from https://eur-lex.europa.eu/legal-content/EN/TXT/?uri=CELEX%3A02016R0679-20160504&qid=1532348683434

Fochmann, M., Fochmann, N., Kocher, M. G., & Müller, N. (2021). Dishonesty and risk-taking: Compliance decisions of individuals and groups. *Journal of Economic Behavior & Organization*, *185*, 250–286. https://doi.org/10.1016/j.jebo.2021.02.018

Gaucher, D., Friesen, J., & Kay, A. C. (2011). Evidence that gendered wording in job advertisements exists and sustains gender inequality. *Journal of Personality and Social Psychology*, *101*(1), 109–128. https://doi.org/10.1037/a0022530

Guo, K. H., Yuan, Y., Archer, N. P., & Connelly, C. E. (2011). Understanding non-malicious security violations in the workplace: A composite behaviour model. *Journal of Management Information Systems*, *28*(2), 203–236. https://doi.org/10.2753/MIS0742-1222280208

Iglesias, J. R., Semeshenko, V., Schneider, E. M., & Gordon, M. B. (2012). Crime and punishment: Does it pay to punish? *Physica A: Statistical Mechanics and Its Applications*, *391*(15), 3942–3950. http://dx.doi.org/10.1016/j.physa.2012.03.001

ISO. (2013). ISO/IEC 27001:2013 Information technology – security techniques – information security management systems – requirements. Retrieved from https://www.iso.org/standard/54534.html

Jowett, B. (1885). *The politics of Aristotle*. Oxford: Clarendon Press. Retrieved from https://books.google.lv/books?hl=en&lr=&id=lsAUAAAAQAAJ&oi=fnd&pg=PP2&dq=politics+aristotle

Karjalainen, M., Siponen, M., & Sarker, S. (2020). Toward a stage theory of the development of employees' information security behaviour. *Computers and Security*, *93*, 101782. https://doi.org/10.1016/j.cose.2020.101782

Ki-Aries, D., & Faily, S. (2017). Persona-centred information security awareness. *Computers and Security*, *70*, 663–674. https://doi.org/10.1016/j.cose.2017.08.001

McLeod, A., & Dolezel, D. (2020). *Toward security capitulation theory*. Association for Information Systems. Retrieved from https://aisel.aisnet.org/amcis2020/info_security_privacy/info_security_privacy/2/

Meghani, A., Rodriguez, D. C., Bilal, H., Tripathi, A. B., Namasivayam, V., Prakash, R., Peters, D. H., & Bennett, S. (2021). Examining policy intentions and actual implementation practices: How organizational factors influence health management information systems in Uttar Pradesh, India. *Social Science & Medicine*, *286*, 114291. https://doi.org/10.1016/j.socscimed.2021.114291

Oireachtas | Irish Government. (2019). Plain Language Bill 2019 (planned – not enacted). Retrieved from https://data.oireachtas.ie/ie/oireachtas/bill/2019/7/eng/initiated/b0719d.pdf

Park, S., Ruighaver, A. B., Maynard, S. B., & Ahmad, A. (2012). Towards understanding deterrence: Information security managers' perspective. *Lecture Notes in Electrical Engineering*, 120. https://doi.org/10.13140/2.1.2522.3049

Rajab, M., & Eydaghi, A. (2019). Evaluating the explanatory power of theoretical frameworks on intention to comply with information security policies in higher education. *Computers & Security*, *80*, 211–223. https://doi.org/10.1016/j.cose.2018.09.016

Rostami, E., Karlsson, F., & Gao, S. (2020). Requirements for computerized tools to design information security policies. *Computers & Security*, *99*, 102063. https://doi.org/10.1016/j.cose.2020.102063

Rusu, G., & Avasilcai, S. (2014). Linking human resources motivation to organizational climate. *Procedia – Social and Behavioral Sciences*, *124*, 51–58 http://dx.doi.org/10.1016/j.sbspro.2014.02.459

Sykes, G. M., & Matza, D. (1957). Techniques of neutralization: A theory of delinquency. *American Sociological Review*, *22*(6), 664–670. https://doi.org/10.2307/2089195

Tang, J., Yang, J., Ye, W., & Khan, S. A. (2021). Now is the time: The effects of linguistic time reference and national time orientation on innovative new ventures. *Journal of Business Venturing*, *36*(5), 106142. https://doi.org/10.1016/j.jbusvent.2021.106142

US Congress. (2010). Plain writing Act of 2010, Public law 111-274. Retrieved from https://www.govinfo.gov/app/details/PLAW-111publ274

Vault, A. (2015). Ethics, security and getting the job done. Retrieved from https://cdn-cybersecurity.att.com/docs/whitepapers/rsa-survey-report.pdf

Wang, C., Hu, R., & Zhang, T. (2020). Corporate social responsibility in international hotel chains and its effects on local employees: Scale development and empirical testing in China. *International Journal of Hospitality Management*, *90*, 102598. https://doi.org/10.1016/j.ijhm.2020.102598

Xu, M., & Warkentin, M. (2020). Integrating elaboration likelihood model and herd theory in information security message persuasiveness. *Computers & Security*, *98*, 102009. https://doi.org/10.1016/j.cose.2020.102009

CHAPTER 9

THEORETICAL ESSENCE OF ORGANISATIONAL RESILIENCE IN MANAGEMENT

Eleftherios Thalassinos[a,b], Marta Kadłubek[c] and Diego Norena-Chavez[d]

[a] *University of Piraeus, Greece*
[b] *University of Malta, Malta*
[c] *Czestochowa University of Technology, Poland*
[d] *Escuela de Posgrado, Universidad de Lima, Peru*

ABSTRACT

The purpose of the chapter is to identify the fundamental characteristics of organisational resilience in management science with particular emphasis on selected approaches to the concept of resilience and organisational resilience in management, development of the definition of organisational resilience, comparison of the definitions of the concept of organisational resilience according to the adopted features, location of the defined features of organisational resilience in the planning perspective of the organisation and application of the concept of resilience to entrepreneurs, enterprises, and their strategies. Understanding resilience differs between disciplines and research contexts. In the management theory, the perception of resilience and organisational resilience is broadly diversified, which implies a niche for discussing their crucial pivot, which will be addressed in this chapter. A systematic literature review was conducted as well as a critical analysis of literature sources, as a result of which relevant significant foundation of organisational resilience area within the theory of management was determined. Analysed directions significantly

Digital Transformation, Strategic Resilience, Cyber Security and Risk Management
Contemporary Studies in Economic and Financial Analysis, Volume 111A, 133–145

Published under exclusive licence by Emerald Publishing Limited
ISSN: 1569-3759/doi:10.1108/S1569-37592023000111A009

indicate the importance of organisational resilience in management, enriching its heritage in accordance with current scientific discoveries. Entrepreneurs can use the selection of the theoretical foundation of organisational resilience as an indication of the management areas that may be developed to search for organisational excellence.

Keywords: Resilience; organisational resilience; management; enterprise; strategy; development

1. INTRODUCTION

Resilience is a concept widely applied in many scientific disciplines including physical sciences, ecology, psychology, economics, technical sciences, and social sciences. The development and understanding of resilience differ not only between disciplines but also between research contexts. Even in social sciences, research trends differ in areas such as strategic management, supply chain management, crisis management, and organisational psychology (Bratnicki, 2000; Martinelli, Tagliazucchi, & Marchi, 2018; Rokita, 2007; Sienkiewicz-Małyjurek, 2015; Skowron-Grabowska, 2021; Thalassinos & Thalassinos, 2019; Witkowski, 2010).

It is one of the newer concepts developing the adaptivity of organisational trend, which has entered the canon of organisational excellence assessments due to the development of the systemic approach in management and the related theory of organisational balance as well as the development of strategic management theory. Researchers dealing with this topic use the scientific achievements of psychology as well as logistics and management.

In its most fundamental sense, resilience refers to the ability of individuals, organisations, or systems to cope with and absorb threats, develop, and adapt to an environment of constant change (Gajendran & Oloruntoba, 2017; Gallopin, 2006; Linnenluecke & McKnight, 2017; Vlasov, Bonnedahl, & Vincze, 2018). It is an ability that allows one to maintain a chosen goal, continue functioning, and even develop under unfavourable operating conditions (Grima, Kizilkaya, Sood, & ErdemDelice, 2021).

Contemporaneously organisational resilience is identified with the organisation's ability to absorb or minimise the negative impact of crisis situations and to continue to act after the crisis (Romanowska, 2020). The concept of a self-oriented organisation, about behaviours particularly useful in a crisis situation, is also recognised, among others, by Rzegocki and Grucza (2015), Piorkowska (2015), as an adaptation of an organisation to unfavourable conditions in a crisis situation, that is, in the context of resistance (Yerpudee, Sood, & Grima, 2022). The term 'resilience' in relation to the behaviour of the system towards disorders and changes is meant to maintain the state of functioning and regain functionality as well as the ability to absorb shock, according to Czerniawska, Błażewicz, Pacuska, and Pańków (2015). The term 'resilience' in relation to supply chains was used by Christopher and Peck (2004) and Świerczek (2020), assuming that a resilient supply chain is characterised by operational continuity related to the ability to deal with uncertainty (Jajuga, 2015; Noja, Thalassinos, Cristea, & Grecu, 2021), having the ability to achieve a new state that is a consequence of the occurrence of disturbances.

2. METHODOLOGY

The purpose of the chapter is to identify the fundamental characteristics of organisational resilience in management science with particular emphasis on selected approaches to the concept of resilience and organisational resilience in management, development of the definition of organisational resilience, comparison of the definitions of the concept of organisational resilience according to the adopted features, location of the defined features of organisational resilience in the planning perspective of the organisation, and application of the concept of resilience to entrepreneurs, enterprises, and their strategies. A systematic literature review was conducted as well as critical analysis of literature sources as a result of which relevant significant foundation of organisational resilience area within theory of management was determined.

3. RESULTS

The other, selected approaches to the concept of organisational resilience are presented in Table 1.

On the other hand, more summary concepts of the scope of the term organisational resilience proposed by international organisations are presented in Table 2.

Table 3 presents the development of the term resilience along with related concepts since 1973 that have had a strong impact on the perception and definition of organisational resilience.

The term organisational resilience was first defined by Holling (1973) concerning to two aspects: (a) the organisation's ability to return to a state of equilibrium, which was defined by the term Engineering Resilience and (b) the volume of the disturbance that the system can absorb before destruction, which he called Ecologic Resilience.

Staw, Sandelands, and Dutton (1981) presented a concept explaining the impact of unexpected changes and disruptions on risk management by individual individuals, groups, and organisations. In 1982, Meyer extended the above concept by illustrating it with examples of hospitals that have to function in the face of unexpected strikes by doctors. However, he rejected Staw's thesis that external threats automatically resulted in an increased risk for the functioning of the enterprise (Meyer, 1982).

Work on organisational resilience in the 1980s focussed mainly on internal disruptions and risks related to the reliability of advanced technologies (Linnenluecke & McKnight, 2017). The shift of interest to external disruptions and the search for solutions within the organisation was strengthened by subsequent events having a significant impact on the functioning of the organisation. The following years strengthened the interest in the areas of risk management, crisis management, rescue planning, and business continuity management (Smith & Elliott, 2006).

Table 1. Characteristics of the Concept of Organisational Resilience.

No.	Author (Year of Publication)	Definition of Organisational Resilience
1	Wildavsky (1988)	Resilience is an organisation's dynamic adaptability that grows and develops over time
2	Sitkin (1992)	Organisational resilience is defined as an organisation's ability to draw conclusions and learn lessons from a disruption
3	Weick (1993)	Organisational resilience is defined by identifying four related factors: improvisation, the role of virtual systems, the absorption and management of knowledge, and the corresponding dependencies
4	Horne and Orr (1998)	Organisational resilience is a fundamental quality feature of an organisation based on the organisation's ability to respond to significant changes that disrupt the pattern of the events' conduct without introducing regressive behaviour that lasts in the organisation for a long time
5	Weick and Sutcliffe (2001)	Organisational resilience is defined as the ability to return to a state of equilibrium
6	Coutu (2002)	The organisation's resilience to staunch opposition to reality, learn lessons and values from temporary distress and implement solutions aimed at ensuring a return to a state of equilibrium through improvisation in the face of new conditions of functioning
7	Sutcliffe and Vogus (2003)	Organisational resilience is the positive ability of an individual to respond and adapt to disturbances adapting to the consequences of catastrophic errors such as lack of access to electricity, fire or bomb threats. As part of the definition, the authors define 14 factors that measure the resilience of an organisation. These are leadership in a crisis, supporting decisions in a crisis, personnel involvement in resilience strategies, awareness of the organisation's situation, delegating decision-making in a crisis, innovation and creativity, effective partnership in a crisis, aligning critical knowledge resources, minimising silos, internal resource crisis management, unity, proactive crisis strategies, crisis and business continuity strategy, and crisis resilience testing regime
8	Fiksel (2003)	Resilience is an organisation's ability to survive, adapt, and grow in the face of turbulent changes.
9	Burnard and Bhamra (2011)	Organisational resilience is most often defined as an organisation's ability to recover after a period of disruption
10	British Standard Institution (2014)	Organisational resilience is defined as the organisation's ability to anticipate, prepare, and adapt to emerging changes and disruptions to survive and continue development
11	Bhamra (2015)	Organisational resilience should not be viewed solely as an organisation's ability to recover from pre-disruption. Organisational resilience is an overarching concept that not only allows enterprises to continue their business but also to grow, learn, and progress regardless of the environment
12	International Organisation for Standardisation (2017)	The resilience of an organisation is understood as the organisation's ability to absorb and adapt to a changing environment

Source: Authors' creation.

Table 2. A Summary Frame of the Term Range of Organisational Resilience by International Organisations.

Organisation	The Scope of the Term of Organisational Resilience	Remarks
	The universal nature of the term organisational resilience	
Resilience Alliance (2019)	The ability of the system to absorb disturbances and reorganise	The universalism of the definition and its multifunctionality
	Perspectives of the catastrophic risk management	
United Nations International Strategy for Disaster Reduction (UNISDR, 2009)	The ability of the system/community exposed to threats to resist them, absorb the effects of the above-mentioned threats, and adapt to them. Category of resilience also includes the ability to return to the original functions and structures of the system in a timely manner	Possibility of use of this definition in systems risk management in systems socio-ecological
	Highlighting the role of reorganisation/reform	
Intergovernmental Panel on Climate Change (IPCC, 2012)	The ability of a social or ecological system to absorb disturbances while maintaining the same basic structure and modes of operation. The ability of the system to self-organise and the ability to adapt to stress and change	Highlighting the association of the resilience to the shocks of climate changes
World Bank (2012)	The ability of the community to endure crisis, sanitation, and reorganisation to all its members could sustain development	High usability definition to measure domestic resilience
	Sectoral approach	
International Food Policy Research Institute (IFPRI, 2014)	Community ability to resist stressors, for example, environmental changes or social, economic, or political shocks	The distinctness of the definition immunity for systems social and ecological
World Economic Forum (2013)	(1) Ability to adapt to changing contexts, (2) the ability to withstand sudden shocks, and (3) the ability to recover balance (old or new) while maintaining continuity	Perspectives of resilience analysis of state immunity or organisation transnational (e.g. EU)

Source: Authors' creation.

When attempting to identify features that connect different interpretations of the concept of organisational resilience, three features can be distinguished to which the definitions contained in the analysed literature refer: (a) Feature 1 – organisational resilience focusses on capturing the strength of the organisation before the disruption; relates to the predictive ability of an organisation to deal consciously with possible disruptions. It should be noted that disruptions

Table 3. Development of the Definition of Organisational Resilience and Related Risk Management Terms.

1973	Holling first defines the concept of resilience later transferred in relation to organization (Holling, 1973).
1981	Staw et al. publish on risk management, explaining the relationship between disruptions and the functioning of groups and organizations (Staw et al., 1981).
1982	Meyer, referring to Staw's publication, extends the concept based on the way the hospitals function (Meyer, 1982).
1995	Australia and New Zealand publish risk management standards – Risk Management Standard AS / NZS 4360.
1999	A team led by Nigel Turnbull (Page & Spira, 2004) publishes the Turnbull report on how to manage an organization, focusing on internal resource control.
2005	The Turnbull report is updated (Financial Reporting Council, 2005).
2007	British Standard Institution publishes Standard BS25999-2 "Specification for Business Continuity Management".
2009	The International Standard Organization (ISO) publishes the Risk Management Standards ISO 31000.
2014	British Standards Institution publishes Standard BS 65000 "Organizational Resilience". "Turnball Report" in terms of risk management – update (Financial Reporting Council, 2014).
2016	The International Standard Organization (ISO) publishes the ISO 22316 Organizational Resilience Standard.
2019	The International Standard Organization (ISO) publishes an update to the ISO 31000 standard for organizational resilience.

Source: Authors' creation.

in the above definitions should be understood as unexpected changes in conditions and circumstances essential for the continuity of business operations. (b) Feature 2 – the resilience of the organisation refers to the context of managing the enterprise during a disruption in the face of a crisis; underlines the organisation's ability to function after system homeostasis is broken. (c) Feature 3 – resistance of the organisation in terms of the functioning of the enterprise after returning to the equilibrium state; takes into account the company's ability to learn from disruptions, implement remedial programmes, and prevent recurrences.

Commonly cited definitions of the term are presented in Table 4, assigning them the adopted features. The considered interpretations of the concept of organisational resilience are described with the names of the authors (or organisations) and the year in which a given definition was published.

As indicated in the above tabular comparison, only 3 of the 12 definitions contain all three features. The authors of the above definitions most often equate the resilience of an organisation with functioning during an on-going disruption (this aspect is characterised by nine of the above-mentioned definitions). Seven definitions take into account post-recovery activities, while only five also apply to the functioning of the organisation before the disruption. The concept of organisational resilience can also be identified at various levels of organisation functioning (Annarelli & Nonino, 2016). Organisational resilience, as

Table 4. Comparison of the Definitions of the Concept of Organisational Resilience According to the Adopted Common Features.

No.	Author (Year of Publication)	Feature 1	Feature 2	Feature 3
1	Wildavsky (1988)		X	
2	Sitkin (1992)			X
3	Weick (1993)	X	X	
4	Horne and Orr (1998)		X	
5	Weick and Sutcliffe (2001)			X
6	Coutu (2002)	X	X	X
7	Sutcliffe and Vogus (2003)	X	X	X
8	Fiksel (2003)		X	X
9	Burnard and Bhamra (2011)			X
10	British Standard Institution (2014)	X	X	
11	Bhamra (2015)	X	X	X
12	International Organisation for Standardisation (2017)		X	

Note: Own elaboration based on (Odważny, 2022).

understood by senior management, will most often refer to the strategic perspective and long-term planning. The strength of the organisation will be built based on a clear vision and strategy of the enterprise, its understanding by the company's human resources, and by skilful use of the strengths of the organisation (Czakon, 2010).

It is relatively common to distinguish operational resilience as a component of organisational resilience (Annarelli & Nonino, 2016; Birkie, Trucco, & Kaulio, 2013). The former is therefore one of the forms of shaping the latter. However, both types of resilience focus on different time horizons and different types of resources.

Research indicates that strengthening the resilience of an organisation is the result of development both at the strategic and operational levels of the enterprise (Duchek, 2019; Ismail, 2011). On the other hand, however, the authors emphasise that if an organisation focusses on tasks and operational processes, without being able to see a wider perspective, and analysing the environment and business, it will not be able to identify critical areas for development, which will significantly weaken the resilience of the organisation (Duchek, 2019).

Based on the literature review, an attempt was made to locate the individual features of the organisation's resilience (defined earlier) in three planning perspectives similar to the one proposed by Odważny (2022). Strategic planning in the context of building organisational resilience focusses primarily on the first of the three characteristics of organisational resilience, that is, activities that are carried out before the disruption occurs. The exact opposite situation applies to the second feature, that is, functioning during a disturbance. Then, first of all, operational activities become important, which seems obvious in the context of the duration of the disruption (usually less than a year). Organisational strategic planning usually does not refer to specific events and in particular to the state of equilibrium after a disruption. Actions taken during this period

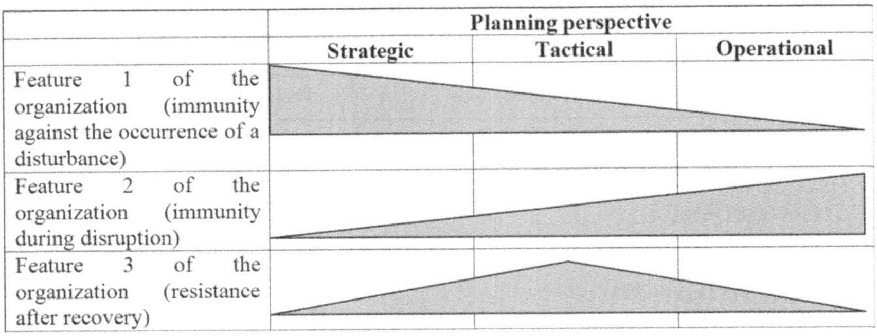

Fig. 1. Location of the Defined Features of Organisational Resilience in the Planning Perspective of the Organisation. *Note*: Own elaboration based on Odważny (2022).

are either tactical or operational. A plan to return to full equilibrium will usually mean a perspective of several months, that is, a tactical perspective, as also shown in Fig. 1.

The interdisciplinary nature of immunity allows for the determination of its universal features, which include (Kirkwood, Dwyer, & Walton, 2017; Manfield & Newey, 2018): (a) dependence on the type of threats; (b) having a dynamic, process-related nature that allows development over time; (c) launching learning processes while dealing with threats; (d) using threats as a source of change and development; and (e) turning challenges into opportunities and seizing opportunities.

In social sciences, the above-mentioned features make systems and organisations able to cope with threats and even use them for rapid development. The development and maintenance of resilience traits are based on four abilities (Martinelli et al., 2018): cognitive, behavioural, contextual, and dynamic. Cognitive abilities are the result of creating a sense and ideological identity, and behavioural abilities – the diversification of resources and functional habits. Contextual capacities include social capital and a network of external resources, while dynamic capacities relate to the creation and modification of the resource base. The foundations of these abilities are built by routines and experience. They relate to the individual, organisational, and social levels.

In considerations regarding resilience, various types of organisational reactions are indicated: adaptive (offensive) or reactive (defensive). Having both of these characteristics at the same time allows the organisation to survive. These considerations serve to build the organisational resilience architecture framework matrix, which covers four states of the enterprise: stiffness (resistance to change, defensive behaviour, failure to meet stakeholder expectations), short-lived (seeking new directions), sensitivity (reactions to changes in the environment of the nature of exploitation behaviours), and adaptability (simultaneous exploitation and exploration behaviours) (Limnios et al., 2014).

4. DISCUSSION AND CONCLUSION

It is worth noting that the concept of resilience can also apply to individuals. In the case of entrepreneurs, resilience is treated as a personal trait, and its resilience dynamic can, for example, be analysed in the context of making decisions to become an entrepreneur based on critical events. The triggers of the resilience process are considered. Using the model based on the theory of trauma, it is indicated that the precursors of the entrepreneurial initiative are the following elements (Bernard & Barbosa, 2016):

- emotional support by a mentor of resilience (resistance, resilience mentor) to build a social network;
- a commitment to action, which enables experience and interaction as a source of learning; and
- achieving temporary (temporary) victories and work allowing for legitimacy based on self-confidence and achieving self-confidence.

The concept of resilience, with a view to social science, can be associated with resilience which refers to groups or communities that have the ability to deal with external disorders and threats. They are associated with social, political as well as environmental changes. Resettlement may refer to the individual as well as the mesostructural level (local communities and communities) based on culture, values, norms, ties, trust, social interactions, and social capital, but it may also refer to ensuring social order. The macrostructural level is related to economic and military aspects.

The concept of resilience in the face of environmental turbulence also considers the need for the entity to temporarily adjust to the changes that occur. Increasing the security of the functioning of enterprises in emergencies may be associated with the implementation of social responsibility, for example, based on cooperation with stakeholders (Ridley, 2011).

The review of the definition of the concept of resilience shows that it does not only refer to survival but also includes potential risks and proactive actions in the face of adversities. Learning an organisation from unexpected events can be used to carry out organisational changes based on dynamic competencies (abilities, dynamic capability). The source of resilience can be bricolage, virtual system, wisdom, and mutual interactions. Bricolage is a source of improvisation and creative problem-solving, and the virtual system is used to create a vision by members of the organisation. Wisdom is about answering questions about what, on the one hand, is already known, but on the other hand, it concerns the limitations of knowledge and activities related to the search for new information. The company's ability is to anticipate, copy, or learn from unexpected events. Thanks to long-term learning, adaptation capabilities are built. In turn, copying uses acceptance, the search for solutions (including those based on bricolage), and their implementation (Duchek, 2019).

Resilience related to self-renewal of an enterprise requires meeting the challenges of a cognitive, strategic (based on an anticipatory approach, including strategies and business models), political (concerning the allocation of resources in breakthrough activities), and ideological challenges related to the renewal and optimisation of the model business. The concept of resilience is also discussed from the point of view of entrepreneurial intentions in extreme situations (after a catastrophe, war, and in connection with terror) (Bullough, 2014), describes key antecedences in companies related to resilience, and presents the relationship between antecedences related to leadership and the level of resilience (Howard & Irving, 2014). Implementation of resilience in strategic terms should include four strategies:

1. Resistance including robustness and hardening.
2. Reliability to ensure the ability to continue its functions as much as possible.
3. Redundancy, creating the possibility of alternative actions.
4. Flexibility is related to adapting to new conditions.

How can an organisation support the resilience of its members? Froman (2010) distinguished three strategies:

- developing a supportive environment that positively affects satisfaction and commitment to work;
- ethical and trustworthy organisational culture involving key stakeholders in the decision-making process; and
- investments in human and social capital, for example, in training programmes, increasing cooperation in teams and at the level of the entire organisation.

Organisational resilience mechanisms lead to increased awareness of the current situation in which the organisation has found itself, reducing susceptibility to risks in the environment and restoring its former effectiveness (Burnard, Bhamra, & Young, 2012). Organisational resilience can be manifested in increased productivity, employee well-being, reduced absenteeism, and higher turnover (Luthans, 2002). The key, however, is the knowledge of the factors enhancing immunity and the implementation of effectiveness-verified programmes to build it. A factor that appears at both levels is supporting interpersonal relationships. The above-mentioned directions significantly indicate the growing importance of the trend in management and enriching its heritage in accordance with current scientific discoveries.

REFERENCES

Annarelli, A., & Nonino, F. (2016). Strategic and operational management of organizational resilience: Current state of research and future directions. *Omega*, *62*, 1–18.

Bernard, M. J., & Barbosa, S. D. (2016). Resilience and entrepreneurship. A dynamic and biographical approach to the entrepreneurial act. *Management*, *19*(2), 89–123.

Bhamra, R. (2015). *Organisational resilience concepts, integration, and practice*. Boca Raton: CRC Press.

Birkie, S. E., Trucco, P., & Kaulio, M. (2013). State-of-the-art review on operational resilience: Concept, scope and gaps. In C. Emmanouilidis, M. Taisch, & D. Kiritsis (Eds.), *Advances in production management systems. Competitive manufacturing for innovative products and services* (Vol. 398, pp. 273–280). Berlin: Springer.

Bratnicki, M. (2000). *Kompetencje przedsiębiorstwa – Od określenia kompetencji do zbudowania strategii.* Warszawa: Placet.

British Standard Institution. (2014). BS65000: Guidance on organizational resilience. Retrieved from https://shop.bsigroup.com/ProductDetail/?pid=000000000030258792. Accessed on 25 July 25. 2022.

Bullough, A., Renko, M., & Myatt, T. (2014). Danger zone entrepreneurs. The importance of resilience and self-efficacy for entrepreneurial intentions. *Entrepreneurship, Theory & Practice*, *38*(3), 473–499.

Burnard, K., Bhamra, R., & Young, R. I. (2012). Critical factors of organisational resilience. *Proceedings of International Conference on Economics Marketing and Management*, *28*, 1–10.

Christopher, M., & Peck, H. (2004). Building the resilient supply chain. *The International Journal of Logistics Management*, *15*(2), 1–14.

Coutu, D. L. (2002). How resilience works. *Harvard Business Review*, *80*(5), 46–55.

Czakon, W. (2010). Zasobowa teoria firmy w krzywym zwierciadle. *Przegląd Organizacji*, *4*, 8–12.

Czerniawska, D., Błażewicz, M., Pacuska, M., & Pańków, M. (2015). *Mazowieccy przedsiębiorcy w obliczu globalnych i regionalnych trendów gospodarczych. Technologie, globalizacja konkurencji, marketing i PR, dane*. Warszawa: MGG Conferences.

Duchek, S. (2019). Organizational resilience: A capability-based conceptualization. *Business Research*, *13*, 215–246.

Fiksel, J. (2003). Designing resilient, sustainable systems. *Environmental Science & Technology*, *37*(23), 5330–5339.

Froman, L. (2010). Positive psychology in the workplace. *Journal of Adult Development*, *2*, 59–69.

Gajendran, T., & Oloruntoba, R. (2017). Governance and resilience: A case of re-development after a bushfire disaster. *Technological Forecasting and Social Change*, *121*, 50–64.

Gallopin, G. C. (2006). Linkages between vulnerability, resilience, and adaptive capacity. *Global Environmental Change*, *16*(3), 293–303.

Holling, C. S. (1973). Resilience and stability of ecological systems. *Annual Review of Ecological Systems*, *4*(1), 1–23.

Horne, J. F., & Orr, J. E. (1998). Assessing behaviors that create resilient organizations. *Employment Relations Today*, *24*, 29–39.

Howard, Ch. S., & Irving, J. A. (2014). The impact of obstacles defined by developmental antecedens on resilience in leadership formation. *Management Research Review*, *37*(5), 466–478.

Intergovernmental Panel on Climate Change. (2012). Managing the risks of extreme events and disasters to advance climate change adaptation. A special report of working groups I and II of the Intergovernmental Panel on Climate Change . Retrieved from https://www.ipcc.ch/site/assets/uploads/2018/03/SREX_Full_Report-1.pdf. Accessed on July 29, 2022.

International Food Policy Research Institute. (2014). *2013 global food policy report*. Washington, D.C.: International Food Policy Research Institute.

International Organization for Standardization. (2017). *ISO 22316:2017. Security and resilience – Organizational resilience – Principles and attributes*. Geneva: International Organization for Standardization.

Ismail, H. S., Poolton, J., & Sharifi, S. (2011). The role of agile strategic capabilities in achieving resilience in manufacturing-based small companies. *International Journal of Production Research*, *49*(18), 5469–5487.

Jajuga, K. (2015). *Zarządzanie ryzykiem*. Warszawa: Wydawnictwo Naukowe PWN.

Kirkwood, J., Dwyer, K., & Walton, S. (2017). An ecopreneur's growing resilience after a series of earthquakes. *Journal of Enterprising Communities: People and Places in the Global Economy*, *11*(1), 129–148.

Mamuni, E. A. L. (2014). The resilience architecture framework. Four organizational archetypes. *European Management Journal*, *32*(1), 104–116.

Linnenluecke, M. K., & McKnight, B. (2017). Community resilience to natural disasters: The role of disaster entrepreneurship. *Journal of Enterprising Communities: People and Places in the Global Economy*, *11*(1), 166–185.

Luthans, F. (2002). The need for and meaning of positive organizational behavior. *Journal of Organizational Behavior*, *6*, 695–706.

Limnios, E. A. M., Mazzarol, T., Ghadouani, A., & Schillizzi, S.G.M. (2014). The resilience architecture framework: four organizational archetypes. European Management Journal, 32, 104-116.

Martinelli, E., Tagliazucchi, G., & Marchi, G. (2018). The resilient retail entrepreneur: Dynamic capabilities for fading natural disasters. *International Journal of Entrepreneurial Behavior & Research*, *24*(7), 1222–1243.

Meyer, A. D. (1982). Adapting to environmental jolts. *Administrative Science Quarterly*, *27*, 515–537.

Noja, G. G., Thalassinos, E., Cristea, M., & Grecu, I. M. (2021). The interplay between board characteristics, financial performance, and risk management disclosure in the financial services sector: New empirical evidence from Europe. *Journal of Risk and Financial Management*, 2(14), 1–20.

Odważny, F. (2022). *Metoda kształtowania odporności organizacji poprzez zarządzanie zasobami materialnymi w przedsiębiorstwie produkcyjnym*. Poznań: Politechnika Poznańska.

Piorkowska, K. (2015). Koncepcja resilience z perspektywy proaktywnych strategii behawioralnych. *Marketing i Rynek*, *5*, 808–824.

Resilience Alliance. (2019). *Resilience*. Retrieved from https://www.resalliance.org. Accessed on July 20, 2022.

Ridley, G. (2011). National security as a corporate social responsibility. Critical infrastructure resilience. *Journal of Business Ethics*, *103*(1), 111–125.

Rokita, J. (2007). *Zarządzanie strategiczne – Zdobywanie i utrzymanie przewagi konkurencyjnej*. Warszawa: PWE.

Romanowska, M. (2020). Atrybuty doskonałości organizacji. In S. Gregorczyk & G. Urbanek (Eds.), *Zarządzanie strategiczne w dobie cyfrowej gospodarki sieciowej* (pp. 499–512). Łodź: Wyd. Uniwersytetu Łódzkiego.

Rzegocki, M. M., & Grucza, B. (2015). Organizational resilience. *Organizacja i Kierowanie*, *166*, 56–71.

Sienkiewicz-Małyjurek, K. (2015). *Skuteczne zarządzanie kryzysowe*. Warszawa: Difin.

Sitkin, S. B. (1992). Learning through failure: The strategy of small losses. *Research in Organizational Behavior*, *14*, 231–266.

Skowron-Grabowska, B. (2021). *Łańcuchy wartości w zarządzaniu organizacjami. Wyzwania innowacyjno-kryzysowe*. Warszawa: PWE.

Smith, D., & Elliot, D. (2006). *Key readings in crisis management: Systems and structures for prevention and recovery*. London: Routledge.

Staw, B. M., Sandelands, L. E., & Dutton, J. E. (1981). Threat rigidity effects in organizational behavior: A multilevel analysis. *Administrative Science Quarterly*, *26*, 501–524.

Sutcliffe, K. M., & Vogus, T. J. (2003). Organizing for resilience. In K. S. Cameron, J. E. Dutton, & R. E. Quinn (Eds.), *Positive organizational scholarship: Foundations of a new discipline* (pp. 94–110). San Francisco, CA: Berett-Koehler Publishers.

Świerczek, A. (2020). Wykorzystanie podejścia multimetaforycznego w refleksji nad rzeczywistością organizacyjną rezylientnego łańcucha dostaw. *Gospodarka Materiałowa i Logistyka*, *3*, 7–16.

Thalassinos, I. E., & Thalassinos, Y. (2019). Financial crises and e-commerce: How are they related. *SSRN*, February, 1–15.

UNISDR. (2009). *Terminology on disaster risk reduction*. Geneva: United Nations Office for Disaster Risk Reduction.

Vlasov, M., Bonnedahl, K. J., & Vincze, Z. (2018). Entrepreneurship for resilience: Embeddedness in place and in trans-local grassroots networks. *Journal of Enterprising Communities: People and Places in the Global Economy*, *12*(3), 374–394.

Weick, K. E. (1993). The collapse of sensemaking in organizations: The Mann Gulch disaster. *Administrative Science Quarterly*, *38*, 628–652.

Weick, K. E., & Sutcliffe, K. M. (2001). *Managing the unexpected*. San Francisco, CA: Jossey-Bass.

Wildavsky, A. (1988). *Searching for safety*. New York, NY: Transaction Books.

Witkowski, J. (2010). *Zarządzanie łańcuchem dostaw. Koncepcje-procedury-doświadczenia*. Warszawa: PWE.

World Bank. (2015). *The state of social safety nets 2015*. Washington, DC: World Bank.

World Economic Forum. (2014). *Global risks 2014 ninth edition, insight report*. Retrieved from http://www3.weforum.org/docs/WEF_Global Risks_Report_2014.pdf. Accessed on August 17, 2022.

Yerpudee, S., Sood, K., & Grima, S. (2022). Blockchain-augmented digital supply chain management: A way to sustainable business. *Journal of Risk and Financial Management*, *16*(1), 7.

CHAPTER 10

DIGITAL TRANSFORMATION AND DATA GOVERNANCE: TOP MANAGEMENT TEAMS PERSPECTIVES

Emil Velinov[a,b], Marta Kadłubek[c], Eleftherios Thalassinos[d,e], Simon Grima[f] and Dimitrios Maditinos[g]

[a]*RISEBA, University of Applied Sciences, Latvia*
[b]*SKODA AUTO University, Czech Republic*
[c]*Faculty of Management, Czestochowa University of Technology, Poland*
[d]*University of Piraeus, Greece*
[e]*Faculty of Economics Management and Accountancy, University of Malta, Malta*
[f]*Department of Insurance, Finance and Risk Management, Faculty of Economics, Management and Accountancy, University of Malta, Malta*
[g]*International Hellenic University, Management Science and Technology Department, Kavala University Campus, Greece*

ABSTRACT

The chapter sheds light on how top management teams (TMTs) across multinational firms tackle the ongoing disruptive digital transformation during the pandemic era. The chapter includes basic definitions and global and regional trends on data governance and digital transformation across multinational firms from advanced and emerging markets. Finally, it provides several case studies demonstrating the theoretical and practical applicability of how data governance and digital transformation emerged from top management team perspectives. The chapter outlines the importance of

Digital Transformation, Strategic Resilience, Cyber Security and Risk Management
Contemporary Studies in Economic and Financial Analysis, Volume 111A, 147–158

Published under exclusive licence by Emerald Publishing Limited
ISSN: 1569-3759/doi:10.1108/S1569-37592023000111A010

leadership and top management in dealing with emerging technologies and business processes across global firms.

Keywords: Digital transformation; data governance; top management teams; global firms; multinational firms; emerging markets

JEL classifications: M15; O32

INTRODUCTION

Since the start of the twenty-first century, an emerging number of automatisation and robotisation has penetrated a wide variety of businesses by introducing digitalisation processes, which served as springboards for multinational corporations to emphasise creating competitive advantage through disruptive innovation and strategic shifts to developed and emerging global markets (Dobrzanski, Bobowski, Chrysostome, Velinov, & Strouhal, 2021). The digitalisation era (2001–ongoing) is characterised by the emerging role of hardware, middleware and software, a disruptive global supply chain, and unbundled networking via the internet and global mobile technologies. Therefore, digitalisation goes much further in innovative disruptions in increasing the quality of physical and information technology infrastructure and the demanded technical digitalised processes during the 'Fourth Industrial Revolution' (Petrillo, De Felice, Cioffi, & Zomparelli, 2018). The Digital era is characterised by swift and unpredictable digital transformation; thus, multinational firms are putting much effort into driving artificial intelligence and digitalisation throughout all levels of management (Holmund, Strandvik, & Lahteenmaki, 2017). Moreover, firms across various industries have become customer-centric, and many new vacancies have shown up in the TMTs and at the daily operational level.

Firms have changed their approach to communicating with clients via online digital platforms, advanced software, hardware, middleware and artificial intelligence advancement, which is inevitable for the entire business (Rogers, 2016). Furthermore, companies promote digitalisation in TMTs, middle-level and entry-level management in various corporations as they try to move forward workflows and customer relationship management platforms, which would bring them not only turnover but also sustainable development as well (Sebastian, Ross, Beath, Mocker, Moloney, & Fonstad, 2020). Moreover, the pressure on TMT has increased due to complex and highly unpredictable strategic decision-making, volatile global markets, and challenging customer requirements within various industries. This pressure has implied the executives and non-executives to start promoting and enhancing IT and digitalisation competencies and skills to make efficient and productive strategic decisions during digital transformation (Velinov, Maly, Petrenko, Denisov, & Vassilev, 2020). Therefore, it has created a higher demand for developing and working on TMT awareness and knowledge of digitalisation (see Figure 1 below).

The TMT's theory argues that a firm's strategic decisions and subsequent results reflect the features of its elite management, particularly its senior management structures (Certo, Lester, Dalton, & Dalton, 2006; Hambrick & Mason, 1984). As the TMT social adaptation is a crucial firm capability (Carpenter, 2002) and has very important components of a strategic asset and digitalisation, TMT social integration might be an important mechanism through which a senior management approach apprehends an organisation's advantageous benefits. Chief Digitalisation officers' (CDO) positions have been established, how CDOs fulfil their positions and how they can be successfully installed to guide organisations through their digital transformation (Velinov, Maly, & Vojvodic, 2018). Digitisation has an extended impact not only on the way of working but also fosters the temp of transformation, which companies are dealing with. Both implications steer to three main demands that must be tackled to succeed: new capabilities and competencies, new ways of leadership, and new firm resources. Depending on the degree to which organisations meet these demands, they could improve their culture towards 'digital thinking'.

On the other hand, digital transformation efforts and programmes are facing big hurdles to reaching the expected business benefits. Several studies in the literature explicitly pinpoint the importance of managing people and organisational challenges in the business environment of digital changes. During the digital era, multinational companies' TMTs have introduced firm-wide trainings and programmes to adjust to practices connected to digitalisation and artificial intelligence implementation. Due to disruptive global supply chains, volatile market conditions, and changing industries' policies and regulations, multinational firms need to foster and prepare their TMTs for embracing risks and taking high-impact decisions in VUCA (volatile, uncertain, complex and ambiguous) environment. Thus, senior management teams are promoting and implementing hiring practices requiring new top managers to possess digitalisation and IT skills, which help them take high risks during strategic decision-making (Vallone, Elia, Greve, Longoni, & Marinelli, 2019).

METHODOLOGY

Upper Echelons and Digitalisation

Based on upper-echelon theory, many previous studies have theoretically and empirically tested the impact of individual characteristics of senior managers in the ongoing process of making strategic decisions (Muhyudi, Maulida, & Aryasa, 2021). The outcomes of the latter studies serve as support that TMT demographic diversity has an impact on decision-making. Similarly, studies on upper-echelon theory have recently revealed more dimensions among top managers, which research the management enlists in the same framework as TMTs (Hassan & Marimuthu, 2018). Furthermore, in terms of TMTs, previous studies argue that top managers' strategic preferences are affected by their perceptions and gained professional experience with company strategy (Zhu, Hu, & Shen, 2020). After the year 2000, there are several studies which have applied agency and the upper-echelon theories to explain the TMT's role in strategic planning and execution, and their study results showed that both TMT position and TMT demography characteristics are essential factors in affecting strategy formation and execution. On the contrary, a study by Oduor and Kilika (2018) examined the TMT demographic diversity and its impact on decision-making processes in the top management. The study has proposed a future research venue for measuring the heterogeneity among TMT members.

Generally, the theory of upper echelons advocates both objective situations and TMT characteristics such as individuals' values, mentality, perceptions and psychological cognitive fundaments affect the strategic decision-making process and influence organisational performance. Research on TMT diversity stems from the strategy literature and is normally linked to studies of strategy execution and board leadership that are predominantly contextualised within the upper echelons concept of the organisation (Hambrick & Mason, 1984). As the paper sheds light on TMT characteristics (management and supervisory boards of directors within German firms with two-tier corporate structure) and its impact on firm performance in a period of intensive industries digitalisation, upper-echelon theory is considered to contribute to the understanding of the influence of TMT diversity dimensions such as TMT gender diversity, TMT age diversity, TMT Nationality diversity, etc. on firm performance. Similarly, considering the TMT gender diversity impact on firm performance, the real contribution of a female team member to firm performance could depend on the level of her similarity to male counterparts in TMT as of level of education, career length, nationality, social status, professional networking, international experience, etc. (Lee & Chung, 2021). For example, in the corporate governance domain, authors simultaneously test multiple dimensions of board members' profiles to assess their potential contributions to firms' digitalisation orientation (De Lomana, Strese, & Brinckmann, 2019).

Similarly, in the literature review on TMTs (Carpenter et al., 2014) outline top managers as a 'bundle' of characteristics, where the interactions between the different attributes of TMT members' personalities to achieve a complete understanding of their mixed and cumulative influence on strategic decisions. Some studies criticise the research on upper echelons due to the undetermined findings regarding the de-contextualisation of diversity in management (Neely, Lovelace, Cowen, & Hiller, 2020). In the research domain of firm and group diversity, the impact of context on the consequences of TMT diversity is widely popular. Particularly, research by Jackson, Joshi, and Erhardt (2003) underlines the emerging need to investigate the role of context in shifting the influence of diversity. Firk, Gehrke, Hanelt, and Wolff (2021) suggest that digitalisation is embedded in various aspects of TMT diversity such as digital skills, strategic orientation and digital innovation. Moreover, studies by Chhabra and Popli (2019) criticise diversity research for suggesting that all diversity dimensions are equally crucial, while in reality, particular TMT diversity dimensions could be more or less important, considering the context.

Information and Data Governance

Information aspects have taken over the domain of information technology (Helin, 2019) and started entering the space of hierarchal higher-order constructs, a natural consequence of data management. Therefore, information and data governance have recently been at the centre of attention (Abraham, Schneider, & Vom Brocke, 2019). The design of the data governance structure needs to be carefully performed to trigger participation from all levels of the organisation, especially from the TMT and to efficiently expedite conflict resolution to encourage support from all domains (Al Ruithe, Benkhelifa, & Hameed, 2019).

Both data and information governance frequently refer to the same concept (Abraham et al., 2019). Korhonen, Melleri, Hiekkanen, and Helenius (2018) attempt to achieve a consistent long-term view of how the most important data and information are created, defined, used, and controlled. Plotki (2013) embeds the definition of data governance into information governance as a system of data-related decision rights and accountabilities for information-related processes, implemented according to agreed models, clearly designating who can take what actions with what information, and when, under what circumstances, using what methods. In the research of governance, the term data has, in the past years, been frequently replaced by the term 'information' (Tallon, Ramirez, & Short, 2013). Both IT and data governance are also considered by some authors (Kooper et al., 2011) subsections of corporate governance; the highest level of governance in an organisation. On the other hand, recent studies have researched the emerging patterns of data governance more than technology matters for the public and private sectors. They suggest that data governance requires a multidisciplinary approach from a business and technological point of view inside organisations (Alhassan, Sammon, & Daly, 2018).

This research will use the more general term 'governance' to mark organisational, managerial and strategic management aspects of data governance, its higher-order and bird-eye view – far from the technical matters of data and far from the 'too abstract' intersection with information governance. This work develops a framework that attempts to bridge these two extreme points. The standalone term 'governance' also highlights redirection from its data, information and corporate angle towards the concept of control. As one of the governance elements, the concept of control, in this chapter, is at the centre of data privacy regulation-driven research. Governance is linked with accountability-oriented control systems (Charlesworth & Pearson, 2013) that are designed to lead to desired behaviours in different circumstances (Benston & Bush, 2008).

Data Governance in the Top Management Context

The idea that data governance requires more attention from business stakeholders has existed since the concept commenced (Alhassan et al., 2016). Line-of-business users of information systems are a vital source of information for data governance systems due to their familiarity with the business surface that data governance needs to support (Hendry, 2008). The stakeholder concept comes from strategic management. A stakeholder is any individual or group who can affect or is affected by a project related to digitalisation or digital transformation. To get vital process expertise, business stakeholders must be established as information owners (Micheli, Ponti, Craglia, & Berti Suman, 2020). Making the selection of users engage from the set of stakeholders is an important process that impacts the whole project's success (Bano & Zowghi, 2015). Ravishankar et al. (2011) suggest that if there is no alignment between any IT system and line-of-business stakeholders, IT initiatives usually fail, and there are wasted resources, all heading to negative financial and organisational outcomes.

Data governance is a concept that finally provides solutions through the joint work of representatives from business lines directly with 'the initiative representatives' from a data governance team (Abraham et al., 2019). Disagreements in project participants' goals, expectations, values and understandings get injected into meaningful intra-organisational dialogue and positive results follow (McLeod & MacDonell, 2011). The secret of the solution provided by the data governance framework is that business and IT together document the corporate-wide data standards and policies into finally integrated models (Abraham et al., 2019). Critical decisions are made in a fast and pre-agreed way in a line of a consensus-building process across the enterprise. In parallel, data governance workflows provide granular management activity sequences of different processes and departments (Otto, 2011a). Furthermore, according to Ofner et al. (2012), workflow modelling is proven as a practical 'user participation' driven activity that integrates data governance and quality into business processes of interest.

Contextual explanation of data is a data governance-driven step towards alignment with business professionals who try to clarify the meaning of data (Dahlberg & Nokkala, 2015). Data meaning and context reflect optimal policy creation on where data should be used and by whom (Abraham et al., 2019).

User participation is often associated with responsibility. Otto (2011a) states that data quality management in a cross-divisional environment suffers from

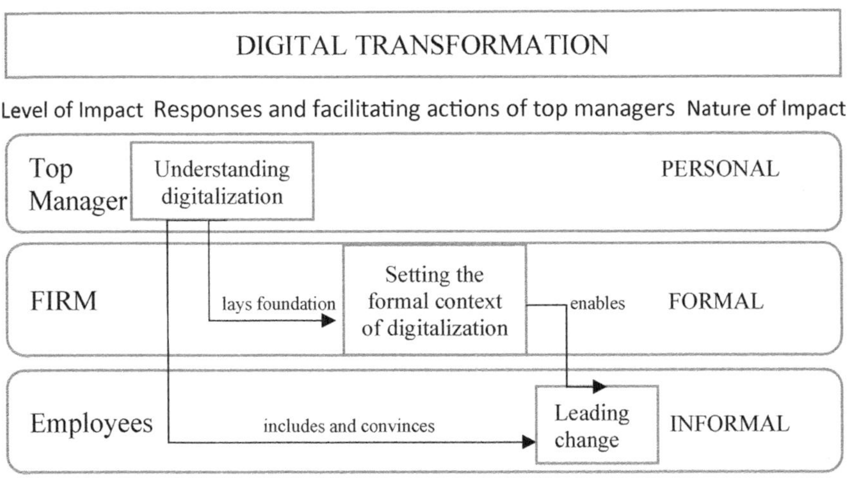

Fig. 1. Digital Transformation and Top Managers. *Source*: A model of top managers' practices to promote digital transformation by Wrede, Velamuri, and Dauth (2020).

the missing definition of clear organisational responsibilities that drive participation at the line-of-business level. Data governance in place with carefully selected attributes that explain data can help establish responsibility, data ownership, usage rules, and effective workflow that drive participation (Leenheer, Christiaens, & Meersman, 2010). Umar et al. (1999) provided results from a case study conducted in the telecommunications industry that confirmed the primary reasons for data quality issues are lack of roles and responsibilities and lack of data quality owners, which lead to inefficient organisational procedures in scheduling scenarios. Smith (2008) also outlines that one of the major problems is ownership issues in data quality projects. Lee (2010a) perceives information quality assessment barriers like a lack of responsibility for information quality in business stakeholders, followed by a lack of procedures.

Several attempts have been made in the literature to associate user participation with data governance in setting objectives and their evaluation. Otto (2011a) notes that the data owners should participate in the design of the major goals of the data quality initiative. Hence, business professionals and middle management formulate data objectives and evaluate results (Raes, 2011). The only way the business processes can operate with high-quality data is in the secret of data governance alignment with a business via objectives and its evaluation. Only business professionals can formulate data objectives and evaluate results on what data are needed to perform their specific tasks (Dahlberg & Nokkala, 2015). Similarly, Vaygan et al. (2007) argue that without the proper involvement of line-of-business stakeholders in setting and reviewing its measurement, master data do not have sufficient quality.

The literature highlights that organisational issues are more important to the success of data governance rather than technical ones (Lee, 2010b). Different data governance roles have been identified in the literature (Korhonen et al., 2018). The most often noted are terms of data owners and data stewards (Berson & Dubov, 2011). Otto (2011b) clarifies that data owners hold accountability for immediately correcting and providing consistency of certain data, while data stewards are accountable for the overall data management and development and provision of the rules for data handling.

Data stewards act as the point of contact for data-related issues, arbitrate and mediate conversations between business and IT, and work across enterprise departments and domains to promote data exchange (Seiner, 2014). Data stewardship is a concept with deep origins in the science and practice of data collection, sharing and analysis intended to transmit responsibility to the data where data governance conceptualises and carries out these responsibilities from stewardship (Rosenbaum, 2010).

The data governance stewardship team is a selected group of individuals with characteristics of the formal cross-functional team of specific key representatives in a specific business area, responsible for the quality, use and meaning of that data in the organisation (Plotkin, 2013). Organisations typically have more than one model in the matrix, usually one steward for business and one for technology (Dyche, 2015). Data stewardship is an operational aspect of data governance (McGilvray, 2008), where most of the day-to-day data work is done (Plotkin,

2013). Data governance stewards formally belong to the cross-functional governance team. Although their reporting lines sometimes remain in their functions, they have another formal link that defines them as cross-functional team members. Operational data stakeholders are those that have some level of responsibility for the data they define, produce and use during data entry, data integration and data analysis (Seiner, 2014). Line-of-business stakeholders would belong to this group, as explained by Wende (2007).

Data governance stewards and their cross-functional team – need leaders' behaviour in their approach to the operational data stakeholders (including line-of-business stakeholders).

An increasing body of work provides evidence that leadership is essential when managing transformation within any organisation, as leadership affects all levels of organisations regardless of the type of business (Schell, 2019).

Authentic leaders are necessary for effective change management. They need to create readiness for change which in the next phase develops into their commitment to change and behaviour that supports the change (Bakari, Hunjra, & Niazi, 2017).

Data governance stewards and their cross-functional teams – need leaders' behaviour in their approach to the operational data stakeholders (including line-of-business stakeholders). Data governance brings organisational change that threatens a person's comfort zone and spurs resistance (Krantz, 2016). Data governance stewards are leaders of different strategies to reduce line-of-business (operational data stakeholders) resistance to reduce emerging conflicts (Seiner, 2014). There are high requirements for their collaborative skills and the ability to influence both business and technology teams across business units (Villar, 2009). A leader positively impacts performance perception resisters, effort and social influence expectancy (Venkatesh, Morris, Davis, & Davis, 2003) by sending strong motivational messages and modelling higher-order values. This stimulates a follower's personal identification towards the leader and shifts their social identification towards the collective (Neufeld, Dong, & Higgins, 2007). Authentic leaders create readiness for change, which develops into their commitment to change and behaviour supporting it (Bakari et al., 2017).

Strong team identity is already defined as a 'superordinate identity' and is described as the strength of members' identification with the cross-functional team and its success (Miller & Brewer, 1984). Transformational leaders can link follower and work values and change strong functional identities taking a big portion of self-identity (Klein & House, 1995). The strong identity of the data governance stewardship team, based on their confidence and meaningful team values, will emit and influence meaning to operational data stakeholders (Bono, 2003; Hacker & Roberts, 2004). They started identifying themselves as a part of the same 'data' vision and extended part of a strong cross-functional data governance stewardship team (Shamir & Howell, 1999).

Data governance stewardship team members require leadership skills in clear, proactive communication towards operational data stakeholders. *They would proactively pass on their knowledge in successful communication when they schedule works to be done, organise, clarify and define the activities, and maintain definite performance standards. Drucker (2002) and Sugarman (2001) marked that leaders willing and capable of communication are enablers of organisational change.* Detlor (2002) believes that as a result of knowledge sharing, there is learning – a fundamental capability/competence of the organisation (Day, 1994). Learning is also associated with detecting and correcting errors (Argyris & Schön, 1978), which is relevant to data governance frameworks. Sarin and McDermott (2003) observe the effect of the team leader's behaviour on team learning. There is a relationship between resistance to change from one side and goal setting and critical communication on the other (Aan, 2016). In parallel with a compelling vision, goal communication causes resisters to consider organisational goals (Shamir & Howell, 1999). One of how knowledge sharing and learning can be operationalised is through the existing concept of 'initiation of structure', defined as the degree to which the team leader assigns tasks and prescribes behaviours to the team members to achieve the desired results (Wofford & Liska, 1993). The structure facilitates the creation of recurring communication patterns.

Data governance stewards are necessary leaders in the context of enterprise-wide data governance. A leadership profile is necessary for a data governance team as it is impacted by high requirements in terms of collaboration skills and the ability to be influential across both business and technology teams and varying business units (Villar, 2009).

This chapter offers 'cross-functional governance integration' as a management tool to increase efficiency within the spheres of privacy accountability and reconciliation projects. The research suggests this in the case of GDPR. Line-of-business stakeholders' governance participation can increase the strength of this impact. It consists of involving business stakeholders in formal engagement, which assumes their responsibility pertaining to the formulation of objectives, the evaluation of results and the use of outputs.

If it is necessary to increase 'cross-functional governance integration', then 'governance team leadership' should be called for (leadership in building team identity, communication and knowledge transfer in the work schedule). The role of 'cross-functional governance integration' becomes even more important when considering it to be an underlying mechanism on a path where 'governance team leadership' also increases the efficiency of data privacy projects.

The conceptual framework presented is based on three major organisational design theory concepts incorporated into the governance line of research and extended to examine project efficiency in a data compliance environment. A secondary focus was the intersection of the focal organisational theories with theories from leadership and transformational leadership theories developed by Burns (2003).

The Existence (Appointment) of a Chief Information/Digitalisation/Technology Officer

Over time the role of the CDO has been increasingly covered by media outlets, academia and practitioner-oriented journals (e.g. Mlhunglu et al., 2019). Therefore, organisations might have gotten the impression that shareholders will encourage them as an organisation pioneering digital initiatives and driving digital innovation if they create the position of the Chief Digitalisation or Information or Technology Officer. Similarly, the appointment of a CDO might express a new management trend in the twenty-first century across varieties of industries, which is defined as a relatively transitory collective belief that a management approach leads to rational management progress. Korhonen et al. (2018) suggest in case that organisations appoint CIO/CDO/CTOs to please shareholders, the creation of the new position is likely not to be the product of an overall digital transformation strategy and occur without considering the underlying organisational conditions (e.g. the existence of CIO position and CDOs role profile). As a result, multinational firms may not benefit from such an appointment, and, in turn, shareholders will no longer perceive the appointment of a CDO as a positive strategic move.

CONCLUSION

The importance of data governance and digital transformation across the firms are the main drivers for plenty of managerial and organisational changes the TMTs have to deal with. Therefore, further research on data governance and digital transformation is needed, as it is emerging every day, especially in digital turbulences. TMTs know they need to invest in cyber security, managing the company's data and customer relationship management by bolstering digital skills among its members and tackling the new challenges of digital disruption.

ACKNOWLEDGEMENTS

This book chapter is dedicated to the memorial of Tatjana Vasiljeva, the former rector of RISEBA University of Applied Sciences in Riga, Latvia.

REFERENCES

Aan, B. (2016). The effect of organizational communication towards resistance to change: A case study in banking sector. *Economic Review: Journal of Economics and Business*, *14*(1), 53–67.

Abraham, R., Schneider, J., & Vom Brocke, J. V. (2019). Data governance: A conceptual framework, structured review, and research agenda. *International Journal of Information Management*, *49*, 424–438.

Alhassan, I., Sammon, D., & Daly, M. (2018). Data governance activities: a comparison between scientific and practice-oriented literature. *Journal of Enterprise Information Management*, *31*(2), 300–316. https.//doi.org/10.1108/JEIM-01-2017-0007

Al-Ruithe, M., Benkhelifa, E., & Hameed, K. (2019). A systematic literature review of data governance and cloud data governance. *Personal and Ubiquitous Computing*, *23*(5), 839–859.

Bano, M., & Zowghi, D. (2015) A systematic review on the relationship between user involvement and system success. *Information and Software Technology*, *58*, 148–169. https.//doi.org/10.1016/j.infsof.2014.06.011

Burns, J. M. (2003). *Transforming leadership: A new pursuit of happiness*. New York, NY: Grove Press.

Carpenter, M. A. (2002). The implications of strategy and socio context for the relationship between top management team diversity and firm performance. *Strategic Management Journal*, *23*(3), 275–284.

Carpenter, M. A., Geletkanycz, M. A., & Sanders, W. G. (2014). Top management teams: A "bundle" of characteristics. *Journal of Management*, *30*(6), 741–763.

Certo, S. T., Lester, R. H., Dalton, C. M., & Dalton, D. R. (2006). Top management teams, strategy, and financial performance: A meta-analytic examination. *Journal of Management Studies*, *43*(4), 813–839.

Charlesworth, A., & Pearson, S. (2013) Developing accountability-based solutions for data privacy in the cloud. *Innovation: The European Journal of Social Science Research*, *26*(1–2), 7–35, https.// doi.org/10.1080/13511610.2013.732753

Chhabra, A., & Popli, M. (2019). Impact of top management team sociodemographic faultlines on speed of foreign direct investment expansion: An emerging market perspective. *Strategic Change*, *28*(3), 209–215.

De Lomana, G. G., Strese, S., & Brinckmann, J. (2019). Adjusting to the digital age: The effects of TMT characteristics on the digital orientation of firms. *Academy Management Proceedings*, *2019*(1), 13589.

Dobrzanski, P., Bobowski, S., Chrysostome, E., Velinov, E., & Strouhal, J. (2021). Toward innovation-driven competitiveness across African countries: An analysis of efficiency of R&D expenditures. *Journal of Competitiveness*, *13*(1), 5–22.

Firk, S., Gehrke, Y., Hanelt, A., & Wolff, M. (2022). Top management team characteristics and digital innovation: Exploring digital knowledge and TMT interfaces. *Long Range Planning*, *55*(3), 102166.

Hambrick, D. C., & Mason, P. A. (1984) Upper echelons: The organization as a reflection of its top managers. *Academy of Management Review*, *9*(2), 193–205.

Hassan, R., & Marimuthu, M. (2018). Contextualizing comprehensive board diversity and firm financial performance: Integrating market, management and shareholder's perspective. *Journal of Management & Organization*, *24*(5), 634–678.

Helin, A. (2019). Inter-organizational IT governance research: a literature review. *International Journal of IT/Business Alignment and Governance (IJITBAG)*, *10*(1), 40–54.

Holmund, M., Strandvik, T., & Lahteenmaki, I. (2017). Digitalization challenging institutional logics: Top executive sense making of service business change. *Journal of Service Theory and Practice*, *27*(1), 219–236.

Jackson, S. E., Joshi, A., & Erhardt, N. L. (2003). Recent research on team and organizational diversity: SWOT analysis and implications. *Journal of Management*, *29*(6), 801–830.

Kooper, M. N., Maes, R., & Vries, H. J. (2011). Information management, IT and data governance: Subsections of corporate governance. *International Journal of Information Management*, *31*(4), 288-295.

Korhonen, J. J., Melleri, I., Hiekkanen, K., & Helenius, M. (2018) Designing data governance structure an organizational perspective. *GSTF Journal on Computing (JoC)*, *2*(4), 11–17.

Lee, J., & Chung, J. (2021). Impact of female presence in a top management team on innovation. In *Academy of management proceedings* (Vol. 2021, No. 1, p. 14327). Briarcliff Manor, NY: Academy of Management.

Micheli, M., Ponti, M., Craglia, M., & Berti Suman, A. (2020). Emerging models of data governance in the age of datafication. *Big Data & Society*, *7*(2), 2053951720948087.

Mhlungu, N. S., Chen, J. Y., & Alkema, P. (2019). The underlying factors of a successful organisational digital transformation. *South African Journal of Information Management*, *21*(1), 1–10.

Muhyudi, M., Maulida, M., & Aryasa, K. (2021). The impact of digital transformation on organizational performance: A case study. *Journal of Business and Management*, *45*(2),123–136.

Neely, B. H., Jr., Lovelace, J. B., Cowen, A. P., & Hiller, N. J. (2020). Metacritiques of upper echelons theory: Verdicts and recommendations for future research. *Journal of Management*, *46*(6), 1029–1062.

Oduor, B. A., & Kilika, J. M. (2018). TMT diversity, decision quality and service sector firm performance: A research agenda. *Journal of Management and Strategy*, *9*(2), 34–45.

Petrillo, A., De Felice, F., Cioffi, R., & Zomparelli, F. (2018). Fourth industrial revolution: Current practices, challenges, and opportunities. In A. Petrillo, R. Cioffi, & F. de Felice (Eds.), *Digital transformation in smart manufacturing* (pp. 1–20). Rijeka, Croatia: InTechOpen.

Plotkin, D. (2013). *Data stewardship: An actionable guide to effective data management and data governance*. Safari Tech Books online. Amsterdam: Morgan Kaufmann/Elsevier. Retrieved from http.//proquest.safaribooksonline.com/9780124103894

Ravishankar, M. N., Pan, S. L., & Leidner, D. E. (2011). When IT Alignment Lacks: The Relationship between IT-enabled flexibility, IT-Business strategic alignment and organizational outcomes. *International Journal of Project Management*, *29*(8), 977-988.

Rogers, D. (2016). *The digital transformation playbook: Rethink your business for the digital age*. New York, NY: Columbia University Press.

Sebastian, I. M., Ross, J. W., Beath, C., Mocker, M., Moloney, K. G., & Fonstad, N. O. (2020). How big old companies navigate digital transformation. In *Strategic information management* (pp. 133–150). Oxfordshire: Routledge.

Tallon, P. P., Ramirez, R. V., & Short, J. E. (2013) The information artifact in IT governance: Toward a theory of information governance. *Journal of Management Information Systems*, *30*(3), 141–178. https.//doi.org/10.2753/MIS0742-1222300306

Vaygan, N., Johnson, D., & Smith, K. (2007). Engaging key shareholders in assessing quality sufficiency: A study on adequateness. *Journal of Organizational Effectiveness: People and Performance*, *12*(3), 127-145.

Vallone, T., Elia, S., Greve, P., Longoni, L., & Marinelli, D. (2019). Top management team influence on firms' internationalization complexity. In *International business in a VUCA world: The changing role of states and firms*. Bingley: Emerald Publishing Limited.

Velinov, E., Maly, M., Petrenko, Y., Denisov, I., & Vassilev, V. (2020). The role of top management team digitalization and firm internationalization for sustainable business. *Sustainability*, *12*(22), 9502.

Velinov, E., Maly, M., & Vojvodic, M. (2018). *Management and business research quarterly*. Ankara: EUROKD.

Villar, M. (2009) Establishing effective business data stewards (No. 2). *Business Intelligence Journal*, *14*, 23–29.

Wrede, M., Velamuri, V. K., & Dauth, T. (2020). Top managers in the digital age: Exploring the role and practices of top managers in firms' digital transformation. *Managerial and Decision Economics*, *41*(8), 1549–1567.

Zhu, Q., Hu, S., & Shen, W. (2020). Why do some insider CEOs make more strategic changes than others? The impact of prior board experience on new CEO insiderness. *Strategic Management Journal*, *41*(10), 1933–1951.

CHAPTER 11

STRATEGIC LEADERSHIP ATTRIBUTES FOR ADOPTING DIGITAL TECHNOLOGY AND ENSURING ORGANISATIONAL RESILIENCE

Kristian Pultz Schlosser[a], Tatjana Volkova[b], Gratiela Georgiana Noja[c], Mirela Cristea[d] and Dimitrios Maditinos[e]

[a]*RISEBA University of Applied Sciences, Latvia*
[b]*BA School of Business and Finance, Latvia*
[c]*West University of Timisoara, Romania*
[d]*University of Craiova, Romania*
[e]*International Hellenic University, Greece*

ABSTRACT

Creating organisational resilience and creating a positive social impact is becoming a condition for sustainable business development. The adoption of digital technologies requires specific leadership characteristics to resolve complex societal challenges. The purpose of the research is to identify the critical strategic leadership characteristics for developing organisational resilience while creating social- and financial value. There is a research gap in strategic leadership, digital technologies, social impact, and organisational resilience studies which will be addressed in this research. The methodology embeds a

Digital Transformation, Strategic Resilience, Cyber Security and Risk Management
Contemporary Studies in Economic and Financial Analysis, Volume 111A, 159–173

Published under exclusive licence by Emerald Publishing Limited
ISSN: 1569-3759/doi:10.1108/S1569-37592023000111A011

critical literature review, complemented by bibliometric analysis. The adoption of digital technology is seen to be a key driver in the societal question and a tool to boost organisational resilience. Sensing, seizing, and driving digital adoption agenda as well as digital adoption are critical and require unique leadership characteristics where contextual ambidexterity was key to the strategic leader when building organisational resilience and creating social- and financial value. The research results can be used for identifying which characteristics strategic leaders must develop for digital technology adaptation to generate both a profit and positive social impact while boosting organisational resilience.

Keywords: Digital technology; organisational resilience; social impact; sustainability; strategic leadership; ambidexterity

INTRODUCTION

Creating organisational resilience and delivering social impact is becoming a must for all businesses. Based on the adoption of digital technologies, enterprises are enabled with agile and innovative approaches to address complex societal challenges and opportunities. The purpose of the research is to identify the critical strategic leadership characteristics for adopting digital technology and building organisational resilience.

The adoption of digital technology is seen to be a key driver in the societal question and tools to boost organisational resilience. Sensing, seizing, and driving digital adoption agenda as well as digital transformation are critical and require unique leadership characteristics such as dynamic capabilities.

The authors believe this will be the first scientific attempt to create a theoretical and practical foundation by bridging the research gap in strategic leadership, digital technologies, social impact, and organisational resilience.

This section was carried out by using relevant aspects of the methodology of the systematic literature review proposed by Kitchenham et al. (2009). The methodology of the systematic literature review is outlined below.

Being able to access the knowledge produced about a certain subject is essential for the development of quality research. In this case, certain subjects are 'strategic leadership' and 'organisational resilience'. Therefore, to be efficient in searching the electronic database, three search strings are identified: 'strategic leadership' and 'organisational resilience' and last to identify any research gap Boolean AND's and OR's were applied to the final search string 'strategic leadership AND shared value'. The selected search strings were executed in the electronic database Scopus.

Once the relevant studies have been obtained from the database, they must be evaluated for their relevance according to the research questions (RQ) (Santos, Pimenta, & Nobre, 2007). Scopus was selected as it's the largest abstract and citation database of the peer-reviewed literature (Scopus, 2020) From the scientific database Scopus, the selection of the publications was conducted through a process consisting of three stages. The three stages were first exclusion criteria

(EC), then inclusion criteria (IC) and last a validation of the quality criteria (QC) applied. In the first stage of the selection process, the EC was defined and applied. The definition and order of the EC are as follows: EC1: studies published before the year 2000 and after the year 2020. This has been selected to ensure a range of data that can identify trends and exclude studies published after 2020 to avoid the data from being skewed due to only half of 2021 having passed. EC2: studies published in other languages than English. Third and final EC3: studies that are not available as 'open access' publications.

Analysis of applied search strings and selection criteria will follow a three-stage analysis process. First, Scopus Analysis will be applied to understand trends and regions and to start identifying any gaps in publications. Second, a bibliometric analysis will be conducted by using VOSviewer2020 (VOSviewer, 2021). The objective of this analysis is to identify research directions and gaps in the selected publications.

Publications on organisational resilience have grown rapidly over the past years. Excelled by the financial crisis in 2008 and recently due to COVID-19 and war in Europe, researchers are giving, even more, focus and importance to this topic. In this chapter, the authors present a review of definitions, directions, and future research to be conducted on organisational resilience regarding strategic leadership. The authors present definitions that define organisational resilience as a heterogeneous phenomenon with two main forms, strategic resilience, and operational resilience (Table 1). Each with different focus areas for strategic leaders (Hepfer & Lawrence, 2022).

Organisational resilience is the ability of a company to respond to disruptions, adversity, and to recover from both internal and external shocks (Grecco et al., 2013). Belalcazar et al. (2017) define organisational resilience as 'the unique characteristic of an organisation that allows it to successfully cope with internal and external changes and events. It is the ability of systems to return to a normal state after an event of fault or disturbance'. It is important to notice that according to scholars, organisational resilience consists of two parts. One is strategic resilience

Table 1. Definitions of Organisational Resilience.

Definition	Author(s)
'Organizational resilience has been defined as a firm's ability to proactively scan their environment, identify looming and evolving threats, institute contingency measures to tackle known threats, withstand crisis and prepare for uncertainty'	Appiah, Amankwah-Amoah, and Liu (2022)
'Resilience is defined as the unique characteristic of an organization that allows it to successfully cope with internal and external changes and events. It is the ability of systems to return to a normal state after an event of fault or disturbance'	Belalcazar, Ron, Díaz, and Molinari (2017)
'Operational resilience is the ability of a company to respond to adversity and recover from internal and external shocks. Strategic resilience is the ability to respond to an opportunity or continuously anticipating and planning'	Grecco, Santos, Carvalho, Vidal, and Cosenza (2013)

Source: Authors' creation.

where the focus is on anticipating, planning, and preparing for potential disruptions. The other part is operational resilience which focusses on withstanding and rebounding from any disruption, shock, or disturbance due to internal or external circumstances (Hepfer & Lawrence, 2022).

Strategic leadership is viewed as the foundation for the successful performance of any organisation operating in the constantly changing and complex environment of the twenty-first century (Jaleha & Machuki, 2018). In the same approach, Ireland and Hitt (1999) entailed the capabilities that are required for effective strategic leadership in the new competitive landscape expected for the twenty-first century. The authors highlight that effective strategic leaders should:

> (1) develop and communicate a vision, (2) build dynamic core competencies, (3) emphasize and effectively use human capital, (4) invest in the development of new technologies, (5) engage in valuable strategies, (6) build and maintain an effective organizational culture, (7) develop and implement balanced controls, and (8) engage in ethical practices.

The topic of leadership has been researched since the beginning of the last century. It has evolved from birth traits and rights with Thomas Carlyle Great-Man theory (Khan, Nawaz, & Khan, 2016) to Greenleaf (2002) defining Contingency Theories (Situational) to Transformational leadership by Burns in 1978 and Bass later elaborated on this in 1985 (Bass & Avolio, 1994). Furthermore, two overlaying research streams have been identified as 'strategy as practice' and 'strategy as process' and leadership scholars are attempting to bridge these (Burgelman et al., 2017).

From the literature review, it can be concluded that there is no common understanding of strategic leadership. More recently strategic leadership scholars defined it as 'the core purpose of strategic leadership theory and research is to understand how much influence top executives have over performance' (Singh, Darwish, & Potocnik, 2016).

Further, empirical and conceptual studies have shown that strategic leadership actions significantly influence performance (Ireland & Hitt, 1999; Quigley & Graffin, 2017). However, gaps in strategic leadership according to Knies, Jackobsen, and Tummers (2016) are identified. These divergent findings indicate either a lack of evidence in establishing a direct association between strategic leadership and performance or of the many confounding variables that make it difficult to demonstrate a clear cause and effect (Knies et al., 2016). Hambrick and Quigley (2014) continue by pointing out that 'scholars are yet to agree on the conceptualisation and operationalisation of contextual conditions strategic leaders face'. There is no common understanding among researchers of the conditions and factors impacting the operations of strategic leaders (Quigley & Graffin, 2017).

In Table 2, the focus of strategic has changed and it is becoming broader.

From Table 2, it is clear that in early stages there was a narrower focus and strategic leaders' main priority was to make decisions and create financial results. Later, Teece and Nonaka (2001) identified firms, markets, and environments to be dynamic; hence, the role of strategic leaders became broader with a focus on

Table 2. Strategic Leadership Focus Development.

Definition	Author(s)
'Strategic leadership encompasses the study of management of an enterprise focusing on decision-making responsibilities as a primary concern'	Tushman and O'Reilly (1996)
'The performance of a firm's products or services relative to its competitors at any point in time will depend upon its competences which over time depend on its capabilities'	Teece and Nonaka (2001)
'The adaptive capacity to appropriately respond to the dynamism and complexity of the external environment'	Schoemaker, Krupp, and Howland (2013)
'Strategic leadership and corporate sustainability have recently come together in conspicuously explicit fashion through the emergence of top management team (TMT) positions with dedicated corporate sustainability responsibilities'	Strand (2014)

Source: Authors' creation.

how to build unique capabilities to ensure a competitive advantage. The dynamic capability view posits that a firm's success is largely driven by its ability to adapt to a changing environment to secure value-creating potential and thus achieve a competitive advantage (Teece, 2018). Moreover, the dynamic capability is driving innovation and is closely connected with ambidexterity (Birkinshaw & Gibson, 2004; Schoemaker, Heaton, & Teece, 2018).

With these, developments in transformational strategic leadership also promote ambidexterity where strategic leaders are focussed on the internal resources of the firm and how to exploit those, while at the same time exploring new opportunities and trends in the market (O'Reilly & Tushman, 2007). Most recently, the focus on the societal aspect has been increasing (Burgelman et al., 2017). Strategic leaders now must focus on creating financial performance, inspiring and motivating employees, and must focus on social aspects of how the firm is engaging with activities both locally and globally.

The search string 'organisational resilience' returned 610 publications in total over the past 20 years with 138 being published in 2021. From Fig. 1, organisational resilience: document by year, there is an upward steepening trend in publications. Moderate upward trend post-2008 and with a significant increase in publications post-2017 and 2020. This indicates significant importance in the topic by researchers and with the past four years accounting for nearly three-fourth of all publications, this is a trending research topic. The key here is that it is not only the number of articles but the diverse areas in which scholars are researching and publishing on strategic leadership.

The search string 'strategic leadership' returned 657 publications in total over the past 20 years with 111 being published in 2021 (Fig. 2). From Fig. 1, 'strategic leadership: document by year', there is an upward steepening trend in publications, especially after 2012. This indicates a significant interest in the topic by researchers and with the past four years accounting for nearly half of all publications, this is a trending research topic. The key here is also that, it is not only the

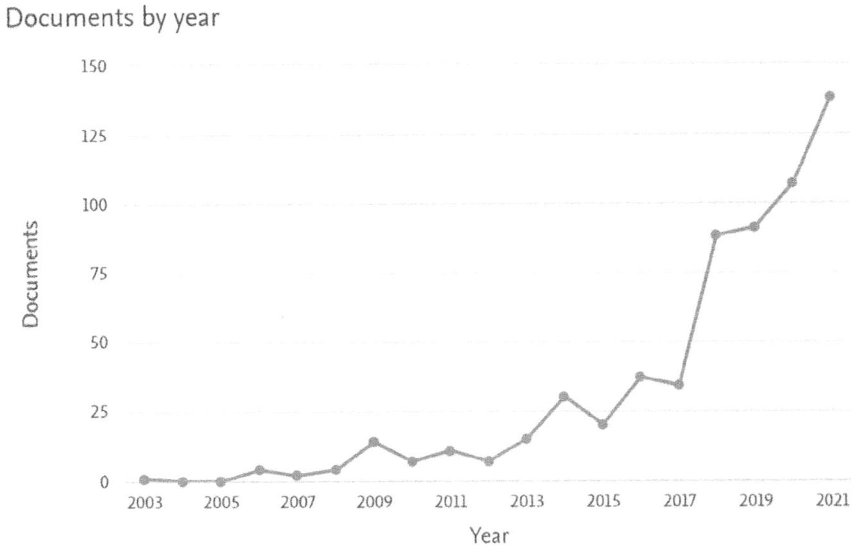

Fig. 1. Organisational Resilience Publications 2002–2021. *Source*: Scopus.

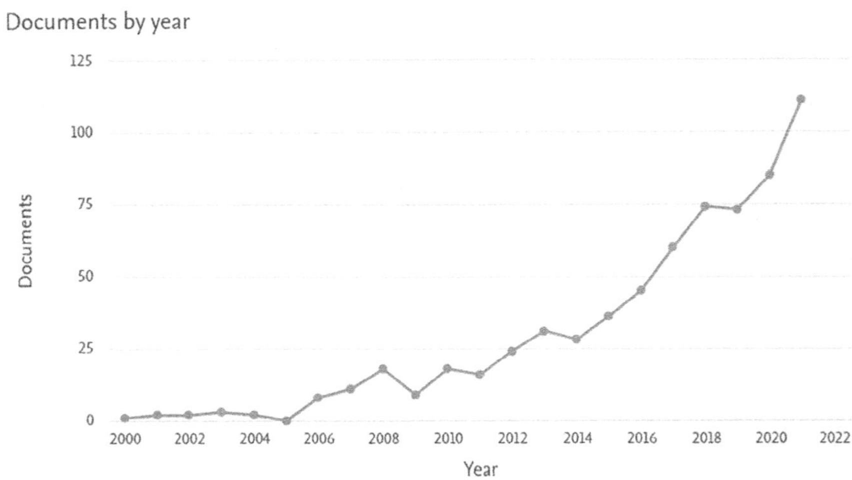

Fig. 2. Strategic Leadership Publications 2002–2021. *Source*: Scopus.

quantity of articles, but the diverse areas of which scholars are researching and publishing on strategic leadership.

From Fig. 3, the bibliometric analysis has been divided into three research clusters: performance strategic leadership, transformational strategic leadership, and dynamic strategic leadership. Conducting analysis of the bibliometric

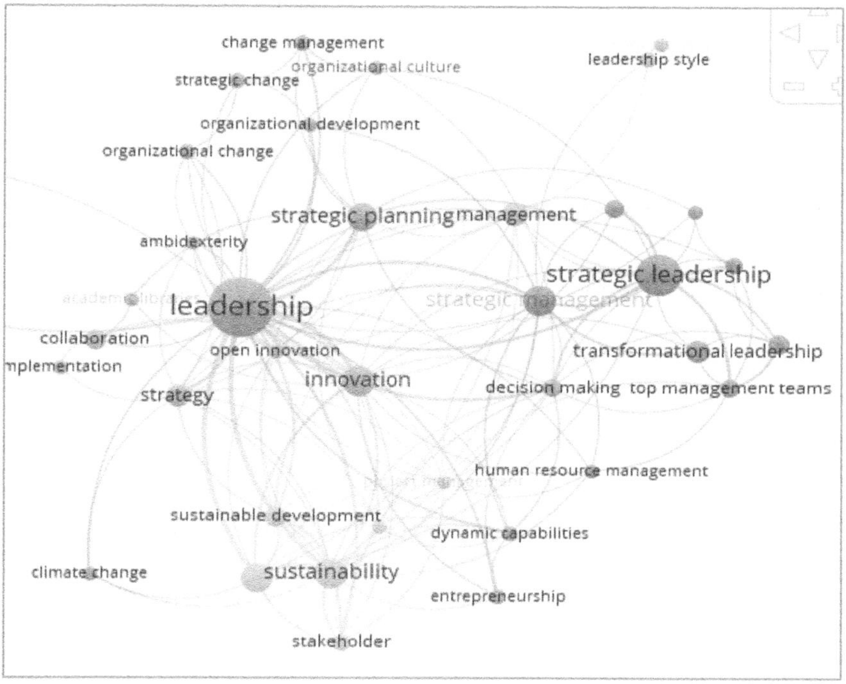

Fig. 3. Strategic Bibliometric Analysis. *Source*: VOSviewer.

analysis and the clustering, based on the research clusters, identified the main contributions on the three main theories (Table 3).

From Table 3, it becomes evident that *performance strategic leadership* plays a predominant role in the financial performance and strategic planning of a firm (Hiller et al., 2011). This theory suggests focussing on the internal resources of the firm to deliver financial value to shareholders. Performance management of employees through close leadership is key. The TMT sets a clear vision of where the firm strives to be financially and executes it via standardisation and efficiency of processes and performance (Hitt & Ireland, 2002).

Transformational strategic leadership (Bass, 1999) is the other main theory identified. According to Bass and Avolio (1994), transformational leadership 'is a type of contingent-reward leadership that had active and positive exchange between leaders and followers whereby followers were rewarded or recognised for accomplishing agreed upon objectives', closely related to transactional leadership theory.

Khan et al. (2016) reveal that 'transformational leadership distinguishes itself from the rest of the previous and contemporary theories, on the basis of its alignment to a greater good as it entails the involvement of the followers in processes or activities related to personal factor towards the organization and a course that will yield certain superior social dividend yield' since it provides clear correlation with performance, decision, and data.

Table 3. Main Strategic Leadership Theoretical Foundations.

Main Theoretical Directions	Contributions
Performance strategic leadership: Yukl (2008), Hernandez, Eberly, Avolio, and Johnson (2011), Hiller, DeChurch, Murase, and Doty (2011), and O'Reilly and Tushman (2007)	• Focus on financial performance • Strategic planning • Employee performance • Firm vision • Standardisation and efficiency
Transformational strategic leadership: Bass (1997), Hitt and Ireland (2002), and Burgelman and Grove (2007)	• Learning and employee development • Behavioural change through inspiration • Support moral positions of employees • Creative thinking and physiological safe environment
Dynamic strategic leadership: Burgelman and Grove (2007) and Schoemaker et al. (2013)	• Socially responsible • Engaging with stakeholders and external focus • Digital technology adoption

Source: Authors' creation.

The main contribution of transformational leadership is how leaders are driving performance through rewards, developing internal knowledge and being an inspiration. Allowing for creativity in a psychologically safe environment, transformational leaders are making a positive impact on the employees of the firm and the financial performance (Mueller, Renzl, & Will, 2020).

The third main theory is *dynamic strategic leadership* that is concerned with the firm and its employees and has a great focus on how leaders ensure that the firm is socially responsible (Fernandes, Veiga, Ferrira, Rammal, & Pereira, 2022). Predominant factors are the sustainability of the firm and its surroundings related to environmental, social, and economic aspects. Moreover, the dynamic strategic leader focusses on exploring trends in the market and how digital adoption can support the firm, its employees, and external stakeholders. Whereas a performance strategic leader would aim to reduce variance and exploit internal resources, the dynamic strategic leader focusses on increasing variance to explore social and digital trends (Metcalf & Benn, 2017).

Exploring the intersection (dotted line) between the three main directions (Fig. 4), it is clear that strategic leadership research must focus on technology and sustainable development. Ambidexterity is the key, when to explore and when to exploit. As it is the strategic leader who here is ambidextrous, it is known as possessing contextual ambidexterity characteristics. Sustainable development also refers to building resilience and sustaining any development over time.

From Fig. 4, the intersection between the main theoretical directions of strategic leadership shows the focus on digital technologies and how this relates to sustainability, leadership, and data. With increased automation and the move to a digital economy, organisational resources' leadership and strategic use are of critical significance (Fernandes, Veiga, Ferrira, Rammal, & Pereira, 2022). Moreover, changes in fundamental industry dynamics, technologies, and strategies create opportunities to develop new visions, create new strategies, and move their organisations in new directions (Burgelman & Grove, 2007). The question

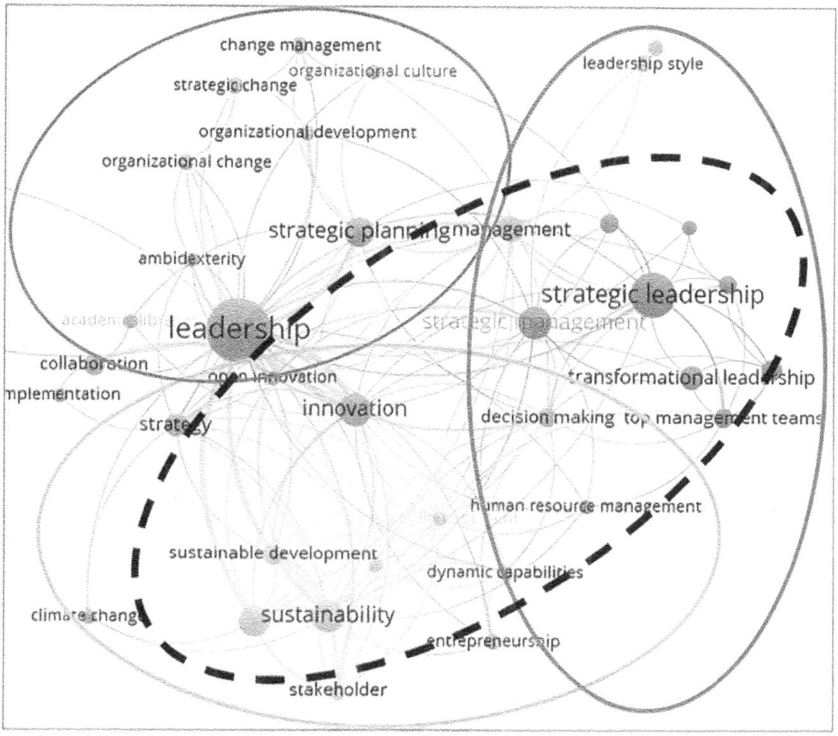

Fig. 4. Intersection Between Main Theoretical Directions of Strategic Leadership. *Source*: VOSviewer.

arises, do we need to revise our theories to or even develop new theories to explain the emerging phenomena (enterprises in the digital age) (Menz et al., 2021).

To summarise the findings and explore how to potentially bridge the streams, Table 4 has been developed.

Table 4 is divided into four sections, highlighting the three main theoretical direction, which are:

1. *Performance strategic leadership* with a primary focus on financial performance of the firm, performance management of employees as well as focussing on reducing variance in processes thereby increase quality and efficiency across the firm.
2. *Transformational strategic leadership* with a focus on the development and inspiration of the individual employee, and how leaders use inspiration to drive change and transformation of the firm and the culture. Transformational strategic leadership also promotes ambidexterity where strategic leaders are focussing on the internal resources of the firm and how to exploit those, while at the same time exploring new opportunities and trends in the market (O'Reilly & Tushman, 2007).

Table 4. Characteristics, Moderators, and Main Theory.

Theory and Concepts	Insights	Main Underlying Theories, Concepts
Performance strategic leadership theory	Financial performance Strategic planning and execution Create a vision for financial health Reduce variance and exploit internal resources Individual performance management	Upper echelon theory Agency theory Resource-based view Dynamic capability theory
Transformational strategic leadership theory	Focus on behaviour Driving transformation Learning and inspiration Promote ambidexterity	
Dynamic strategic leadership theory	Focus on sustainability is fundamental Social issues at the core Digital technology is adopted to amplify social impact Developing internal knowledge and social capital Increase variance to explorer	
Creating shared value	Transformation of leadership Social value is created at the core of the enterprise Financial value must be created to ensure survival and avoid mission drift Measurement of social value	Theory of change Blended value concept Stakeholder theory Social entrepreneurship theory

Source: Authors' creation.

3. *Dynamic strategic leadership* has social issues and sustainability as a fundamental element of doing business. The strategic leader is focussed on adopting digital technology to amplify the social and financial impact. Hence, during this sensing of new technology, the strategic leader aims to increase variance and risk quality to capture new trends and be able to seize any opportunity. Dynamic capabilities are supporting this view that sensing, seizing, and transforming businesses towards a specific direction is key, and the adoption and usage of digital technology is a key driver in delivering value (Fitzgerald, Kruschwitz, Bonnet, & Welch, 2014). The drivers of technology, are, however, not technology itself, but the characteristics of strategic leaders (Kane, Palmer, Phillips, Kiron, & Buckley, 2015). Closely related to dynamic capabilities, the *resource-based view theory* views the internal resources of the firm that 'starts from the concept that a firm's performance is determined by the resources it has at its disposal. The way these resources are used and configured enable the firm to perform and may provide a competitive advantage' (Barney, 1991). Digital technology is nowadays increasingly important in achieving business goals (Nylén & Holmström, 2015).

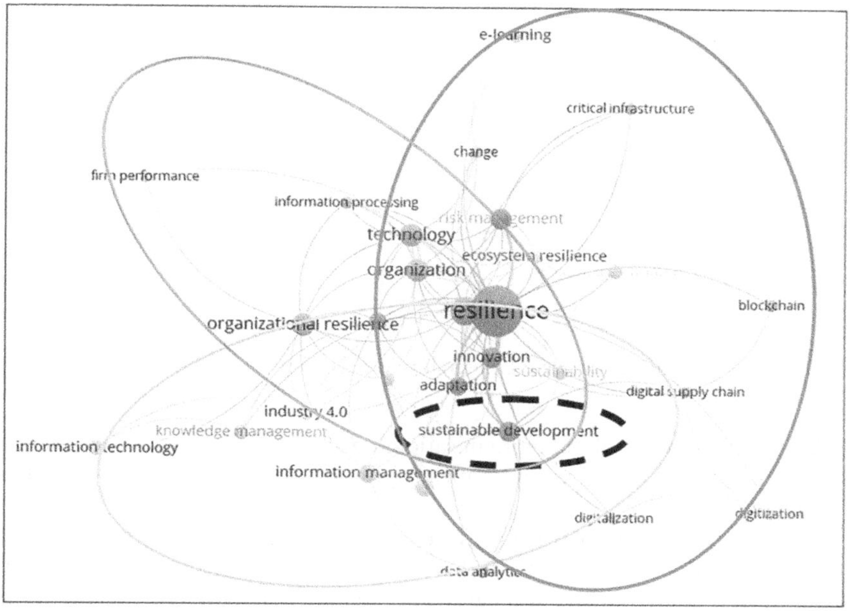

Fig. 5. Three Clusters for Organisational Resilience. *Source*: Authors' creation.

Fig. 5, three clusters for organisational resilience, is a bibliometric analysis conducted to identify directions. The first, and largest, cluster focuses on digital technology. Both exploring trends and developments as well as adoption and application of digital technologies to build resilient processes (Heinz, Hunke, & Breitschopf, 2021). The second cluster refers to strategic leadership. Key here is that more recently, resilience, technology and firm performance has been shown to be correlated. The third cluster is related to data. The trend here is to use data in a smarter way. Moving away from big data, focussing on quality data and moving away from data silos to have data lakes, ensuring data flow through the enterprise (He, Huang, Choi, & Bilgihan, 2022).

The dotted area represents sustainable development. This is the exact same key element which was highlighted in strategic leadership. Hence, sustainable development of the enterprise, for both resilience and strategic leadership, is centred around digital technology and ambidexterity.

FINDINGS

Based on the literature review and bibliometric analysis, the management model has been developed. The independent variable is 'strategic leadership', under which specific characteristics of SL has been identified.

The management model displayed in Fig. 6, respectively, the 'dynamic strategic leadership', consists of four main elements, where each one has its own characteristics as the driving force. SL, as the main enabler, moderated by

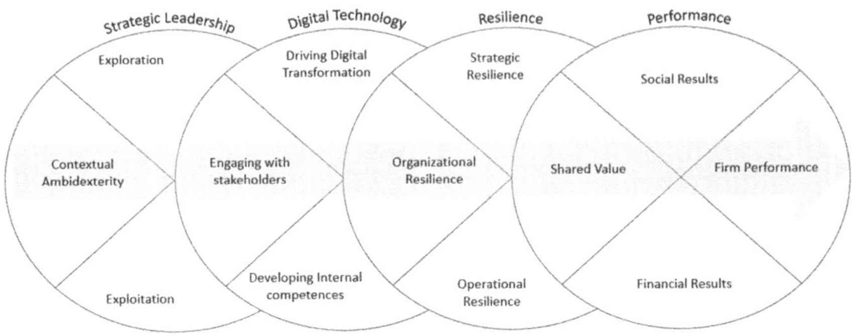

Fig. 6. Dynamic Strategic Leadership Model. *Source*: Authors' creation.

digital technology, developing organisational resilience, resulting in the creation of shared value, that is, creating both positive social and financial results, ultimately improving firm performance.

Contextual ambidexterity is identified as a key characteristic when it comes to strategic leaders. Ambidexterity in this regard can also be identified under contextual ambidexterity, where strategic leaders on one side exploit the resources of the enterprise and thereby decrease variance, creating resilient operations, while delivering financial value. On the other hand, the ambidextrous strategic leader is focussed on exploring trends within their sector and beyond, utilising new knowledge acquired on technology and people through the exploration to drive the digital transformation of the enterprise.

Exploration is centred around digital technology adoption, assessing new digital technologies, applications hereof and emerging trends. With exploration, strategic leaders increase variance to sense and seize new opportunities, preparing on a strategic level for disturbances, opportunities, and shocks – that is, strategic resilience. Therefore, it is paramount that the strategic leader will explore and drive digital transformation based on the exploration. Sensing and seizing emerging opportunities will translate into a transformation, hence the strategic leader will be driving the transformation from a strategic perspective. Success transformation is initiated by the strategic leader, but must be executed by employees on a tactical and operational level.

For the employee to have the skills to use the power given by the strategic leader, the management model suggests that the strategic leader must develop internal competencies, that is, bringing in what was explored into the firm, adding, and strengthening internal resources. The visionary strategic leader emphasises the characteristics of CEOs on the development of human and social capital and investing and developing the internal knowledge of the enterprise they are leading.

The theoretical framework under the research of 'performance strategic leadership' identified the driving force in digital technology adoption, engaging with internal and external stakeholders. This showed to be especially important when the enterprise promised to develop new partnerships, develop organisational resilience, and create a positive social impact.

Organisational resilience is a result of the two first dimensions. The exploration part from the ambidextrous leader, connected with sensing from dynamic capabilities, will induce strategic resilience. Exploitation and seizing and transforming are related to operational resilience. Transformation is in the intersection between exploring and exploiting, but it will eventually translate new resources into operational resilience.

Ultimately, the final dimension is related to the overall performance of the enterprise. The three previous dimensions are translating into the creation of shared value and ultimately improve firm performance.

CONCLUSION

The authors believe this will be the first scientific attempt to create a theoretical and practical foundation by bridging the research gap in strategic leadership, digital technologies, positive social impact, and organisational resilience. Strategic leadership has been demonstrated to be the key to successful enterprises.

The role of the strategic leader has evolved from focussing on decision-making and financial performance to including well-being, motivation, and upskilling of employees and most recently, ensuring the firm is making a positive social impact.

The interchange between three theoretical directions was identified as being a critical area for a future research agenda. Therefore, strategic leaders must maintain focus on internal as well as external areas. Explore the market, the trends, and stakeholder ecosystems and then to exploit new knowledge gained during exploration.

Hence, sustainable development, ambidexterity, and digital technology are all acting as critical areas for any enterprise aiming to become resilient and eventually deliver above-average financial returns while creating a positive social impact.

Limitations

As with all studies, this research is also constrained by several limitations. The authors used a comprehensive data sample of published studies. However, it may be that future research can review the EC and include studies in other languages than English. Concerning the actual findings, this research is purely based on secondary sources, following the bibliometric analysis.

Future Research

This research has pointed out several important directions for future researchers. The proposed future research agenda will include measuring the strength of the impact of strategic leadership characteristics on creating organisational resilience and improving the creation of shared value, hence firm performance. Moreover, ambidexterity was identified as a key characteristic. Hence, future research must focus on how strategic leaders and TMTs become ambidextrous to understand when to explore and when to exploit firm resources. Last, a call for future research to empirically test the direction.

REFERENCES

Appiah, G., Amankwah-Amoah, J., & Liu, Y.-L. (2022). Organizational architecture, resilience and cyber-attacks. *IEEE Transactions on Engineering Management*, *69*(5), 2218–2233. doi:10.1109/tem.2020.3004610

Barney, J. (1991). Firm resources and sustained competitive advantage. *Journal of Management*, *17*(1), 99–120.

Bass, B. M. (1997). *Full range leadership development: Manual for the multifactor leadership questionnaire*. Menlo Park, CA: Mindgarden.

Bass, B. M. (1999). Two decades of research and development in transformational leadership. *European Journal of Work and Organizational Psychology*, *8*(1), 9–32.

Bass, B. M., & Avolio, B. J. (Eds.). (1994). *Improving organizational effectiveness through transformational leadership*. Thousand Oaks, CA: Sage Publications.

Belalcazar, A., Ron, M. B., Díaz, J., & Molinari, L. (2017). Towards a strategic resilience of applications through the NIST cybersecurity framework and the strategic alignment model. In *International conference on information systems and computer science (INCISCOS)* (pp. 181–187). Quito, Ecuador. doi:10.1109/INCISCOS.2017.29. Retrieved from https://www.computer.org/csdl/proceedings/inciscos/2017/12OmNzsrwbn

Birkinshaw, J., & Gibson, C. (2004). Building ambidexterity into an organization. *MIT Sloan Management Review*, *45*(4), 47–55.

Burgelman, R., Floyd, S., Tomi, L., Saku, M., Eero, V., & Richard, W. (2017). Strategy processes and practices: Dialogues and intersections. *Strategic Management Journal*, *39*(Special Issue), 531–558.

Burgelman, R. A., & Grove, A. S. (2007). Let chaos reign, then rein in chaos-repeatedly: Managing strategic dynamics for corporate longevity. *Strategic Management Journal*, *28*(10), 965–979.

Fernandes, C. I., Veiga, P., Ferrira, J., Rammal, H., & Pereira, V. (2022). Assessing strategic leadership in organizations: Using bibliometric data to developing a holistic model. *Journal of Business Research*, *141*, 646–655.

Fitzgerald, M., Kruschwitz, N., Bonnet, D., & Welch, M. (2014). Embracing digital technology: A new strategic imperative. *MIT Sloan Management Review*, *55*(2), 3–12.

Grecco, C. H. S., Vidal, M. C. R., Cosenza, C. A. N., Santos, I. J. A. L,, & Carvalho, P. V. R. (2013, November 24–29). A fuzzy logic based method to monitor organizational resilience: Application in a Brazilian radioactive facility. In *2013 international nuclear Atlantic conference – INAC 2013* (pp. 1–10), Recife, PE, Brazil, November 24-29, 2013. Associação Brasileira de Energia Nuclear - Aben.

Greenleaf, R. K (2002). *Servant leadership: A journey into the nature of legitimate power & greatness*. Mahwah, NJ : Paulist Press.

Hambrick, D. C., & Quigley, T. J. (2014). Toward more accurate contextualization of the CEO effect on firm performance. *Strategic Management Journal*, *35*(4), 473–491.

He, Z., Huang, H., Choi, H., & Bilgihan, A. (2022). Building organizational resilience with digital transformation. *Journal of Service Management*, *20*(1), 0216. https://doi.org/10.1108/JOSM-06-2021-0216.

Heinz, D., Hunke, F., & Breitschopf, G. F. (2021, March). Organizing for digital innovation and transformation: bridging between organizational resilience and innovation management. In *International conference on wirtschaftsinformatik* (pp. 548–564). Cham: Springer.

Hepfer, M., & Lawrence, T. B. (2022). The heterogeneity of organizational resilience: Exploring functional, operational and strategic resilience. *Organization Theory*, *3*, 1–29. https://doi.org/10.1177/26317877221074

Hernandez, M., Eberly, M. B., Avolio, B. J., & Johnson, M. D. (2011). The loci and mechanisms of leadership: Exploring a more comprehensive view of leadership theory. *The Leadership Quarterly*, *22*(6), 1165–1185.

Hiller, N. J., DeChurch, L. A., Murase, T., & Doty. (2011). Searching for outcomes of leadership: A 25-year review. *Journal of Management*, *37*(4), 1137–1177.

Hitt, M. A., & Ireland, R. D. (2002). The essence of strategic leadership: Managing human and social capital. *Journal of Leadership & Organizational Studies*, *9*(1), 3–14.

Ireland, R. D., & Hitt, M. A. (1999). Achieving and maintaining strategic competitiveness in the 21st century: The role of strategic leadership. *Academy of Management Perspectives, 13*(1), 43–57.

Jaleha, A. A., & Machuki, V. N. (2018). Strategic leadership and organizational performance: A critical review of literature. *European Scientific Journal, 14*(35), 124–149.

Kane, G. C., Palmer, D., Phillips, A. N., Kiron, D., & Buckley, N. (2015). Strategy, not technology, drives digital transformation. *MIT Sloan Management Review and Deloitte University Press, 14*, 1–25.

Khan, Z. A., Nawaz, A., & Khan, I. (2016). Leadership theories and styles: A literature review. *Journal of Resources Development and Management, 16*, 1–7.

Kitchenham, B., Brereton, O. P., Budgen, D., Turner, M., Bailey, J., & Linkman, S. (2009). Systematic literature reviews in software engineering – A systematic literature review. *Information and Software Technology, 51*(1), 7–15.

Knies, E., Jackobsen, C., & Tummers, L. (2016). Leadership and organizational performance: State of the art and research agenda. In J. D. J. Storey, J. Hartley, J.-L., Denis, P. Hart, & D. Ulrich (Eds.), *Routledge companion to leadership* (pp. 426–440). New York, NY: Routledge.

Menz, M., Kunisch, S., Birkinshaw, J., Collis, D. J., Foss, N. J., Hoskisson, R. E., & Prescott, J. E. (2021). Corporate strategy and the theory of the firm in the digital age. *Journal of Management Studies, 58*(7), 1695–1720.

Metcalf, L., & Benn, S. (2017). Leadership for sustainability: An evolution of leadership ability. *Journal of Business Ethics, 112*(3), 369–384.

Mueller, J., Renzl, B., & Will, M. G. (2020). Ambidextrous leadership: A meta-review applying static and dynamic multi-level perspectives. *Review of Managerial Science, 20*(1), 37–59.

Nylén, D., & Holmström, J. (2015). Digital innovation strategy: A framework for diagnosing and improving digital product and service innovation. *Business Horizons, 58*(1), 57–67.

O'Reilly, C. A., III, & Tushman, M. L. (2007). Ambidexterity as a dynamic capability: Resolving the innovator's dilemma. *Research in Organizational Behavior, 28*, 185–206. https://doi.org/10.1016/j.riob.2008.06.002.

Quigley, T. J., & Graffin, S. D. (2017). Reaffirming the CEO effect is significant and much larger than chance: A comment on Fitza (2014). *Strategic Management Journal, 38*(3), 793–801.

Santos, C. M. D. C., Pimenta, C. A. D. M., & Nobre, M. R. C. (2007). The PICO strategy for the research question construction and evidence search. *Revista Latino-Americana de Enfermagem, 15*, 508–511.

Schoemaker, P. J., Heaton, S., & Teece, D. (2018). Innovation, dynamic capabilities, and leadership. *California Management Review, 61*(1), 15–42.

Schoemaker, P. J., Krupp, S., & Howland, S. (2013). Strategic leadership: The essential skills. *Harvard Business Review, 91*(1), 131–134.

Scopus. (2020). What is Scopus. Retrieved from https://service.elsevier.com/app/answers/detail/a_id/15534/supporthub/scopus/#tips

Singh, S., Darwish, T. K., & Potocnik, K. (2016). Measuring organizational performance: A case for subjective measures. *British Journal of Management, 27*(1), 214–224.

Strand, R. (2014). Strategic leadership of corporate sustainability. *Journal of Business Ethics, 123*(4), 687–706.

Teece, D. J. (2018). Business models and dynamic capabilities. *Long Range Planning, 51*(1), 40–49.

Teece, D. J., & Nonaka, I. (2001). *Managing industrial knowledge. Creation, transfer, utilization.* London: SAGE Publications Ltd.

Tushman, M. L., & O'Reilly, C. A., III (1996). Ambidextrous organizations: Managing evolutionary and revolutionary change. *California Management Review, 38*(4), 8–29.

VOSviewer. (2021). VOSviewer.com. Retrieved from https://www.vosviewer.com/

Yukl, G. (2008). How leaders influence organizational effectiveness. *The Leadership Quarterly, 19*(6), 708–722.

CHAPTER 12

CYBER INCIDENT RESPONSE MANAGERIAL APPROACHES FOR ENHANCING SMALL–MEDIUM-SIZE ENTERPRISE'S CYBER MATURITY

Ieva Auzina[a], Tatjana Volkova[b], Diego Norena-Chavez[c], Marta Kadłubek[d] and Eleftherios Thalassinos[e]

[a]*Atea Global Services Ltd., Latvia*
[b]*School of Business and Finance, Latvia*
[c]*Escuela de Posgrado, Universidad de Lima, Peru*
[d]*Czestochowa University of Technology, Poland*
[e]*University of Piraeus, Greece ; University of Malta, Malta*

ABSTRACT

There is a research gap in the explanation of cyber incident response approaches in management to increase cyber maturity for small–medium-size enterprises (SMEs). Therefore, based on the literature analysis, the chapter aims to (1) provide cyber incident response characteristics, (2) show the importance for SMEs, (3) identify cyber incident response feasibility and causal factors, (4) provide scenarios for consideration to create an incident response plan (IRP),

Digital Transformation, Strategic Resilience, Cyber Security and Risk Management
Contemporary Studies in Economic and Financial Analysis, Volume 111A, 175–190

Published under exclusive licence by Emerald Publishing Limited
ISSN: 1569-3759/doi:10.1108/S1569-37592023000111A012

and (5) discuss the cyber incident response and managerial approaches in SMEs. The authors used content analysis of scientific and professional articles to develop the theoretical foundation of incident response approaches in management for SMEs. The authors start from the fundamentals to obtain knowledge and understanding of the latest threats and opportunities, and how to defend themselves using the limited capacity of resources might be the starting point to building an extensive incident response capability. Incident response capabilities and maturity levels vary widely between various organisations. There is no simple one-size-fits-all process for incident response; each case is unique and requires continuous refinement. Differentiation and adaptation to different types of SMEs are pivotal to developing cyber maturity and defining requirements that fit the market's needs and are therefore more efficient in achieving the goal of increasing cyber security (CS) among business management. SMEs may not have a mature IRP, but at least one readiness indicator could lead to the preparation of a mature IRP. Implementation of the secure undertakings and information processes requires using modern information and communication technologies, incident response processes, and other modules that could enhance support for decision-making processes in management. The approach requires a systematic approach to issues related to constructing these solutions. The authors highlight that building efficient incident response approaches in management to improve cyber maturity will begin with infrastructure and people factors.

Keywords: Cyber security; cyber maturity; cyber incident response; cyber incident response plan; cyber resilience; cyber incident response approaches; management

INTRODUCTION

CS is generally used as a substitute for the terms Information Security and Computer Security (Khari, Shrivastava, Gupta, & Gupta, 2017). The National Cyber Security Centre (NCSC, 2016) defines a cyber incident as a breach of a system's security policy to affect its integrity or availability and/or the unauthorised access or attempted access to a system in line with the Computer Misuse Act (1990).

In general, types of activity that are commonly recognised as being breaches of a typical security policy are:

- Attempts to gain unauthorised access to a system and/or to data.
- The unauthorised use of systems for the processing or storing of data.
- Changes to a system's firmware, software, or hardware without the system owner's consent.
- Malicious disruption and/or denial of service (National Cyber Security Centre, 2016).

With punitive measures introduced by the European Union General Data Protection Regulation (EU GDPR) and the The Network and Information Systems Regulations (2018), how an organisation responds to a cyber incident can often spell the difference between failure and success (IT Governance, 2018). The speed at which companies can identify and respond to cyber incidents significantly affects controlling risks, cost, and exposure. Effective cyber IRP can reduce the risk of future incidents, help detect incidents at an earlier stage and develop a robust defence against attacks (IT Governance, 2018). Recently, the emergence of a new form of malware in cyber space, known as ransomware crypto virus, starts to draw attention among information systems security practitioners and researchers (Liao, 2020). Response to incidents which are vital for ensuring continuous business operations should be considered as important as any other internal process in management. Imposing serious threats to information assets protection, and ransomware victimises. Internet users by hijacking user files, encrypting them, and then demanding payment in exchange for the decryption key (Liao, 2020). About 71% of ransomware attacks are aimed at SMEs because hackers understand smaller organisations often aren't as prepared and protected (Holtman, 2020). Based on Symantec Internet Security Threat Report US Securities and Exchange Commission, 68% of SMEs have no systematic approach for ensuring CS, 81% don't receive any training on CS and 60% of SMEs who were victims of cyberattacks did not recover and shut down within six months (SMESEC, 2020).

CYBER INCIDENT RESPONSE CHARACTERISTICS AND IMPORTANCE FOR SMES

Cyber incident response is the process of responding to and handling security-related incidents involving information and communications technology infrastructure and data (Jaatun, Albrechtsen, Line, Tondel, & Longva, 2009). Cyber incident response approaches in management are reactive efforts to handle information security incidents using existing or new tools, processes, and people.

Effective CS provides SMEs with the confidence that allows them in an online and interconnected world to grow, innovate, and find new ways of creating value for their customers (ENISA, 2021).

Based on European Commission (2012), small and medium-sized enterprises represent 99% of all businesses in the EU. Bright Technology (2017) considers that strategic planning is fundamental to business success. Accessing and analysing information, in whatever form, is crucial to successful strategic planning. The development of various methods for rapid, inexpensive communications in management allows IT systems to facilitate communication between employees and third-party customers. Although, marketing comprises a fundamental activity for most SMEs. Various solutions and software allow for the improvement of a company's marketing efforts. Nevertheless, to improve the chances of successful business, SMEs must empower and engage their employees to enable them to represent the company to the best of their ability (Bright Technology, 2017).

INCIDENT MANAGEMENT

Incident management is the widespread practice of managing CS incidents. Incident management involves developing, implementing, and operating capabilities that include people, processes, and technology. However, incident handling, response, and analysis are operational level activities. These involve tactical practices to detect, respond to, and recover from a cyber incident (National Cyber Security Centre (NCSC), 2017). Nevertheless, an organisation's cyber risk strategy must be driven from the board level focussing on technology is not enough – security must be an integral part of core business governance strategy. Embedding incident management in the cyber maturity framework is the starting point for designing, developing, and delivering a forward-looking security strategy (NCC Group, 2015).

Incident management implementation is long, complex, expensive, and often fails. Failure to properly operate the information management process can result in constant interruptions by IT support technicians, poorly defined resolution priorities, poor management information, and forgotten poorly managed events.

Before a security incident occurs, an organisation should plan and implement an incident handling capability that includes skills, roles, procedures, processes, and tools to respond to security incidents (Voigt, 2018).

INCIDENT RESPONSE PLAN

An IRP is a documented, written plan that helps organisations to recognise and respond to CS incidents. The main goal is to design an IRP that enables to:

- Detect compromises as quickly and efficiently as possible.
- Respond to incidents as quickly as possible.
- Identify the cause of the issue as effectively as possible (Voigt, 2018).

An effective IRP needs to deal with several organisational challenges to enable decision-makers to detect anomalies and extract useful knowledge for problem-solving. In this context, decision-makers should evaluate the risks, select the appropriate alternatives during an incident, and provide differentiated services to satisfy the requirements of different incident response phases (Aguiar, Pereira, Vasconcelos, & Bianchi, 2018).

An IRP should be set up to address a suspected security incident (Tello-Oquendo et al., 2019). Within each phase, there are specific areas of need that should be considered (Table 1).

Preparation is critical to successfully identifying, handling, and recovering any computer incident (Johnson, 2014). Apart from compiling assets, creating a communication plan, setting metrics, or creating an incident plan for each type of incident, security event simulation is also a valuable part of this stage. Simulation or modelling helps to identify gaps, determine, and optimise which security events and at what trigger should be investigated; therefore, they provide a controlled opportunity to strengthen weaker areas and improve cyber maturity

Table 1. Incident Response Phases.

Phase	Description	Considerations for implementation
1. Preparation	Readiness to minimise the impact of security incident and maintain organisation continuity	• Has everyone been trained on security policies? • Has management approved security policies and IRP? • Have all employees participated in awareness training? • Have organisations identified critical assets and communication channels?
2. Identification	The process where organisations determine if a security incident has happened. A breach or incident could originate from many different areas	• When did the event happen? • How was it discovered? • Who discovered it? • Have any business areas been impacted, for example, does it affect business operation? • What is the scope of the compromise? • Has the source of the event been discovered?
3. Containment	Create short-term and long-term containment strategies	• What's been done to contain the breach short term? • What's been done to contain the breach long term? • Have all access controls been reviewed? • Have report strategies been developed?
4. Eradication	Elimination of incident root cause	• Have artefacts/malware from the attacker been securely removed? • Has incident response team gathered necessary artefacts from the affected system? • Has the system been hardened, patched, and updates applied?
5. Recovery	The process of restoring and returning affected systems and devices back into the business environment	• When can systems be returned to production? • How long will the affected systems be monitored? • Which tools will ensure avoiding similar attacks in future?
6. Lessons Learned	Once the investigation is complete, an after-action meeting is required to discuss what employees have learned from the security incident. Determine what has worked in the response plan and where is the place for improvement.	• What changes need to be made to the security? • How should employees be trained differently? • What weakness did the breach exploit? • Which tools or policies will ensure similar activity avoidance?

Source: Authors' adaptation from Tello-Oquendo et al. (2019).

(Ahmadi-Assalemi, Al-Khateeb, Epiphaniou, & Maple, 2020). The preparation includes the creation and approval of well-established corporate security policies including warning banners, user privacy expectations, an established incident notification process, the development of an incident containment policy, the creation of incident handling checklists, and ensuring the corporate disaster recovery plan is up to date (Johnson, 2014).

According to Johnson (2014), another important part of preparation is training for the incident responders and training for the organisation's system administrators. The third area important to preparation is having pre-deployed incident handling assets. The assets include:

- Sensors, probes, and monitors on critical systems – these automated mechanisms will allow monitoring of system applications with service and network monitoring programme, investigation of unusual activity, and application activity check.
- Tracking databases on core systems based upon minimum security baselines (snapshots of the systems or networks during normal operations).
- Active audit logs for all server and network components – where the logs are retained, how often the logs are updated, etc. (Johnson, 2014).

Identification is a key phase in incident response because the response cannot be manifested without accurate detection. Although incident detection is considered a reactive approach in management, there are detectable events that precede an incident (Johnson, 2014). Based on Johnson (2014), the main questions to be answered are:

- Is the event simply an unusual activity or can someone/something identify it as suspicious?
- What are the surrounding activities?
- Are there multiple reports of issues on the network or is it confined to one machine or location?
- Who notices a suspicious or unusual event and when did they notice it?

A couple of questions are asked when an incident occurs, which helps identify the event or potentially an incident. The basic requirement for incident response is the identification of the type of incident that has or is occurring at the time of response (Johnson, 2014).

Containment, eradication, and recovery is the part of the process where standards differ. The terminology used by NIST refers to containment as an aim to stop the attack or threat, eradication removes it stopping cross-systems proliferation and recovery aims to get the system operation returning to business as usual. Once the identification shows no further external or internal actions are necessary to complete the containment, the eradication step is initiated (Ahmadi-Assalemi et al., 2020).

Two important parts are *clean-up and notification*. Clean-up usually consists of executing antivirus software, deinstallation of infected software, or rebuilding the entire operating system. By getting the system back into operation, the next stage is recovery. Recovery is returning the system/network/component to normal business operations. There are always two steps to any recovery effort. First part of recovery involves service restoration, based upon implementation of corporate contingency plans. Second part of recovery involves system and/or network validation, testing and certifying the system as operational. Each system or component which has been determined to have been compromised must be recertified to the both operational and secure, not to reintroduce the issue into the operating environment (Ahmadi-Assalemi et al., 2020).

Lessons learned activity is one of the most important phases of the incident response process, but it is most often omitted. This phase provides an opportunity to contribute to continuous learning. A review of what occurred and defining actionable advice that can be used to inform decisions in the incident response's preparation phase is important to achieve a closure of the Incident response process (Ahmadi-Assalemi et al., 2020).

Based on Johnson (2014), the questions to be answered in the lessons-learned activity are:

- Was there sufficient preparation?
- Did detection occur promptly?
- Were communications adequate?
- What was the financial or informational cost of the incident?
- How to prevent similar activities in future?

To complete the incident response, objective and subjective data are recorded regarding each incident (IT SCC, 2011).

These data serve to:

- Identify the processes, procedures, and policies that were and were not effective during the incident identification, containment, eradication, and recovery stages of the incident response.
- Update incident response policies and procedures based on successes and failures of previous incident response activities.
- Develop new prevention techniques, improving the overall incident management lifecycle for future attacks, for example, training and awareness, mechanisms to integrate incident lessons learned into subsequent product/service design or improve testing procedures based on known vulnerabilities and threats.
- Improve information and intelligence flow between and across the SMEs to support the rapid identification of emerging cyber-related threats and other circumstances requiring intervention by government authorities (IT SCC, 2011).

INCIDENT RESPONSE FEASIBILITY AND CAUSAL FACTORS

The inability to prevent or render incident management ineffective is a serious threat to the IT sector's incident management function. A lack of common situational awareness among incident responders could leave critical assets, systems, networks, and functions vulnerable. Additionally, the inability to determine an incident's source or cause could prevent an effective response. Table 2 shows SME's feasibility factors of incident response (IT SCC, 2011).

Table 2. Feasibility Factors of Incident Response for SME.

Feasibility Factors	Feasibility	Description	Explanation
Legal	High	Statutes, regulation	The existing IT frameworks are extremely favourable for implementation of incident management plan
Organisational Compliance	High	Best practices, organisational charters, corporate values	To maintain and continue operations, almost all entities have developed best practices to protect against cyber incidents. Therefore, the implementation of incident management plan shall align closely with existing standards and best practices
Political	High	Public confidence, privacy-related issues	There may be privacy concerns involved; however, charges will likely be deemed acceptable during an emergency incident
Financial	Medium	Cost, budget limitations	The cost of developing, implementing, and maintaining an incident management plan. However, the cost of operational down time should prove as justification for the investment
Time	Medium	Reasonable schedule expectations	The implementation of incident management plan shall be completed in a reasonable time frame (i.e. 12–24 months to full implementation)
Technology	High	Ease of implementing existing technology or developing new technology	The technology or solutions to use depends on financial factor as well as organisations management decision
Market	High	Market conditions, competition	Organisations shall implement strategies that include mitigation activities and continue to find ways to make detection capabilities more resilient
Compatibility	Medium	Confidentiality, integrity, availability of services, systems, and data	Capability issues associated with incident mitigation would include technological limitations on various defence layers (i.e. endpoint, network, perimeter, etc.)
Cultural	High	The alignment of incident response strategy and company's culture	Cultural aspects of SME influence overall response strategies and capabilities, including limitations of CS specialist skill sets and overall human resource management

Source: Authors' adaptation from IT SCC, 2011.

From a design perspective, the *causal factors* that affect CS can be viewed within the context of organisation/enterprise, people, process, and technology (Mbanaso, Abrahams, & Apene, 2019).

These environments form the basis for a comprehensive definition of causal factors and quantitative effects, for instance:

(1) *Organisation/enterprise* – Corporate governance is key to the effectiveness of operational CS, aimed at minimising organisations' cyber risk exposure. In an organisational context, the executive management must set the policy direction and governance structure that assure that CS actions are consistently and correctly executed.
(2) *People* – The people element is the weakest link in an organisation security posture. Everyone with access to cyber infrastructure needs to be aware of their CS responsibilities, to have their effectiveness evaluated continually, and be managed consistently.
(3) *Process* – Corporate process, applications, and data that support the operations and decision-making of CS must be assessed to assure effectiveness and consistency.
(4) *Technology* – Concerned with an assessment of physical and technical infrastructure, that is, hardware, and software components required to support CS measures (Mbanaso et al., 2019).

From the author's point of view, the fifth factor plays a crucial role in affecting CS, and it is organisational culture and CS culture as a part of it. The goal for managers should be to drive cyber secure behaviours. That is achieved, in part, by creating a CS culture (the beliefs, values, and attitudes). Managers need practical solutions for dealing with the human side of CS. Building a culture of CS within an *organisation* guides employee behaviour and increases cyber maturity.

SCENARIOS FOR CONSIDERATION TO CREATE AN IRP

For SMEs to understand the importance of incident response process development and implementation in the organisation. Diogenes and Ozkaya (2019) have created scenarios and considerations to create an IRP (Table 3).

From the author's point of view, the scenarios for the company must take into consideration the international presence, generic business strategies, different business models, strategic priorities of development, etc. and must be further elaborated.

CYBER INCIDENT RESPONSE APPROACHES

Each incident response is different and presents its challenges, which are addressed. However, the standard security methodologies and best practices help to make the engagement successful during the environment's containment,

Table 3. Security Scenarios and Considerations for SMEs.

Scenario	SMEs' Security Considerations
Company is in possession of personally identifiable information, health information, or trade secret information that is federally or state-protected	• There is a need to determine the responses and actions that the business has taken in response to the data breach and to discover the most important points during the event
A variety of hardware and software is used for business operations	• Determine the date and time of asset utilisation and whether it has been recorded • Determine whether there is a security wall around any impacted systems • Has the software used by employees on corporate devices that been approved by management
The business is collaborating with several outside vendors and looking for new clients	• Determine whether organisations have communicated the process to follow in case of a security incident • Determine whether the organisation has clarified essential points of contacts in case of a security incident • Determine the company's plan for interacting with its clients, reliable vendors, and employees

Source: Authors' adaptation from Diogenes and Ozkaya (2019).

eradication, and recovery. McAfee (2017) focusses on approaches to prepare for incident response:

- *Define roles, responsibilities, guidelines, and procedures*. Due to the size of SME, there may not be the ability to divide the responsibilities among many people, some individuals may take on multiple roles. When an individual must assume many roles, their effectiveness diminishes. In these circumstances, it may be necessary to add additional personnel from the organisation to assist or temporarily augment resources with outside contractors to lead and/or respond during an incident.
- *Communicate plans and procedures effectively*. Preplanning considerations should be done before an incident. There is a need to include the potential out-of-band communication (non-business accounts) and encrypted communications. Consideration should be given during planning for a meeting space large enough for a team of people to meet and work. The one central point for all response activity coordination is a good approach.
- *Incorporate thorough intelligence and research*. During an incident, SMEs must identify the true nature of the incident or the attack. The initial contact related to an incident often contains inaccurate or incomplete information. This is generally caused by hastily compiled information and not examining the systems. SMEs need to be able to further review the tools to use the indicators of compromise and attack vectors to feed back into security applications and infrastructure to better defend and protect the environment.

- *Isolate or monitor affected systems (virtually or physically).* During an incident, SMEs must identify a variety of executables, files, processes, ports, IP addresses, and other indicators. Once indicators are identified, SMEs must decide whether to isolate systems from connecting to the network to protect infrastructure from potentially destructive activity, exfiltration of data, and other potential threats. This can be done by physically isolating the system. The virtual isolation of a system is highly desirable.
- *Document and maintain records of response activities.* Documentation during a response is essential for several reasons. The ability to recall facts concerning events during an incident can prove helpful when SME must repeat results or document completed aspects. Type of recordkeeping will also prove helpful when there is a need to relay facts around events to management, auditors, or regulatory representatives.
- *Document chronology of incident events.* Once the notes are recorded, SMEs should document the order of events by date and time. As a record of events is being made, other activities and/or events are often put in context.
- *Maintain logs and archives.* It is extremely important to be able to review historic logs and data to reconstruct the activities of cyberattack. Records will be available during an incident by routinely preserving logs and forwarding data to an archive (McAfee, 2017).

CYBER MATURITY LEVEL EVALUATION

A maturity model consists of a sequence of maturity levels for a class of objects. It represents an anticipated, desired, or typical evolution path of these objects shaped as discrete stages. Usually, organisations use maturity models to evaluate their methods and processes in accordance with good management practices and a set of external parameters. The assignment of a particular maturity level indicates maturity. By doing it, organisations taking advantage of maturity models' simplicity facilitate their understanding and communication and the fact that they may be used for benchmarking (Aguiar et al., 2018).

To adequately respond to an incident, SMEs must be evaluated by the existing cyber maturity level to understand the level of improvements in incident response capabilities. Cyber maturity goes beyond risk management and technical solutions, requiring a holistic view of systems and processes to prepare for the reality of cyber incidents (NCC Group, 2015).

The analysed methodology is used in practice to evaluate the cyber maturity level (see Table 4).

The authors suggest that after identifying the cyber maturity level, the plan of activities on strategic, tactical, and operational levels must be elaborated to move further to the next level. The key success factors must be identified to increase the level of cyber maturity and necessary financial resources allocated. It is also necessary to consider that cyber maturity works together with several cyber resilience elements.

Table 4. Description of Cyber Maturity Stages.

Level	Description
Stage 1 – Unstructured	Typically, processes are chaotic. The company does not offer a consistent setting to support processes. The process is not implemented or fails to accomplish its process purpose
Stage 2 – Structured	A work group or division is established by the organisation to develop and manage the incident management procedure. To assure the processes lifespan, workgroups identify an overall security aim, develop policies, and oversee the activity
Stage 3 – Well-defined	The approach has been acknowledged, and standard operating guidelines have been written and shared through internal training (Aguiar, 2017). Organisations manage everyday operational tasks using established internal processes. They check the processes for incident resolution and prevention as well as the demands placed on them by outside service providers. A specified process that can accomplish the process outcomes is not used to implement the managed process that was previously described
Stage 4 – Structured quantitatively	Process managers create measurable goals for performance and quality and use them as standards for controlling processes. Quality and process performance are managed across the course of a process's life and are comprehended in statistical terms. In order to attain its process outputs, the previously mentioned established process now runs within set bounds
Stage 5 – Improved	Leading techniques are applied automatically. Establishment of a self-contained continuous improvement process. On the basis of a quantitative comprehension of its business goals and performance requirements, the organisation continuously develops its IRP.

Source: Authors' adaptation from Aguiar et al. (2018).

CYBER RESILIENCE

CS maturity is a comprehensive assessment of an organisation's readiness to prevent, detect, contain, and respond to threats to information assets (KPMG, 2021). *Cyber resilience* is the ability to anticipate, withstand, recover from, and adapt to adverse conditions, stresses, attacks, or compromises on cyber resources (MITRE, 2017). Cyber resilience is the ability to continuously deliver the intended outcome despite adverse cyber events. The ability to continuously deliver the intended outcome can pertain to a nation, an organisation, or even a specific IT system. Incident response capabilities – both at the organisational level as well as at sector level – have redundant and resilient infrastructures built into them already.

Contrary to traditional views of CS, cyber resilience's main purpose is to prepare the company to be a 'safe-to-fail' system to maintain business continuity despite any type of adverse situations including unexpected and unknown ones. Sharkov (2016) emphasised that the enterprise's focus on resiliency at a very high level is not only a competitive advantage but also is vital for business sustainability and growth.

However, cyber resilience is not easy to operationalise because it is a multidimensional concept that involves governance, awareness and training, and business continuity management, among other dimensions for which SMEs usually do not have assigned resources. In addition, cyber resilience also involves investment in several policies such as preparing for unknown threats, maintaining business continuity, cooperating with external stakeholders, etc., which were not usually considered in traditional CS methodology. These added policies are complex since they require strategy, planning, testing, and coordination with external entities and SMEs usually lack the specialised resources to implement them (Carias, Borges, Labaka, & Arrizabalaga, 2020).

The notion of continuous means that the ability to deliver the intended outcome should be working even when regular delivery mechanisms have failed, during a crisis and after a security breach. The notion also denotes the ability to restore the regular delivery mechanisms after such events and continuously change or modify these delivery mechanisms if needed in the face of changing risks (Bjorck, Henkel, Stirna, & Zdravkovic, 2015).

MANAGEMENT AND ORGANISATIONAL LEVEL IMPROVEMENTS

Organisational CS requires more than just the latest technology. To secure an organisation, all members of the organisation must act to reduce risk. To obtain the goal of organisational level incident response capability development in a structured fashion, the framework should consist of the questions 'what to do', 'for whom', 'in what local setting', and 'in cooperation with whom' (Huang & Pearlson, 2019). Leaders have a special responsibility to define, shape, and align the entire organisation's beliefs, values, and attitudes with overall information security and CS goals. Since CS is more than a technical issue, the *organisation* needs to rely on the employees' behaviours to prevent and protect the organisation from potential cyberattacks. Ultimately, employee behaviour is what creates or reduces cyber-based vulnerability. Values, attitudes, and beliefs are unwritten rules that can be observed in actions taken by leaders, groups, and individuals in the organisation (Huang & Pearlson, 2019).

For incident response, it is crucial to receive input from internal personnel about security issues or suspicious activities in the environment, which may help save the company from cyberattack damage. For this reason, information security policies are very helpful.

Huang and Pearlson (2019) consider that to emphasise the necessity of management level changes, three basic top management qualities for SME should include:

- *Top management's priorities* – Strategic discussions of CS role in organisation and allocation of funding to help defend against adverse events.
- *Top management's participation* – Refers to the top management's personal involvement in CS-related activities. Participation could be in the form of communicating CS policies and attitudes or in actions that specifically secure the organisation, for instance, training attendance, participating in IRP testing,

and communication to internal/external parties about CS role and necessity for safeguard mechanisms.

- *Top management's knowledge* – Refers to the CS-related knowledge, skills, and competencies leaders have. Leaders who know and understand gaps and vulnerabilities in their organisation are more likely to have the values, beliefs, and attitudes around building a more cyber-resilient organisation (Huang & Pearlson, 2019).

Within the CS domain, examining effective teaming among cyber analysis involves understanding specific compositions of skills and roles among team members as well as team processes such as collaborative interactives and leadership (Buchler et al., 2018). Efficient human resource management needs accurate assessment and representation of available competencies as well as effective mapping of required competencies for specific jobs and positions (Boglouli et al., 2016). Effective communication, collaboration, and leadership are necessary to manage the demands of applying practical information security skills in a live fire scenario with intense time pressure to perform against the clock (Buchler et al., 2018).

CONCLUSIONS

Many SME organisations often fail to see the need for an IRP to mitigate cyber incidents. When security incidents occur, it's critical that organisations can handle it in a timely manner. The speed with which an organisation can recognise, analyse, and respond to an incident will affect the damage and lower recovery costs. Organised IRP requires defined, repeatable processes and the ability to learn from incidents that threaten the confidentiality, availability, and integrity of critical systems and data (Ruefle, Dorofee, & Mundie, 2014). The key to reducing the duration of an incident is prompt detection and response. Readiness is fundamental to efficient and effective incident management (NCSC, 2017).

From the author's point of view, for SMEs, starting from the fundamentals to obtain knowledge and understanding of the latest threats and opportunities on how to defend themselves using the limited capacity of resources, might be the starting point to build extensive incident response capability. Incident response capabilities and maturity levels vary widely between various organisations. SMEs may not have a mature IRP, but at least one readiness indicator could lead to the preparation of a mature IRP. Two different SMEs of similar sizes may have different approaches that reflect their risk appetites, business objectives, and cultures (NCSC, 2017).

There is no simple one-size-fits-all process for incident response – each case is unique and requires continuous refinement. Differentiation and adaptation to different types of SMEs are pivotal to developing cyber maturity and defining requirements that fit the market's needs and are therefore more efficient in achieving the goal of increasing CS among businesses.

REFERENCES

Aguiar, J., Pereira, R., Vasconcelos, J. B., & Bianchi, I. (2018). An overlap less incident management maturity model for multi-framework assessment (ITIL, COBIT, CMMI-SVC). *Interdisciplinary Journal of Information, Knowledge, and Management*, *13*, 137–163. https://doi.org/10.28945/4083

Ahmadi-Assalemi, G., Al-Khateeb, H., Epiphaniou, G., & Maple, C. (2020). Cyber resilience and incident response in smart cities: A systematic literature review. *Smart Cities*, *3*, 894–927. https://doi.org/10.3390/smartcities3030046

Bjorck, F., Henkel, M., Stirna, J., & Zdravkovic, J. (2015). *Cyber resilience – Fundamentals for a definition*. Cham: Springer International Publishing.

Boglouli, M., Mittas, N., Kakarontzas, G., Theodosiou, T., Angelis, L., & Fathi, M. (2016). Competence assessment as an expert system for human resource management: A mathematical approach. *Expert Systems with Applications*, *70*, 83–102. https://doi.org/10.1016%2fj.eswa.2016.10.046

Bright Technology. (2017). IT & SME business fundamentals – Executive summary. Retrieved from https://www.slideshare.net/vickimmel/it-sme-business-fundamentals-executive-summary. Accessed on July 20, 2022.

Buchler, N., La Fleur, C. G., Hoffman, B., Rajivan, P., Marusich, L., & Lightner, L. (2018). Cyber teaming and role specialization in a cyber security defense competition. *Frontiers in Psychology*, *9*, 2133. https://psycnet.apa.org/doi/10.3389/fpsyg.2018.02133

Carias, J. F., Borges, M. R. S., Labaka, L., & Arrizabalaga, S. (2020). Systematic approach for cyber resilience operationalization in SMEs. *IEEE Access*, *8*, 174200–174221. http://dx.doi.org/10.1109/ACCESS.2020.3026063

Diogenes, Y., & Ozkaya, E. (2019). *Cybersecurity – Attack and defense strategies*. Birmingham: Packt Publishing.

European Commission. (2012). SME definition. Retrieved from https://ec.europa.eu/growth/smes/sme-definition_en. Accessed on August 31, 2022.

ENISA. (2021). Cybersecurity for SMEs – Challenges and recommendations. Retrieved from https://www.enisa.europa.eu/publications/enisa-report-cybersecurity-for-smes. Accessed on October 14, 2022.

Huang, K., & Pearlson K. (2019). *For what technology can't fix: Building a model of organizational cybersecurity culture*. Honolulu: University of Hawaii.

Holtman, M. (2020). Ransomware: SME guide to protection, prevention and response. Retrieved from https://www.theukdomain.uk/ransomware-sme-guide/. Accessed on August 11, 2022.

IT Governance. (2018). Becoming a victim of a cyber-attack is an imminent reality for all companies. Retrieved from https://www.itgovernance.co.uk/cyber-incident-response-management. Accessed on October 17, 2022.

IT SCC, IT GCC. (2011). *Risk management strategy for the provide incident management capabilities critical function*. Washington, DC: Homeland Security.

Jaatun, M. G., Albrechtsen, E., Line, M. B., Tondel, I. A., & Longva, O. H. (2009). A framework for incident response management in the petroleum industry. *International Journal of Critical Infrastructure Protection*, *2*(1), 26–37. https://doi.org/10.1016/j.ijcip.2009.02.004

Johnson, L. R. (2014). *Computer incident response and forensics team management – Conducting a successful incident response*. Waltham: Elsevier.

Khari, M., Shrivastava, G., Gupta, S., & Gupta, R. (2017). *Role of cyber security in today's scenario*. Hershey, PA: IGI Global.

KPMG. (2021). Cyber maturity assessment. Retrieved from https://home.kpmg/au/en/home/services/advisory/management-consulting/technology/cyber-security/cyber-strategy-governance/cyber-maturity-assessment.html. Accessed on August 11, 2022.

Liao, O. (2020). *Ransomware: A growing threat to SMEs*. Brownsville, TX: The University of Texas at Brownsville and Texas Southmost College.

Mbanaso, U. M., Abrahams, L., & Apene, O. Z. (2019). Conceptual design of a cybersecurity resilience maturity measurement (CRMM) framework. *The African Journal of Information and Communication*, *23*, 1–26. https://doi.org/10.23962/10539/27535

McAfee. (2017). Ten ways to prepare for incident response. Retrieved from https://www.mcafee.com/enterprise/en-us/assets/white-papers/wp-10-ways-prepare-incident-response.pdf. Accessed on August 14, 2022.

National Cyber Security Centre (NCSC). (2016). What is a cyber incident. Retrieved from https://www.ncsc.gov.uk/information/what-cyber-incident. Accessed on October 17, 2022.

National Cyber Security Centre (NCSC) – A Part of the GCSB. (2017). Incident management. Be resilient, be prepared. Retrieved from https://www.ncsc.govt.nz/assets/NCSC-Documents/NCSC-Incident-Management-Be-Resilient-Be-Prepared.pdf. Accessed on October 19, 2022.

NCC Group. (2015). Cyber resilience and incident response. Retrieved from https://www.nccgroup.trust/globalassets/service-pages/documents/security-consulting/technical-security-consulting/cyber-resilience-and-incident-response.pdf. Accessed on July 10, 2022.

Ruefle, R., Dorofee, A., & Mundie, D. (2014). Computer security incident response team development and evolution. *IEEE Security and Privacy*, *12*(5), 16–26. https://doi.org/10.1109/MSP.2014.89.

SMESEC. (2020). Cybersecurity for SMEs – Increase your awareness, be ready, protected and aware. Retrieved from https://www.cyberwiser.eu/sites/default/files/SMESEC.pdf. Accessed on July 17, 2022.

Tello-Oquendo, L., Tapia, F., Fuertes, W., Andrade, R., Erazo, N. S., Torres, J., & Cadena, A. (2019). *A structured approach to guide the development of incident management capability for security and privacy*. Prague: ICEIS.

The MITRE Corporation. (2017). Cyber resiliency FAQ. Retrieved from https://www.mitre.org/sites/default/files/PR_17-1434.pdf. Accessed on August 19, 2022.

The Network and Information Systems Regulations. (2018). Retrieved from https://www.legislation.gov.uk/uksi/2018/506/made. Accessed on October 18, 2022.

Voigt, L. (2018). Incident response steps: 6 steps for responding to security incidents. Retrieved from https://www.exabeam.com/incident-response/steps/. Accessed on July 10, 2022.

CHAPTER 13

CENTRAL BANK DIGITAL CURRENCY CAN LEAD TO THE COLLAPSE OF CRYPTOCURRENCY*

Peterson K. Ozili

Central Bank of Nigeria, Nigeria

ABSTRACT

The chapter evaluates how the demise of cryptocurrencies as a medium of exchange may result from the issue of digital money by central banks. To evaluate the likelihood that central bank digital money would cause the demise of cryptocurrencies, the research employs discourse analysis and literature review. In this chapter, I demonstrate how the issuing of a digital currency by a central bank might result in the demise of private digital currencies like bitcoin. I contend that central banks will make use of their monetary authority and the confidence that people have in currency guaranteed by the government. This might provide considerable motivation for central banks to launch their own digital money. The creation of a digital currency by a central bank has the potential to reduce confidence in cryptocurrencies, which might eventually cause them to collapse. The chapter is the first to argue that fiat digital money should prevail over private digital currency.

Keywords: Central bank digital currency; cryptocurrency; bitcoin; blockchain; distributed ledger; payment system; central banks; digital innovation; cryptoassets; stablecoin; COVID-19; fiat digital currency

JEL classifications: E42; E58; G21; G28' O33

*An early version of this chapter was deposited by the author as an unpublished working paper in MPRA repository in 2021. It can be found at: https://mpra.ub.uni-muenchen.de/111218/1/MPRA_paper_111218.pdf.

Digital Transformation, Strategic Resilience, Cyber Security and Risk Management
Contemporary Studies in Economic and Financial Analysis, Volume 111A, 191–198

Published under exclusive licence by Emerald Publishing Limited
ISSN: 1569-3759/doi:10.1108/S1569-37592023000111A013

1. INTRODUCTION

Infamy surrounds cryptocurrency's volatility and anonymity. A cryptocurrency is a sort of digital currency that, with the help of blockchain technology, allows people to transfer value in a virtual environment. Due to its decentralised nature, it cannot be governed by a single entity (Bunjaku et al., 2017; Ozili, 2019). Due to the distributed-ledger technology used by cryptocurrencies, the correctness of cryptocurrency transactions is continually being checked by a number of people linked via digital devices all over the globe.

Cryptocurrencies are thought to be quite unstable (McCoy & Rahimi, 2020; Yi, Xu, & Wang, 2018). Economic theory backs up the claim that cryptocurrencies cannot be relied upon to function as money for this reason. According to economic theory, money shouldn't be unstable as one of its characteristics (Alchian, 1977; Ammous, 2018; Smithin, 2002).

There is a new kind of centralised digital money that is starting to take off. It is often referred to as fiat digital money or central bank digital currency (CBDC). A CBDC is a fiat currency issued by a central bank or other monetary authority that exists only in electronic form. Central banks are in charge of creating and managing CBDCs.

2. RISKS OF CRYPTOCURRENCIES

Emerging digital currency called cryptocurrencies provide for anonymous access to a range of risky online behaviours (Mills & Nower, 2019). Numerous researches provide evidence of bitcoin danger. For instance, Shanaev, Shuraeva, Vasenin, and Kuznetsov's (2019) research shows that the majority of blockchain assaults result in a drop in coin values, and those prices do not return to pre-attack levels a week later. According to Marella, Kokabha, Merikivi, and Tuunainen (2021), anytime these cyberattacks take place, clients can stop trusting not only a certain cryptocurrency exchange but also cryptocurrencies in general. A link between trading high-risk equities and trading cryptocurrency has been noted by Mills and Nower (2019). They note that gamblers who participated in both types of trading had more symptoms of worry and despair. Zhang, Li, Xiong, and Wang (2021) examine whether owning cryptocurrencies with more downside risk results in better earnings for investors. They discover that the cryptocurrency market exhibits a positive link between potential downside risk and future gains. The impact of cyberattacks on volatility spillovers among three cryptocurrencies – Bitcoin, Litecoin, and Ethereum – is examined by Caporale, Kang, Spagnolo, and Spagnolo (2021). When cyberattacks are taken into consideration, they discover a considerable dynamic dependency between the three cryptocurrencies, with Bitcoin being the most dominating one. According to Caporale et al., (2020), cyberattacks increase the volatility of cryptocurrencies.

3. THE RISE OF CBDC

In reaction to the acceptance of cryptocurrencies that have no official support and the rising cashlessness of many societies, central banks have introduced digital currencies. Many central banks are making conscious efforts to create their own digital currencies (CBDC). According to a poll of central banks conducted in 2021 by the Bank for International Settlements (BIS), 86 per cent of them are actively examining the possibilities of CBDCs, 60 per cent are experimenting with the technology, and 14 per cent are implementing CBDC pilot projects.

While some central banks, such those in China, Sweden, and the Bahamas, have progressed in their development of a CBDC, others, like those in Canada, the United States, Thailand, Singapore, Venezuela, and Uruguay, are still in the early phases. Additionally, although other central banks embrace other technologies, some are using blockchain and cryptography to develop their own CBDC.

4. CBDC: A LITERATURE REVIEW

The introduction of private digital currencies like Bitcoin has disrupted the financial services sector, and central banks wish to use these new technologies to help carry out their basic tasks by creating a CBDC (Ozili, 2022; Wadsworth, 2018). According to Bjerg (2017), adopting a CBDC monetary system might be an important political choice in certain situations.

Fernández-Villaverde, Schilling, and Uhlig (2020) show that the introduction of CBDC creates a challenging trilemma for central banks, who must simultaneously pursue the goals of efficiency, financial stability (i.e. the absence of runs), and price stability. This has an impact on how well central banks function. Boar, Holden, and Wadsworth (2020) assert that central banks will need to cooperate in order to better comprehend the effects of private digital tokens on CBDC transactions, even while they desire to create their own digital money. According to research by Barontini and Holden (2019), only a tiny portion of central banks are now employing central bank digital currencies as pilot projects, and even fewer central banks regard the issuing of a CBDC as a short- or medium-term goal. Despite the fact that the majority of central banks are studying CBDC, this is the case. Some of the arguments in favour of central bank digital money are shown to be unpersuasive by Engert and Fung (2017). For instance, although it could be a big factor in emerging and developing economies, the desire to create a CBDC in order to promote financial inclusion might not be a key driver in wealthy countries. Release of CBDC to increase contestability in retail payments may not be a very solid rationale since this impact depends on the particular properties of the currency. Bordo and Levin (2017) examine the potential contribution of a central bank-issued digital currency to the transparency of monetary policy. They show that digital currencies issued by central banks can only function as free means of exchange, secure stores of value, and stable units of account if they are account-based and interest-bearing. Cukierman (2019) asserts that in a future where private digital currencies are growing, central banks will be compelled to introduce their own digital currencies in order to preserve the effectiveness of monetary policy. Central banks want to leverage these new technologies to better carry out its fundamental functions by establishing a CBDC in response to the disruption caused by the advent of private digital currencies like Bitcoin in the financial services industry (Ozili, 2022; Wadsworth, 2018). Bjerg (2017) argues that in certain circumstances, adopting a CBDC monetary system might be a significant political decision.

As it relates to improving central bank function, Fernández-Villaverde et al. (2020) demonstrate that the introduction of CBDC creates an impossibly difficult trilemma for central banks, who must simultaneously pursue the objectives of efficiency, financial stability (i.e. the absence of runs), and price stability. According to Boar et al. (2020), even while central banks want to issue their own digital money, they will need to work together to better understand the implications of private digital tokens for CBDC transactions. Only a small percentage of central banks are currently using central bank digital currencies as pilot projects, and even fewer central banks see the issuance of a CBDC as a short- or medium-term objective, according to research by Barontini and Holden (2019). This is despite the fact that the majority of central banks are conducting research into CBDC. Engert and Fung (2017) demonstrate that some of the justifications for CBDC are not convincing enough. For example, the desire to issue a CBDC in order to promote financial inclusion may not be a major factor in developed nations, even though it may be a major factor in emerging and developing economies. Additionally, since this influence relies on the precise characteristics of the CBDC, releasing CBDCs to raise the contestability in retail payments may not be a very good justification.

Bordo and Levin (2017) look at how a digital currency issued by a central bank may help make monetary policy more transparent. They demonstrate that only if CBDCs are account-based and interest-bearing can they become a free medium of exchange, a safe store of value, and a stable unit of account. According to Cukierman (2019), central banks will be forced to launch their own digital currencies in order to maintain the efficiency of monetary policy in a world where private digital currencies are proliferating. The introduction of private digital currencies like Bitcoin has disrupted the financial services sector, and central banks wish to use these new technologies to help carry out their basic tasks by creating a CBDC (Ozili, 2022; Wadsworth, 2018). According to Bjerg (2017), adopting a CBDC monetary system might be an important political choice in certain situations.

Fernández-Villaverde et al. (2020) show that the introduction of CBDC creates an impossibly challenging trilemma for central banks, who must simultaneously pursue the goals of efficiency, financial stability (i.e. the absence of runs), and price stability. This has an impact on how well central banks function. Boar et al. (2020) assert that central banks will need to cooperate in order to better comprehend the effects of private digital tokens on CBDC transactions, even while they desire to create their own digital money. According to research by Barontini and Holden (2019), only a tiny portion of central banks are now employing central bank digital currencies as pilot projects, and even fewer central banks regard the issuing of a CBDC as a short- or medium-term goal. Despite the fact that the majority of central banks are studying CBDC, this is the case.

Some of the arguments in favour of central bank digital money are shown to be unpersuasive by Engert and Fung (2017). For instance, although it could be a big factor in emerging and developing economies, the desire to create a CBDC in order to promote financial inclusion might not be a key driver in wealthy countries. Release of CBDC to increase contestability in retail payments may not be a very solid rationale since this impact depends on the particular properties of the currency. Bordo and Levin (2017) examine the potential contribution of a central bank-issued digital currency to the transparency of monetary policy. They show that digital currencies issued by central banks can only function as free means of exchange, secure stores of value and stable units of account if they are account-based and interest-bearing.

Cukierman (2019) asserts that in a future where private digital currencies are growing, central banks will be compelled to introduce their own digital currencies in order to preserve the effectiveness of monetary policy. Bossu et al. (2020) examine whether a CBDC can become an official form of payment with regard to the design of CBDC. According to them, account-based CBDC and token-based CBDC are two distinct ideas that represent different sorts of money, and how the two types of CBDC are treated legally will rely on their respective design elements. They demonstrate how a central bank obligation is contained inside a digital token and distributed to users as central bank digital money. According to Lee, Yan, and Wang (2021), central banks that adopt CBDC will have to decide which ledger to use. They will decide whether the conventional central bank infrastructure or distributed-ledger technology should support the central bank's digital currency. According to Lee et al. (2021), nations that are familiar with distributed-ledger technology will have an advantage over rivals when creating CBDC. They demonstrate that, following the introduction of the CBDC, it will be necessary to continuously review current regulations in order to support it. They also suggest that whenever international dynamics alter the environment for the CBDC, it may be necessary to modify the CBDC. According to Auer et al. (2020), more central banks are developing retail CBDC systems in which the CBDC is a direct claim on the central bank that functions similarly to cash.

In order to determine the welfare consequences of a CBDC, Davoodalhosseini (2021) looked at a monetary policy design where economic agents may access just cash, only CBDC, or both cash and CBDC. They demonstrate that economic actors will choose to utilise CBDC over cash if the cost of doing so is not prohibitive. Furthermore, compared to when either cash or only central bank digital money is accessible, having access to both might result in poorer well-being. According to Auer and Böhme (2020), CBDC may provide peer-to-peer payments with ease and security similar to cash. Söilen and Benhayoun (2021) utilise a survey instrument to determine if households accept digital currency issued by central banks. They demonstrate that social recommendations had a role in families' adoption of CBDC.

Yao (2018) examines CBDC in China and makes the case that it might help make money a more stable value and provide useful instruments for macroeconomic management. This is in relation to the advantages of CBDC for macroeconomic and financial stability. To examine the implications of the central bank's digital money, Williamson (2019) built a model comprising numerous payment methods. They demonstrate how central bank digital money reduces crime related to physical cash and enables interest to be paid on a significant central bank debt. A monetary general equilibrium model is used by Kim and Kwon (2019) to analyse the effects of CBDC on financial stability. They demonstrate that the introduction of deposits into CBDC accounts would result in less private credit being extended by commercial banks, which will increase the nominal interest rate and reduce the commercial banks' reserve-to-deposit ratio. By raising the possibility of a bank panic, in which commercial banks run out of cash reserves to pay out to depositors, this might have a detrimental impact on financial stability. Regarding competition with banks, Chiu, Davoodalhosseini, Jiang, and Zhu (2019) point out that if banks have market power in the deposit market, an interest-bearing CBDC can enhance competition, raise the deposit rate, expand intermediation, and increase output.

Andolfatto (2021) shows that introducing interest-bearing CBDC can increase financial inclusion and diminish the demand for cash. Also, the introduction of interest-bearing CBDC may not disintermediate banks; rather it can expand their depositor base if the added competition compels banks to raise interest on customer deposits. Agur, Ari, and Dell'Ariccia (2021) examined CBDC in an environment where users are allowed to freely choose between using cash, CBDC, and bank deposits according to their preferences for anonymity and security. They show that a CBDC that competes with deposits could depress bank credit and output. In contrast, a cash-like CBDC may lead to the disappearance of cash over time. Grym, Heikkinen, Kauko, and Takala (2017) state that CBDC can make banknotes become a technically outdated payment instrument.

Ferrari, Mehl, and Stracca (2020) analyse CBDC in an open economy with regard to the risks and spillovers. They demonstrate how the existence of a CBDC may greatly exacerbate the effects of shocks throughout the world. However, the size of these impacts would rely on the precise design of the central bank's digital currency and may be greatly reduced if it has risk-mitigation mechanisms.

5. CBDCs CAN LEAD TO THE COLLAPSE OF CRYPTOCURRENCY

In two ways, CBDCs may result in the demise of cryptocurrencies. First, confidence in CBDCs, and second, the authority of central banks.

The first factor is confidence in CBDCs. The future of fiat money will be represented by CBDCs. People already trust fiat money; thus, it will be relatively easy for them to believe in fiat digital currency when it is introduced since it is backed by governments, a central bank responsibility, and is subject to regulation.

The ability of central banks to declare all non-fiat digital currencies unlawful is the second justification. The central bank is authorised by law to be the only issuer of a legal tender currency in the majority of nations. This gives the central bank the authority to declare all non-fiat currencies unlawful when necessary and to create new money such a digital currency.

Some countries, including Algeria, Bolivia, Morocco, Nepal, Pakistan, and Vietnam, have outright banned cryptocurrencies despite the fact that many central banks have strongly advised against using them for financial activities. Central banks are under a lot of pressure to take the lead in the digital currency field since private digital currencies are attracting a lot of attention from economic actors, particularly from people and enterprises. Because of this, it is likely that central banks will give in to pressure by launching their own fiat digital currency and then declare that other non-fiat private digital currencies, notably bitcoin, are prohibited from being used as money in the economy. A central bank or government action like that might cause cryptocurrencies to disappear. Cryptocurrencies may be utilised as investment assets by central banks who do not wish to outlaw them, but not as a medium of exchange for fair-trade transactions.

6. CONCLUSION

In this chapter, I examined the growth of CBDCs and how, after CBDCs have been produced, cryptocurrencies may cease to exist as a means of exchange for goods and services. Two things that may cause cryptocurrencies to fail as a medium of trade are people's belief in government-backed money and the might of central banks.

The world of cash has recently been transformed by cryptocurrencies. It started off with a lot of promise and potential, but because of its tremendous volatility, it is not as useful as a currency. Only if they continue to be seen as investment assets can cryptocurrencies withstand the rise of CBDC. However, as soon as its proponents demand that it become a currency, it will collapse due to its legal inability to compete with fiat digital money or CBDCs.

REFERENCES

Agur, I., Ari, A., & Dell'Ariccia, G. (2021). Designing central bank digital currencies. *Journal of Monetary Economics, 125*, 62–79

Alchian, A. A. (1977). Why money? *Journal of Money, Credit and Banking, 9*(1), 133–140.

Ammous, S. (2018). Can cryptocurrencies fulfil the functions of money? *The Quarterly Review of Economics and Finance, 70*, 38–51.

Andolfatto, D. (2021). Assessing the impact of central bank digital currency on private banks. *The Economic Journal, 131*(634), 525–540.

Auer, R., & Böhme, R. (2020, March). The technology of retail central bank digital currency. *BIS Quarterly Review*, pp. 85–100. Retrieved from https://www.bis.org/publ/qtrpdf/r_qt2003j.htm

Auer, R. A., Cornelli, G., & Frost, J. (2020). *Rise of the central bank digital currencies: Drivers, approaches and technologies*. CESifo Working Paper No. 8655. https://www.bis.org/publ/work880.htm

Barontini, C., & Holden, H. (2019, January 8). Proceeding with caution – A survey on Central Bank digital currency. *BIS Papers 101*, 1–24. https://www.bis.org/publ/work880.htm

Bjerg, O. (2017, June). *Designing new money – The policy trilemma of central bank digital currency*. CBS Working Paper. https://dx.doi.org/10.2139/ssrn.2985381

Boar, C., Holden, H., & Wadsworth, A. (2020). Impending arrival – A sequel to the survey on central bank digital currency. *BIS Papers, 107*, 1–19.

Bordo, M. D., & Levin, A. T. (2017). *Central bank digital currency and the future of monetary policy (No. w23711)*. Cambridge, MA: National Bureau of Economic Research.

Bossu, W., Itatani, M., Margulis, C., Rossi, A. D., Weenink, H., & Yoshinaga, A. (2020). *Legal aspects of central bank digital currency: Central bank and monetary law considerations*. IMF Working Paper No. 20/254. Retrieved from https://ssrn.com/abstract=3758088

Bunjaku, F., Gjorgieva-Trajkovska, O., & Miteva-Kacarski, E. (2017). Cryptocurrencies – Advantages and disadvantages. *Journal of Economics*, *2*(1), 31–39.

Caporale, G. M., Kang, W. Y., Spagnolo, F., & Spagnolo, N. (2020). Non-linearities, cyber attacks and cryptocurrencies. *Finance Research Letters*, *32*, 101297.

Caporale, G. M., Kang, W. Y., Spagnolo, F., & Spagnolo, N. (2021). Cyber-attacks, spillovers and contagion in the cryptocurrency markets. *Journal of International Financial Markets, Institutions and Money*, *85*, 101298.

Chiu, J., Davoodalhosseini, S. M., Jiang, J. H., & Zhu, Y. (2019). Bank market power and central bank digital currency: Theory and quantitative assessment. https://dx.doi.org/10.2139/ssrn.3331135

Cukierman, A. (2019). *Welfare and political economy aspects of a central bank digital currency*. CEPR Discussion Papers 13728. Retrieved from https://ssrn.com/abstract=3387317

Davoodalhosseini, S. M. (2021). Central bank digital currency and monetary policy. *Journal of Economic Dynamics and Control*, *142*, 104150.

Engert, W., & Fung, B. S. C. (2017). *Central bank digital currency: Motivations and implications*. Bank of Canada Staff Discussion Paper No. 2017-16. Retrieved from https://www.econstor.eu/handle/10419/200452

Fernández-Villaverde, J., Schilling, L., & Uhlig, H. (2020). *Central bank digital currency: When price and bank stability collide*. CEPR Discussion Paper No. DP15555. Retrieved from https://ssrn.com/abstract=3753955

Ferrari, M. M., Mehl, A., & Stracca, L. (2020). *Central bank digital currency in an open economy*. ECB Working Paper No. 20202488. Retrieved from https://ssrn.com/abstract=3733463

Grym, A., Heikkinen, P., Kauko, K., & Takala, K. (2017). Central bank digital currency. *BoF Economics Review*, *5*, 1–10. Retrieved from https://publications.bof.fi/bitstream/handle/10024/43569/BoFER_5_2017.pdf?sequence=1

Kim, Y. S., & Kwon, O. (2019). *Central bank digital currency and financial stability*. Bank of Korea WP 2019-6. Retrieved from https://ssrn.com/abstract=3330914 or http://dx.doi.org/10.2139/ssrn.3330914

Lee, D. K. C., Yan, L., & Wang, Y. (2021). A global perspective on central bank digital currency. *China Economic Journal*, *14*(1), 52–66.

Marella, V., Kokabha, M. R., Merikivi, J., & Tuunainen, V. (2021, January). Rebuilding trust in cryptocurrency exchanges after cyber-attacks. In *Hawaii international conference on system sciences* (pp. 1–10). Manoa: Association for Information Systems IEEE Computer Society Press.

McCoy, M., & Rahimi, S. (2020). Prediction of highly volatile cryptocurrency prices using social media. *International Journal of Computational Intelligence and Applications*, *19*(4), 2050025.

Mills, D. J., & Nower, L. (2019). Preliminary findings on cryptocurrency trading among regular gamblers: A new risk for problem gambling? *Addictive Behaviors*, *92*, 136–140.

Ozili, P. K. (2019). Blockchain finance: Questions regulators ask. In *Disruptive innovation in business and finance in the digital world*. Bingley: Emerald Publishing Limited.

Ozili, P. K. (2022). Central Bank Digital Currency in Nigeria: Opportunities and Risks. In S. Grima, E. Özen & H. Boz (Eds.), *The new digital era: Digitalisation, emerging risks and opportunities* (Contemporary Studies in Economic and Financial Analysis, Vol. 109A, pp. 125–133). Bingley: Emerald Publishing Limited. https://doi.org/10.1108/S1569-37592022000109A008

Shanaev, S., Shuraeva, A., Vasenin, M., & Kuznetsov, M. (2019). Cryptocurrency value and 51% attacks: Evidence from event studies. *The Journal of Alternative Investments*, *22*(3), 65–77.

Smithin, J. (Ed.). (2002). *What is money?* Oxfordshire: Routledge.

Söilen, K. S., & Benhayoun, L. (2021). Household acceptance of central bank digital currency: The role of institutional trust. *International Journal of Bank Marketing*, *40*(1), 172–196. http://dx.doi.org/10.1108/IJBM-04-2021-0156.

Wadsworth, A. (2018, June). The pros and cons of issuing a central bank digital currency. *Reserve Bank of New Zealand Bulletin*, *81*, 1–21.

Williamson, S. (2019). *Central bank digital currency: Welfare and policy implications* (p. 4). Unpublished, University of Western Ontario.

Yao, Q. (2018). A systematic framework to understand central bank digital currency. *Science China Information Sciences*, *61*(3), 1–8.

Yi, S., Xu, Z., & Wang, G. J. (2018). Volatility connectedness in the cryptocurrency market: Is Bitcoin a dominant cryptocurrency? *International Review of Financial Analysis*, *60*, 98–114.

Zhang, W., Li, Y., Xiong, X., & Wang, P. (2021). Downside risk and the cross-section of cryptocurrency returns. *Journal of Banking & Finance*, *133*, 106246.

CHAPTER 14

LIQUIDITY POSITION OF THE BANKING SECTOR DURING THE COVID-19 PANDEMIC: EVIDENCE FROM WESTERN BALKAN COUNTRIES

Shkelqesa Citaku[a], Simon Grima[b] and Gani Asllani[c]

[a] *University Hasan Prishtina, Kosovo*
[b] *University of Malta, Malta*
[c] *University Haxhi Zeka, Kosovo*

ABSTRACT

This chapter aims to examine the position of the banking system and the effect of the COVID-19 pandemic on bank liquidity in six Western Balkan Countries. We aim to analyse the current financial parameters of the banking system to determine the impact of the pandemic's various risks on the banking liquidity stability in response to the capital reserves of central banks of the respective countries. This chapter deals with cross-country comparison analysis of how the government responded including fiscal stimulus packages to prevent the financial downturn and the impact on liquidity retention. The methodology is based on a comparative data analysis using primary and secondary sources. Although it is too early to have full evidence of the depth of the pandemic impact, the findings show that because of the immediate actions undertaken by the liquidity management of each country and also as a result of the favourable

Digital Transformation, Strategic Resilience, Cyber Security and Risk Management
Contemporary Studies in Economic and Financial Analysis, Volume 111A, 199–212

Published under exclusive licence by Emerald Publishing Limited
ISSN: 1569-3759/doi:10.1108/S1569-37592023000111A014

liquidity position before the pandemic Crisis, the banking sector had sufficient reserves to overcome the risk of crisis. Moreover, all six Balkan Countries have adapted the regulatory framework in line with international emergency measures to maintain financial stability. The measures and instruments implemented by countries have generally complied with the Basel Committee's instructions. The measures and instruments implemented by countries have generally complied with the Basel Committee's instructions.

Keywords: Pandemic; sustainability; finance; banking; liquidity; Basle Committee

INTRODUCTION

The financial crisis of 2008 was the biggest shock to the worldwide financial system and a unique challenge to financial institutions. The event of the crisis in 2008, in essence, was caused by the interaction of market participants. This happened due to synchronised decisions to sell assets, causing an acute lack of liquidity. Market participants before the crisis assumed that they all had sufficient liquidity (Citaku, Asllani, Luboteni, & Grima, 2020). When the market questioned this assumption, the liquidity disappeared. The crisis followed. Central Banks immediately reacted by increasing liquidity and trying to keep interest rates low to stimulate the economy. Since 2008, Central Banks have continued to provide massive liquidity as the prerequisite for ensuring financial stability. However, in 2020, the world faced another economic crisis driven by the spread of the COVID-19 pandemic. However, this time the crisis differs from 2008 because it was not caused by the failure of the financial system, but it was caused by an external factor. Now the question is whether the financial system was affected or to what extent the coronavirus impacted the stability. Although it is too early to fully understand the depth of the pandemic impact, the pandemic-related losses are likely to continue materialising for some time. It is obvious that banks are those areas in the financial system most affected by any crisis.

However, have the financial indicators of the banking sector remained stable due to the pandemic and have they affected the banking stability in the region? During the pandemic, it is evident that all banks have faced a cash flow problem that threatened banking liquidity stability. For that reason, all counties have announced a broad range of support measures to enable banks for additional resources to maintain balanced liquidity. At the very beginning of the pandemic, the Central Bank Governors endorsed a set of measures for additional operational capacity for banks. Mainly they deferral the implementation of the Basel III framework that creates capital safeguards and liquidity in case of banking shocks. Because the immediate actions were undertaken by the liquidity management of each country and as a result of the favourable liquidity position before the pandemic crisis, the banking sector potentially had reserves to overcome the risk of a crisis. A study shows that banks' capitalisation ratio considered a supportive parameter for liquidity, remained stable and above the required minimum capital adequacy ratio of 12%.

LITERATURE REVIEW

In previous events, counties have implemented many measures to ease the obstacles to banking activity. Among others, these included measures to relieve the strains on the banking system with special liquidity lines, blanket guarantees for liabilities and also maintaining adequate liquidity levels in the financial system (Awad, Ferreira, Gaston, & Riedweg, 2020). Liquidity is an important attribute of financial assets and is vital in the financial system. The high liquidity attracts more attention from investors. Liquidity risk occurs when a bank may suffer an adverse blow to its position (Schwarz, 2014). Shocks in the liquidity position of a bank can affect the credit supply due to the central role of banks in providing liquidity (Berger & Bouwman, 2016). In practical terms, the impact of any outbreak could affect the bank's financing and liquidity position, which could lead banks to decline. During the financial Crisis of 2008, the main source of banking stress in financial conditions arose from the lack of financial liquidity experienced in the financial market (Adrian & Shin, 2009). Adrian and Shin emphasise that during the crisis, liquidity is considered a main concern for banking stability. It is revealed that the crisis has influenced firm performance, liquidity, dividends and the structure of corporate governance (Khatib & Nour, 2021). In practical terms, the impact of any outbreak could affect the bank's financing and liquidity position, leading banks to fail (Gorton & Metrick, 2012). However, since the Basel Liquidity standards have come into force, it permits banks to use their stock during the stress period after assessing the situation and adjusting the measures depending on the duration of the shortage (European Banking Authority, 2020). It is the banking supervisors who should provide clarity and guide the banks on the use of capital and liquidity assets.

The liquidity protection measures mean the continuation of the issuance of financing instruments such as issuance income, short-term notes, commercial paper, treasury operations, etc. Banks whose capital rations fall below the minimum requirements should take immediate action to restore capital over the medium term (European Systemic Risk Board, 2016). It is very important that regular liquidity reporting is constantly presented (Bolton, Cecchetti, Danthine, & Vives, 2019). On the other hand, liquid assets are defined as assets that, when necessary, can be converted into cash to prevent any possible failure of the banking system Carletti, Claessens, Fatás, & Vives, 2020). However, banks must manage liquidity flows in the most profitable way that, at the same time, does not jeopardise financial stability (Boissay, Cantú, Claessens, & Villegas, 2019). The literature above suggests that the liquidity must be consistent with bank capital because the larger capital requirements might prevent liquidity creation (Shaban, Morina, & Misiri, 2019). The bank capital can impact a bank's liquidity because banks with highly capital can take on greater liquidity risk (Cetorelli & Goldberg, 2012). Although the bank needs to hold a large amount of liquid assets, a bank with little capital will find a risk to take on greater liquidity. That is why larger capital is consistently associated with lower probabilities of failure due to liquidity (Gatev, Strahan, & Schuermann, 2006). The bank liquidity indicators measure how liquid a bank is. It is a simple ratio that uses a few of the bank's assets (Berger & Bouwman, 2016). The bank capital is segmented into tiers as the primary indicator of a bank's health. Capital and reserves include funds contributed by owners, retained earnings, general and special reserves, provisions, and valuation adjustments. Capital includes tier 1 capital (paid-up shares and common stock), which is a common feature in all countries' banking systems, and total regulatory capital, which includes several specified types of subordinated debt instruments that need not be repaid if the funds are required to maintain minimum capital levels (these comprise tier 2 and tier 3 capital). Total assets include all nonfinancial and financial assets (Campello, 2002). The ratio of bank liquid reserves to bank assets is the ratio of domestic currency holdings and deposits with monetary authorities to claims on other governments, nonfinancial public enterprises, the private sector, and other banking institutions. We consider that the liquidity must be consistent with bank capital as the greater capital requirements might prevent liquidity creation. The banks need to hold a large amount of liquid assets; otherwise, banks with low capital will find a risk to take on greater liquidity. That is why the higher capital requirements are consistently associated with lower probabilities of failure due to liquidity.

RESEARCH METHODOLOGY AND DATA

To develop this work and to define the main characteristics of the banks' position in the Balkan Counties a comparative analysis was adopted, using primary data and other secondary sources. The analysis focusses on six Western Balkan countries: Kosovo, Albania, Bosnia and Herzegovina, North Macedonia, Montenegro and Serbia. The data are taken from different recourses: Annual Financial Report of each Central Bank, World Bank, IMF, EU progress reports, CEIC global database and other sources.

The empirical question of this chapter is that: at which parameters, respectively, the liquidity position affected the sustainability of the banking sector, significant for the financial system as a result of the COVID-19 pandemic?

The hypotheses set out are *H1* and *H2*:

H1. The measures and instruments implemented by Balkan Countries in accordance with instructions of the Basel Committee have saved the bank's liquidity and bank reserves.

H2. As a result of the favourable liquidity position before the pandemic crisis, the banking sector had sufficient reserves to overcome the risk of crisis from the COVID-19 pandemic.

THE MEASURES TO ALLEVIATE THE CHALLENGES POSED BY PANDEMIC

The Western Balkan financial sectors are at different levels of development. Financial systems are bank-oriented, where banks have more than 90% of financial institutions' assets in most countries. Between 70% and 90% of banking sector assets in the Western Balkan countries are composed of foreign capital or branches (Financial Sector Restructuring and Regional Integration in the Western Balkans, 2007). Because of these circumstances, the banking system in the Balkan region could be affected by any international economic Crisis (World Bank, 2021). As a consequence of the pandemic, all countries have implemented fiscal support (The COVID-19 Crisis in the Western Balkans, 2019). The impact on the service industry was evident, as shown by the turnover data and the restructuring of loans. However, the impact on the liquidity assets was minimal. The first measure was to restructure the loans by postponing the deadline for repayment and restructuring the loan. The bank temporarily made loan payments for borrowing from the pandemic and approved regulatory changes that allowed banks to classify outstanding loans (European Commission, 2021). The reason was to support borrowers in their difficulties with loan repayments. Although these measures were intended to support the economy to cope with declining incomes due to the pandemic, they also prevented any possible situation affecting the loan portfolio. In the study, we analysed the data extracted from the Annual Financial Report of each respective Central Bank of six Balkan Countries. Bank capital and liquidity position are essential concepts to understand what banks do, the risks they take and the best way to reduce them.

The instability arises if banks experience a lack of financial resources – capital or liquidity – as well as impairment of the essential economic functions they play. However, the main banking parameters and bank capital to assets ratio in all countries remain stable. See Table 1.

As the bank to assets is the ratio of bank capital and reserves to total assets, the data indicate that capital is consistent in western Balkan countries except for Serbia.

Bank capital and liquidity position are essential concepts to understand what banks do, the risks they take and the best way to reduce them. The instability arises if banks experience a lack of financial resources – capital or liquidity – as well as impairment of the essential economic functions they play. However, the ratio of liquid bank reserves to banking assets in all countries remains sustainable (see Tables 2 and 3).

Table 4 shows that the ratio of liquid assets to total assets of the Western Balkan countries' banking sector remained around 30%.

KOSOVO

As measures undertaken in dealing with the pandemic crisis, Kosovo adopted the regulatory framework in line with emergency measures taken internationally to maintain financial stability. With the outbreak of the COVID-19

Table 1. Deposits, Loans, Capital Adequacy Ratio, and Non-Performing Loans (2019/2020).

Country	Total Deposits Growth (%)		Total Loans Growth (%)		Capital Adequacy Ratio (%)		Non-Performing Loans Ratio (%)		Liquidity/Assets		Bank Capital/Equity to Assets Ratio (%)	
	2019	2020	2019	2020	2019	2020	2019	2020	2019	2020	2019	2020
Kosovo	12.0	16.0	8.0	9.82	19.0	16.5	4.6	3.0	25.4	29.0	28.8	30.1
Albania	6.8	6.5	4.3	6.55	18.2	18.1	8.1	8.2	30.2	34.2	35.7	33.3
North Macedonia	7.1	7.4	5.2	5.71	16.0	16.7	4.6	3.3	29.8	30.6	31.9	32.5
Montenegro	1.2	2.8	3.3	6.20	19.6	19.3	5.1	5.7	25.3	22.6	20.8	21.8
Serbia	17.7	18.5	7.73	8.06	21.0	22.4	4.6	4.1	35.1	35.7	36	37.3
Bosnia and Herzegovina	5.0	5.1	0.9	1.13	18.3	19.2	7.4	6.1	28.3	29.7	29.6	29.1
Average	8.3	9.38	4.9	6.25	18.6	18.7	4.38	4.98	29	30.3	30.4	30.6

Source: Calculations are based on data extracted from the Annual Financial Report of each respective Central Bank (2021).

Table 2. Bank Capital to Assets Ratio in All Six Balkan Countries (2008–2020).

Bank Capital/Equity to Assets Ratio (%)	2008	2009	2010	2011	2012	2013	2014	2015	2016	2017	2018	2019	2020
Kosovo	8.8	9.2	9.3	9.5	9.5	9.1	10.8	12.2	12.1	12.6	12.2	11.2	11.7
Albania	n/a	n/a	9.4	8.6	8.5	8.3	8.5	9.5	9.7	10.1	10.1	10.4	10.3
North Macedonia	11.5	11.39	10.5	11	11.1	11.27	10.8	10.5	10.6	10.8	10.7	10.9	11.6
Montenegro	8.9	9.6	9.3	10.1	9.06	8.2	8.9	8.6	8.6	8.6	8.4	10.1	10.03
Serbia	n/a	n/a	n/a	n/a	n/a	n/a	n/a	n/a	n/a	n/a	n/a	n/a	n/a
Bosnia and Herzegovina	9.3	10.7	11.7	13.6	14.21	14.36	14.38	14.09	14.3	14.1	13.1	12.8	12.5
Average	7.7	10.2	10.4	10.4	10.3	10.2	10.6	10.9	11.06	10.9	10.9	10.8	11.22

Source: Calculations are based on data extracted from https://data.worldbank.org/indicator (2008–2020).

Table 3. The Ratio of Bank Liquid Reserves to Bank Assets in All Six Balkan Countries (2008–2020).

The Ratio of Bank Liquid Reserves to Bank Assets (%)	2008	2009	2010	2011	2012	2013	2014	2015	2016	2017	2018	2019	2020
Kosovo	8.6	12.4	9.3	9.4	12.7	13.1	12.1	11.4	9.8	10.3	9.9	10.6	13
Albania	15.8	14.3	14.3	13.4	13.4	13.8	13.6	18	18	17.3	17.8	15.2	19.6
North Macedonia	21	21.2	24.9	26.5	24.7	22.1	24.5	20.9	23.8	22.4	24.3	29.1	25.1
Montenegro	n/a	n/a	n/a	n/a	n/a	12.8	16.5	20.4	25.1	24.9	21.9	22.3	21.3
Serbia	41	39.9	25.8	31.7	25.6	30.4	20.9	23.30	20.9	20.8	22.3	23.5	24.1
Bosnia and Herzegovina	19.6	21.5	21.7	19.8	19.0	21	22.3	23	25.3	22.4	27.5	26.8	29.2
Average	21.2	21.8	19.2	20.16	19.08	18.8	18.3	19.5	20.4	19.7	20.6	21.2	22.05

Source: Calculations are based on data extracted from https://data.worldbank.org/indicator (2008–2020).

Table 4. Liquidity to Total Assets in All Six Balkan Countries (2017–2020).

Liquidity to Total Assets in %	2008	2009	2010	2011	2012	2013	2014	2015	2016	2017	2018	2019	2020
Kosovo	n/a	34.6	32.3	26.6	22.6	21.9	23	22.9	26.3	25.4	29,0	28.8	30.1
Albania	n/a	22.65	25.95	26.3	29.3	27.6	31.9	32.6	31.2	30.2	34.2	35.7	33.3
North Macedonia	n/a	n/a	30.9	31.2	32.4	31.2	29.8	28.2	28.9	29.8	30.6	31.9	32.5
Montenegro	n/a	11.6	13.7	11.5	16	20	22.1	24.8	25	25.3	22.6	20.8	21.8
Serbia	n/a	49	43.7	42.3	38.9	41	42.2	40.5	38.9	35.1	35.7	36	36.3
Bosnia and Herzegovina	n/a	30.94	28.14	27.19	25.43	26.39	26.78	26.48	27.21	28.3	29.7	29.6	29.1
Average	n/a	29.7	29.11	27.5	27.3	28	29	28.4	29.7	29	30.3	30.4	30.6

Source: Calculations are based on data extracted from https://www.ceicdata.com (2008–2020).

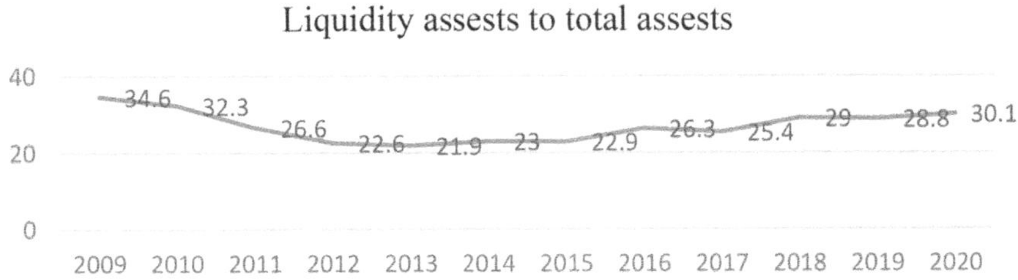

Fig. 1. Liquidity Position (to Total Assets) of the Banking Sector in Kosovo. *Source*: Data extracted from Financial Stability Report of Central Bank of Kosovo (2021).

pandemic, the Central Bank of Kosovo took measures to prevent any potential crisis arising from such an unforeseen situation that could affect the banks' stability (Central Bank of Kosovo, 2021). The first measure was to restructure the loans by postponing the deadline for repayment as well as restructuring the loan by changing one or more terms of the contract. The first phase of the restructuring was done for March–June 2020. The share of restructuring loans in the first phase was 40.9% (IMF, 2021). In the second phase of the restructuring, in June and December 2020, the share of restructuring loans was lower at 11.5% of total loans. This measure on loan repayment or suspension of loan instalment payments was without charging the penalty interest, specifically for the borrowers who faced financial difficulties in generating revenues due to COVID-19. Because of the immediate actions undertaken by the management and as a result of the favourable liquidity position before the pandemic crisis, the banking sector had sufficient reserves to overcome the risk of the crisis besides the restructuring of the loans (Commission Staff Working Document Kosovo, 2021). In 2020, the banking indicators remained stable, including the key liquidity indicators, which stand advantageous. The liquidity assets to total assets in 2020 was 30.1% (see Fig. 1).

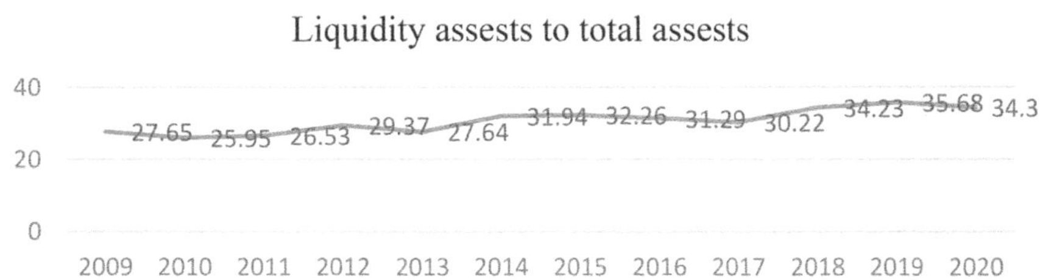

Fig. 2. Liquidity Position (to Total Assets) of the Banking Sector in Albania. *Source*: Data extracted from Financial Stability Report of Bank of Albania (2021).

ALBANIA

The banking system's liquidity during 2019 was stable and had low exposure to risks. In 2020, due to the unexpected situation of COVID-19, the Bank of Albania undertook prudential and regulatory measures. The bank temporarily suspended the credit payments to borrowers affected by the pandemic and approved the regulatory amendments, which enabled banks to classify loans and non-performed loans. The purpose was to support borrowers with difficulties they face with credit payments (Financial Stability Report of Bank of Albania, 2021). Although these measures aim to support the economy to handle the decrease in incomes as a result of the pandemic, they also prevented any potential situation that could affect the loan portfolio. The banking liquidity position stands considerably above the minimum regulatory ratios (Commission Staff Working Document Albania, 2021). The liquid assets in the bank's balance remain in a good position, even considering the slow lending performance during 2020. This resulted in a slight fall in liquid assets by 34.3% in 2020 compared to 35.7% in 2019. The increase in the level of deposits, the high level of the liquidity ratio and the high level of the liquidity ratio helped protect against liquidity risk.

The figure shows that liquidity assets to total assets within 12 years period have been between 27.65% in 2009 and 34.3% in 2020 (see Fig. 2).

NORTH MACEDONIA

The banking system in Northern Macedonia is considered stable, and the integrated prudential policies are in line with the standards set by European regulations. Due to the pandemic crisis in March 2020, the National Bank undertook measures to temporarily limit the payment of dividends to banks and savings householders (Financial Stability Report of National Bank of Republic of North Macedonia, 2021). The loan reclassification was effective through 2020, and repayment was effective through June 2021. With the crisis-support programme in place and strong deposit growth, lending continued to rise with credit available

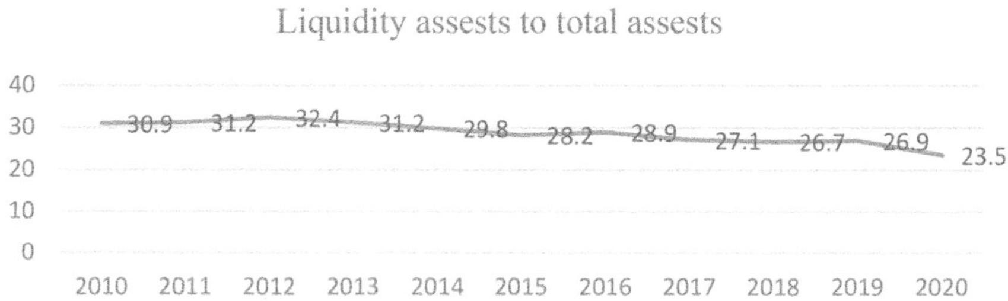

Fig. 3. Liquidity Position (to Total Assets) of the Banking Sector in North Macedonia. *Source*: Data extracted from the Financial Stability Report of National Bank of Republic of North Macedonia (2021).

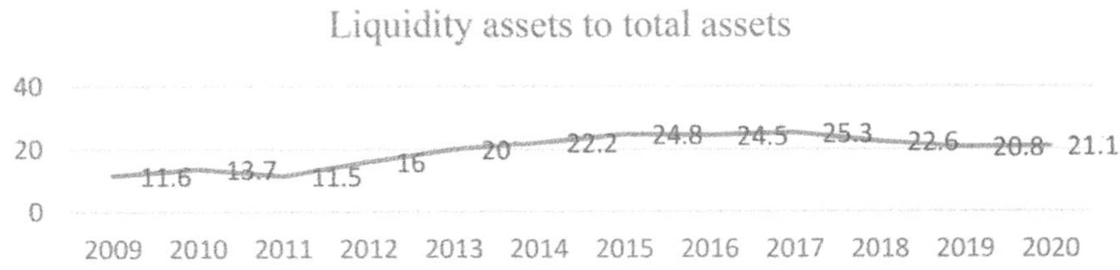

Fig. 4. Liquidity Position (to Total Assets) of the Banking Sector in Montenegro. *Source*: Data extracted from the Financial Stability Report of Central Bank of Montenegro (2020).

to households and firms. Based on the implementation of Basel II rules, which is ongoing, the liquidity risk management has been upgraded as a result, banks are required to integrate the internal liquidity adequacy assessment process into the risk management system.

Banks dominate the country's financial sector. The liquidity assets remained stable, slightly increasing by 23.55% in 2020 compared to 26.5% in 2019.

The figure shows that liquidity assets to total assets within 11 years period have been between 30.9% in 2010 and 23.5% in 2020 (see Fig. 3).

MONTENEGRO

Banks dominate the country's financial sector and play the main role with the composition of total assets of 92.3% in the financial sector. In Montenegro, regulations are still being issued in line with EU banking requirements. It has worked mainly on capital requirements, bank recovery and settlement (Financial Stability Report of Central Bank of Montenegro, 2020). According to the 2019 Progress Report, the solvency and liquidity indicators of the financial sector have improved year by year. In March 2020, Montenegro adopted the first package of measures to deal with the COVID-19 crisis's consequences (Commission Staff Working Document Montenegro, 2021). The measures related to loan repayments, credit provision, and tax obligations. This supported borrowers and companies coping with a situation during the lockdown. The Central Bank of Montenegro introduced a 90-day call for the repayment of loans. This could have a negative effect on banks' liquidity and profits of banks, but according to the Central Bank, the liquid assets in 2020 were estimated to read 21.8% compared to 20.8% in 2019.

The figure shows that liquidity assets to total assets within 12 years have been between 11.6% in 2010 and 21.1% in 2020 (see Fig. 4).

BOSNIA AND HERZEGOVINA

In March 2020, like the other countries, because of the effect of the pandemic, Bosnia and Herzegovina undertook measures to ensure banking stability. The

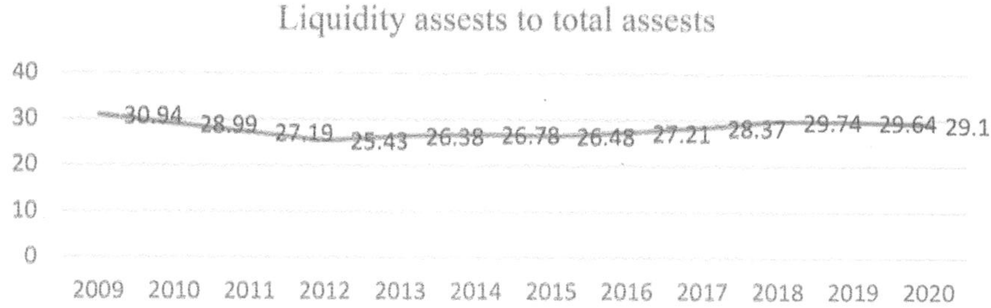

Fig. 5. The Banking Sector's Liquidity Position (to Total Assets) in Bosnia and Herzegovina. *Source*: Data extracted from Financial Stability Report of Central Bank of Bosnia and Herzegovina (June 2020).

banking sector has allowed a 6-month loan repayment moratorium for credits to be restructured (Financial Stability Report of Central Bank of Bosnia and Herzegovina, 2020). Banks also considered additional support for dividends or bonuses. To ease the situation and unexpected requirements due to COVID-19, banking authorities amended decisions related to liquidity as well (Commission Staff Working Document Bosnia and Herzegovina, 2021). Support came from the IMF Rapid Financing Instruments that used Macro-Financial Assistance from the European Union to leverage. Liquidity remained stable, with total assets around 29.1% in 2020 compared to one year before from 29.6%. The figure shows that liquidity assets to total assets have been more or less at the same level over the last 12 years between 30.94% in 2009 and 29.1% in 2020 (see Fig. 5).

SERBIA

As across the region, also in Serbia, the crisis response package included substantial health sector support, credit lines with changes in interest rates and other supporting measures (Commission Staff Working Document Serbia, 2021). Just

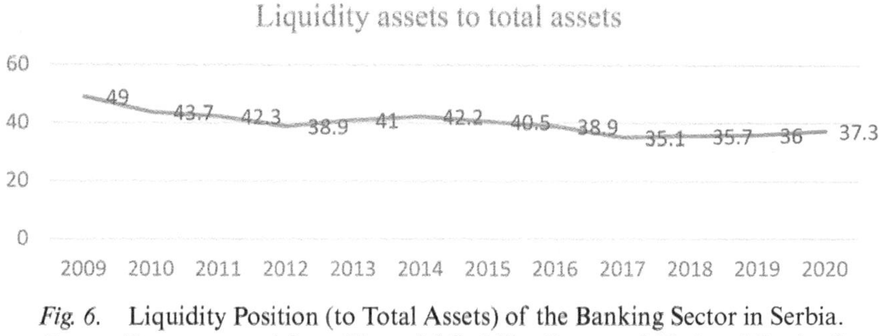

Fig. 6. Liquidity Position (to Total Assets) of the Banking Sector in Serbia. *Source*: Data extracted from Financial Stability Report of National Bank of Serbia (June 2020).

before the crisis, Serbia made fiscal consolidation which allowed a big support package in the form of loan guarantees, a range of revenues and expenditure measures. Due to the COVID-19 crisis, in 2020, Serbia adopted a package of fiscal measures (Financial Stability Report of National Bank of Serbia, 2020). The government's fiscal package also included the 5% in liquidity-enhancing measures. Liquidity remained high, with total assets around 37% in 2020 compared to one year before from 36%.

FINDINGS

The bank capital to assets ratio in all six Balkan Countries during the period between 2008 and 2020 varied from 7.7% in 2008 to 11.2% in 2020 (see Table 2). The ratio of bank liquid reserves to bank assets in 2008 averaged around 21.2%, while in 2020 was 22.05%. Also, capital adequacy in all countries remained stable. In Kosovo, the capital adequacy ratio in 2020 was 16.5% lower than in 2019, around 19%. Montenegro's capital adequacy ratio remained high, at 18.5% at the end of 2020 and 19.2% in June 2021. In Serbia, the capital adequacy (regulatory capital to risk-weighted assets) was 22.4% in 2020, much above the minimum set by the central bank. In North Macedonia, the implementation of the liquidity indicators of Basel III has been applied, maintaining stability during COVID-19 crisis with ratios above the required. The capital adequacy ratio was 16.7% in 2020. Albania continued to align its banking regulation with Basil III on the liquidity coverage ratio and the macroprudential framework. The capital adequacy ratio was 18.1% in 2020. In Bosnia and Herzegovina, the capital adequacy ratio was above the regulatory minimum of 12% and appeared liquid. The capital adequacy ratio was 19.2% in 2020. The study shows that banks' capitalisation ratio, considered as a supportive parameter for liquidity, remained stable and above the required minimum capital adequacy ratio of 12% (see Fig. 6).

CONCLUSION

As a consequence of the pandemic, many uncertainties have increased the financial system's risk of instability. To undertake all measures in dealing with the pandemic crisis, all six countries have adapted the regulatory framework in line with international emergency measures to maintain financial stability. Most countries have implemented and extended fiscal support in 2020, which will continue in 2021. The measures and instruments implemented by countries have generally complied with the Basel Committee's instructions and the requirements of the national authorities in charge. According to the data gathered, the banking sector indicators remained at high levels, without a major downturn due to the pandemic crisis. The ratio of liquid assets to total assets of the banking sector in Western Balkan Countries continued to be around 30%. Also, the level of capital shown means banks can absorb defaults and have fewer chances of causing bankruptcies.

REFERENCES

Adrian, T., & Shin, H. S. (2009). Money, liquidity, and monetary policy. *American Economic Review, 19*(2), 600–605. http://doi.org/10.1257/aer.99.2.600

Awad, R., Ferreira, C., Gaston, E., & Riedweg, L. (2020). *Banking sector regulatory and supervisory response to deal with coronavirus impact (with Q and A)* (pp. 16–17). International Monetary Fund. Retrieved from https://www.imf.org/~/media/Files/Publications/covid19-special-notes/enspecial-series-on-covid19banking-sector-regulatory-and-supervisory-response-to-deal-with-coronavir.ashx

Berger, A. N., & Bouwman, C. H. S. (2016). *Bank liquidity creation and financial crisis*. Cambridge, MA: Academic Press.

Boissay, F., Cantú, C., Claessens, S., & Villegas, A. (2019, March). Impact of financial regulations: Insights from an online repository of studies. *BIS Quarterly Review*, pp. 53–68. Retrieved from https://www.bis.org/publ/qtrpdf/r_qt1903f.pdf

Bolton, P., Cecchetti, S., Danthine, J. P., & Vives, X. (2019). *Sound at last? Assessing a decade of financial regulation*. London: Centre for Economic Policy Research.

Campello, M. (2002). Internal capital markets in financial conglomerates: Evidence from small bank responses to monetary policy. *Journal of Finance, 57*, 2773–2805. https://doi.org/10.1111/1540-6261.00512.

Carletti, E., Claessens, S., Fatás, A., & Vives, X. (2020). *The bank business model in the postCOVID-19 world*. London: Centre for Economic Policy Research.

Central Bank of Kosovo. (2021). Financial stability report. Retrieved from https://bqk-kos.org/publications/financial-stability-report/?lang=en. Accessed on July 12, 2022.

Cetorelli, N., & Goldberg, L. (2012). Liquidity management of U.S. Global Banks: Internal capital markets in the great recession. *Journal of International Economics, 88*(2), 299–311. http://doi.org/10.1016/j.jinteco.2012.05.001

Citaku, S., Asllani, G., Luboteni, G., & Grima, S. (2020). Financial integration, banking supervision and sustainability of the Western Balkan Countries. *International Journal of Economics and Business Administration, 8*(1), 3–14.

Commission Staff Working Document Albania. (2021). *Report accompanying the document communication from the commission to the European Parliament* (pp. 80–81). Brussels: The European Economic and Social Committee and the Committee of the Regions.

Commission Staff Working Document Bosnia and Herzegovina. (2021). *Report accompanying the document communication from the commission to the European Parliament* (pp. 75–76). Brussels: The European Economic and Social Committee and the Committee of the Regions.

Commission Staff Working Document Kosovo. (2021). *Report, communication from the commission to the European Parliament* (pp. 79–80). Brussels: The European Economic and Social Committee and the Committee of the Regions 2021 Communication on EU Enlargement Policy.

Commission Staff Working Document Serbia. (2021). *Report accompanying the document communication from the commission to the European Parliament* (p. 64). Brussels: The European Economic and Social Committee and the Committee of the Regions.

European Banking Authority. (2020). Basel III reforms: Updated impact study results based on data as of 31 December 2019 EBA/Rep/2020/34. Retrieved from https://www.eba.europa.eu/sites/default/documents/files/document_library/Publications/Reports/2020/961423/Basel%20III%20reforms%20-%202019Q4%20update%20and%20COVID%20impact.pdf. Accessed on October 28, 2022.

European Commission. (2021). Enlargement-stabilization and association agreement. Retrieved from https://ec.europa.eu/neighbourhood-enlargement/enlargement-policy/negotiations-status_en.Countries reports. Accessed on October 28, 2022.

European Systemic Risk Board. (2016). Macroprudential policy issues arising from low-interest rates and structural changes in the EU financial system. Retrieved from https://www.esrb.europa.eu/pub/pdf/reports/161128_low_interest_rate_report.en.pdf. Accessed on July 10, 2022.

Financial Sector Restructuring and Regional Integration in the Western Balkans. (2007). Office for South East Europe European Commission – World Bank. Retrieved from https://documents1.worldbank.org/curated/en/760431468275694776/pdf/42007optmzd0SE1ial0Markets01PUBLIC1.pdf. Accessed on August 18 2022.

Financial Stability Report of Bank of Albania. (2021). Retrieved from https://www.bankofalbania.org/Financial_Stability. Accessed on October 23, 2022.

Financial Stability Report of Central Bank of Bosnia and Herzegovina. (2020). Retrieved from https://www.cbbh.ba. Accessed on July 28, 2022.

Financial Stability Report of Central Bank of Montenegro. (2020). Retrieved from https://cbcg.me/en. Accessed on October 16, 2022.

Financial Stability Report of National Bank of Republic of North Macedonia. (2021, June). Retrieved from https://www.nbrm.mk/pocetna-en.nspx. Accessed on August 24, 2022.

Financial Stability Report of National Bank of Serbia. (2020). Retrieved from https://nbs.rs/en/indeks/. Accessed on October 14, 2022.

Gatev, E., Strahan, P. E., & Schuermann, T. (2006). *Managing bank liquidity risk: How deposit-loan synergies vary with market conditions*. FDIC Center for Financial Research Working Paper 2006-03, pp. 1–35 Retrieved from https://click.endnote.com/viewer?doi=10.2139/ssrn.882087&route=2.

Gorton, G., & Metrick, A. (2012). Getting up to speed on the financial crisis: A one-weekend-reader's guide. *Journal of Economic Literature*, *50*(1), 128–150. http://doi.org/10.1257/jel.50.1.128.

IMF. (2021). Staff report and statement by the executive director for Republic of Kosovo. Retrieved from https://www.elibrary.imf.org/view/journals/002/2021/041/002.2021.issue-041-en.xml?rskey=eTdLG8&result=6. Accessed on October 11, 2022.

Khatib, S. F. A., & Nour, A.-N. I. (2021). The impact of corporate governance on firm performance during the COVID-19 pandemic: Evidence from Malaysia. *Journal of Asian Finance, Economics and Business*, *8*(2), 0943–0952.

Schwarz, K. (2014). Mind the gap: Disentangling credit and liquidity in risk spreads. Retrieved from http://ssrn.com/abstract=1486240. Accessed on October 11, 2022.

Shaban, H., Morina, F., & Misiri, V. (2019). The effect of capital adequacy on returns of assets of commercial banks in Kosovo. *European Journal of Sustainable Development*, *8*(2), 201. https://doi.org/10.14207/ejsd.2019.v8n2p201

The COVID-19 Crisis in the Western Balkans. (2019). Economic impact, policy responses, and short-term sustainable solutions OECD. Retrieved from https://www.oecd.org/south-east-europe/COVID-19-Crisis-Response-Western-Balkans.pdf. Accessed on August 12, 2022.

Western Balkan Regular Economic Report. (2021). Retrieved from https://openknowledge.worldbank.org/bitstream/handle/10986/35509/Subdued-Recovery. Accessed on July 11, 2022.

World Bank. (2021). Retrieved from https://data.worldbank.org/indicator. Accessed on October 19, 2022.

CHAPTER 15

METACOGNITIVE READING STRATEGY IN THE AWARENESS OF TERTIARY LEVEL ENGLISH AS A FOREIGN LANGUAGE IN KOSOVO

Nazli Tyfekçi

University of Gjakova 'Fehmi Agani', Gjakova, Kosovo

ABSTRACT

Metacognitive strategies are learning strategies that involve planning, self-monitoring, and self-evaluation. Metacognition is characterised as a build that alludes to considering one's reasoning or the human capacity to be aware of one's mental processes. According to Flavell (1976) metacognitive learning is 'one's learning concerning one's own particular intellectual procedures and items or anything identified with them, e.g., the learning-applicable properties of data or information'. The purpose of the study is to investigate to what extent the university English as a Foreign Language (EFL) learners employ metacognitive reading strategies in reading comprehension. Further, it aims to research the most used strategy of MARSI inventory subscale: reading performance in reading EFL. Statistical analysis has been calculated by using ANOVA, correlation, and metacognitive awareness reading strategy inventory (MARSI), which in fact is the self-report instrument. The study has identified that EFL students of Kosovo universities possess considerable amount of awareness over metacognitive strategies in reading comprehension.

Keywords: Metacognitive reading strategies; English as a foreign language; reading comprehension; reading skill; awareness; tertiary level English

Digital Transformation, Strategic Resilience, Cyber Security and Risk Management
Contemporary Studies in Economic and Financial Analysis, Volume 111A, 213–229

Published under exclusive licence by Emerald Publishing Limited
ISSN: 1569-3759/doi:10.1108/S1569-37592023000111A015

1. INTRODUCTION

1.1. Reading Strategies in the Second Language – L2 Context

Important scholars in the subject have compiled language learning methodologies in foreign language education in a variety of ways. Language learning techniques are described by Oxford (2003) as 'actions pupils do to improve their own language acquisition'. According to O'Malley and Chamot (1990), language learning techniques are 'unique concepts and behaviors that help learners grasp, acquire, and recall new information'.

The first benefit of language learning systems is the improvement of linguistic abilities. Listening, speaking, reading, and writing all reflect this. Second, behaviours, like methods, may be visible aspects like ideas and mental processes or unseen ones.

These tactics are broken down into many categories and stratified into distinct sorts in a number of different ways. Oxford University created the most thorough taxonomy of language learning techniques (Oxford, 2013). She separated this system into 'indirect' and 'direct' primary categories. She categorised memory, compensation, and cognitive techniques under the direct strategies heading, while metacognitive, emotive, and social strategies fell under the indirect strategies heading.

Regardless existing definitions, Oxford (2017) states that she has not reached an agreement to what exactly strategies are, how many of them exist, how they can be categorised or if there is any possibility to order them hierarchically. In the meantime, she asserts that conflicts of categorisation would be inevitable. In her second edition of 'Teaching and Researching Language Learning Strategies', she highlights that strategy categorisation should be flexible since the clear cut division of strategies for specific skills may not be so true. For example, writing competence strategies might also be used for reading competence (Oxford, 2017).

When the employment of strategy was explored within the context of reading abilities, it was discovered that proficient readers used the methods more often than less proficient readers, and that they did so purposefully and successfully (Carrell, Gajdusek, & Wise, 1998). Additionally, Carrell et al. (1998) claim that metacognitive abilities are related to successful reading strategy utilisation. 'Thought about how the thinking process takes place and what is occurring throughout this process' is how she defines metacognition. To sum up, language learning strategies are methods that students employ – consciously or unconsciously – while taking part in the process of learning a foreign language. As a result, they assist students in learning and using the abilities of the new language in a simpler, more efficient, and organised manner.

1.2. Reading Strategies

A lot of research on reading strategies in the first language has uncovered their significance in the reading procedure and the importance of their transfer to the second language – L2 reading process.

Oxford (2003) states that reading is one of the most important skills since most information lies in written sources. She therefore brings attention to the complex process underling the reading procedure. While the reader makes hypotheses, they bring their different perspectives to the reading piece while comprehending. Thus different readers may end up with different meanings or may comprehend something else apart from what the author intended. This is a very important fact when we consider comprehension in L2 language.

> L2 reading strategies are teachable, dynamic thoughts and behaviors that learners consciously select and employ in specific contexts to improve their self-regulated, autonomous L2 reading development, for effective task performance and long-term proficiency. (Oxford, 2003)

Another perspective has been put forward by Douglas Brown (2007), who claims that teaching reading skills in recent years is considered much more contemporary when we consider the strategies of their usage. In the present day, researchers of learning strategies are more concerned with interpreting discourse devices such as reference, ellipses, and then discourse markers such as therefore, moreover, and much more (Brown, 2007, p. 203).

Anderson (1991) took a different approach to studying reading by examining the distinctions in the second language reading strategies under two reading test and academic reading assignment. Twenty-eight subjects in Anderson's research were Spanish L1 learners of mixed abilities from different nations studying ESL at an American college. A key finding was that there is no single strategy combination which can be used in specific tasks as well as there is no single manner in which the strategies are going to be transferred in L2. This result led Anderson (1991) to claim that

> strategic reading is not the matter of knowing what strategy to use, but the knowledge the reader must possess on how to use the strategy successfully and orchestrate its use with other strategies.

Block (1992) explored the use of reading strategies including capable and less capable readers. The findings revealed that poor readers were highly connected with their lexical knowledge during their comprehension process. The author discovered that if the students did not comprehend the word they felt frustrated and had a feeling of not understanding the sentence as well.

1.3. Metacognitive Reading Strategies

For the purpose of understanding metacognitive strategies better, definitions that emphasise the difference between cognitive and metacognitive strategies have been considered useful in elaborating briefly in the preceding part of this chapter.

Cognitive and metacognitive reading methods are the two layers of reading strategy according to cognitive theory. The first level relates to task-specific methods for each person. In contrast, metacognitive methods include the learning process or thinking about learning, planning, and understanding monitoring. Production and self-evaluation of learning also occur after the language exercise is over (O'Malley, Chamot, Stewner-Manzanares, Russo, & Küpper, 1985). In short, cognitive strategies provide the foundation for a text's meaning, while metacognitive strategies start to build the usage of the methods.

Metacognition, according to Flavell (1979), is 'knowledge and cognition about cognitive phenomena'. Anything relevant that goes beyond cognitive understanding is what it is about. It entails being conscious of the information one has about cognitive processes and actions, emotional states, and control over this knowledge in order to accomplish a certain objective.

Metacognitive methods arise during or after the language action and include thinking about the processes of reading, planning about reading, and comprehending while reading. Cognitive methods, on the other hand, involve direct control and processing and are directly related to reading activities (O'Malley et al., 1985).

Metacognition has two key parts when it comes to reading, including the owner's information strategy (metacognitive knowledge) and control over their own behaviours when reading for a different purpose (Carrell, 1989).

1.4. The Relationship Between Metacognitive Reading Strategies and Reading Comprehension

As indicated in the first study question, EFL students from Kosovo universities are metacognitively aware of the reading comprehension methods they use. Alhaqbani and Riazi (2012) found comparable outcomes among Arabian EFL students with African ancestry. The difference was that, similar to the current research, the study found that this area of knowledge is crucial for developing metacognitive awareness since most students lack familiarity with problem-solving techniques. This implies that there is a statistically significant association between awareness and metacognitive reading methods across various fields of study or areas of competence. In addition, Malcolm (2009) contended that metacognitive reading awareness grows with practice.

O'Malley and Chamot (1990) dispute the notion that strong learners use learning techniques whereas poor learners do not. In contrast to poor learners, good learners employ metacognitive strategies to match their needs in learning processes. Based on their academic results, Sheorey and Mokhtari (2001) also found a difference in the reading methods used by native and non-native English speakers. The findings indicate that both native English speakers and non-native English speakers have a strong understanding of all the different metacognitive reading methods included in the survey. Sheorey and Mokhtari (2001) also found a beneficial relationship between good metacognitive skill use and reading performance.

In his research on using reading strategies Brown (1980) states that metacognitive reading strategies allow readers to understand the comprehension process to decide what to do and which actions to undertake in order to facilitate it.

He asserts that experience contributes to the development of metacognitive control and the use of metacognitive strategies. The findings conclude that metacognitive processes help to regulate and control learning while planning and monitoring cognitive activities. For example, after reading a text, student may ask themselves about the concepts discussed in the paragraph. Here the student's cognitive goal is to understand the text. If the students cannot answer their own questions or if they do not understand the text, they will have to decide how to reach the cognitive goal. In this case, they may decide to go back to the text and read again. If they can answer their questions the second time they read it, they will achieve their goal by using the metacognitive reading strategy.

In recent years, the importance of learning English in Kosovo has grown considerably, and the country is providing some of the best scholarships to promote this trend. Schools in Kosovo offer EFL. The problem is that students who choose EFL face challenges when trying to cope with reading comprehension requirements, as decoding, fluency, vocabulary, sentence construction and cohesion, background knowledge, and attention. But, primarily this is due to the lack of understanding of how background knowledge affects reading ability and comprehension.

Consequently, the current study attempts to explore this problem by discovering the extent of awareness on metacognitive reading strategies and the positive correlation these strategies might have on students' reading comprehension abilities in Kosovo Universities and Colleges.

2. METHODOLOGY

The study aims to analyse the awareness among EFL students of metacognitive reading strategies.

With respect to the purpose of the study, the following research questions are going to be addressed:

1) How metacognitively aware are university EFL learners in Kosovo with respect to the reading strategies they employ?
2) Which MARSI subscale strategies are mostly used by university EFL learners in Kosovo?

The research hypotheses for this study are as follows:

H1 University EFL learners in Kosovo are not metacognitively aware regarding the reading strategies they employ.

H2 There is a positive correlation between metacognitive strategy use and students' reading performance in reading EFL.

2.1. Design

This research employs a quantitative approach where survey item is used aiming at demanding objective responses to the research questions which are the focus in the study.

The questionnaire is based on the MARSI (Mokhtari & Reichard, 2002). The MARSI is a self-report questionnaire that students fill in, and it measures the behaviours and strategies the readers employ when they read academic or school-related materials. Mokhtari and Reichard said that the inventory had a quite positive effect on getting students to be aware of the strategies they use and whether these strategies helped or are going to help them to attain their reading goals. It has mainly been used to research the intended aim regarding metacognitive awareness of strategy uses in reading for academic purposes. The MARSI questionnaire is divided into three subscales such as global, support, and problem-solving strategies.

Global reading strategies (13 items) refer to strategies that aim at prepare the scene for the act of reading, for

Problem-solving strategies (8 items) are differently referred as repair strategies. They are used when problems occur for a deeper understanding of the textual information such as checking for better understanding or re-reading.

Support reading strategies (9 items) are supportive tools that are used to maintain the responsiveness to reading. Examples include taking notes, reading aloud, underlining, or highlighting information and using a dictionary.

2.2. The Participants

The MARSI survey was conducted to 473 undergraduate students currently studying in private and public universities in Kosovo. In total three public and one private university were included. All of them are accredited by the Kosovo Accreditation Agency. The Universities are situated in four different main cities of Kosovo: Pristina, Prizren, and Gjakova.

2.3. Data Analysis Procedure

Based on the first study question, EFL students from Kosovo universities are metacognitively aware of the reading comprehension methods they use. Alhaqbani and Riazi (2012) found comparable outcomes among Arabian EFL students with African ancestry. The difference was that, similar to the current research, the study found that this area of knowledge is crucial for developing metacognitive awareness since most students lack familiarity with problem-solving techniques. This implies that there is a statistically significant association between awareness and metacognitive reading methods across various fields of study or areas of competence. In addition, Malcolm (2009) contended that metacognitive reading awareness grows with practice.

3. RESULTS AND DISCUSSIONS

3.1. Metacognitive Awareness of Students of University EFL Learners in Kosovo with Respect the Reading Strategies They Employ

The subscales of the MARSI questionnaire concerning global strategies, support strategies, and problem-solving strategies were calculated among university students in this way: the score of every subscale's total answer was divided with the number of the scale's total number of statements and then the revealed result was divided with frequency number of university participants. The aim was to get the average of strategy use by university students for each subscale.

Based on the MARSI calculating method (Table 1), mean score from the global reading strategies the University of Prizren has the highest level of usage (3.64); on the other hand the lowest level is in Gjakova University even though it corresponds to a medium level of strategy use (3.43). Support reading strategies had the highest score in AAB College and lowest in University of Gjakova. Problem-solving strategies are the most frequently used strategies in all of the universities with a mean of (3.8) and above for all of the participants in study, the highest score being that of the University of Prizren (3.86) and the lowest for the University of Gjakova (3.8).

The above histogram represents the distribution of three subscale scores obtained by students from five different universities.

Therefore, the answer to the second research question, which MARSI subscale strategies are mostly used by university EFL learners in Kosovo, reveals that support reading strategies are highly scored by all university students. Furthermore, there are similar scores which were obtained by five different university students on global reading strategies and support reading strategies in the MARSI scale.

Consequently it has been found that students of different Universities and Colleagues of Kosovo prefer strategies which help them solve difficulties they face during reading comprehension; thus they do apply the strategies as: I try to get back on track when I lose concentration; When text becomes difficult, I re-read to increase my understanding; I read slowly but carefully to be sure I understand what I'm reading; I stop from time to time and think about what I'm reading; I try to guess the meaning of unknown words or phrases, some of the strategies which are listed on MARSI inventory (Appendix 1). Notwithstanding other subscales are also applied by the students, Fig. 1 reveals that there is awareness towards three groups of strategies among the Kosovo university students. This is confirming that the metocognitive reading strategies are used based on individual needs when reading for comprehension.

Based on the MARSI scoring rubric and the scores gathered from five universities obtained from questionnaire answers the analysis shows that there is a high level of strategy use, with the score being more or less similar in each of the subscales of the questionnaire. This trend was present in all of the universities

Table 1. MARSI Mean Scores of Five Different Universities.

University Name	Global Reading Strategies Mean Score	Support Reading Strategies Mean Score	Problem-solving Reading Strategies Mean Score	Overall Mean Score
University of Gjakova	3.43	3.47	3.8	0.35
AAB College	3.59	3.74	3.85	0.37
University of Prizren	3.64	3.73	3.86	0.37
University of Pristina	3.48	3.51	3.8	0.36
University of Peja	3.48	3.69	3.81	0.37
Total	3.52	3.63	3.82	0.36

Source: Authors' compilation.

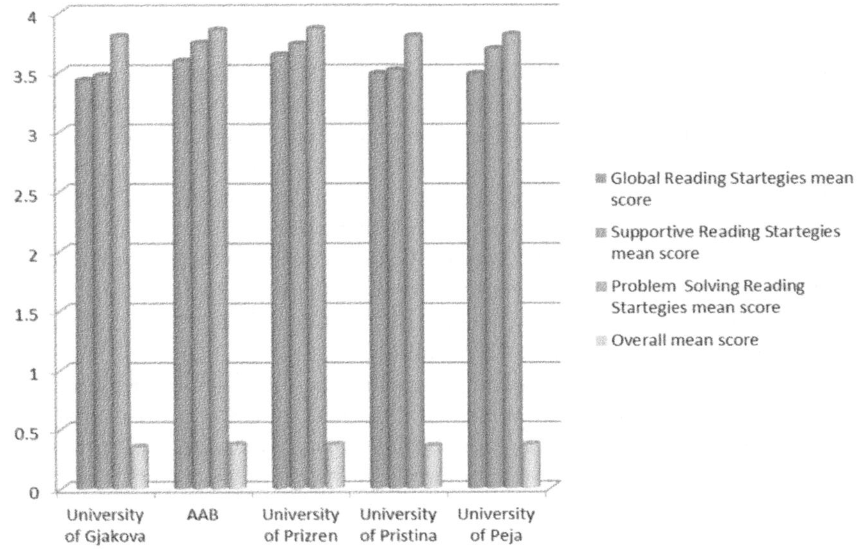

Fig. 1. MARSI Mean Scores of Five Different Universities.
Source: Author's compilation.

that took part in the research. Therefore, the results in Table 1 suggest that the hypothesis of the research is rejected.

As indicated in the first study question, EFL students from Kosovo universities are metacognitively aware of the reading comprehension methods they use. Alhaqbani and Riazi (2012) found comparable outcomes among Arabian EFL students with African ancestry. The difference was that, similar to the current research, the study found that this area of knowledge is crucial for developing metacognitive awareness since most students lack familiarity with problem-solving techniques. This implies that there is a statistically significant association between awareness and metacognitive reading methods across various fields of study or areas of competence. In addition, Malcolm (2009) contended that metacognitive reading awareness grows with practice.

One-way ANOVA (Table 2) was the additional tool used for the investigation of students' knowledge of metacognitive strategies. It was carried out by comparing the survey data's total mean scores for the global, support, and problem-solving strategies. The MARSI questionnaire indicates that pupils are highly aware of metacognitive methods if they get average scores more than 3.5. Using mean comparison analysis, students from diverse academic fields were evaluated for their knowledge of metacognitive methods.

The mean total scores for awareness over problem-solving strategies were discovered to be (30.71M3.52 S.D) at the 95% confidence interval. The overall mean of global reading strategies was observed to be 46.03M5.9 S.D., the total mean support strategies was seen to be (32.64M4.9 S.D). As a result, it was shown that

Table 2. ANOVA Report.

Study Branch		Glob_Total_Score	Sup_Total_Score	Prob_Total_Score
Albanian Language	Mean	44.9118	32.4412	31.5294
	N	34	34	34
	Std. deviation	6.10200	4.56728	2.40246
Albanian Literature	Mean	44.2286	30.4000	29.2571
	N	35	35	35
	Std. deviation	5.89659	4.82152	4.24502
Faculty of Economy	Mean	45.5326	33.0978	31.0652
	N	92	92	92
	Std. deviation	5.84310	4.61021	2.90057
Faculty of Education	Mean	47.5484	33.2581	31.4624
	N	93	93	93
	Std. deviation	5.78513	4.82499	3.28885
Faculty of Law	Mean	47.8200	33.3800	30.4800
	N	50	50	50
	Std. Deviation	4.81363	4.57540	3.85047
Faculty of Philosophy	Mean	44.1786	30.7679	29.8750
	N	56	56	56
	Std. deviation	5.93022	5.23621	3.84737
Faculty of Tourism	Mean	46.3617	33.6596	30.8298
	N	47	47	47
	Std. deviation	6.43167	4.78347	3.69676
German Language	Mean	45.2222	31.4722	29.8611
	N	36	36	36
	Std. deviation	6.39692	5.61369	2.21879
Software Design	Mean	47.1667	34.3333	30.8333
	N	30	30	30
	Std. deviation	6.18721	4.45153	5.02465
Total	Mean	46.0317	32.6469	30.7104
	N	473	473	473
	Std. deviation	5.98808	4.92702	3.52573

Source: Author's compilation.

although students have a greater awareness of global reading methods, they are less knowledgeable about problem-solving and support tactics.

ANOVA Table 2 clearly points out the metacognitive strategic awareness among students studying various courses in five different universities. Table A1 in Appendix 2 represents the detailed results.

For further support of the claim the ANOVA Table 3 also clearly points out the metacognitive strategic awareness among students studying various courses in five different universities. Table 3 represents the detailed results.

One-way ANOVA Table 3 reveals that there exists a statistically significant difference between and within groups for global and support strategies awareness among different courses since $p = 0.03$, $p = 0.01 < 0.05$ at 95% CI. On the other hand, problem-solving strategies and study branches of students fail to achieve statistically significant difference $p = 0.17 > 0.05$, 95% CI.

Prevailed results show that there is a correlation but based on mean scores it is not strong correlation. However, based on ANOVA, which is one of the tests

Table 3. ANOVA Table.

			Sum of Squares	*df*	Mean Square	*F*	Sig.
Glob_Total_ Score* STUDY BRANCH	Between Groups	(Combined)	812.849	8	101.606	2.926	0.003
	Within Groups		16,111.675	464	34.723		
	Total		16,924.524	472			
Sup_Total_Score* STUDY BRANCH	Between Groups	(Combined)	639.375	8	79.922	3.428	0.001
	Within Groups		10,818.663	464	23.316		
	Total		11,458.038	472			
Prob_Total_Score * STUDY BRANCH	Between Groups	(Combined)	229.720	8	28.715	2.363	0.017
	Within Groups		5,637.599	464	12.150		
	Total		5,867.319	472			

Source: Author's compilation.

used in this study to analyse the data for testing hypothesis 1, the hypothesis 1 is rejected, which means that university students of Kosovo are aware of metacognitive strategies they employ.

On the other hand, based on MARSI scores presented in Table 1 it was claimed that the overall mean scores of a strategy use are of a high average, which based on MARSI scoring rubric means that student are high users of metacognitive strategies. Hence, hypothesis stating *University EFL learners in Kosovo are not metacognitively aware with respect to the reading strategies they employ* can be rejected due to the statistically significant association of MARSI scores and ANNOVA test results, where both claim that university students are highly aware of the metacognitive strategy use.

4. CONCLUSION

This research has shown that English language learners at universities in Kosovo have a high level of metacognitive awareness while reading in English. According to Flavell (1979), metacognitive awareness is the knowledge of one's own emotional and cognitive processes. By understanding one's own thinking processes, this may be determined. Such encounters are said to be able to alter one's thought process. Many studies (Anderson, 1991; Levine & Haus, 1985; McVay & Kane, 2012) have shown how crucial it is to be aware of these techniques in general and reading metacognitive methods in particular since they help with reading comprehension. As a result, these experiences may lead a person to alter their objectives, make choices that will affect their ability to achieve their objectives, and as a result, alter their performance going forward. Last but not the least, Sheorey and Mokhtari (2001) discovered that the main difference between proficient and less competent EFL readers is in their ability to take part in activities that involve flexibility and regular self-observation. As a result, developing metacognitive awareness is essential for improving reading abilities, and it's crucial for EFL readers to become conscious of the employment of certain strategies.

Through survey analysis among 473 students enrolled in five different Kosovo institutions, this study sought to provide answers to the research questions.

The findings have repercussions for EFL instructors, which should inspire them to provide their students instruction in reading strategies that may improve reading comprehension performance. It is thus feasible for readers to take action to satisfy the requirements of the reading scenario provided they are aware of what is involved in the reading process and what is required to read well. The findings of the present research also have consequences for language learners, urging them to be more aware of the strategies they use for lifetime learning.

With regard to their reading practices, how metacognitively aware are university-level EFL students in Kosovo? According to the results of the standardised MARSI questionnaire, university students in Kosovo are aware of the metacognitive techniques they use. The first study hypothesis, 'University EFL learners in Kosovo are not metacognitively aware with regard to the reading methods they utilize', is refuted by the mean MARSI scores (Table 1) and descriptive data (Table 2). It has been discovered that the subscales of the MARSI questionnaire (global reading strategies, support reading strategies, and problem-solving strategies) that students at Kosovo universities favour the most are problem-solving strategies.

But when the subscales of the MARSI questionnaire are considered, there are different statistical results between MARSI and one-way ANOVA scores.

Based on one-way ANOVA analysis, results reveal a statistically significant difference between and within groups for global reading strategies and support reading strategies awareness among strategies since $p = 0.03$, $p = 0.01 < 0.05$ at 95% C.I. In addition to the hypothesis rejection it could be said that not all the strategies are used in equal level. Therefore, based on one-way ANOVA, support and global strategies are most applied strategies by students as far as they are involved in the reading process. the problem-solving strategies are not in the same level of preference, which is not in line with the results of MARSI scores, where problem-solving strategies were found to be among most used strategies.

With reference to the MARSI subscales calculating method, Table 1 mean score from the global reading strategies the University of Prizren has the highest level of usage (3.64); on the other hand the lowest level is in University of Gjakova even though that corresponds to a medium level of strategy use (3.43). Support reading strategies had the highest score in AAB College and lowest in University of Gjakova. Problem-solving Strategies are the most frequently used strategies in all of the universities with a mean of 3.8 and for all of the participants in study, the highest score being that of the University of Prizren (3.86) and the lowest for the University of Gjakova (3.8). Consequently, with respect to overall mean score of all participant students of University of Prizren seems to be the most aware of metacognitive strategy use, whereas students in University of Gjakova are least aware of metacognitive strategy use.

Eventually, the two methods of the current study – the MARSI questionnaire and one-way ANOVA – proved different score results on the basis of strategy subscales. However, the importance is that descriptive statistics which showed the analyses of mean of each strategy separately and ANOVA, which looked for the effects of between groups (subscales of MARSI) as well as MARSI calculation score, all proved that students are metacognitively aware.

But since the current study has the MARSI questionnaire instrument as the main data analysis tool, the score results obtained from the same are considered as the most reliable findings of the research.

Similar result of MARSI findings was observed by Alhaqbani and Riazi (2012) among Arabian EFL students from an African background. The difference was that the study revealed that the problem-solving strategies play vital role in determining metacognitive awareness. This suggests that the familiarity of students with texts and contents of their studies (expertise) in university causes statistically significant relationships with the awareness of metacognitive reading strategies.

With reference to the second research question, which MARSI subscale strategies are mostly used by University EFL learners in Kosovo research findings suggest that the students who participated in the current study preferred support reading strategies to problem-solving reading strategies and global reading strategies subscale. This statement is fostered by the fact that most of the problem-solving strategies were ranked higher than global strategies. Among others there is also a consistency when the first and second research question results are considered. While MARSI results reported awareness of students of metacognitive reading strategies in general and the strategies they apply in specific, it was confirmed that problem-solving strategies are among the most preferred ones.

Consequently, student confirmed that when they have problems with deeper understanding of the textual information reforming reading task indicated the ability to finite comprehension when problems occur for a deeper understanding they apply strategies that help them solve the problem, respectively, use problem-solving strategies as listed in MARSI inventory (Appendix 1). This is, of course, not to underestimate the importance of support strategies, which are also preferred by students. As per global subscale, they are among the least used, but we may spot from the MARSI inventory that some of the students do apply only them. Therefore, all these data are recalling student's individual need in metacognitive strategies selection.

The study showed that Kosovo university students are aware of metacognitive reading strategies and use a variety of these strategies when reading authentic texts. They are more oriented towards strategies that help them to solve the problems they face when encountering difficulties in comprehension. Therefore, it is recommended that Kosovo EFL teachers continuously help students raise awareness of applying the strategies that might fit their needs. Given that metacognitive training is a learning to learn approach, it is vital that teachers acquaint students with various reading strategies from which students can choose in line with their needs.

The present study could possibly inspire future studies in metacognitive reading strategy training. Since this study did not consider students' nationality, language proficiency as well as the number of languages known by the students, the researcher considers these variables limitation of the study.

REFERENCES

Alhaqbani, A., & Riazi, M. (2012). Metacognitive awareness of reading strategy use in Arabic as a second language. *Reading in a Foreign Language*, 24(2), 231–255.

Anderson, N. J. (1991). Individual differences in strategy use in second language reading and testing. *Modern Language Journal, 75*, 460–472.

Block, E. L. (1992). See how they read: Comprehension monitoring of L1 and L2 readers. *TESOL Quarterly, 26*, 2.

Brown, A. L. (1980). *Metacognitive development and reading*. In R. J. Spiro, B. Bruce, & W. Brewer (Eds.), *Theoretical issues in reading comprehension* (pp. 453–481). Hillsdale, NJ: Lawrence Erbaum.

Brown, H. D. (2007). *Principles of language learning and teaching* (5th ed). London: Pearson Education.

Carrell, P. L. (1989). Metacognitive awareness and second language reading. *Modern Language Journal, 73*, 120–134.

Carrell, P. L., Gajdusek, L., & Wise, T. (1998). Metacognition and EFL/ESL reading. *Instructional science, 26*(1), 97–112.

Flavell, J. H. (1976). *Metacognitive aspects of problem solving*. In L. B. Resnick (Ed.), *The nature of intelligence* (pp. 231–236). Hillsdale, NJ: Erlbaum.

Flavell, J. H. (1979). Metacognition and cognitive monitoring: A new area of cognitive-developmental inquiry. *American Psychologist, 34*, 906–911.

Levine, M. G., & Haus, G. J. (1985). The effect of background knowledge on the reading comprehension of second language learners. *Foreign Language Annals, 18*(5), 391–397.

Malcolm, D. (2009). Reading strategy awareness of Arabic-speaking medical students studying in English. *System, 37*, 640–651.

McVay, J. C., & Kane, M. J. (2012). Why does working memory capacity predict variation in reading comprehension? On the influence of mind wandering and executive attention. *Journal of experimental psychology: general, 141*(2), 302.

Mokhtari, K., & Reichard, C. A. (2002). Assessing students' metacognitive awareness of reading strategies. *Journal of Educational Psychology, 94*(2), 249–259. http://dx.doi.org/10.1037/0022-0663.94.2.249

O'Malley, M., & Chamot, A. (1990). *Learning strategies in second language acquisition*. New York, NY: Cambridge University Press. http://dx.doi.org/10.1017/CBO9781139524490

O'Malley, J. M., Chamot, A. U., Stewner-Manzanares, G., Russo, R. P., & Küpper, L. (1985). Learning strategy applications with students of English as a second language. *TESOL Quarterly, 19*(3), 557–584. https://doi.org/10.2307/3586278

Oxford, R. (1990). *Language learning strategies: What every teacher should know*. Boston, MA: Heinle & Heinle.

Oxford, R. L. (2003). Language learning styles and strategies: Concepts and relationships. *Iral, 41*(4), 271–278.

Oxford, R. L. (Ed.). (2013). *The language of peace: Communicating to create harmony*. Charlotte, NC: IAP.

Oxford, R. L. (2017). *Teaching and learning language learning strategies: Self-regulation in context*. Oxfordshire: Routledge.

Sheorey, R., & Mokhtari, K. (2001). Differences in the metacognitive awareness of reading strategies among native and non-native readers. *System, 29*(4), 431–449.

APPENDIX 1

MARSI VERSION 1.0

Kouider Mokhtari and Carla Reichard © 2002

Directions: Listed below are statements about what people do when they read *academic or school-related materials* such as textbooks, library books, etc. Five numbers follow each statement (1, 2, 3, 4, and 5) and each number means the following:

- *1* means '*I never or almost never* do this'.
- *2* means 'I do this *only occasionally*'.
- *3* means 'I *sometimes* do this'. (About *50%* of the time.)
- *4* means 'I *usually* do this'.
- *5* means 'I *always or almost always* do this'.

After reading each statement, *circle the number* (1, 2, 3, 4, or 5) that applies to you using the scale provided. Please note that there are *no right or wrong answers* to the statements in this inventory.

Type	Strategies	Scale				
GLOB	1. I have a purpose in mind when I read	1	2	3	4	5
SUP	2. I take notes while reading to help me understand what I read	1	2	3	4	5
GLOB	3. I think about what I know to help me understand what I read	1	2	3	4	5
GLOB	4. I preview the text to see what it's about before reading it	1	2	3	4	5
SUP	5. When text becomes difficult, I read aloud to help me understand what I read	1	2	3	4	5
SUP	6. I summarise what I read to reflect on important information in the text	1	2	3	4	5
GLOB	7. I think about whether the content of the text fits my reading purpose	1	2	3	4	5
PROB	8. I read slowly but carefully to be sure I understand what I'm reading	1	2	3	4	5
SUP	9.I discuss what I read with others to check my understanding	1	2	3	4	5
GLOB	10. I skim the text first by noting characteristics like length and organisation	1	2	3	4	5
PROB	11. I try to get back on track when I lose concentration	1	2	3	4	5
SUP	12. I underline or circle information in the text to help me remember it	1	2	3	4	5
PROB	13. I adjust my reading speed according to what I'm reading	1	2	3	4	5
GLOB	14. I decide what to read closely and what to ignore	1	2	3	4	5
SUP	15. I use reference materials such as dictionaries to help me understand what I read	1	2	3	4	5
PROB	16. When text becomes difficult, I pay closer attention to what I'm reading	1	2	3	4	5

(*Continued*)

Type	Strategies	Scale				
GLOB	17. I use tables, figures, and pictures in text to increase my understanding	1	2	3	4	5
PROB	18. I stop from time to time and think about what I'm reading	1	2	3	4	5
GLOB	19. I use context clues to help me better understand what I'm reading	1	2	3	4	5
SUP	20. I paraphrase (restate ideas in my own words) to better understand what I read	1	2	3	4	5
PROB	21. I try to picture or visualise information to help remember what I read	1	2	3	4	5
GLOB	22. I use typographical aids like bold face and italics to identify key information	1	2	3	4	5
GLOB	23. I critically analyse and evaluate the information presented in the text	1	2	3	4	5
SUP	24. I go back and forth in the text to find relationships among ideas in it	1	2	3	4	5
GLOB	25. I check my understanding when I come across conflicting information	1	2	3	4	5
GLOB	26. I try to guess what the material is about when I read	1	2	3	4	5
PROB	27. When text becomes difficult, I re-read to increase my understanding	1	2	3	4	5
SUP	28. I ask myself questions I like to have answered in the text	1	2	3	4	5
GLOB	29. I check to see if my guesses about the text are right or wrong	1	2	3	4	5
PROB	30. I try to guess the meaning of unknown words or phrases	1	2	3	4	5

Source: Adapted from Mokhtari and Reichard (2002).

Metacognitive Awareness of Reading Strategies Inventory
SCORING RUBRIC

Student Name: _______ Age: _______ Date:

Grade in School: □ 6th □ 7th □ 8th □ 9th □ 10th □ 11th □ 12th □ College □ Other

1. Write your response to each statement (i.e. 1, 2, 3, 4, or 5) in each of the blanks.
2. Add up the scores under each column. Place the result on the line under each column.
3. Divide the score by the number of statements in each column to get the average for each subscale.
4. Calculate the average for the inventory by adding up the subscale scores and dividing by 30.
5. Compare your results to those shown below.
6. Discuss your results with your teacher or tutor.

Global reading strategies (GLOB subscale)	Problem-solving strategies (PROB subscale)	Support reading strategies (SUP subscale)	Overall reading strategies
1. ______	8. ______	2. ______	GLOB ______
3. ______	11. ______	5. ______	
4. ______	13. ______	6. ______	PROB ______
7. ______	16. ______	9. ______	
10. ______	18. ______	12. ______	SUP ______
14. ______	21. ______	15. ______	
17. ______	27. ______	20. ______	
19. ______	30. ______	24. ______	
22. ______		28. ______	
23. ______			
25. ______			
26. ______			
29. ______			

Source: Author.

______ GLOB Score ______ PROB Score ______ SUP Score ______ Overall Score

______ GLOB Mean ______ PROB Mean ______ SUP Mean ______ Overall Mean

Key to averages: 3.5 or higher = High 2.5 – 3.4 = Medium 2.4 or lower = Low

Interpreting your scores: The overall average indicates how often you use reading strategies when reading academic materials. The average for each subscale of the inventory shows which group of strategies (i.e. global, problem-solving, and support strategies) you use most when reading. With this information, you can tell if you are very high or very low in any of these strategy groups. It is important to note, however, that the best possible use of these strategies depends on your reading ability in English, the type of material read, and your purpose for reading it. A low score on any of the subscales or parts of the inventory indicates that there may be some strategies in these parts that you might want to learn about and consider using when reading brown adapted from Oxford (1990, pp. 297–300).

APPENDIX 2

Table A1. ANOVA Report.

Study Branch		Glob_Total_Score	Sup_Total_Score	Prob_Total_Score
Albanian Language	Mean	44.9118	32.4412	31.5294
	N	34	34	34
	Std. deviation	6.10200	4.56728	2.40246
Albanian Literature	Mean	44.2286	30.4000	29.2571
	N	35	35	35
	Std. deviation	5.89659	4.82152	4.24502
Faculty of Economy	Mean	45.5326	33.0978	31.0652
	N	92	92	92
	Std. deviation	5.84310	4.61021	2.90057
Faculty of Education	Mean	47.5484	33.2581	31.4624
	N	93	93	93
	Std. deviation	5.78513	4.82499	3.28885
Faculty of Law	Mean	47.8200	33.3800	30.4800
	N	50	50	50
	Std. deviation	4.81363	4.57540	3.85047
Faculty of Philosophy	Mean	44.1786	30.7679	29.8750
	N	56	56	56
	Std. deviation	5.93022	5.23621	3.84737
Faculty of Tourism	Mean	46.3617	33.6596	30.8298
	N	47	47	47
	Std. deviation	6.43167	4.78347	3.69676
German Language	Mean	45.2222	31.4722	29.8611
	N	36	36	36
	Std. deviation	6.39692	5.61369	2.21879
Software Design	Mean	47.1667	34.3333	30.8333
	N	30	30	30
	Std. deviation	6.18721	4.45153	5.02465
Total	Mean	46.0317	32.6469	30.7104
	N	473	473	473
	Std. deviation	5.98808	4.92702	3.52573

CHAPTER 16

FINANCIAL SOUNDNESS OF GENERAL INSURANCE INDUSTRY IN SRI LANKA: A CARAMELS APPROACH

Vithyalani Muthusamy[a], Narayanage Jayantha Dewasiri[a], K. M. Rajeewa Chanaka Lankanatha[a], Kiran Sood[b] and Simon Grima[c]

[a]*Department of Accountancy and Finance, Faculty of Management Studies, Sabaragamuwa University of Sri Lanka, Belihuloya, Sri Lanka*
[b]*Chitkara Business School, Chitkara University, Punjab, India*
[c]*Department of Insurance Finance and Risk Management, Faculty of Economics, Management and Accountancy, University of Malta, Valetta, Malta*

ABSTRACT

The study explores the impact of the general insurance industry's financial soundness on Sri Lanka's financial performance by using the CARAMELS approach for seven years (2011–2019) and using secondary data. The study utilised panel data regression analysis. Return on Asset was used as the proxy of financial performance while the 10 dimensions were employed. The best-fitted model is the fixed effect model (FEM), which indicates capital adequacy ratio (CAR) and profitability ratio has a positive impact and that the retention ratio (RR), claims ratio, and expenses ratio harm financial performance in the general insurance sector. The study concluded that capital adequacy, earnings and profitability, reinsurance, and actuaries are important predictors of

Digital Transformation, Strategic Resilience, Cyber Security and Risk Management
Contemporary Studies in Economic and Financial Analysis, Volume 111A, 231–242

ISSN: 1569-3759/doi:10.1108/S1569-37592023000111A016

financial performance for general insurers. The findings help the regulator and general insurers set better performance targets and enable insurance company managers to allocate capital more efficiently.

Keywords: CARAMELS; financial soundness; general insurance; return on asset; Sri Lanka; insurance sector

INTRODUCTION

The financial system plays a critical role in the economy, which is of immense importance as it portrays the stability and sustainability of the country. Currently, financial systems are pressurised under the turbulent market. To cope with market volatility, financial systems are becoming more complex (Trichet, 2005). Therefore, regulators have an important role in measuring financial stability to overcome market changes. Previously the financial system was highly dependent on the banking sector, but currently, many financial intermediaries, such as the insurance industry, have taken a major role in the economy. The insurance industry is vital in uplifting the economic growth in developed countries (Ali, Chanar, Ghauri, & Obaid, 2019) and developing countries (Adejare & Aliu, 2020; Chakraborty, 2017; Dar & Thaku, 2015). Therefore, it is important to shed light on the insurance industry's financial stability.

Financial stability is one of the most important factors in forecasting the future direction and is compiled with market strategies and regulatory requirements. Therefore, financial stability is most important for stakeholders of the insurance industry because insurance assures society by taking risks or stressing about financial losses. Moreover, insurance brokering companies highly depend on the insurance industry. About 65 brokering companies are currently operating in Sri Lanka, and the unstable insurance industry also adversely affects the broking companies. Therefore, insurance companies should be able to absorb the risks, which can be measured using one of the survival ratios of the CARAMELS framework. Many scholarly articles used the CARAMELS framework to measure the financial soundness of the insurance industry (Adejare & Aliu, 2020; Ali et al., 2019; Chakraborty, 2017; Dar & Thaku, 2015). Financial soundness is key to the success and stability of the insurance industry. Monitoring the non-life and life insurance companies has dynamic importance for assessing the financial soundness of the industry. The framework recommended measuring the financial soundness of the insurance industry by the World Bank and International Monetary Fund (Das, Davies, & Podpiera, 2003; Tesfaye, 2018). In this study, the general insurance sector is taken to analyse the financial stability because the general insurance sector has slow growth with low profitability in Sri Lanka (Muthusamy & Fernando, 2019, chapter 13).

There is a contradiction in the findings of the studies conducted in the past few decades on the financial soundness of the insurance industry in developing countries such as India, Pakistan, Nigeria, and Nepal (Adejare & Aliu, 2020; Ali et al., 2019; Chakraborty, 2017; Dar & Thaku, 2015). For instance, Dar and

Thaku (2015) argued that capital adequacy is an insignificant factor in measuring financial stability. Contrary to Dar and Thaku (2015), findings concluded that capital adequacy is a significant factor in measuring financial stability (Sang, 2021). Moreover, Dar and Thaku (2015) stated that profit is a significant factor, but Adejare and Aliu (2020) argued that profit is an insignificant factor in measuring financial stability.

The present study is different from the studies mentioned above since it focusses on a holistic view of financial soundness using the CARAMELS model of the general insurance industry in Sri Lanka (Adejare & Aliu, 2020; Ali et al., 2019; Ansah-Adu, Andoh, & Abor, 2011; Chakraborty, 2017; Dar & Thaku, 2015; Weisbart, 2018). Moreover, there is a paucity of studies conducted in the Sri Lankan context on the same phenomenon. Therefore, the controversy in the findings of the empirical studies and the paucity of studies conducted in the Sri Lankan context have motivated this study to a great extent. Thus, this research is aimed to contribute to the existing literature, filling the above-mentioned research gaps of contradictory findings and dearth of studies conducted in the Sri Lankan context. Thereby, the research problem of this study is identified as 'What is the impact of CARAMELS model indicators on the financial soundness of the general insurance industry?' The main objective of this study is to investigate the financial soundness based on the CARAMELS framework in Sri Lankan general insurance industry.

LITERATURE REVIEW

The insurance industry captures paramount importance in the economy of a country (Muthusamy & Fernando, 2019). Insurance companies provide an avenue through which financial risks are pooled and dispersed, and they provide backup plans for the development activities in a country. These insurance companies boost active economic activities such as entrepreneurial ventures and infant businesses by pledging to undertake the risk involved. Insurance companies handle the insured risks; hence, failure of these insurance companies could be fatal for the insureds. The collapse of the insurance industry will result in a tragedy for the economic growth of a country. Therefore, the insurance industry is important, and a stable one is more important to an economy.

Burca and Batrinca (2014) have examined the determinants of the financial performance in the Romanian insurance market based on 2012 data and concluded that the company's size and margin of solvency positively influence its financial performance. Thus, the effect of the combined ratio, financial leverage, and rate of written premium growth on insurers' return on assets is negatively impacted. Here return on assets has been used as a proxy of financial performance. Lee (2014) investigated the relationship between firm-specific factors and macroeconomics on profitability in the Taiwanese property–liability insurance industry. The research has been based on 15 public insurance companies from 1999 to 2009. Here, it was estimated that underwriting risk, reinsurance usage, input cost, economic growth rate, and return on assets significantly influence profitability, and the results indicate that low underwriting risk, low input cost, and low reinsurance usage produce a positive effect on profitability (Mittal & Jhamb 2016; Mittal et al., 2020).

A strength financial position is not only important to policyholders but also important to stakeholders. This study has examined the financial soundness of the private and public sectors using 10 companies from 2002 to 2012 and the CARAMELS model Mann–Whitney test. Here all variables (capital adequacy, asset quality, reinsurance, adequacy of claims and actuarial, management soundness, earnings and profitability, liquidity, and sensitivity to market risk) have a significant impact except the liquidity ratio for both sectors. The researcher excluded the hypothesis of comparison of the financial soundness of both sectors except for earnings, profitability, reinsurance, and actuarial parameters. On the other hand, private companies have reached a higher position which has been earlier employed by public companies (Chakraborty & Sengupta, 2014).

Daare (2016) explored the factors affecting general insurance companies by using 2006–2016 period data. The researcher noted that there is a positive relationship between capital adequacy and GDP with profitability and a negative relationship between liquidity and inflation with profitability. The profitability is always fluctuating because the company's profitability, such as inflation, company size, company age, etc., influences internal and external factors. Ali et al. (2019) mentioned three key important factors as transfers of insurance companies threaten the economy, investment promotion, and allocated savings. Moreover, premium growth rate, liquidity, liability, and fixed assets are significant factors in insurance companies' performance, but these negatively impact the company's performance.

Kaya (2015) has explained that recently several researchers have concentrated their focus on the financial performance of the insurance industry, which is more important for the stockholders, and financial performance contributes to the country's economic growth. Here, the result demonstrates that the premium growth rate, liquidity ratio, and loss ratio negatively impact the financial performance of the insurance sector, and the RR has found as an insignificant variable. Siddiqua and Parvin (2017) have explained the determinants of general insurance companies' performance using secondary data from 2012 to 2014. Here seven variables were utilised, and all variables significantly impact financial performance with a positive relationship: the return on asset, profit after taxation, earnings per share, investment, total asset, number of insurance policies, and net earned premium. Mwangi & Iraya (2014) have explained the determinants of financial performance in the general insurance sector and found that earning asset, investment yield ratio, loss ratio, and expenses ratio have a significant impact on financial performance as well as earning asset and investment ratio have a positive impact and expenses and loss ratios hurt financial performance in the general insurance sector. Further, it was found that the growth of premiums, size of the insurer, and RRs are not significant financial performance variables.

In the Sri Lankan context, the insurance industry shows low growth compared to other countries such as India, Nepal, and Pakistan. Existing literature indicates that only some types of research are available in the Sri Lankan insurance industry (Muthusamy & Fernando, 2019). Specifically, according to the researcher's best knowledge, there is no literature identified for the firm-specific factors that affect CARAMELS financial soundness indicators for general insurance companies in Sri Lanka. The empirical contradiction of evidence from other countries and the paucity of studies conducted in the Sri Lankan context provide the rationale for this study. Therefore, to address the literature gap, the researchers of this study attempted to examine the impact of CARAMELS model indicators on the financial soundness of the insurance industry.

METHODOLOGY

The study was conducted using a quantitative research method. The quantitative data focussed on descriptively discovering facts regarding social phenomena (Dewasiri, Weerakoon, & Azeez, 2018; Sekaran & Bougie, 2016). This study aims to examine the financial soundness of both life and general insurance companies based on CARAMELS framework parameters with strong theoretical and empirical literature reviews. Capital adequacy, asset quality, reinsurance and actuarial, management efficiency, earnings, profitability, liquidity, and market risk sensitivity are the CARAMELS framework indicators. This study used seven parameters to measure the financial soundness of insurance companies. The period of the study is confined to seven years from 2011 to 2018. The data points were collected yearly from the general insurance industry in Sri Lanka. The yearly data verified from firm annual reports, the annual report of the Central Bank of Sri Lanka, the industry annual report of the Insurance Regulatory Commission of Sri Lanka, Insurance Act was considered. The sample comprises 26 insurance companies registered under the Insurance Regulatory Commission of Sri Lanka by the end of 2018. Here, the sample was 10 general insurance companies due to the availability of data.

This study tested the panel data regression model to find out the impact of CARAMELS parameters on the financial soundness of general insurance companies. The researcher developed a regression modal for the general insurance industry;

The model:

$$\begin{aligned}\text{ROA} = \beta 0 + \beta 1\text{CAR} + \beta 2\text{AQR} + \beta 3\text{RR} + \beta 4\text{PR} + \beta 5\text{CR} + \beta 6\text{ER} + \beta 7\text{IYR} \\ + \beta 8\text{PSR} + \beta 9\text{LR} + \varepsilon nt \qquad (1)\end{aligned}$$

where ROA is the return on asset; $\beta 0$, the constant; CAR, capital adequacy ratio; AQR, the asset quality ratio; RR, the retention ratio; PR, the profitability ratio; CR, the claim ratio; ER, the expense ratio; IYR, investment yield ratio; PSR, the premium stability ratio; LR, the liquidity ratio; ε, the error term; n, the number of company; and t, the number of years.

The RR has the highest mean value (0.8431) while the standard deviation is 0.04111, and the lower mean value is the ROA ratio which was a 0.0535 mean value with a 0.04101 standard deviation. The maximum retention percentage is 90%, and the minimum is 78%. The reason for the low RR was that Sri

Table 1. Descriptive Analysis and Normality Data.

Variables	*N*	Minimum	Maximum	Mean	Median	Std. dev.
ROA	8	−0.015	0.115	0.0535	0.0505	0.04101
CAR	8	0.170	0.306	0.2324	0.2325	0.05033
AQR	8	0.382	0.500	0.4270	0.4245	0.04078
PR	8	−0.017	0.162	0.0804	0.0820	0.05696
RR	8	0.781	0.903	0.8431	0.8405	0.04111
CR	8	0.611	0.683	0.6497	0.6405	0.02686
ER	8	0.303	0.494	0.3895	0.3923	0.06352
IYR	8	0.050	0.128	0.0883	0.0865	0.02822
PSR	8	0.028	0.388	0.2033	0.2076	0.11719
LR	8	0.548	0.949	0.7393	0.7300	0.13873

Source: Data analysis by 2020.

Lanka Insurance Corporation's (SLIC) Reinsurance premium increased due to the Suraksha health scheme (Reinsurance premium Rs. 2.25 billion), but SLIC did not continue until 2018 (IRCSL, 2018). Also, the reason for decreased RR is that the Allianz reinsurance ceded premium has decreased due to the company changing the reinsurance structure from a proportional treaty basis to a non-proportional treaty basis (Allianz, 2018). The maximum liquidity ratio is 95% because specially Allianz's liquidity has increased due to the amalgamation with Janashakthi general insurance company and higher government securities of Fair First Insurance company as well as the acquisition and merger of Union General insurance company's position has drastically changed (Fair First, 2017).

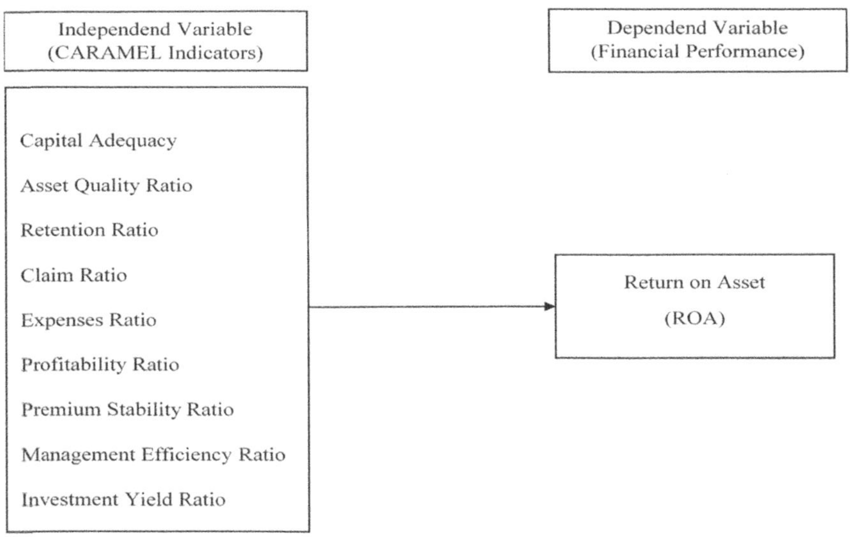

Figure 1. Conceptual Framework
Sources: Adopted from Das, Nigel, and Richard (2003)

The Jarque–Bera statistic is used to test normality based on EViews software. The estimated p-values of the Jarque–Bera tests ($p > 0.01$) confirmed the normality of the distribution of all variables at a significant level.

PANEL DATA REGRESSION ANALYSIS

Regression analysis is the best method to identify the most important variables which have influenced the dependent variable. Three models have been tested in this study. They are the ordinary least squares, FEM, and random effect model (REM). For the objective of finding out the most appropriate model for the estimate and representing the results, the F test, LM test, and Hausman test were performed.

According to the LM test, the REM was selected, and the Hausman test indicated a p-value (0.000) less than 0.05; therefore, the FEM is appropriate rather than the REM to analyse the general insurance industry.

The R-square is a statistical measure that shows how close the data are to the fitted regression line. It is also known as the coefficient of determination for multiple regression. According to Table 2, the R-square value for the model was 97%.

Table 2. Fixed Effect Model.

Dependent variable: ROA				
Sample period: 2011–2018				
Total panel (balanced) observations: 80				
Variable	Coefficient	Std. Error	t-Statistic	Prob.
CAR	0.061580	0.024384	2.525494	0.0142
AQR	−0.022747	0.015508	−1.466767	0.1476
RR	−0.134552	0.050240	−2.678186	0.0095
PR	0.637885	0.044074	14.47320	0.0000
CR	−0.038181	0.015166	−2.517616	0.0145
ER	−0.051971	0.025105	−2.070150	0.0427
IYR	−0.010619	0.068608	−0.154775	0.8775
PSR	0.009358	0.020412	0.458455	0.6483
LR	0.025491	0.018034	1.413538	0.1626
C	0.136210	0.048216	2.824967	0.0064
Effects Specification				
Cross-section Fixed (Dummy Variables)				
R-squared	0.970791	Mean dependent var		0.053500
Adjusted R-squared	0.962172	S.D. dependent var		0.055143
S.E. of regression	0.010725	Akaike info criterion		−6.028635
Sum squared residual	0.007017	Schwarz criterion		−5.462904
Log-likelihood	260.1454	Hannan–Quinn criteria		−5.801817
F-statistic	112.6340	Durbin–Watson stat		1.260848
Prob(F-statistic)	0.000000			

Source: Data analysis by 2020.

It signifies variation of ROA dependent variable, and it was explained by CAR, asset quality ratio, RR, profitability ratio, claim ratio, expenses ratio, investment yield ratio, premium stability ratio, and liquidity ratio. In that case, there was a 3% of unexplained variation in this model for the general insurance sector.

The adjusted *R*-square value is adjusted for the number of variables included in the regression equation. This is used to estimate the expected variation in *R*-square that would not generalise to the population because the model is over-fitted to the data set by including too many independent variables. According to Table 2, the 96% of adjusted *R*-square value was lower than the 97% of *R*-square value, and it was an indication that the regression equation may be over-fitted to the sample and limited generalisability. Moreover, the adjusted *R* – the squared percentage is 96% of the model.

The standard error of the estimate was a measure of the accuracy of predictions. The value of the standard error of the estimate was 0.010725. It implies that the model was fitted well because the value of the standard error of the estimate was less than the mean value of the return on asset variable, which was 0.53500.

Durban–Watson statistic value is 1.3, which is a value near 2 points, and it will be an acceptable level.

According to Table 3, the constant (β_0) was 0.136210, and the *p*-value of the constant was 0.0064, which is statistically significant at the 0.05 level of significant constant beta coefficient values representing positive value.

When considering the variable of CAR, the β-coefficient of 0.061580 indicated that when CAR was increased by one unit while other variables remained constant, ROA was increased by 0.061580 U. Furthermore, CAR contributed significantly to the model since the *p*-value of 0.0142 was less than the 0.05 level of significance. Therefore, there is a positive relationship between the CAR and with ROA of the company. Hence, the null hypothesis was rejected, and the alternative hypothesis was accepted.

The panel regressions model can be illustrated based on the above information.

$$\text{ROA} = 0.1362 + 0.0616\text{CAR} - 0.01346\text{RR} + 0.6379\text{PR} - 0.0382\text{CR} - 0.0520\text{ER} \quad (2)$$

The results of the hypotheses are shown in Table 3.

Table 3. Results of Hypotheses.

Hypothesis	Coefficient	*P* value	Decision
H1. There is a significant relationship between capital adequacy with financial performance	0.0616	0.0142	Accepted
H2. There was a significant relationship between Asset quality ratio and return on assets	−0.0227	0.1476	Rejected
H3. There was a significant relationship between retention ratio and return on assets	−0.1346	0.0095	Accepted
H4. There was a significant relationship between the profitability ratio and return on assets	0.6379	0.0000	Accepted
H5. There was a significant relationship between claim ratio and return on assets	−0.0382	0.0145	Accepted

Table 3. (*Continued*)

Hypothesis	Coefficient	*P* value	Decision
H6. There was a significant relationship between expenses ratio and return on assets	−0.0519	0.0427	Accepted
H7. There was a significant relationship between investment yield ratio and return on assets	−0.0106	0.8775	Rejected
H8. There was a significant relationship between premium stability ratio and return on asset	0.0094	0.6483	Rejected
H9. There was a significant relationship between liquidity ratio and return on assets	0.0255	0.1626	Rejected

Source: Data analysis by 2020.

DISCUSSION

According to the results of the study, the CAR has a significant impact on financial performance, and it has a positive impact on financial performance (financial performance has measure using return on asset). Capital adequacy is the most important factor because all-insurance companies should maintain the minimum net capital requirement prescribed by IRCSL. After all, it will decide the insurance company's capacity to continue its operations. Recently MBSL has been suspended by IRCSL due to inadequate capital requirements. Therefore, the company's performance is always decided by the capital adequacy of the company. It is important not only for the insurance sector but also for the banking sector. Accordingly, Barus, Muturi, Kibati, and Koima (2017), Lotto (2018), and Udom and Eze (2018) also found that capital adequacy is a significant variable in the financial performance of banks. This study found that the asset quality ratio has no significant variable on financial performance or ROA.

The RR negatively and significantly impacts financial performance. The RR will decide the value of the reinsurance arrangement, and all-insurance companies deduct some amount from the gross written premium as a 'Premium ceded to the reinsurer'. Therefore, the ratio inversely impacts financial performance. Most researchers witnessed that the RR hurts the financial performances of general insurance companies (Kocovic, Paunovic, & Jovovic, 2014; Kumarasinghe, 2015).

The profitability ratio has been used under Earning and Profitability parameter of the CARAMELS model. The profitability ratio positively impacts general insurers' financial performances (coefficient, 0.6379, *p*-value 0.000). The study proves that the claim ratio has a negative and significant impact on general insurers' firm performance. The net claim ratio directly impacts the underwriting profit of the company. Therefore, increased claims will adversely impact firm performance. The Amana life insurance company has represented a higher claim ratio due to the incensement of prematurity claims in unit-linked products and also in that year the ROA was a negative percentage (IRCSL, 2018). Empirical evidence supports that the claim ratio negatively impacts the financial performance of an insurance company. Burca and Batrinca (2014) have mentioned that the combined ratio negatively impacts financial performance. The combined ratio is the collection of both the claim and expense ratios (Malik, 2011; Marie & Cyrus, 2014). The study findings witness that the Expense Ratio has a significant and negative impact on financial performance. The expenses ratio represents administrative expenses, selling and distribution expenses, finance expenses, and underwriting and acquisition expenses. Empirical evidence supported the current study (Burca & Batrinca, 2014; Mwangi & Iraya, 2014; Upreti, Adams, & Jia, 2022). The study explored that the investment yield ratio plays a dismal role in the Sri Lankan general insurance sector. In the Sri Lankan context, marketable securities fluctuate due to external environmental factors. Therefore, some companies earned very lower investment income. SLIC has a total equity investment of around 52% of total investments, whereas subsidiary investments represent 63% of total equity, but the return for the same is 1–2% in 2017 and 2018 (SLIC, 2017). The study found that the premium stability ratio is not a significant variable for both insurance sectors. Similarly, Tesfaye (2018) stated that there is an insignificant impact on premium growth rate with financial performance. The liquidity ratio is an insignificant variable of general insurers' financial performance (Derbali & Jamel, 2018; Ridwan, Ulupui, & Ahmad, 2022) have mentioned that the liquidity ratio has no significant impact on financial performance.

IMPLICATIONS AND RECOMMENDATIONS

The purpose of this study is to investigate the financial soundness based on the CARAMELS framework in Sri Lankan general insurance industry. A quantitative study is conducted to achieve the objective of the study. Based on the findings from the FEM, it is possible to conclude that CAR, RR, profitability ratio, claim ratio, and expense ratio significantly impact general insurers' financial performance and asset quality ratio, investment yield ratio, premium stability ratio, and liquidity ratios were insignificantly impacted on general insurers financial performance.

The financial soundness of the insurance industry fluctuated highly. Many companies are operating under loss before taxation. Thus, a strong financial position is the most important to a company because it will decide its operations. However, when considering the overall results of this study, some indicators of the CARAMELS framework are the most important to decide the sound financial system of the company. Further, the administration of the companies should highly focus on CARAMELS parameters and introduce new strategies to minimise losses and increase the performance of the overall industry as a sub-sector of financial institutions. Since the study found that capital adequacy, earnings and profitability, reinsurance, and actuarial issues are key drivers of the financial soundness of the insurance industry in Sri Lanka, it is recommended that the management of insurance companies should consider the above parameters in managing well.

The management should consider the proper claim settlement strategies and control indirect and direct expenses and develop a new distribution channel to increase the market share of the insurance sector.

A study was on the impact of CARAMELS parameters on the financial performance of the general insurance industry. Future researchers can investigate the financial soundness of the life insurance industry in Sri Lanka. Further, this study is conducted using the risk-based capital concept to explore financial soundness. The further researcher can be considered the above matters in their study.

REFERENCES

Adejare, R. B., & Aliu, I. D. (2020). Effect of board members dynamics on the financial performance of insurance company in Nigeria using CARAMELS financial performance indicators. *Fountain University Osogbo Journal of Management*, *5*(1), 135–158.

Ali, N., Chanar, Z. A., Ghauri, S. P., & Obaid, S. (2019). The effects of firm-specific factors on the financial soundness by using CARAMELS framework indicators: A case of non-life insurance industry of Pakistan. *International Journal of Experiential Learning and Case Studies*, *4*(1), 131–56. https://doi.org/10.22555/ijelcs.v4i1.2452.g536

Allianz. (2018). Annual report. Retrieved from https://www.allianz.com/content/dam/onemarketing/azcom/Allianz_com/investor-relations/en/results-reports/annual-report/ar-2018/en-AR-Group-2018.pdf. Accessed January 20, 2021.

Ansah-Adu, K., Andoh, C., & Abor, J. (2011). Evaluating the cost efficiency of insurance companies in Ghana. *The Journal of Risk Finance*, *13*(1), 61–76. https://doi.org/10.1108/15265941211191949

Barus, J. J., Muturi, W., Kibati, P., & Koima, J. (2017). Effect of liquidity on financial performance of savings and credit societies in Kenya. *International Journal of Finance*, *2*(7), 34. https://doi.org/10.47941/ijf.188

Burca, A.-M., & Batrinca, G. (2014). The determinants of financial performance in the Romanian insurance market. *International Journal of Academic Research in Accounting, Finance and Management Sciences*, *4*(1), 299–308. https://doi.org/10.6007/ijarafms/v4-i1/637

Chakraborty, J. (2017). Financial soundness of Indian life insurance firms: An investigation based on the CARAMELS framework. *Indian Journal of Finance*, *11*(11), 7. https://doi.org/10.17010/ijf/2017/v11i11/119339

Chakraborty, J., & Sengupta, P. P. (2014). Financial soundness in Indian insurance sector: A comparison between two leading life insurers. In A. N. Barman & P. P. Sengupta (Eds.), *2014 2nd international conference on business and information management (ICBIM)* (pp. 86–90). Piscataway, NJ: IEEE.

Daare, W. J. (2016). Factors affecting general insurance companies profitability: Empirical study in India. *International Journal of Marketing, Financial Services and Management Research*, *5*(12), 1–8.

Dar, S. A., & Thaku, I. A. (2015). A comparative analysis of the financial performance of public and private non-life insurers in India. *International Journal of Management*, *6*(1), 507–526.

Das, U., Davies, N., & Podpiera, R. (2003). Insurance and issues in financial soundness. *SSRN Electronic Journal*, *2003*(138), 1–44. https://doi.org/10.2139/ssrn.879214

Derbali, A., & Jamel, L. (2018). Determinants of performance of Tunisia insurance companies: Case of life insurance. *International Journal of Productivity and Quality Management*, *24*(4), 531. https://doi.org/10.1504/ijpqm.2018.093452

Dewasiri, N. J., Weerakoon, Y. K. B., & Azeez, A. A (2018). Mixed methods in finance research: The rationale and research designs. *International Journal of Qualitative Methods*, *17*, 1–13.

IRCSL. (2018). Supervisory review of the insurance industry. Retrieved from http://www.ibsl.gov.lk/images/annual_reports/Annual%20Report%202017.pdf. Accessed on February 15, 2021.

Fair First. (2017). Annual report. Retrieved from http://www.annualreports.com/HostedData/AnnualReports/PDF/TSX_FFH_2017.pdf. Accessed February 17, 2021.

Kaya, E. O. (2015). The effects of firm-specific factors on the profitability of non-life insurance companies in Turkey. *International Journal of Financial Studies*, *3*(4), 510–529. https://doi.org/10.3390/ijfs3040510

Kocovic, J., Paunovic, B., & Jovovic, M. (2014). Determinants of business performance of non-life insurance companies in Serbia. *Ekonomika Preduzeca*, *62*(7–8), 367–381. https://doi.org/10.5937/ekopre1408367k

Kumarasinghe, K. K. A. M. R. (2015). The determinants of financial performance in insurance companies in Sri Lanka. In *Proceedings of the 4th students' research symposium* (p. 25), Department of Finance, Faculty of Commerce and Management Studies, University of Kelaniya, Sri Lanka.

Lee, C.-Y. (2014). The effects of firm-specific factors and macroeconomics on the profitability of property–liability insurance industry in Taiwan. *Asian Economic and Financial Review*, *4*(5), 681–691.

Lotto, J. (2018). The empirical analysis of the impact of bank capital regulations on operating efficiency. *International Journal of Financial Studies*, *6*(2), 34. https://doi.org/10.3390/ijfs6020034

Malik, H. (2011). Determinants of insurance companies profitability: An analysis of insurance sector of Pakistan. *Academic Research International*, *1*(3), 315–321.

Mittal, A., Aggarwal, A., & Mittal, R. (2020). 'Predicting university students' adoption of mobile news applications: the role of perceived hedonic value and news motivation'. *International Journal of E-Services and Mobile Applications (IJESMA)*, *12*(4), 42–59.

Mittal, A., & Jhamb, D. (2016). Determinants of shopping mall attractiveness: The Indian context. *Procedia Economics and Finance*, *37*, 386–390.

Muthusamy, V., & Fernando, K. (2019). Factors in affecting the cross-selling of dwelling house and personal accident insurance to private motor car policyholders in Sri Lanka. In M. Aslam, M. J. M. Cooper, W. A. K. C. Gnanapala & T. C. Gamage (Eds.), *Managerial dilemmas in developing countries: Business, marketing, finance and tourism* (pp. 152–163). Cambridge: Cambridge Scholars Publishing.

Mwangi, M., & Iraya, C. (2014). Determinants of financial performance of general insurance underwriters in Kenya. *International Journal of Business and Social Science*, *5*(13), 210–215.

Ridwan, M. I., Ulupui, G. K. A., & Ahmad, G. N. (2022). The impact of total equity, risk-based capital ratio, adequacy investment ratio, direct premium receivable ratio, liquidity ratio, and loss ratio toward the early warning system of general insurance. *The International Journal of Social Sciences World (TIJOSSW)*, *4*(1), 11–27.

Sang, M. N. (2021). Capital adequacy ratio and a bank's financial stability in Vietnam. *Banks and Bank Systems*, *16*(4), 61–71. https://doi.org/10.21511/bbs

Sekaran, U., & Bougie, R. (2016). *Research methods for business: A skill-building approach* (7th ed). West Sussex: Wiley and Sons.

Siddiqua & Parvin, (2017). A study on the performance of private non-life insurance companies in Bangladesh. Asian Business Consortium, 7(2), 55–58.

SLIC. (2017). Annual report (pp. 14–37). Retrieved from https://www.google.com/search?q=slic+annual+report+2017andsa=Xandved=2ahUKEwj6nqSa-ZHjAhVSFHIKHe3fB-YQ1QIoAnoECAoQAwandbiw=1366andbih=657. Accessed on February 17, 2021.

Tesfaye, T. T. (2018). Analysis of factors affecting financial performance evidence from selected Ethiopian insurance companies. *International Journal of Science and Research*, *7*(12), 834–852.

Trichet, J.-C. (2005). Financial stability and the insurance sector. *The Geneva Papers on Risk and Insurance – Issues and Practice*, *30*(1), 65–71. https://doi.org/10.1057/palgrave.gpp.2510021

Udom, I. S., & Eze, O. R. (2018). Effect of capital adequacy requirements on the profitability of commercial banks in Nigeria. *International Research Journal of Finance and Economics*, *165*, 79–89.

Upreti, V., Adams, M., & Jia, Y. (2022). Risk management and the cost of equity: Evidence from the United Kingdom's non-life insurance market. *The European Journal of Finance*, *28*(6), 1–20. https://doi.org/10.1080/1351847x.2021.1936588

Varma, P., & Nijjer, S. (2022). Examining the role of fintech in the future of retail banking. *ECS Transactions*, *107*(1), 9855.

Weisbart, S. (2018). How insurance drives economic growth. Report No. 053018. Insurance Information Institute New York. Retrieved from https://www.iii.org/sites/default/files/docs/pdf/insurance-driver-econ-growth-053018.pdf

CHAPTER 17

MULTIMEDIA SUSTAINED BENEFITS FOR FINANCIAL SERVICES

Priya Jindal[a] and Lochan Chavan[b]

[a]*Chitkara Business School, Chitkara University, Punjab, India*
[b]*Smt. Kamala Mehta V.W.A. College of Commerce, Mumbai, India*

ABSTRACT

Government organisations, small and medium-sized businesses, education, and the entertainment industries all use multimedia technology to communicate information and ideas across digital, print, catalogue, and advertising mediums. Any message delivered by businesses, whether digital or printed graphics, images, text, movies, or animation, is more likely to be accepted by the target audience. The financial sector is no exception. Multimedia technology refers to activities involving computers, software development, and online media distribution. Professionals and experts in computer or software development use multimedia technology to create a variety of mechanisms including product demos, web pages, news sites, and presentations to attract attention or convey any message to a specific audience. Multimedia technology such as multimedia software, transaction processing, electronic payments, voicemail, and networked communication required banks and the financial sector to adopt new practices for delivering banking services and making the financial system more user-friendly for consumers and the financial industry's operation. Banks and other financial institutions are compelled to innovate as computer technologies advance to maintain competitiveness. Multimedia technology offers lower occupancy costs with a smaller staff and lower transaction processing expenses.

Digital Transformation, Strategic Resilience, Cyber Security and Risk Management
Contemporary Studies in Economic and Financial Analysis, Volume 111A, 243–262

ISSN: 1569-3759/doi:10.1108/S1569-37592023000111A017

New technologies in the financial sector are replacing traditional methods of operation because multimedia technology makes work simpler, faster, and more effective. The industry is trying to switch to a self-service model through technology by providing the same level of convenience at a lower price.

Keywords: Financial sector; multimedia technology; electronic payment; self-service model; online media distribution; user-friendly operation

17.1 INTRODUCTION

The first wave of the multimedia revolution hit the financial industry with the introduction of automated teller machines and telephone banking. The electronic cash system and subsequent online services signalled the start of the second wave. With the help of cutting-edge technologies like 3D graphics, AR, VR, AI, and video-mediated communication, Multimedia Message Service customers' interactions with banks are constantly changing and becoming more like real-world experiences. With multimedia technologies, customers can now communicate at their convenience via email, phone, or the internet without being physically present.

In this chapter, the researcher will focus on the financial industry and how multimedia technology improves customer intimacy by giving customers a quick response to their needs. With how the multimedia marketplace enhances the financial sector's operations since a new method of service delivery is needed to keep it competitive.

17.2 BENEFITS OF MULTIMEDIA TECHNOLOGIES IN THE FINANCIAL SECTOR

The electronic payment system and transactional flow changed the way that multimedia technology was used to deliver services. The new firms will compel banks and other financial institutions to embrace innovative improvements due to multimedia technology, resulting in smaller occupancy, cheaper costs, and lower transaction process costs. Everyone is aware that multimedia technology has led to innovations like the automatic time machine and telephone or online banking (Sajić, Bundalo, Bundalo, & Pašalić, 2017). As technology has advanced, more improvements are being made to ATMs, which were previously solely used for cash withdrawals. Now, deposits of cash are being made using ATMs. A depositor's passbook has a record of each transaction that is made, both deposits and withdrawals. In the past, the passbook was filled out by bank staff during established business hours.

However, thanks to technology, banks now have automatic passbook printing machines that allow depositors to print their passbooks whenever they like. They may also get them by email if they need a copy of the transaction data.

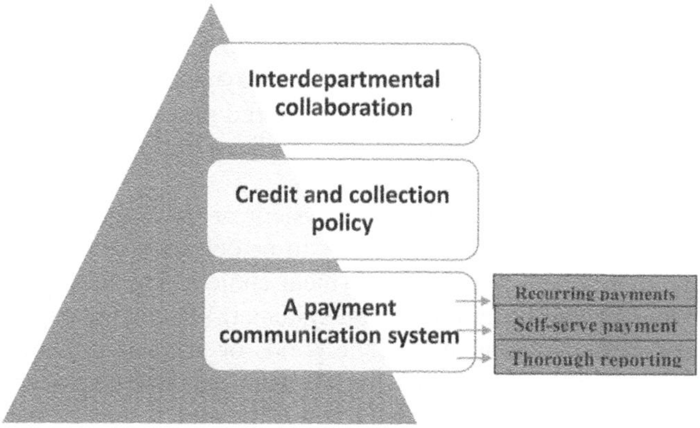

Fig. 1. Steps Used in Billing. *Source*: fico.com

Financial service providers can automate a tedious, information-intensive operation with the aid of multimedia technology (Nicholas, Williams, Martin, & Cole, 2020). The bank can carry out operations including monitoring loan disbursement, issuing loans, trading stocks, investment analysis, verification, and retail operation with the aid of multimedia technology. Robo advisors is one of the newest and most significant areas of financial technology (Belanche, Casaló, & Flavián, 2019). The business that offers this service queries the clients and creates personalised investment ideas using a specialised algorithm. Advisors can choose inexpensive assets because there is no minimum amount needed to invest. It must strike a balance and promote the asset that offers strategies for future investment planning. The algorithm is used to manage and plan, which lowers operational costs for the institution.

17.2.1 Billing and Accounts Receivable

Account receivable is the term used to describe an outstanding amount when a financial institution offers products and services without first receiving complete payment. Invoices are delivered to the client asking them to pay the amount due within a certain time frame to collect the payment. The collection boosts the company's revenue and improves efficiency by offering billing services, late payment fees, and an increase in the quantity of money flowing through the bank account each month (Listiadi, 2022). The department that was specifically created for billing and accounts receivable attempts to recover the money in a shorter amount of time by adopting the following strategies as shown in fig.1.

1. *Interdepartmental collaboration:* To get rid of the backlog of outstanding customer accounts, one department needs the help of another to gather specific client data, such as the customer service department and the sales department, which will provide insights into the customer status (Ramaswamy & Gouillart, 2010).

2. *Credit and collection policy:* Under this policy, if a customer doesn't pay on time, the financial institution will make an effort to recover the amount by choosing a different technique to collect late payments. For everyone working with the institution to be aware of the rules and procedures, financial institutions should set up credit and collection policies and incorporate them into their procedures (Ferguson & Toktay, 2006).
3. *A payment communication system:* A system or software is built that enables prompt account receivable invoices to be delivered to clients along with reminders giving them a range of payment choices. The following should be included in a payment communication system: (a) Recurring payments: If the client's payment requirements for the goods or services provided are more extensive, a business should look for software that will help schedule recurring payments, ensuring that revenue is not lost due to missed payments. (b) Self-serve payment option: Financial institutions should offer their customers online payment portals and IVR phone systems so that even busy customers can readily access online payment portals. (c) Thorough reporting: The institution's software should offer customised options and comprehensive reporting features so a financial institution may get the precise reporting needed to optimise its accounts receivable billing operations.

17.2.1.1 Multimedia Technologies' Advantages in Billing and Accounts Receivable

1. *Boost cash flow:* Businesses that have invested in technology have had the best results in terms of maintaining a healthy cash flow. To employ best practices, multimedia technology reminds clients when payments are due, identifies previous unpaid invoices, and assists clients in making payments (Truant, Broccardo, & Dana, 2021).
2. *Increase control over cash and working capital:* Understanding cash position is crucial for improving working capital. When working capital is managed well, it may be used to inform investment strategies such as acquiring assets, hiring personnel, providing additional facilities to support business expansion, etc.
3. *Improve customer communication:* As you are all aware, it takes a long time to determine who has been called, who is still waiting to be called, or when the previous call was placed. As a result, automated solutions for managing accounts receivable have made it easier to prioritise calls, prepare for them, and handle other organisational problems.
4. *Enhance customer service and satisfaction:* Using technology makes it simple to communicate with consumers because it may sometimes be helpful to examine account information, compose emails, attach bills, then combine the papers, and place calls. The conversation with the remark is also recorded for later review and analysis, which helps to prevent a repetition of previously done or said things.
5. *Lower administrative expenses:* The consumption of paper, toner, envelopes, postage, and other supplies has been reduced as a result of technological innovation. The software creates the task so that no human involvement is necessary when it is being produced.

17.2.2 Accounts Payable

In accounting, the word 'accounts payable' is also used to describe the funds that must be paid to suppliers or vendors for financed products and services. The balance sheet's liabilities show the outstanding payments to various suppliers, and the cash flow statement will show additional increases and decreases (Fields, 2016). Since this is the core function of every firm, as shown in fig. 2, it is essential to keep accurate records of payments and closely monitor expenditures to preserve balance. The organisation can benefit from an automated accounts payable system by not having to make any inaccurate payments or decisions. Payments will only be made if the supplier has requested them (Sood, Seth, & Grima, 2022). The accounts payable department supports the organisation financially, administratively, and clerically. The accounts department now operates efficiently and precisely with the use of multimedia technologies. Payments are made on time to prevent late fees and may enable the use of promotions or discounts. Payments are made through a variety of methods, including ACH, checks, and virtual cards with cashback rewards that benefit the organisation (Rysman & Schuh, 2017; Sood, Kaur, & Grima, 2022). Cash flow management for organisations gets simpler. Examples of accounts individuals include raw materials, power, energy, fuel, items or equipment, leasing, and licencing, among others.

17.2.2.1 Multimedia Technologies' Advantages in Accounts Payable

1. *Shorten the procure-to-pay cycle:* By capturing and directing data to the business system, multimedia technology used in accounts payable helps to speed up business operations. Without requiring human data entry, it is beneficial to allocate data and validate data immediately through the ERP system (Hader et al., 2022). This states that the work is completed efficiently and that employee time promotes data accuracy.
2. *Capture early payment discounts:* Through multimedia technology, customers or organisations are informed of the discounts that encourage them to make payments early, which benefit both the customer and the organisation by allowing them to receive timely supplier payments and maintaining cash flow (Jain & Woodcock, 2017).

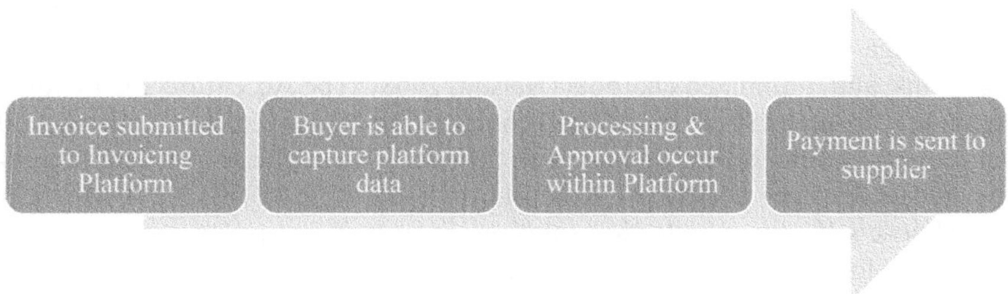

Fig. 2. Process of Multimedia Technology in Accounts Payable.
Source: stampli.com

3. *Strengthen relationships with vendors and customers:* According to the law, satisfied customers are more likely to buy from the business again. To keep the business running, it is crucial to manage vendors by making payments on time. This strengthens relationships with vendors and customers ultimately encouraging loyalty to suppliers. Technology advancements also assist customers in resolving issues as they arise, rather than waiting for them to get worse.
4. *Gain more internal control:* Technology has made the account payable process more transparent. It has also helped the company make decisions about business issues, improving it day by day and forecasting financial results. Removing late fees and taking advantage of discount offers on payments, also provides a clear picture of the state of the financial position, and aids in better cash management in general.

17.2.3 Collection

When a customer owes business money, the phrase 'collection' is used by the business to describe the situation. The amount of the bill gets past-due and is occasionally turned over to a collection agency when a customer fails to pay the company within the time frame given.

A debtor may opt for part payment, EMI (Easy Monthly, Instalments) or may full payment (Tejaswini, 2021).

Debt collection has traditionally required a lot of physical labour including making a lot of phone calls and negotiating payment terms with past-due customers. Even with all of those efforts, the actual debt collection might not meet expectations. Furthermore, due to their incapacity to scale, banks can no longer rely on these conventional approaches to handle the pandemic's ever-rising delinquencies and defaults. The manual collection has never been a cost-effective solution, not even for minor ticket infractions, as it necessitates a capital expenditure on both resources and personnel.

The typical methods used by banks and other financial institutions to collect payments from consumers are phone calls and emails. These techniques are regarded as obtrusive and frequently harm clients.

Therefore, implementing alternate communication channels is the practice that will provide the solution. As a result, banks and other financial institutions now engage with their clients using mobile apps, internet portals, social media platforms, and automated chatbots (Nelson, 2008). The Accenture 2020 Global Banking Consumer Study found that, compared to 32 per cent two years ago, 50 per cent of consumers now interact with their bank through a mobile app or website at least once per week (Eger, Komárková, Egerová, & Mičík, 2021). Most clients choose self-service collection solutions in today's fast-paced economy since they allow for an easy engagement at any convenient time and location of their choice, free of any obligations. These three concepts have been at the centre of the entire process: control, ease, and mobility.

17.2.3.1 Identifying the Potential Defaulters

Credit Information Companies receive repayment data from banks and other financial organisations regarding loans and credit card balances. Both timely payments and payments that defaulted will be represented in this data.

Software used for debt collection integrates information from client accounts with their internet and social media activity. Banks and other financial institutions can accurately assess the position of their consumer's by combining internet and social media data. They can use it to find possible defaulters. Timely notification of the clients who might become defaulters enables banks to take proactive measures in advance.

A prominent private-sector banker claimed that 'now, credit bureaus can identify a serial defaulter even if he changes his residence'. The system will detect the fraudster if the defaulter uses the same name and identity proof as his PAN number. The first credit-information provider in the nation, Credit Information Bureau (India), has a tool called CIBIL that offers timely, comprehensive, and most updated contact details of the customers to the credit grantors (Sharma, 2016). Credit grantors can contact the consumer at the proper moment to assure recovery by using the power of this information. Technology can help to streamline the debt collection process, decrease the amount of time spent dealing with consumers, and adheres to regulatory regulations, lowering the risk of non-compliance and improving results. Debt collection can be made a more enjoyable yet purpose-driven experience using gamification and behavioural finance theories to increase collection efficiency.

17.2.4 Cash Flow Management

Management of cash flow is crucial in all enterprises. Keeping track of all the money coming in and going out is made easier by this. It makes sure that a company's cash intake exceeds its outflow. This helps in timely supplier payments and serves as a reminder to collect debtor payments, purchase stocks, maintain corporate operations, and make investments (Margasova et al., 2019). Additionally, it aids in forecasting and decision-making for the company. Cash flow management is helpful to understand how much money a company needs to balance its books.

The nine steps of cash flow management are as follows:

1. *Put in place effective credit control measures:* This involves explaining credit control methods to customers and establishing payment terms in writing as well as electronically. When the due date is set, the consumer will instantly begin getting reminder calls or texts.
2. *Create a monthly sales projection:* Multimedia technology aids in concentrating the company's cash flow regularly for the months ahead. The chosen goal should genuinely be accomplished in a way that closely resembles the business's future forecast.
3. *Negotiate with reputable suppliers:* Negotiate with reputable suppliers to avoid time lags and errors by giving customers and businesses more time to pay or receive payments.

4. *Implement strict stock controls:* We all know that when cash is invested in stock, it is difficult to sell the stock quickly. Owing to multimedia technology, it is now simple to track the stock, which aids in managing stock levels to keep a healthy balance.
5. *Spending restraint:* This refers to expenses like equipment purchases and other outlays. Cost management assists in keeping spending in check with income; this complements cash flow management.
6. *Reduce unnecessary costs:* Since all records of daily, monthly, and annual incomes and expenses are kept digitally, it is simple to exercise unnecessary spending restraints that might result in savings or reserves.
7. *Create and read financial reports:* To ascertain whether the profit and loss statement, balance sheet statement, cash inflow and outflow, understanding of the present financial position and sales over purchases may be provided as financial reports.
8. *Develop the ability to recognise warning indicators:* Factors such as currency exchange rates, governmental regulations, inflation, and uncertain events can significantly affect cash flow. Multimedia technology can be used to discover warning indications and gauge a company's finances.
9. *Truthful and practical:* Maintaining integrity in a firm's financial accounts is very important. An assessment should receive an accurate report on how a business is operating. There are fewer opportunities for data adulteration when everything is digital.

Users or investors can evaluate a company strategy through the cash flow management activity depicts in fig. 3. which approximates the degree to which the company depends on operating, finance, and investment activities to raise cash flow.

The following are the type's cash flow management:

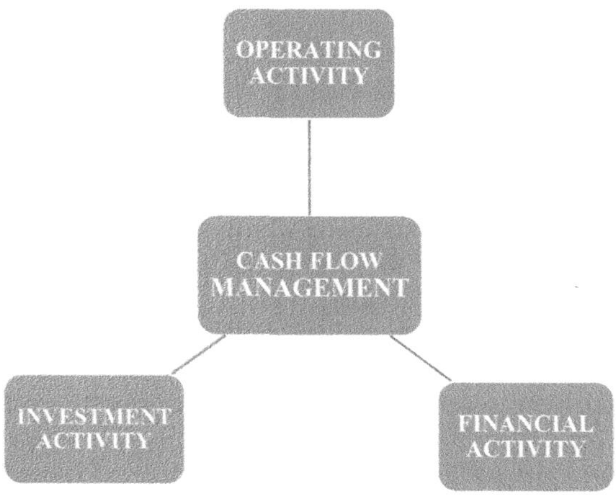

Fig. 3. Cash Flow Management. *Source*: double-entry-bookkeeping.com

1. *Operating activity:* To build income business uses operating activities in cash flow. For example, cash flow from the activities includes cash used in the sale and purchase of stock, to pay expenses like electricity bills, salaries, income tax, etc.
2. *Investment activity:* Cash flow from investment activity or test transaction considering the business investments in long-term assets. These are recorded under fixed assets and long-term assets on the balance sheet. Examples purchase of land and building, equipment, investment in assets, and the amount received from the sale of assets like land and building, furniture and fixture, equipment, etc.
3. *Financial activity:* Changes in long-term liabilities and equity indicate when cash flow from financial accounts is being used for business-related operations. Financial activity's cash flow is used to pay off debt, issue capital stock, distribute dividends, etc., raise capital from investors, or sell stocks.

17.2.4.1 Benefits of Cash Flow Management

1. *A dashboard with high cash flow visibility:* An automated system aids in obtaining a quick picture of the company's financial situation and enables connections to all bank accounts, loans, etc. The development of technology makes it easier to obtain and maintain data.
2. *Expense categorisation:* Technology has made it possible for businesses to cut costs more quickly, and automated systems, in particular, have made it possible to classify costs in a way that makes them more transparent, makes budgeting simple, and also enables businesses to benefit from tax exemptions.
3. *Budget tracking and cash positioning:* Monitoring and controlling a company's cash intake and outflow is known as tracking cash flow. When expenses and other operating costs are paid, money that entered the organisation through sales, income, and interest on savings can easily be tracked.
4. *Effective decision-making:* Businesses can determine more precisely by looking at the cash flow statement that they have enough cash on hand to engage in new business ventures or whether the business needs to discover alternative funding sources. In addition, cash flow statement is a helpful tool for assisting the business in securing finance (Lepădatu, 2017).
5. *Easy making payments and reconciling payments:* Recorded balances of the firm and the bank statement matchup are the major objective of any business to reconcile the cash. A cash reconciliation method enables businesses to find any inconsistencies and pinpoint the areas where the ledger and statement don't agree.

17.2.5 Tax Preparation

Tax preparation refers to the process of getting ready to file a tax return by an individual or a business which can be done both manually and online. A certified public accountant, licenced professional attorney, or designated agent prepares taxes. As part of the tax assessment process, the government uses provided data from many sources, which is influenced by multimedia technology. Data from various sources are compared using digital technology, which is also used to create computerised audit assessments and monitor the taxpayer. Tax authorities have accepted the digitalisation process. Technology has made it easier for taxpayers to understand policies, allowed businesses to embrace them, and improved municipal law compliance (Atkinson & McKay, 2007). Additionally, it facilitated the collection of information from different taxpayers by tax officials and its transmission to relevant judicial bodies.

It has been noted that new tax laws are being created around the world, not just in India, to deal with digitalisation business models, grievances, and difficulties relating to secrecy, help with information sharing among the tax authorities, and ensure openness in GST filing (Das, 2018). India is regarded as being at the forefront of technological innovation when it comes to developing technology-based tax solutions (Bird & Zolt, 2008). The tax authority employs technology to facilitate e-filing for taxpayers and otherwise enhance the way taxes are administered. Using technology extensively and successfully during lockdown caused a significant difference to be noticed.

17.2.5.1 Importance of Multimedia Technologies in the Tax Preparation

1. The firms are adopting technological advancement and attaining distinct levels as opposed to less technical businesses. The use of ERP systems in the financial, social, and economic sectors of business has increased efficiency and accuracy while reducing the amount of time needed to complete tasks.
2. Maintaining data manually was highly challenging; while modest amounts of data from various sources could be handled, it was impossible to retain or complete any required filings for vast amounts of data. Faster business growth was made possible by technology.
3. Because of information technology, ERP platforms, and other technological advancements, life is now easier and work is moving along more quickly.

Additionally, initiatives are made to incorporate technology improvement in the areas of litigation administration, the documentation procedure, data gathering control and workflow in the tax department, tax compliance, and handling reports and financial data (Malini & Menon, 2017). Additionally, it aims to close the communication gap between taxpayers and the tax department (Grima, Kizilkaya, Sood, & ErdemDelice, 2021). The quality of data and the auditing procedure in the tax department have both improved as a result of assessing the taxpayer through the process of filing returns from any location in the nation as shown in fig. 4. In the area of general direct and indirect taxes, multimedia technology has driven improvements and has been helpful. Technology is utilised to enhance tax administration and the procedure for taxpayers to file their tax returns. Additionally, it aids in the detection of fraud and tax evasion. The usage of multimedia

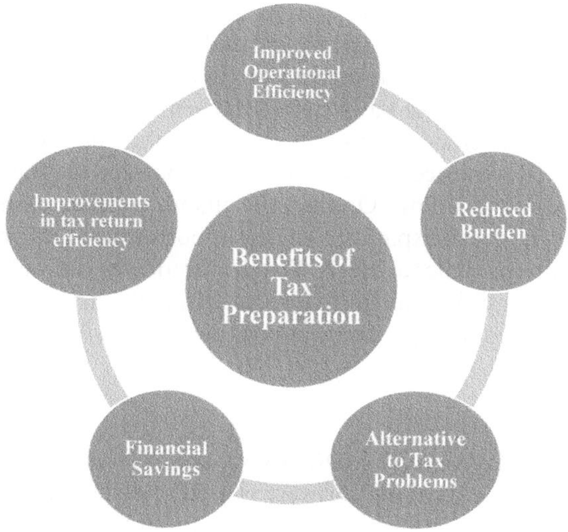

Fig. 4. Benefits of Tax Preparation. *Source*: enterslice.com

technology has improved the chances for the younger generation to carry out tax-related duties and reach new heights.

17.2.5.2 Benefits of Multimedia Technology in Tax Preparation

1. It serves as a hedging tool and safeguards the company's reputation.
2. The expenses of licencing and investment have also benefitted from it.
3. It improves the working environment's productivity and helps formulate tax policy (Smith, Lin, & Miller, 1993).
4. Tax professionals can develop different techniques for the best use of resources (Syaripuddin, 2017).
5. Makes it more productive by lowering costs and saving time, which is then used to generate income.

17.2.6 Cash Disbursements

In accounting, the word 'disbursement' simply means 'to send out'. A payment made by one party to another is referred to as a cash disbursement in accounting terms. This payment or cash disbursement is done via a cheque, an electronic cheque, an ACH (automated clearing house), a digital payment, or any other method that causes the money to be taken out of the account right away (James & Weiman, 2005).

Stock purchases, costs, supplier payments, loan repayment, dividend payments, and other miscellaneous payments – aside from credit card payments – all require cash payments or disbursements. A payment made on the other party's behalf will likewise be counted as a cash disbursement. Maintaining or tracking cash flow in a firm is crucial but often difficult. Every business must maintain an accurate and effective record of each cash disbursement. Business closure is a result of poor financial flow. On the other hand, effective cash flow management enables businesses to expand, seize new opportunities, and profit from shifting market conditions (Palepu, Healy, Wright, Bradbury, & Coulton, 2020). It is vital to monitor cash disbursement to forecast future financial positions. A warning indicator that a company's financial position is in peril is when cash outflow exceeds cash inflow.

17.2.6.1 Accounting Software That Disburses Funds Automatically

Generally, automatic accounting software is used to disburse cash that has been kept in auto-pilot mode. The accounting team can save time with automatic cash disbursement software. When billing and the payable record are due, applications like ACH Connect Accounting Seed Extension and Clear Cloud make sending and receiving payments easier.

There are various forms of cash disbursement used as payment, including:

1. *Customer refund:* After making a purchase, a customer requests a refund, which is referred to as disbursement of cash and results in a drop in sales.
2. *Dividend payment:* A decrease in the capital of the equity and preference shares is regarded as a cash payout.
3. *Student loan repayment:* When a student receives a loan, the bank notifies them in writing of the amount and date of the disbursement as well as informing them at school.
4. *Rent in a physical place:* Rent, expenses, and fees paid in cash, checks, or any other form are recorded as cash disbursements.
5. *Paying salaries:* Payroll payments to employees, including salary payments, are considered financial outlays.
6. *Purchasing asset:* Acquiring an asset entails purchasing or paying for items such as furniture and fixtures, real estate and buildings, and various kinds of equipment that are deducted from unadjusted income.

Journal of Cash Expenditures: Some firms record cash disbursement in a cash disbursement journal before posting it to the company's ledger. Journals for cash disbursements keep track of details regarding transactions, including date, price, pay invoice number, check number, and remarks.

17.2.7 Budgeting Process

Business budgeting and planning haven't changed all that much in recent years. The majority of businesses still base their projections on manual data entry into

Excel spreadsheets. It illustrates how forecasts and budgets must be created over weeks or months, often using outdated data (Nolan, 1999). This inaccuracy causes some problems such as making poor strategic decisions as a result of false assumptions. Unexpected sales or cash flow declines that weren't anticipated in forecasts could significantly impact the organisation's overall health. These are all unacceptable outcomes. Technology can radically alter this situation. Today, a lot of businesses try to use technology to help them make better decisions, and multimedia technology is very helpful in this regard. The goal of organisations is to become more flexible. Today's market demands can shift quickly, and businesses that are prepared to spot opportunities can take advantage of them. That is very challenging with the traditional business budgeting and forecasting process (Saidu & Musa, 2017). Because of this, automation in particular has become crucial for assisting in the budgeting and forecasting process. Automation has improved everything from scheduling to accounts payable and inventory control. As a result, the organisational operation was able to operate more effectively and efficiently, which is a key goal for any business. Today, it would be challenging to locate a business that hasn't automated (or isn't currently automating) its accounting systems. As a result, every sector recognises the value of automation. When it comes to improving the budgeting and financial forecasting process for businesses, automation helps a lot.

The key to this technology is that it enables budget managers and CFOs to enhance two crucial aspects. First the process involves in creating the budget. Systems that automatically sync with the general ledger can be built into the technology. Maintaining data accuracy to the minute rather than just the week significantly lowers the possibility of errors. Second, automation enables businesses to enhance the real-time monitoring and reporting of their business budget and forecast. This is crucial for the organisation's long-term health. Data automation and better technology can produce reports that compare historical data and enhance dashboards (Stehle & Kitchin, 2020).

Multimedia Technology and automation are crucial components of the future for any organisation that wants its key decision-makers to be quick and flexible. The overall budgeting and planning process for businesses will improve with improved technology and automation. It will enable everything from increased departmental coordination to data collection, modelling, and projections. This allowed more time for analysis and improvement because every department in the company spent far less time on the laborious budgeting and forecasting tasks. This has been long overdue in so many organisations. As the link between technology and data, CFOs who take a leadership role and actively participate in the process of making strategic decisions can instead advocate for a new method of budgeting that enables better and more accurate financial intelligence. The long-term advantages will undoubtedly accrue to technologically advanced organisations that adopt automation and create wiser planning and budgeting methods. With the aid of multimedia and automation, the organisation can easily build a driver-based budget model, test various scenarios, and produce precise forecasts, and charts of accounts can simply get. The process known as 'driver-based budgeting' connects actual assets and activities to the financials during the budgeting process

(Nikodijević, 2021). This is typically accomplished with the aid of a computer system that makes it possible to manage the planning and budgeting process.

A driver-based budgeting (DBB) process evaluates drivers, which are the business factors that affect financial performance, to connect demand with the resources required to meet it. Organisations using DBB typically concentrate only on the components that most accurately reflect the performance and development of the business, even though a variety of internal and external factors can be considered drivers. As a result, the company can concentrate on making timely, agile, and effective strategic top-down decisions. DBB strategies can be used in almost every industry because they are adaptable by nature. Healthcare, hospitality, consumer packaged goods, insurance, and the financial sector are a few of the more prevalent industries that employ these strategies successfully. The majority of budget contributors use DBB methodologies today; they are neither complex nor novel. However, finding the business drivers with the greatest impact on the company and incorporating them into the budgeting process can be challenging when these business plans are carried out using spreadsheets. The process becomes transformative when DBB is implemented using an automated, cloud-based planning platform that offers visibility and transparency into driver insights.

17.2.7.1 Benefits of Multimedia Technologies in integrated DBB Approach

1. Organisations can quickly evaluate the effects of internal or external changes with DBB plans. Budget holders could spend their time researching the factors that drive the company.
2. Utilising drivers for outcomes helps the finance team work in a setting that is more consistent across business functions and more aligned with the overall strategy of the company.
3. 'What-if' scenario analysis is frequently carried out by altering the drivers and examining the financial impact. Organisations can understand the impact of those drivers and what even minor adjustments can mean to the bottom line in a very effective way when those drivers are visible and transparent throughout the planning process.

An IoT-based monitoring and cloud-based platform can reduce the toxicity levels in the field. Environmental monitoring can reduce greenhouse gas emissions and waste in an organisation.

17.2.8 Financial Analysis and Reporting

A financial report is the accounting information system's ultimate output. The value of accounting information impacts decision-making and the accounting profession's competitiveness (Fridson & Alvarez, 2022). The quality of accounting data has fallen off recently. Currently, the accounting scandals have damaged investor confidence. For accounting theorists, practitioners, and governmental agencies worldwide, providing confidence and improving the quality of financial reporting have emerged as top priorities. However, diverse stakeholders require quick, comprehensive, and convenient financial information to make decisions about the economy that is increasingly influenced by global factors. Businesses urgently require a new financial reporting paradigm to give their many stakeholders greater financial information in light of scientific and technological advancements. The only formats for the present financial reporting model are PDF and HTML. The rise of network financial reporting is supported by the intelligent multimedia technology platform, which combines computer and video technologies (Birt, Muthusamy, & Bir, 2017). In addition to changing how businesses interact with consumers of financial information, the Internet, a new channel for the dissemination of financial reports, also changes how financial reports are produced, what they contain, how they are organised, and how they are made.

Multimedia technology automatically collects and compiles financial data in the finance industry based on the language specification of electronic communication of business and accounting data. Due to the ease with which this technology makes it possible to build reports with multiple data subsets, regulators, intermediaries, and other information users are now able to simply extract the data they need based on their specific needs and authority and output it in the format of their choice. Therefore, firms can deliver diverse financial reports by tailoring the information they need. Information from accounting reports has been elevated to a previously unheard-of high level and scope for gathering, publishing, analysing, and using. It conserves resources, vastly improves efficiency, and does away with the difficult initial task of obtaining and utilising accounting data.

17.2.9 Payroll Administration

Payroll management is one of the most crucial tasks that demands proper attention to its payroll management process, regardless of the size or type of business. Payroll significantly contributes to improving employee satisfaction and motivates them to work harder and be more dependable to advance both personally and professionally. Every business aspires to operate as effectively as possible. The financial stability of the business and the morale of the employees are both supported by an accurate payroll management process (Munap, Badrillah, & Rahman, 2013). However, mistakes can still occur and have detrimental effects. These systems for managing payroll are very error-prone. The performance and morale of employees may suffer if payroll management systems are inaccurate. Instead of managing payroll, a company administers and implements payroll functions, which include keeping track of hours worked, and managing leave, incentives, and deductions, among other payroll administration responsibilities.

The need for automated payroll systems in every business grows as new technological trends usher in the incorporation of fresher concepts. Through an organised system, automation across regions overcomes the challenge of ongoing payroll updates including tax and regulatory changes. Paying employees the right amount at the right time has a vital importance. Multimedia technologies provide a Cloud-Based Global Payroll Software that can be deployed on-premise, in the cloud, or as a managed service offering. It includes integrated Core HR, Time & Attendance, and Expense modules.

1. *Easily track working hours:* In a conventional workplace, the manager or supervisor is responsible for closely supervising the employees, giving them instructions, and recording their attendance and working hours. The manager and supervisor have a challenging job. The company gradually increases its workforce as it grows. And it becomes harder, slower, and more chaotic to keep track of each employee's working hours. This might be easy to manage with automated payroll management software. The automated system can easily keep track of the employees' working hours by providing information about their login and logout times and their break times. The manager and supervisor will be able to focus on more important tasks as a result.
2. *Make necessary changes to the salary structure:* The management can design and implement appropriate wage structures for particular employees with the aid of automated payroll solutions. The system also enables the management to quickly alter or change the wage structure as necessary. This aids in locating and resolving any irregularities in the compensation package offered to employees.
3. *Quick payroll calculations*: Payroll calculation by hand is a difficult and time-consuming process. The HR division must compile data from various sources and then perform intricate calculations. It takes a lot of time to manually compute and compare data when making spreadsheets. The majority of problems can be quickly and easily resolved with HR automation software. With the automation system, you only need to enter the necessary data; the software will handle all other calculations, including base salary, benefits and perks, deductions, overtime pay, and so on.
4. *Payroll automation helps save money for an organisation:* Companies that work with a reputable payroll service provider and use an automated payroll system don't need as many financial and HR staff members, which lowers operating costs and makes payroll processes even more efficient for the business. Automated payroll service is a better option to consider because it is more cost-effective and effective.
5. *Centralised employee records:* All employee records are stored, updated, and maintained in a single repository with automation and multimedia technologies. It lowers the cost of compliance and audit preparation and enables better reporting.

17.2.10 Compliance

To ensure that an organisation's operations comply with all applicable legal and regulatory requirements, as well as professional and industry standards, is to practice effective compliance. This has several different aspects, beginning with management processes for identifying applicable requirements such as laws, regulations, contracts, and policies. To develop the creative for the awareness campaigns among the public, the RBI began inviting applications from advertising agencies. The campaigns would target social media, web portals, and digital media in addition to traditional media outlets like newspapers, magazines, radio, television stations, and movie theatres. The RBI conducts extensive, multilingual, and pan-Indian public awareness campaigns. The main goal of the campaigns is to raise general awareness of the RBI regulations and other initiatives among Indian citizens. Education and financial inclusion are two crucial components of the RBI's developmental role. The RBI's developmental role must include both financial inclusion and education, which are both essential.

The first step is to determine the current level of compliance, evaluate the risks and costs of non-compliance, and then prioritises and implement any necessary actions to achieve compliance are the next steps. The compliance function has long been tasked with proactively managing and keeping up with an ever-changing compliance landscape and demonstrating the effectiveness of their compliance programmes (Prorokowski & Prorokowski, 2014). To do this, the central bank has produced a significant body of literature that is accessible for download and use by banks and other stakeholders across 13 different languages on its website. According to the RBI website, the initiative aims to increase public awareness of financial services and products, wise money management, going digital, and consumer protection.

The foundation of the RegTech industry is compliance, which includes 181 businesses out of 439. The process also includes adhering to statutory requirements for employee payments such as income tax. The payroll management process includes establishing a process and system to handle employee complaints. Businesses must better understand the entire payroll process and why payroll automation is required to ensure compliance and employee engagement if they are to comply with legislative requirements for accuracy and reliability.

Regulatory compliance is a challenge for financial institutions nowadays. The increasing number of regulatory changes and the rising compliance costs are making more institutions opt for technological advancements, so the market growth is understandable. Eliminating manual and paper processes by letting end-users use the mobile app to capture incidents and compliance data in real-time (Black & Baldwin, 2012). As the task of risk management grows along with the number and complexity of regulations, the need for new strategies and tools that enable risk management and regulatory compliance to be more agile, adaptive, and executable in real-time, increases in urgency.

17.3 THREATS AND CHALLENGES

Disintermediation, cannibalisation of existing channels, risk of standardising on the incorrect technology platform, and failure to keep up with developments were just a few of the threats mentioned. Inadequate digital security created a barrier to the bank's engagement with its customers (Nami, 2009). The exposure of interconnectivity raises the risk of fraudulent transactions and the risk of disclosing private financial information in this financial business because it deals with large amounts of cash and cheques.

Instability in networks and systems is another barrier. When the effects of system failure become more severe, businesses that rely on technology suffer loss. More than just the trading and investment sectors are in danger (Mulligan, Carruthers, & Cahill, 2004).

According to *Economic Times*, on 24 February 2021, the New Delhi Stock Exchange (NSE) experienced a significant technical issue that caused several traders to incur unintended losses. Due to the online risk management system's failure, the entire system had to be shut down. Even if the trading hours were extended, the losses could not be recovered. The NSE is awaiting the vendor's and telecom service providers' investigation of the incident's core causes.

Any threat or impediment not only harms a financial institution's standing and reputation but also depletes the assets of its clients. Every bank must adopt robust cyber security procedures and put them into practice to guarantee the protection of clients' data.

Data breaches enable the recovery of monies but are also a major issue for banks since they result in the loss of client data and make it difficult for customers to once again have faith in the bank. Customers may choose to quit bank as a result of the most serious customer service issues. The good news is that by utilising the appropriate technology, there are numerous methods to get around many obstacles in the banking industry (Hõbe, 2015). For example, using the AI chat box to solve queries relieves the burden on the customer service personnel.

REFERENCES

Atkinson, R. D., & McKay, A. S. (2007). Digital prosperity: Understanding the economic benefits of the information technology revolution. *SSRN Electric Journal*. http://dx.doi.org/10.2139/ssrn.1004516.

Belanche, D., Casaló, L. V., & Flavián, C. (2019). Artificial intelligence in FinTech: Understanding robo-advisors adoption among customers. *Industrial Management & Data Systems*, *119*(7), 1411–1430.

Bird, R. M., & Zolt, E. M. (2008). Technology and taxation in developing countries: From hand to mouse. *National Tax Journal*, *61*(4), 791–821.

Birt, J. L., Muthusamy, K., & Bir, P. (2017). XBRL and the qualitative characteristics of useful financial information. *Accounting Research Journal*, *30*(1), 107–126.

Black, J., & Baldwin, R. (2012). When risk-based regulation aims low: Approaches and challenges. *Regulation & Governance*, *6*(1), 2–22.

Das, P. K. (2018). An insight into black money and tax evasion – Indian context. *Marketing*, *3*(4), 30–39.

Eger, L., Komárková, L., Egerová, D., & Mičík, M. (2021). The effect of COVID-19 on consumer shopping behaviour: Generational cohort perspective. *Journal of Retailing and Consumer Services*, *61*, 102542.

Ferguson, M. E., & Toktay, L. B. (2006). The effect of competition on recovery strategies. *Production and Operations Management*, *15*(3), 351–368.

Fields, E. (2016). *The essentials of finance and accounting for nonfinancial managers* (3rd ed). New York, NY: Amacom.

Fridson, M. S., & Alvarez, F. (2022). *Financial statement analysis: A practitioner's guide*. Hoboken, NJ: John Wiley & Sons.

Grima, S., Kizilkaya, M., Sood, K., & ErdemDelice, M. (2021). The perceived effectiveness of blockchain for digital operational risk resilience in the European Union insurance market sector. *Journal of Risk and Financial Management*, *14*(8), 363.

Hader, M., Elmhamedi, A., Tchoffa, D., Ghodous, P., Abouabdellah, A., & Essaoudi, M. (2022, June). Optimisation of procure to pay process through blockchain technology – Case of textile sector. In *2022 IEEE 6th international conference on logistics operations management (GOL)* (pp. 1–7). Piscataway, NJ: IEEE.

Hõbe, L. (2015). The changing landscape of the financial services. *International Journal of Trade, Economics and Finance*, *6*(2), 145.

Jain, K., & Woodcock, E. (2017). A road map for digitizing source-to-pay. Retrieved from https://www.mckinsey.com/capabilities/operations/our-insights/a-road-map-for-digitizing-source-to-pay. Accessed on June 30, 2019.

James, J. A., & Weiman, D. F. (2005). Financial clearing systems. In *The limits of market organization* (pp. 114–155). New York, NY: Russell Sage Foundation.

Listiadi, A. (2022). The acceptance effectiveness through accounts receivable billing period average. *IJEBD International Journal of Entrepreneurship and Business Development*, *5*(4), 699–707.

Lepădatu, G. V. (2017). Need and benefits of cash flow information. *Knowledge Horizons. Economics*, *9*(4), 52–57.

Malini, A., & Menon, D. G. (2017, December). Technological innovations in the banking sector in India: An analysis. In *2017 international conference on technological advancements in power and energy (TAP energy)* (pp. 1–5). Piscataway, NJ: IEEE.

Margasova, V., Muravskyi, O., Vodolazska, O., Nakonechna, H., Fedyshyn, M., & Dovgan, L. (2019). Commercial banks as a key element in regulating cash flows in the business environment. *International Journal of Recent Technology and Engineering*, *8*(4), 4537–4543.

Mulligan, G., Carruthers, J., & Cahill, M. (2004). Urban quality of life and public policy: A survey. *Contributions to Economic Analysis*, *266*, 729–802.

Munap, R., Badrillah, M. I. M., & Rahman, B. A. (2013). Organizational rewards system and employees' satisfaction at Telekom Malaysia Berhad. *Journal of Educational and Social Research*, *3*(3), 281.

Nami, M. R. (2009, May). E-banking: Issues and challenges. In *2009 10th ACIS international conference on software engineering, artificial intelligences, networking and parallel/distributed computing* (pp. 263–266). Piscataway, NJ: IEEE.

Nelson, J. R. (2008). Going paperless: Online processing breeds multiple advantages. *Journal of Property Management*, *73*(6), 36–40.

Nicholas, D., Williams, P., Martin, H., & Cole, P. (2020). *The Media and the Internet*. Oxfordshire: Routledge.

Nikodijević, M. (2021). Implications and challenges of using driver-based budgeting in contemporary business environment. *Trendovi u Poslovanju*, *1*(17), 49–57.

Nolan, G. J. (1999). The end of traditional budgeting. *Journal of performance management*, *12*(2), 59.

Palepu, K. G., Healy, P. M., Wright, S., Bradbury, M., & Coulton, J. (2020). *Business analysis and valuation: Using financial statements*. Victoria: Cengage.

Prorokowski, L., & Prorokowski, H. (2014). Organisation of compliance across financial institutions. *Journal of Investment Compliance*, *15*(1), 65–76.

Ramaswamy, V., & Gouillart, F. J. (2010). *The power of co-creation: Build it with them to boost growth, productivity, and profits*. New York, NY: Simon and Schuster.

Rysman, M., & Schuh, S. (2017). New innovations in payments. *Innovation Policy and the Economy*, *17*(1), 27–48.

Saidu, S. K., & Musa, B. (2017). Budgeting participation, goal commitment and accounting performance of Nigerian listed banks. *Saudi Journal of Business and Management Studies*, *2*(1), 19–23.

Sajić, M., Bundalo, D., Bundalo, Z., & Pašalić, D. (2017, November). Digital technologies in transformation of classical retail bank into digital bank. In *2017 25th telecommunication forum (TELFOR)* (pp. 1–4). Piscataway, NJ: IEEE.

Sharma, M. P. (2016). Comprehensive study of Kisan Credit Card at Central Bank of India – A useful credit tool for rural development. *IBMRD's Journal of Management & Research*, *5*(1), 21–29.

Smith, L. M., Lin, P. P., & Miller, J. R. (1993). Multimedia: A new technology for the CPA. *The CPA Journal*, *63*(11), 26.

Sood, K., Kaur, B., & Grima, S. (2022). Revamping Indian non-life insurance industry with a trusted network: Blockchain technology. In K. Sood, R. K. Dhanaraj, B. Balamurugan, S. Grima, &

R. U. Maheshwari (Eds.), *Big data: A game changer for insurance industry* (pp. 213–228). Bingley: Emerald Publishing Limited.

Sood, K., Seth, N., & Grima, S. (2022). Portfolio performance of public sector general insurance companies in India: A comparative analysis. In S. Grima, E. Özen, & I. Romānova (Eds.), *Managing risk and decision making in times of economic distress, Part B* (pp. 215–229). Bingley: Emerald Publishing Limited.

Stehle, S., & Kitchin, R. (2020). Real-time and archival data visualisation techniques in city dashboards. *International Journal of Geographical Information Science*, *34*(2), 344–366.

Syaripuddin, J. (2017). Tax accounting with computer tax programs, publication by Scholars Middle East Publishers, Dubai, United Arab Emirates, ISSN-2523-2665.

Tejaswini, G. (2021). *Loans and advances of HDFC bank* Inf Syst Front, *23*, 941–961.

Truant, E., Broccardo, L., & Dana, L. P. (2021). Digitalisation boosts company performance: An overview of Italian listed companies. *Technological Forecasting and Social Change*, *173*, 121173.

WEBLINKS

https://www.fico.com/blogs/8-success-tips-debt-collection-pandemic

https://www.stampli.com/blog/ap-automation/accounts-payable-technology/

https://www.double-entry-bookkeeping.com/investing-cash-flow/cash-flow-from-investing-activities/

https://enterslice.com/tax-preparation-services

INDEX

Printed and bound by CPI Group (UK) Ltd, Croydon, CR0 4YY

13/09/2026

14961062-0006